Michael Twaddle

The critical phase in Tanzania 1945–1968

The critical phase in Tanzania
1945–1968

*NYERERE AND THE EMERGENCE OF
A SOCIALIST STRATEGY*

CRANFORD PRATT

CAMBRIDGE UNIVERSITY PRESS

CAMBRIDGE

LONDON · NEW YORK · MELBOURNE

Published by the Syndics of the Cambridge University Press
The Pitt Building, Trumpington Street, Cambridge CB2 1RP
Bentley House, 200 Euston Road, London NW1 2DB
32 East 57th Street, New York, NY 10022, USA
296 Beaconsfield Parade, Middle Park, Melbourne 3206, Australia

First published 1976

Printed in Great Britain by
Western Printing Services Ltd,
Bristol

Library of Congress Cataloguing in Publication Data

Pratt, Cranford,
    The critical phase in Tanzania, 1945–1968.

    Bibliography: p.
    Includes index.
    1. Socialism in Tanzania. 2. Nyerere, Julius Kambarage, Pres. Tanzania,
1922– 3. Tanzania – Politics and government. 4. Tanganyika – Politics
and government. I. Title.
HX 457.T3C7   320.9′678   75-22979
ISBN 0 521 20824 6

To Renate

CONTENTS

PREFACE

Tanzanians have been eager to advance the understanding of the present dramatic phase in the development of their country. As a result, I have been encouraged and aided by a great many individuals. That I do not now mention each by name only heightens my gratitude to them.

I want, firstly, to express my particular appreciation to Mwalimu Julius Nyerere who kindly submitted to several extended interviews as my work progressed, who gave my family and me the marvelous opportunity to work and to live in Tanzania during the first four years of its independence and who later involved me further in Tanzanian questions for two additional, briefer periods.

I have had innumerable conversations with friends during my residence in Tanzania about the events and developments that are the subject of this book. My understanding of Tanzanian politics has been largely shaped by these conversations and I recall these personal associations with pleasure and gratitude. I think, for example, of Roland and Irene Brown, the late Herbert Chitepo, Amir Jamal, Cleopa Msuya, Dickson Nkembo, Amon Nsekela and Joan Wicken and, as well, of Derek Bryceson, Frederick Burengelo, the late Solomon Eliufoo, Yash Ghai, Reginald Green, Joseph Namata, the late Jacob Namfua, Julius Sepeku and Knud-Erik Svendsen.

Many already hard-pressed public servants found time to be interviewed and were always helpful. I can name but a few of those to whom I am grateful. These include Vice-President Rashidi Kawawa and Mohammed Babu, Paul Bomani, I. M. Kaduma, C. A. Kallaghe, Oscar Kambona, Norman Kyondo, Job Lusinde, Pius Msekwa, M. Mushi and Nsilo Swai.

My efforts to understand British colonial policies were aided by the interest and assistance of numbers of British officials. I am, for example, indebted to Richard Braine, Peter Johnston, Robert King and Kim Meek.

Expatriate generations are short in Tanzania. I have had few opportunities to meet those who have contributed to the committed scholarship of very high quality that has been an exciting feature of the University of Dar-es-Salaam and a particular pleasure to me as to anyone associated with the University in its earliest years. No one can write about even the

x *Preface*

period preceding their work as I am doing without being indebted to their scholarship and impressed by their intellectual activity and skillful advocacy.

Jonathan Barker, Gerald Helleiner, Colin Leys, Patrick McAuslan, Jock Snaith and William Tordoff have each read large portions of earlier drafts of this book. Though they can be assigned no responsibility for its inadequacies, they identified many errors and helped me to see where my arguments were still unclear or inconclusive. I am grateful to these good friends for the attention they gave to my manuscript.

Tanzania Information Services kindly gave permission to reproduce the plates.

This book has been published with the help of a grant from the Social Science Research Council of Canada using funds provided by the Canada Council. This grant, which has made possible the publication of a less expensive East African edition, is gratefully acknowledged.

I wish also to thank the Canada Council for a generous Killam Award which has permitted me to visit Tanzania and to spend a year free of teaching to work on this book. The Ford Foundation also helped greatly by twice responding favourably to requests from the Office of the President of Tanzania for funds to finance my participation in special advisory projects, one in 1965–6, to prepare a report on the administrative implications of the democratic one-party state and the other, in 1969, to be the chairman of the team which reported to the President on the possible decentralization of the government of Tanzania.

This book is dedicated to Renate Pratt. We met in East Africa, we lived full and happy years in Tanzania and we have continued, individually and jointly, to sustain a variety of active interests relating to Africa. Not only my work on this book but my other involvements with Tanzania and Africa as well, have been enriched and sustained by her comradeship, her enthusiasm and her insight.

Toronto
February 1975

CRANFORD PRATT

1: Themes and perspectives

Political strategies during 'the critical phase'

Early in 1964 Amir Jamal, the brilliant Tanzanian Minister and close colleague of Julius Nyerere, President of the United Republic of Tanzania, entitled a major address 'The Critical Phase of Emergent African States'.[1] The contemporary years are, in his judgment, the critical phase. They are the years in which popular needs, aspirations and demands race ahead of the capacity of the economy and the government. In these years, the divisive forces within society are bound to be powerful. 'In the short run', wrote Jamal, 'the success of leadership will depend on the ability to deal successfully with all these contending forces. In the long run it will depend on the rate of economic and social progress. The critical test is one of being able to reconcile the short-term priorities with the long-term objectives.'[2]

The two parts of this book are respectively about the ways in which the colonial government and the independent government of Tanzania* hoped to cope with their immediate problems while also pursuing the long-term objectives which they had set for the whole country. This book is thus about *political strategies* for development in Tanzania between the years 1945 and 1968. It is about the ideas which were held by those in power in Tanzania on how the politics of Tanzania should be managed and its political institutions shaped so as simultaneously to meet the immediate requirements of government and to move the society towards the long-term goals which they had defined for it. It is concerned more with their views on how to initiate a transformation of Tanzanian society and on how to rule during that transforming process than with their views on what the society would be like once transformed.

To inquire into the political strategies of both the colonial and the

---

* Tanzania has had several official names during the period covered by this book. It was Tanganyika until 26 April 1964, when as a consequence of the union with Zanzibar it became the United Republic of Tanganyika and Zanzibar. A year later it became the United Republic of Tanzania. The practice which will be followed in this book is to use 'Tanganyika' when referring to events confined to the pre-1964 period and 'Tanzania' when referring to the post-April 1964 period. 'Tanzania' will be used when the reference refers to events, activities or institutions that both predate and postdate 26 April 1964.

independent governments of Tanzania within the bounds of a single book is not at all to suggest that the winning of independence did not constitute a great advance, universally welcomed, by the people of Tanzania. The colonial administrators' perception of the interests of Tanzanians was encased within assumptions about the legitimacy of their own rule and was delimited in advance by the fact that they were members of a colonial service whose first loyalty was to the imperial power. They were not, and could not expect to be, supported by the increasing numbers of Africans who were taking an active interest in the politics of the colony. Moreover they had to accept that even the acquiescence of the countryside to their rule was rapidly declining. Though the colonial administrators felt a need to enlist popular support they could in fact permit popular participation within the political institutions of their rule only within narrow and ineffective limits.

In sharpest contrast, the nationalist leaders were an integral part of the African community, articulating and providing leadership for that hostility to foreign rule which was stirring throughout the whole country. The nationalists came to power with a popular support that was nearly universal. They assumed that that support would continue. Yet it quickly became clear that democracy, at least through the Westminster-type political institutions which the British had hurriedly created in the last years of their rule, was inappropriate and perhaps incompatible with the transformation which the leaders hoped Tanzania would be able to achieve. Political strategy, the question of how to hold the support and increase the commitment of the masses during the lengthy period of transition to a socially transformed and economically developed society, became an important concern for Nyerere and his colleagues.

Not every government has a set of ideas which can be called a political strategy. Many make little effort to place their activities in a long-term perspective. They have not articulated an integrated view of the longer-term consequences of their present pursuits. They seek to maintain order, to balance conflicting interests and to remain in power. They strive to maximize their own advantage and the advantage of those in political alliance with them. They do not seek to reform or to transform their societies. They do not have longer-term objectives with which the pursuit of their more immediate objectives must be reconciled. In sharp contrast to such governments, the several governments which have ruled Tanzania during the years 1945 to 1968 each had a clear, though different, perception of a different pattern of economic, social and political life for Tanzania. Each sought to initiate reforms which would begin to bring life in Tanzania nearer to its perception of how it wished Tanzania to develop. Each had clear ideas on how the politics of the country could be managed during this transition. They have all had, in other words, a political strategy.

This distinction between ends and means, between the ideal society and the steps which must be taken to achieve it, obviously cannot be pushed too far. The character of its long-term objectives directly influences the strategies which a leadership chooses, and cannot be ignored in a study which focuses on the political strategy pursued by those with political power. Nevertheless this distinction between long-term objectives and the means chosen for the achievement of these objectives is useful, particularly in a study of the political ideas of men who actually exercise power. For these leaders, and for those whom they govern, the intellectual elaboration of an ideal society is likely to be less significant than decisions about the immediate policies which are needed to promote that idea. The ideals of many highly motivated leaders have been unrealized, not because of any intrinsic faults in their ideals but because of serious errors which they made when deciding how best to move towards their accomplishment.

Political strategies in Tanzania 1945–68

The political strategies which are examined in Part I of this book cover the last sixteen years of British rule in Tanganyika. Part II examines the strategies followed during the first seven years of independence. It concludes with an analysis of the reasons for the emergence of a strong socialist commitment in 1967 and of the political strategy that was integral to that commitment.

During the years 1945 to 1960 the colonial government, with an unexpected disregard for consistency, moved from one strategy to another, giving primary attention first to one and then to another of the preoccupations which intermittently gripped it. The British administrators were an aloof and superior class, planning the fate of a people to which they did not themselves belong. This detachment did not mean that they diagnosed the needs of Tanganyika dispassionately or with exceptional insight. Each of the strategies followed by the British in Tanganyika was seriously misconceived. Each was flawed by the fact that the British officers who devised the strategies were still primarily the servants of an imperial government; each was flawed by the fact that too many of these officers were unresponsive to, indeed unobservant of some of the most acutely felt needs of Tanganyikans. In consequence, British policies in Tanganyika during the last sixteen years of British rule were marked by sudden fluctuations, by monumental misjudgments and by an absence of political imagination and sensitivity.

The primary focus of Part II is upon Nyerere's political strategy as it developed over the period 1958 to 1967. During these years, his assessment of the policies and institutions which were required in Tanganyika shifted dramatically. Initially, he had felt that Tanganyika had no choice but to accept a major dependence upon Britain and to continue the administrative, development and welfare policies which the first African government had inherited from the colonial regime. This strategy was abandoned in 1962. For the next five years, government policy was marked by a sustained effort to lessen Tanganyikan dependence on Britain, by a pragmatic search for solutions to political problems which compelled attention, by a preoccupation with economic development that was not governed by a consciously held doctrine, and by a recurring concern to assert an independent Tanzanian identity in foreign-policy matters. During these years there were few policy initiatives that can be said to have been consciously influenced to a major degree by the political ideas of the leadership. Nevertheless, Nyerere continued to seek ways to bring his fundamental values more effectively to bear upon Tanzanian society. However he was, to use his own phrase, still 'groping forward'.[3] Only after a number of false starts did he come to a settled view of the economic and political policies which these values required.

By 1967 Nyerere had come to that settled view. In January 1967, he presented to the National Executive Committee of the Tanganyika African National Union (TANU) a new and major statement of party principles. The Committee endorsed this statement, which has since become known as the Arusha Declaration. Nyerere followed it with a series of important policy papers in which he discussed the foreign policy, the rural development policies and the educational policies which seemed to be required by this freshly reaffirmed commitment to socialism, equality and self-reliance. By mid 1968 TANU had initiated a major and continuing effort to give effect to these policies and to realize these basic values in Tanzanian society. The result was a government whose policies, style and preoccupations were quite different from those which Nyerere had accepted, not only in the period 1959 to 1962, when the government accepted a close dependence on Britain, but also in the years 1963 to 1966, when it sought a more complete independence.

The Constitution of 1965 and the socialist pronouncements of 1967 have not, of course, closed off creative policy-making nor brought to a halt the further elaboration of socialist ideology in Tanzania. These continue and they may in time take Tanzanian socialism into quite different directions from those which were set for it in the years 1965–7. Nevertheless the political, economic and constitutional reforms and pronouncements of these years are mutually consistent and constitute a coherent strategy. They represent a socialist position which is communitarian, egalitarian, democratic and liberal. It is communitarian in its opposition to private land titles and to the private ownership of the commanding heights of the economy, in its concern to limit the force of selfish acquisitiveness and to promote communal economic activity and a greater sense of mutual responsibilities. It is egalitarian in its wish to limit income differentials between the rich and the poor and to avoid the emergence of economic classes in the countryside. It is democratic in its insistence upon a system in which leaders are electorally responsible to the people and in which leaders limit themselves to argument, example and persuasion in their efforts to win popular acceptance of socialist objectives. It is liberal in its belief in freedom of discussion, its scepticism of intellectual elitism and its respect for the rights of ordinary men and women and for the worth of their contribution to public life.

The importance of Tanzanian socialism

Tanzanian socialism is of profound interest far beyond the boundaries of Tanzania for at least four forceful reasons. Firstly, the government has come to its socialist commitments by an unfamiliar path. Tanzania's present efforts to achieve a socialist transformation of its society is not a result of revolution, a military occupation by socialist forces or an electoral victory by a genuinely socialist party. There is no powerful inner ruling group which is united around a consciously held ideology to which each member is deeply committed. There is no aroused and militant peasantry, no powerful revolutionary working class and no prevailing expectation of revolutionary change. Tanzania is now committed to socialism primarily because its national leader came to the view that it was in his country's best interest to pursue development along socialist lines. Many developments made the country receptive to this initiative, but the ideology which emerged in 1967 and which has been of such importance since is not the product of the civil service, the party, the Cabinet or an intelligentsia. It is, to a remarkable extent, the work of one man, President Julius Nyerere. He has dominated the search for the institutions and for the major policies which will achieve a democratic and socialist Tanzania. The civil service and the other TANU leaders have each been responsible for new policies and for fresh initiatives. Nyerere's socialist initiatives would have been impossible without the loyalty and the devoted hard work of many civil servants and the support and cooperation of his political colleagues. Nevertheless, it has been Nyerere's developing perception of the nature of his country's needs which explains the decision of the party's National Executive Committee in January 1967 to reaffirm its commitment to socialism. It has also been Nyerere who has given detailed content to Tanzania socialism and who has made it central to the formation of policy since that date. A study of the emergence of a socialist ideology in Tanzania and of the political strategy required by that ideology is, to an important degree, a study of the development of the political thought of Julius Nyerere.

Nyerere's influence on government policies was all the greater because no body of African thinking on political matters had existed either inside the party or outside of it, to provide an alternative to his political ideas. At this time, there were very few Marxists or neo-Marxists in Tanganyika and fewer still who were Tanzanians. Many educated Tanzanians had been influenced by Western liberal ideas and by Christianity but little had been written to apply these values to national politics. As a result, Nyerere's thought was not subjected in these years to any continuing Marxian, liberal or Christian criticism and there was little local exposition of Marxian liberal or Christian alternatives to his views.

The role which Nyerere has played in Tanzania is not unique in the newly independent states of the developing world. In those newly independent countries in which the nationalists were united under the leadership of a single man, this national leader has tended to have enormous influence. His ideology, his aspirations and indeed his personal characteristics have been extremely important determinants of government policies and have had a major impact upon the character of political life in the first years of national independence. A plasticity has marked the thinking of the politically active in a number of newly independent states.[4] Novel and sometimes highly personal ideologies which have been developed by leaders have received a remarkably swift if superficial general acceptance and have had a major impact upon government policies.

Nyerere has had such an influence in Tanzania. This influence, of course, has not been felt equally throughout the whole range of governmental activities. There have been many developments which are to be explained by quite different factors. Major crises have diverted his attention and the attention of his government from their longer-term objectives. There have been ideologically desirable initiatives that could not be undertaken because of the poverty of the country and its multiple scarcities of resources and trained manpower. There have also been important political limits to Nyerere's influence. On some important matters he has been unable to convince his colleagues of the wisdom of his views. There have been other issues in which his initiative has been blunted or diverted by politicians or by a civil service who have not understood or who have opposed his underlying purposes. Nevertheless, despite all these observations, it is surely true that Nyerere has had an extraordinary impact upon government policy and upon the nation's aspirations and its public ethics. Tanzania might well eventually have pursued socialism without his leadership but it is hard to imagine that without Nyerere Tanzanian socialism would have taken its present form or that Tanzania would have sought socialism in the ways it is now doing.

A second reason for the widespread interest in Tanzanian socialism is that Tanzania is a poor and predominantly peasant society which is attempting to find an egalitarian, socialist and democratic way to develop. With so many examples throughout the third world of the fact that a capitalist pattern of development results in severe class differentials, repressive regimes and actual impoverishment for a sizable proportion of the population, the Tanzanian endeavour is of global significance. It is all the more unique in that Nyerere is seeking to achieve socialism in Tanzania without coercion and with meaningful mass participation. How he has hoped to accomplish this, his political strategy in other words, is thus a central factor in the uniqueness of Tanzania's socialism.

A third reason for the interest that is being taken in Tanzanian socialism is that it is a socialist ideology which is genuinely indigenous to Africa. It is not a simple, nor indeed a sophisticated, application to Africa of ideas and techniques which were first elaborated in a European context. There are interesting parallels between Nyerere's position and the position of the early Marx and of some of the revisionist Marxist writings; there are also important parallels between his basic policies and policies in such socialist countries as Sweden, China, Cuba and Yugoslavia. But these are parallels, not determining influences. Nyerere and Tanzania are now paying more attention to these parallels and are learning from them; but the initial elaboration of the ideology was the product of one man's shrewd observation of Tanzanian realities and his sensitive assessment of her needs. Since that initial elaboration, Tanzania has become one of the very few states anywhere in the world which are pursuing independent paths to socialism.

A fourth reason why Nyerere's socialist ideology merits the interest which it has received is Nyerere's concern over the moral implications of the techniques which are chosen to achieve socialism. Marx has written of a 'crude communism in which the domination of material property looms so large that it aims to destroy everything which is incapable of being possessed by everyone'. Marx characterized this as 'universal envy setting itself up as a power' and commented:

> [It] is only a camouflaged form of cupidity which reestablishes itself and satisfies itself in a different way. The thoughts of every individual private property are at least directed against any wealthier private property, in the form of envy and the desire to reduce everything to a common level; so that this envy and levelling in fact, constitute the essence of competition. Crude communism is only the culmination of such envy.[5]

This warning that socialists may be motivated by an envy which is but a more intensive expression of the very quality of capitalist society which Marx deplored may well be a particularly appropriate observation in regard to some socialist commentaries on Africa. Whatever the moral quality of life which is expected in the eventual communist society after the achievement of abundance, there is no chance that that abundance can be achieved in Africa for a very, very long time. If techniques of 'crude communism' are used to accelerate socialist change, if for example, the greed of men is aroused in order to mobilize them against class enemies, then the result will be an intensification of values which are opposite to the values envisaged for a socialist society. This will surely render more difficult the achievement of a genuinely socialist society. Moreover, if this struggle for socialism is likely to last for several generations, then any socialist who is concerned with the quality of the life which Africans will actually lead in this and in subsequent generations must be as concerned with the quality of life during the transition to socialism as he is concerned with the quality of life in the fully socialist society which he hopes to achieve.

Nyerere is such a socialist. He is striving to begin to realize *now* a society based, as he has said in one of his most reflective pieces, on the ethics of love.[6] He is seeking to achieve meaningful political participation by peasants and workers *now*. He is striving to promote economic development while yet controlling the intrusion of acquisitive individualism and checking the emergence of class differentiation. He has thus shown a profound recognition of the importance of the way of life which Tanzanians are being encouraged to follow *now* as they strive to build a democratic and socialist Tanzania.

Part One

British political strategies in Tanganyika 1945-60

2: British strategies and African nationalism in Tanganyika 1945–58

An introductory overview

The transition to independence in Tanganyika is often presented as a process in which the colonial government and the African nationalists agreed that the ultimate objective was the achievement of independence but disagreed over its timing.[1] If viewed in this way, the colonial government appears cautious and paternal and the nationalists impatient and brash. Margery Perham, for example, despite the fact that she supported the early granting of independence to the British African territories, nevertheless held this general view of the transition to independence. She wrote in 1961, 'I want to state with all emphasis my belief that once Africans have been fully stirred into racial self-consciousness and political awareness, *prematurely though this may be in their own interests*, there was little more that foreign rulers could do for them.'[2] Miss Perham would have preferred the development of African nationalism postponed until a later historical period. Had that in fact happened, she feels that these states would then begin their independence with a more numerous educated elite, more developed economies and greater national cohesion. However, once nationalism has become a powerful force, there is no real option but rapidly to concede independence. She applied this general point of view to the specific instance of Tanganyika:

> Tanganyika had not only a heavy volume of precedent behind her to
> carry her smoothly forward to the celebrations of 1961. It had also
> the status of a trust territory under the United Nations and its
> destination was obvious almost as soon as it came to be seriously
> discussed. Even so, there is no more instructive illustration of the
> power both of external pressure and of precedent than in the way in
> which leisurely plans for self-government, which would also have
> preserved a place in the Constitution for the European and Indian
> minorities, were pushed forward with ever increasing speed to the
> culmination of complete African majority and one party rule.[3]

Those who take this general view of the transition to independence tend to attribute the rapidity and the cordiality with which it was handled in Tanganyika in large measure to the coincidence in Tanganyika at that time of a Governor, Sir Richard Turnbull, who was less cautious and more trusting than most Governors, and a nationalist leader, Julius Nyerere, who was in turn, less impatient and less brash. To quote Miss Perham once more, 'Some of the reason for this breathless advance may be found in the characters of both the governor, the realistic Sir Richard Turnbull, and of the then Prime Minister, Mr. Julius Nyerere, certainly the most poised, confident, extrovert and indeed, radiant of all the African leaders I have met.'[4]

The reality, it will now be argued, is far more complex than this view of the transition to independence in Tanganyika and is in direct contradiction to it in several important respects. From 1949 to 1958 the Tanganyika government pursued a political strategy in Tanganyika which was doctrinaire in character and profoundly hostile to the aspirations of the African nationalists. The Tanganyika government and TANU disagreed over two issues which were more important to the nationalists than even the question of the timing of independence. The Tanganyika government rejected TANU's claim to speak for the Africans of Tanganyika. Instead, it sought to treat chiefs as the natural and accepted leaders of the African community. Secondly, during these ten years the government promoted political and constitutional policies which sought to entrench a pattern of constitutional development[5] which it was advocating throughout East and Central Africa and which were designed to entrench the representation of the Asian and European minorities in the legislatures and thus to assure them an influence vastly disproportionate to their numbers.* TANU's rejection of these two policies cannot be presented as a disagreement over the timing of independence. The issues which divided TANU and the Tanganyika government were profound and basic.

Just as the policies which the British followed in the six territories of East and Central Africa were interrelated, so also were the aspirations of African nationalism in each of these territories. The struggle was most crucial in Nyasaland and in Northern Rhodesia. It was the strength of African nationalism there which finally forced the British government to withdraw these two territories from the Federation of the Rhodesias and Nyasaland and to advance them quickly to majority African rule. Nevertheless, the determination of Kenyan, Tanganyikan and Ugandan nationalists to reject the British plan as it applied to their own territories can fairly be seen as part of a common African struggle throughout this whole area for political institutions which would be primarily African. Had African nationalism in these five territories been weaker, and had

---

* The population of these three communities in 1961 was estimated to be: African 10,450,000; Asian 102,400; and European 22,300. Tanganyika, *Statistical Abstract 1962* (Dar-es-Salaam, 1962), p. 11.

the British government in consequence persevered successfully with its strategy of the mid 1950s, political development in each of these five territories would have been totally different. The political, social and constitutional scene in East Africa by 1970 would not have been the same as it was in the late 1950s, with the addition of an augmented African elite, a stronger economy and greater national cohesion. If African nationalism had not emerged as a major force until one or several decades after the 1950s, it would then have had to struggle against white minorities in full control in Central Africa and with substantial and well-entrenched constitutional privileges in East Africa. A delayed emergence of African nationalism in East and Central Africa would therefore not have increased the prospects for stable and popular government in East Africa. Rather the reverse. It would have led to a situation similar to that in Rhodesia and, until very recently, in Mozambique and Angola, a situation, that is, of an extensive and protracted African struggle for liberation. Unless one wishes to argue that such a struggle is in fact beneficial for an African state, one must surely conclude that African nationalism emerged only just in time in East and Central Africa.

This view of British policy in Tanganyika does not need to be argued primarily in terms of the wider strategy being pursued by Britain in East and Central Africa. In the 1950s the government of Tanganyika, because of its own assessment of Tanganyika's needs and because of its own preferences and prejudices, expended a great deal of energy and exhausted its remaining capacity for leadership in promoting policies at national and local levels which had little or no chance of success. Indeed, one can go further. Had the Tanganyikan government succeeded in implementing these policies, it would thereby have increased the economic, political and social problems which would have faced future governments in Tanganyika. It is this view of the political strategy of the Tanganyikan government in the 1950s which must now be substantiated.

Political strategy 1945–50

Before the government began vigorously to pursue 'multiracialism' in 1949, there was in fact little that could be called a political strategy in Tanganyika. The colonial rulers were confident that they knew best what the country needed. They were also confident that, supported by the network of native authorities who ruled locally, they would continue to be able to secure the cooperation of Tanganyikans. There was very little speculation about the political institutions that would be appropriate for an independent Tanganyika and even less about the management of the transition from the colonial rule of the immediate post-war years to that eventual independent Tanganyika.

However, there was such a concern within the Colonial Office in

London. A major reassessment of British constitutional and political policies throughout Africa was made by senior officers of this office in the years 1946–9. This reassessment can perhaps be dated from the publication and confidential circulation of a perceptive and liberal study by Lord Hailey.[6] After 1945, a group within the Colonial Office, led by Andrew Cohen,[7] who was then head of the Africa Division of the Colonial Office, came to conclusions similar to Lord Hailey's. They were, in turn, strongly supported by Creech Jones, the Labour Government's Secretary of State for the Colonies. With his assistance, they conducted a sustained campaign over a period of several years to win recognition within the Colonial Service in Africa of the force of their analysis.[8] Their starting point was a recognition that nationalism was going to become a powerful force throughout Africa and that the British colonies therefore very much needed what we are here calling a political strategy. Lord Hailey expressed this point in these terms:

> There are forces both at home and in the dependencies which will exert increasing pressure for the extension of political institutions making for self government, and the fuller association of Africans in them. The strength of this pressure is likely to be largely enhanced as a result of the war. Unless we have a clear view of the constitutional form in which self government is to be expressed, the answer to this pressure will be ill-coordinated, and may lead to the adoption of measures which we may afterwards wish to recall.[9]

The argument was repeated five years later by the Secretary of State:

> The rate of political progress cannot be regulated according to a pre-arranged plan; the pace over the next generation will be rapid, under the stimulus of our own development programs, of internal pressure from the people themselves, and a world opinion expressed through the growing international interest in the progress of colonial peoples.[10]

The proponents of this view went on to suggest that this increased political activity was bound to lead to increased authority within the African community for the educated and urbanized nationalist. 'As political consciousness develops', said Hailey, 'there is likely to be an increasing disinclination to accept as political representatives those whose recognition as native authorities is under government control and whose activities are carried out under official supervision.'[11] Creech Jones, in an exasperated response to the comments of several Governors who had expressed cynical judgments on the integrity of the educated African, expressed the same view when he finally 'intervened to remind the governors that the demand for responsible government was there and though it is said to come from a few, it will spread; we could not wait to find the people of the standard of competence and responsibility that we should like. We had to satisfy the demand whether we liked it or not; we could not afford to wait.'[12]

There were two central propositions in the political strategy which was recommended by Cohen and others in the period 1947–9 and which they felt was required by the early prospect of strong nationalist movements in Africa. These central propositions were that there should be rapid advancement of Africans within the civil service and more particularly, within the elite corps within it, the administrative service, and that popularly elected members should form a majority of the Legislative Council and a minority of the Executive Council.* These concessions, it was hoped, would secure for the colonial governments the cooperation and assistance of the educated and politically conscious Africans for a final and extended period of preparation for internal self-government and independence. Under this strategy, representative local governments were of central importance. These local governments, replacing the Native Authorities, would be a training ground for democracy, inculcating appropriate political values and providing the voter and the politician with valuable experience in the operation of democratic institutions. They would form an electoral college within an indirect system of elections for the national legislature which would link the political leaders and the African masses, helping to limit any tendency towards authoritarian rule and helping also to assure that the interests of the rural masses were not ignored. Finally, they would be more likely to win the active participation of the rural population in economic development than would traditional or neo-traditional Native Authorities.[13]

This strategy and the assumptions underlying it were rejected by the East African Governors. The most outspoken rejection came from Sir Philip Mitchell, then Governor of Kenya. His reply to the Secretary of State's Despatch of 25 February 1947 was an extraordinary document. He was verbose, racist and unrepentently imperialistic. To the suggestion that colonial governments did not have complete control of the timing of political advancement and should therefore anticipate that this advancement might be somewhat faster than expected, Mitchell replied:

> It is not by an apologetic or defensive attitude either before our own
> people at home or in Africa or in international gatherings, largely com-
> posed of representatives of the most corrupt and abominable mis-
> governments extant today, that we shall do what we have to do but
> by a restored and re-invigorated belief in ourselves, in our own strength
> and our determination to persevere in the task to which we have set our

* This summary refers specifically to the strategy as it was recommended for the West African territories. In the case of East and Central Africa, the strategy proposed that the British government retain official majorities in the Legislative Council and the Executive Council but that more elected members should be introduced.

hands which I conceive to be no less than to civilize a great mass of
human beings who are at present in a very primitive moral, cultural
and social state...how primitive the state of these people is and how
deplorable the spiritual, moral and social chaos in which they are
adrift are things which can perhaps only be fully realized by those who
are in close personal touch with the realities of the situation.

  The only way the multitude of East African tribes can enjoy the
benefits of civilized government both central and local now and for
generations to come, before they become themselves civilized is under
the forms of colonial governments administered by a strong and
enlightened colonial power.[14]

After several pages more or less in the same vein, Sir Philip Mitchell
then concluded this section of his dispatch in these terms:

  The government of Kenya...considers itself morally bound to resist
  processes which might be called 'political progress' by the misinformed
  or opinionated but would in fact, be no more than progress towards the
  abdication of its trust in favour of that class of professional politicians
  discussed above. It may often be difficult but will, for a very long time,
  be necessary to dispose of the moral courage and political integrity to
  say no to proposals for apparent progress of that kind.[15]

To the suggestion that colonial governments must seek ways to integrate
the educated minority of Africans into the political system, he commented:

  I take educated minority to mean what it says and not the large number
  of Africans who have barely achieved the education of an English boy
  of 14 and suppose themselves to be educated. Confusion of these can
  and does at times, lead to distortions of judgement and mistakes of
  local policy.[16]

Mitchell added an appendix to his dispatch in which he presented the
case for continued imperial rule in terms which could hardly have been
less in harmony with the political values and perceptions which characterized the Secretary of State's dispatch and the papers prepared for the
several conferences in 1947 by the Africa Division and the African
Studies Branch of the Colonial Office. He wrote in that appendix:

  To one resident in Africa, it does not appear that the matters discussed
  in the Secretary of State's Dispatch can be treated by themselves as if
  they were, so to speak, a detached piece of scientific research...
     Africa's colonial problem is indivisible...there is a strategic unity
  which is as essential to the safety of all parts as the whole is to the
  survival of the Commonwealth and of the nations of Western Europe
  who share the responsibility with us. Unless this is understood, initiative
  must necessarily pass from our hands to those for whom it is beyond

question a matter of life and death notably the Union of South Africa, Southern Rhodesia and the ancient and mature Portuguese colonies...

There is no 'African nation', no purely African history of culture and no African technical or economic development that is capable of standing alone and never has been; but there is an essential strategic unity which it is necessary to preserve...we are not here to create a succession of Bulgarias, but to develop and civilize this continent as part of what I may call western European civilization and economics and to see that the African tribes as they gradually become civilized, have a satisfying part and share in that development to the full extent that their natural ability makes possible.[17]

No other Governor was as outspoken as Mitchell. But each nevertheless, in his own style, was careful to disassociate himself from the political analysis and the underlying assumptions of the Secretary of State's dispatch. The Acting Governor of Tanganyika, for example, commented quietly in the opening paragraph of his reply that he had seen Sir Philip Mitchell's reply and was in agreement with it. He also endorsed Mitchell's judgment of educated Africans, concluding his dispatch with this lethargic expression of prejudice:

It is a melancholy fact...that we have failed to advance to any appreciable degree the moral and ethical standards of a great number of those Africans who have had the longest benefits of our schools and the training centres. Any failure to appreciate this fact might lead us into grave danger.[18]

Perhaps the most significant illustration that the East African governments had not responded at all to the effort of the Colonial Office to convey a sense of urgency about the pace of political advancement was the failure of these governments to devise any special entry for Africans into their provincial administrations. In theory, the administrative service in Tanganyika and in the other East African territories was open to qualified African and Asian candidates. However, very few Africans or Asians had a British university degree, which was one of the qualifications. A serious effort to recruit Africans in significant numbers into the administrative service would have required the creation of a training cadre of locally recruited Assistant District Officers, the best of whom, after several years of experience, would then be promoted into the administrative service. There were precedents for the appointment of men to the administrative service who were not university graduates. Following the war, the administrative service in Tanganyika and in many other colonies accepted numbers of British candidates who were not graduates but who had served as officers in His Majesty's forces during the war. In neighbouring Kenya non-graduates from white settler families were also recruited into the administrative service, particularly during the Mau Mau emergency. These precedents in the employment of non-graduates were not, however, accepted as relevant to the possible employment of non-graduate Africans.

The governments' antipathy to appointing Africans in any numbers to the administrative service was made all the more apparent in 1949 when Makerere University College entered into its special relationship with the University of London in 1949, and began to prepare East African students for the University of London Arts and Science pass degree. At that time the East African governments made it clear that Makerere graduates would not be eligible for admission to the administrative service, arguing that the education requirement for entry into that service was an honours degree rather than a pass degree. The Tanganyika government at this time was sending only a very small number of Africans overseas for further study; and none of them was encouraged to pursue an honours degree.

It is hard to conclude other than that the Tanganyika government, while claiming correctly that there was no colour bar to admission to its administrative service, nevertheless was careful to arrange matters in such a way that no African District Officers were appointed.[19] No effort at all was made until very late in the day to assure even a very limited flow of African candidates for the adminstrative service. A cadre of African Assistant District Officers was not begun until 1955. No African was appointed a District Officer until 1957 and no Makerere graduate until 1959.[20] Yet eighteen years earlier, Lord Hailey had warned the colonial governments that 'it is in our readiness to admit Africans to such posts that they [i.e. Africans] will see the test of the sincerity of our declared policy of opening to them the road to self-government'.[21]

The Tanganyika government also ignored the recommendation that it should be responsive to the emergence of African nationalism and ready to concede rapid constitutional advance. It was untouched by the analysis on which this recommendation was based. Instead, the Tanganyika government presented its own cautious reforms in local government as if they demonstrated that there was, in fact, a coincidence between its objectives and analysis and that of the Colonial Office. It is true that the actual policies recommended to it by the Secretary of State each involved the introduction of representative local government institutions. But this limited coincidence does not demonstrate an underlying harmony. The assumption behind the Secretary of State's proposals was that independence was likely to come more swiftly than expected and that representative local governments should therefore be introduced rapidly so that they could be ready in time to play an important role within the institutions of a future, independent Tanganyika. In contrast, the Tanganyika government's self-assurance as a colonial regime was unshaken. Its local government reforms were intended to improve the efficiency of colonial rule, not to prepare it for dismantlement. Sir Edward Twining, who had become Governor of Tanganyika in 1950, took the recommendation of the Secretary of State and, by giving it a further twist, brought it into line with his own objectives. Twining agreed that the introduction of representative councils was an important reform to which priority should be given. However, he went on to argue:

> Progress is being made but before the indigenous people as a whole can assume any responsibilities in the sphere of central government, the local government system now being built up on the foundations of the native administrations must be fully and firmly established. Only thus can the great mass of the people be assured of true representation in the counsels of government. Critics may suggest that this envisages too slow a rate of progress but those responsible for carrying out the policy in Tanganyika have no doubt that the future will bear witness to its soundness. The truth is that there is no safe shortcut to the establishment of full democratic government among Bantu peoples.[22]

Thus local government reform, instead of being rapidly introduced because of the inevitability of swift political advancement, served instead to provide a further rationale for delaying that advancement.[23]

The strategy followed by the Tanganyikan government in the late 1940s was fundamentally different from that recommended to it by the Colonial Office. The Tanganyikan government anticipated a long period of colonial rule; it saw no need to Africanize the civil service; it had no confidence in educated Tanganyikans; it was willing to consider significant constitutional advancement for Africans at the level of the central government only after the successful implementation of a protracted and gradual conversion of the Native Authority system into a representative local government system; and it relied upon the continuing authority of the colonial regime to maintain national integration, to promote development and to assure stability during a transition to independence which was to be very lengthy.

Economic development, social change and the rise of nationalism

The promotion of economic development within the framework of the colonial relationship became an important feature of government policy in Tanganyika after 1945. It was, however, never pursued so vigorously as to reveal or even to suggest to the government of Tanganyika that the genuine economic advancement of Tanganyika might bring it into conflict with British interests. Individual British officers at the district level often worked with deep commitment to achieve a greater rate of economic development for Africans in their district. At the centre, however, there was an uninspired amateurism in the handling of fiscal and monetary policies and an unquestioning acceptance of the many limitations to economic development which were implicit in the colonial relationship.[24] This was apparent in many ways. The Tanganyikan government did not employ the very wide range of monetary, fiscal and other policies which are available to an independent state in its pursuit of development. Tanganyikan currency remained fully convertible with sterling; the export of profits was uncontrolled; and the reserves of the marketing boards and the investible funds of banks and insurance companies operating in Tanganyika were very largely invested in Britain rather than in Tanganyika. The government of Tanganyika, moreover, entered into economic arrangements with the British government which were highly favourable to that government. For example, between 1941 and 1948 the whole of the Tanganyikan sisal crop was sold to the British government under a bulk purchase agreement at prices far below those obtainable elsewhere. Ehrlich estimates that the Tanganyika producers lost £11,000,000 during these years because of this bulk purchase agreement. He concludes, 'this loss to the industry and, by implication, to the Tanganyika government's revenue, appears to be a fairly clear example of "exploitation" by the metropolitan power'.[25]

The economy of Tanganyika remained very much a classical open economy. What economic development there was took place very largely in agriculture. There were very few import substitution industries and little processing of locally grown produce. In 1958, for example, the manufacturing sector accounted for less than five per cent of the Gross Domestic Product. In the same year this sector employed only 75,000 persons. Twenty-seven thousand of these worked in sisal processing plants and a further 13,000 in other agricultural processing plants.[26]

The colonial government looked to private capital from local non-Africans and from overseas as the source of capital investment funds. The government sought to encourage investment by keeping taxes low and by permitting the full exportation of profits. The development expenditures of the government itself were spent very largely on infrastructure, particularly relating to communications and to education, which the government judged essential to further economic development.

Despite the severe inadequacies of this pattern of colonial development, the nationalist challenge to colonial rule which came at the end of this period cannot be regarded as a consequence of these inadequacies. Neither a balance-of-payments problem nor the social and economic strains which typically emerge if an open economy is maintained had yet developed in Tanganyika to the point where they required policy changes which would be difficult to achieve under colonial rule. Indeed there was still a solid favourable balance of payments each year. The rapid growth of nationalism in the late 1950s was not the consequence of a widespread undermining of older loyalties nor of the growth of powerful new social classes with aspirations which could not be contained within a colonial system. For some colonial societies generalizations of this sort are relevant. They do not apply to Tanganyika in the 1950s.

New ideas had, of course, permeated into Tanganyika, however poor and undeveloped its economy. By 1956 over 400,000 children were in primary school classes. These pupils constituted nearly 50 per cent of the relevant four-year age group.[27] Moreover, though these figures must be little more than guesses, the 1957 census reported that 31 per cent of the African population were Muslim, and 25 per cent Christian.[28] Nevertheless, judged by almost any of the indices of social mobilization, Tanganyika was still at an early stage in its development into a modern national society. Daily newspaper circulation in 1960 was only 4 per 1,000 population and there were only 3.1 radios per 1,000 population.[29] Adult literacy was estimated at between five per cent and ten per cent in 1950.[30] In 1957 only four per cent of the population lived in cities and towns with populations exceeding 5,000.[31] In the same year an estimated 740,000 men were participating in the money economy. These constituted only 32 per cent of the total number of adult males in the country. They divided approximately equally between cash-crop farmers and wage earners.[32]

An African middle class hardly existed in the 1950s. There were, for example, in 1957 less than 15,000 African males earning wages of more than £10 a month.[33] A detailed high-level manpower study undertaken in 1962 commented that Tanganyikan high-level manpower figures proportionately 'are amongst the lowest figures of high-level manpower encountered in any country even the least industrially developed'.[34] It was also the case that there were very few African commercial or manufacturing entrepreneurs.[35] Finally, cash-crop farming, though extensive, had as yet produced very few substantial African commercial farmers. The average per capita income of farmers in areas where cash-crop cultivation was widespread was much higher than in districts where farming was still largely subsistence-crop agriculture. For example, in 1957–8 the average payments to African coffee producers from cooperatives in Kilimanjaro and Meru was £47. The national average per capita income in the same year was £6.[36] In the wealthier districts there were of course income differentials as between farmers. These were aggravated in a few districts in which population increases had outstripped the supply of cultivable land and where in consequence a landless or nearly landless class was beginning to emerge.[37] However, the typical pattern, even in the economically productive districts, was of peasant farmers growing cash crops on land which they held under customary law. Individual negotiable titles had not been introduced. Successful African farmers had not been able easily and with a secure title to accumulate large areas of land. In consequence few farmers were earning incomes that would match earnings of those in the tiny urban middle class.

By the mid 1950s economic development and the processes of social change had not yet produced in Tanganyika a powerful and dynamic modern sector led by a vigorous and self-confident African middle class. The impact of colonial rule and of colonial patterns of economic and social development upon Tanganyika society had not been as great in Tanganyika as it had been in most other British African countries. Yet, despite this fact, by the late 1950s the Tanganyika African National Union, which had only been founded in 1954, had extended its influence throughout the whole of the country and commanded the near-universal support of Tanganyikan Africans. The speed with which African nationalism became a major force throughout Tanganyika cannot be explained primarily as a consequence of general processes of social change that were rapidly transforming Tanganyikan society. Tanganyika was not being burst asunder by social and economic changes which colonial rule could no longer contain. Nationalism in Tanganyika spread rapidly despite the comparative weakness of these forces rather than because of their strength.[38]

These forces, however, had produced a small number of individual Africans by the late 1940s who were seeking to win for themselves greater wealth and higher status than they could secure either from farming or from advancement within the Native Authorities. These included the men and women in such middle-rank positions in the civil service as teachers, clerks and medical and veterinary assistants, and the small numbers in similar positions in the private sector. They included also the few self-employed Africans who were trying to establish small businesses such as retail shops or trucking firms. They were townspeople, living apart from their tribal area, though often still closely associated with it. A few of these men tended to move restlessly amongst a wide range of activities that included wage employment, private economic initiatives and the founding and revitalizing of African cooperatives. They saw that wealth, status and influence in their society were very largely in European and Asian hands. They were searching for ways to acquire these same advantages for themselves. The common element in their various activities was, as Iliffe has observed, a concern for self-improvement.[39]

In time their aspirations widened to include their fellow Africans. They came to see that many of their objectives could best be pursued by a co-ordination of their efforts. The African Association, founded in 1929, was a product of this recognition.

Only gradually did the search for self-improvement take political forms. Often, when it did, the specific objectives were local. However, by the late 1940s, the first radical criticisms of colonial rule in the modern period began to appear. They were voiced by men whose restless striving for self-improvement had already led them into a variety of activities. The typical early nationalist was not a civil servant and probably had never been a civil servant for any significant period of time. He was typically a man of some formal education who had worked for local private employers, had tried his hand at starting a small shop or business, and had almost certainly been active in local branches of whatever were the more vigorous African organizations in his town

As the early nationalists were not members of the civil service, they were beyond its restraining discipline. They were also outside the Native Authority structure and increasingly they were rivals to the local elites who held power within it. They were especially active in the smaller towns rather than in Dar-es-Salaam. They had usually come to a radical view of colonial rule from their encounters with it on local issues.

By 1954 a new type of nationalist began to appear. He was the young and highly educated man who had not had an earlier chequered career, but who had come to nationalist conclusions and to an anti-colonial commitment by more direct routes. The founder of TANU, Julius Nyerere, and Oscar Kambona, its first Secretary-General, were nationalists of this second type. Once TANU had become a major movement it attracted other young and educated nationalists. Nevertheless, most of the earliest activists in TANU were nationalists of the first type, men whose pursuit of self-improvement had brought them to a sense of common cause with their fellow Africans in opposition to colonial rule.

The mixture of the personal and the idealistic in the motivation of the early nationalists, and the fact that most can fairly be called members of an emerging bourgeoisie, have led some in recent years to denigrate their contribution to the welfare of their society. It is, of course, important to an understanding of the uses to which they put the power they gained after independence to see clearly that they had the normal human quota of private ambition interlaced with the aspirations which they voiced for the whole society. It is also important to recognize that they constituted a class with interests which might well diverge from those of the African masses. Nevertheless this realism in assessing their activities after 1960 should not conceal the importance of the contributions made by the leaders of TANU in the 1950s. They gave a national focus to the variety of rural discontents which were separately agitating many districts. Their activities, and the work of their precursors in the African Association, helped to create a national consciousness which was sufficiently widely shared that the men and women who led local protest movements came easily to the conviction that they ought to give a national expression to this opposition as well. The early nationalists, moreover, provided the leadership and the national organization which were needed to transform this developing anti-colonialism into a major nationalist force in Tanganyika.[40] Their efforts in these matters were all the more crucial because of the weakness of the new economic class from which these first nationalists emerged. For the very reason that there was no major social or economic transformation occurring which seemed to demand the creation of a powerful nationalist movement, the contribution of those who were responsible for the success of TANU was all the more important.

One therefore returns again to the question How was it possible for TANU so swiftly to win such unanimous support throughout Tanganyika? To a large extent, this phenomenon can be attributed to the unintended consequences of three government policies each of which contributed very significantly to the alienation of rural Africans both from the British and from their own Native Authorities, leaving them enormously receptive to TANU.

The government's unintended support for TANU

The first of the policies which served greatly to assist the emergence of TANU as a powerful movement was Twining's decision to move only slowly and cautiously with the development of representative African local governments to replace the Native Authorities. In almost every District the chiefs and their nominees still dominated the Native Authority Councils in the 1950s. As a result, when Africans became more active and more ambitious politically, these local Councils did not offer them an adequate forum in which to air their grievances nor a feasible access to influence and power. Local opposition to the Native Authorities and to the colonial power therefore was organized outside of the whole system of local administration and in opposition to it.

This pattern contrasts with that of a number of other African colonies in which the British had introduced local councils with a large elected component and had built up non-traditional local government bureaucracies of some status and power before the appearance of widespread anti-colonial sentiments. In these colonies the aspiring African nationalists had less need for a nationalist movement. They could build bases for themselves in the local councils and could hope to acquire positions of influence within the local bureaucracy. Moreover, the local governments themselves, by asserting a degree of autonomy vis-à-vis the colonial government, often maintained their own legitimacy in the popular view. Both of these developments took place in Uganda for example, at the very time that, in Tanganyika, the nationalists were rejecting these local institutions and were pursuing political influence and local power through a new institution of their own creation, TANU.

The Colonial Office, in 1947, had advised that representative local institutions should be quickly established to provide a channel for political ambitions which would otherwise flow into national anti-colonial channels. The Tanganyikan government ignored this advice. Instead it moved very slowly in introducing elected Councillors into local Councils. A few years later TANU benefited significantly from the predicted consequences of this policy of deliberate caution.

The second inadvertent assistance to TANU by the government occurred when it insisted upon using the Native Authorities to enact and to enforce a wide range of burdensome measures which were intended to improve agricultural practices. The enforcement by chiefs of the rules and orders were already an important part of their responsibilities. In 1946, for example, there were over 75,000 persons convicted before the native courts.[41] Insofar as the chiefs were issuing and enforcing rules and orders whose purposes were widely understood and accepted as necessary, it probably added to their authority and to their status. Indirect rule theory had always suggested that if the government wished to call upon the Authorities to enforce orders whose purposes were new to the community, it should do so only after the chiefs had been convinced of the need for these orders, and after they and the District Officers had secured widespread public acceptance of this necessity. For a crucial period from 1946 until 1956, the government of Tanganyika chose instead to use the Native Authorities in much blunter and more aggressive ways to enforce improved practices relating to agriculture, livestock care and land usage.

The primary impetus for this was the increased concern to promote the growing of export crops which was a feature of government policy immediately after the war. Reinforcing it was the concern of the Agricultural Department over the soil erosion and declining productivity of the land which had taken place in a number of Districts as a result of the pressure of increasing population, existing agricultural practices and the indiscriminate keeping of livestock.

The government chose to promote agricultural development through legal compulsion, exercised through the Native Authorities. The compulsion which was involved was not minimal. It was not a case of a few Africans being compelled by law to comply with new agricultural practices after a process of public education had won widespread popular acceptance of the rules being enforced. The practice in these matters after 1946 came much nearer to an effort to educate through compulsion. Native Authority rules were used to secure the initial cooperation of the rural masses with policies which the government had decided were in their interest. N. V. Rounce, the agricultural officer who had been most involved in the planning of the Sukumaland Development Scheme, wrote in 1945 of the need for 'an understanding by those who govern that in place of the stress which forces Europeans to do things, the African must be compelled – and forcibly – to improve the condition under which he lives with his own hands'.[42] Two years later the Acting Governor laconically expressed the judgment that in regard to economic progress 'a great proportion [of Africans] must be driven rather than led'.[43]

This new attitude had begun to influence the administration of rural areas by 1947. In that year the Sukumaland Ten Year Development Scheme was launched.[44] This was a major scheme involving the expenditure of approximately £2,000,000, primarily on the opening up of new land by bush clearing and on water supply development. The scheme involved the imposition, upon those being resettled on this new land, of stringent controls and requirements relating to land use and to livestock numbers. The use of compulsion was soon further extended. By 1952, the provincial administration had convinced the Native Authorities of Sukumaland to attempt to enforce generally throughout Sukumaland rules relating to scores of practices which these officers felt would increase productivity and prevent soil erosion. Moreover, once the provincial administration and the chiefs had set their minds to the issuing of rules and orders, they went on to deal with a wide range of matters of social policy in the same way. The net result was that the people of Sukumaland were subjected to an extraordinary range of detailed regulations issued by the Native Authorities on the instruction of their British superiors. These rules were enforced by the Native Authorities who had issued them. Offences against the rules were heard before the native courts in which the Authorities themselves were the judicial officers.

It is worth having a more detailed impression of this effort to 'educate' a million people through legal compulsion. The Land Usage Rules were a comprehensive set of rules applying to the new settlements. They regulated the size and siting of homesteads, the numbers and kinds of stock to be permitted, and the husbandry methods to be used. The forty-four sections of the Natural Resources Rules included detailed regulations governing the growing of essential food crops, the planting of diseased crops, the control of locusts, the checking of soil erosion, the destruction of vermin, the manuring of land, the construction of cattle dips, the preservation of local forests, the safeguarding of water supplies and the setting of bush fires. The Sukumaland Federal Council in 1954 consolidated and augmented the orders issued under section 9 of the Native Authorities Ordinance. The result was a list of over fifty different orders on an extraordinarily diverse range of matters, which included the eradication of witchweed and periwinkle, the provision of ten days' free labour a year on public works, the forbidding of the use of a hoe to decorate a house, save by chiefs, and control of disorderly conduct.[45]

The all-embracing character of Sukumaland rules and orders makes them exceptional. Nevertheless the use of detailed Native Authority rules to secure community participation in agricultural improvement projects occurred in at least six other Districts. In 1951 the Uluguru Land Usage Scheme was introduced. It attempted to check soil erosion in the Uluguru Hills of Morogoro District by having the Native Authorities of that District require all peasant families to bench-terrace at least one-eighth of an acre of land each year.[46] In Iringa, compulsory cattle dipping was attempted from 1954 to 1958. In a number of other areas, Mbulu, for example, and Mlalo, cattle-culling was required as part of an effort to check the deterioration of the soil through overgrazing.

Almost all of these efforts to promote development through coercion failed. By 1955 mass withdrawal of cooperation within Sukumaland led to the abandonment of most of the rules and orders. In 1955 riots occurred in Morogoro District bringing compulsory bench-terracing and tie-ridging to a halt. In 1957 there was a nearly universal refusal in Iringa to participate in the cattle-dipping scheme. In 1958 the government decided to abandon throughout Tanganyika its efforts to secure rural development through legal compulsion.

It would be misleading, indeed wrong, to suggest that the nearly universal breakdown of the government's efforts to secure the enforcement of these rules and orders is an illustration of a failure by an enlightened government to prevail against the suspicions of conservative peasants in agricultural matters. In many cases the rules involved very heavy new impositions upon the farmers. The building of bench-terracing and the tie ridges and the driving of one's cattle five to ten miles each week to a cattle dip were exhausting and time-consuming. In the peasants' judgment the advantages did not begin to outweigh their costs. This crisis cannot be interpreted as a breakdown in communications or as a failure in mass education. The peasants' judgment in several important cases proved, in retrospect, to be sound. The abandonment of cattle dipping in Iringa did not bring the predicted epidemic. In Morogoro District terraced land did not prove to be noticeably more fertile than equivalent unterraced land. Indeed, as terracing often exposed subsoils, the terraced land sometimes became less productive.

Many of these schemes were, in fact, mistakes. Their social costs and their longer-term consequences had not been fully calculated before the effort was made to introduce them. In more representative system of government, the administrator and the expert would have been restrained by political opposition expressed through constitutional channels. In British Tanganyika the opposition could only be extra-constitutional and spontaneous.

A further important cause of the failure of legal coercion as a technique to promote rural development was the inadequacy of the instruments of law enforcement. The chiefs, subchiefs, and headmen, usually reinforced with substantial numbers of agricultural or veterinary assistants, were responsible for the implementation of the rules. Everywhere there were widespread complaints of corruption, favouritism and vindictiveness in the administration of the Land Usage Rules. Young and Fosbrooke stressed the importance of this factor in the breakdown of the Uluguru scheme.[47] Government officers and TANU officials in Sukumaland in 1959 also frequently identified corruption in the administration of the rules and orders as one of the major factors explaining the breakdown of the Sukumaland scheme.[48]

The effort to enforce agricultural improvement by an extensive use of the Native Authorities had two profoundly important political consequences. Firstly, in District after District, it accelerated the undermining of the position of the Native Authorities. In 1946 it was still very widely true that the Native Authorities were accepted by their people as their spokesmen. This was no longer true in 1956. In the intervening years the chiefs had been compromised too obviously by the colonial regime. Opposition to the rules and orders had become opposition to the Native Authorities themselves.

Secondly, the tensions which emerged in the rural areas as a consequence of these efforts to use the Native Authorities in new and more forceful ways generated a rural discontent which was directed simultaneously against the colonial administrators and the Native Authorities. This discontent helped to 'open up' the rural areas to the influence of the small groups of nationalists who were seeking to win countryside support for the newly created TANU.

What was still lacking was a genuinely national issue which would have a wide appeal throughout Tanganyika and which would bring politically restless members of the peasantry to the view that they must act in concert on a national basis against the colonial regime. Without such an issue, the middle-class and 'modern' leadership of TANU might not have been able to create a common movement out of the multitude of eddies of rural unrest which had begun to stir. That issue was provided by the efforts of the colonial government to entrench within the political institutions of Tanganyika highly disproportionate political power for the European and Asian minorities. For a crucial decade, 1949–59, the British sought to deny that the obvious political destination for Tanganyika was that it would ultimately be ruled primarily by Africans. Instead, for ten years, the British sought to secure acceptance in Tanganyika of a pattern of constitutional evolution which would give each racial community, African, European and Asian, equal representation on the unofficial side of the legislature. They did not intend necessarily that racial parity should be a permanent feature of the political institutions of Tanganyika. They did intend, however, to place the minority communities in a strong position from which they could bargain effectively at a later date for long-term protection of their privileged position. The Secretary of State for the Colonies gave this definitive statement of the British position on 25 June 1952:

> Her Majesty's Government accepts the recommendation of the
> Tanganyika Constitutional Development Committee that unofficial

seats on the Legislative Council should be divided equally between the three major racial groups. . .

I should make it clear that I regard the reconstitution of the Council in accordance with these proposals as a settlement which is designed to last for a considerable period and until the time comes for the main communities in Tanganyika to consider a different system of representation.[49]

The effort to impose a multiracial pattern of constitutional development upon Tanganyika originated in London. It was an integral part of British political and constitutional policies for East and Central Africa. Throughout this substantial part of British-controlled Africa the British were willing to cede a political power to the settled white minorities which was vastly in disproportion to their numbers. It was at this time that the British linked Nyasaland and Northern Rhodesia with Southern Rhodesia in a federation in which white control of the federal government was constitutionally unchallengeable. The constitutions which were introduced after 1948 in Kenya, Northern Rhodesia, Uganda and Tanganyika each involved a balancing of the racial composition of the unofficial side of the legislature. The actual ratios reflected the comparative political power at that time of the European and African communities. In Northern Rhodesia, European unofficial members formed a substantial majority of the unofficial members of the Legislative Council.[50] In Kenya where the European minority was less powerful the ratio of European to Asian to African unofficial members was at this time 2 : 1 : 1. In Uganda, it was, in contrast, 1 : 1 : 2. It is a fair surmise that the Colonial Office was anxious that British policy in Tanganyika should not diverge from the pattern which the British government was promoting elsewhere in East and Central Africa. As a result, in Tanganyika the British promoted racial parity for the legislature of a society in which the numerical ratio of European to Asian to African was, in fact, approximately 1 : 4 : 430.

The decision to see a racial balance in the composition of the unofficial side of the Legislative Council appears to have been taken by Cohen and Twining at the beginning of Twining's governorship in Tanganyika. Within a few months of his arrival at Dar-es-Salaam in 1949, Twining exchanged lengthy dispatches with Cohen on constitutional developments in Tanganyika.[51] Twining proposed that the official majority on the Legislative Council should continue, but that the unofficial side of the legislature should be enlarged, with the number of African unofficial members to equal that of the Asian and European members combined.[52] He proposed that the African members should be elected by the Native Authorities. Finally, he wished to create multiracial Provincial Councils which would provide a governmental level between the African Native Authorities and the multiracial Legislative Council.

Cohen endorsed Twining's proposals. Twining's next step was to have individual conversations with the unofficial members of the legislature to assure himself that they would be willing to support his proposals. He then established the Committee on Constitutional Development, of which a majority of the members were unofficial members of the legislature. Twining submitted a detailed confidential memorandum to that Committee outlining his constitutional proposals. Tanganyika had entered its decade of 'multiracialism'.

There was no serious opposition to this policy from within the government of Tanganyika. By 1950 many colonial administrators had become more concerned to protect the interests of the racial minorities than to prepare Africans for self-government. In 1950, for example, the Provincial Commissioners asked that the Governor issue a public affirmation on the rights of the minority communities. At no time, in contrast, did the Provincial Commissioners call for the protection of the future political rights of the African majority. In 1951 a dozen senior members of the administrative service individually presented evidence to the Constitutional Development Committee. None of these voiced the trusteeship values to which the administrative service had been profoundly committed before the war. None argued for the paramountcy of African interests. Most of these officers shared Twining's concern to apply a brake to African political advancement and to find ways to entrench safeguards within the Constitution to protect the position of the minority communities.

African representations to the fact-finding subcommittee of the Constitutional Development Committee were uncoordinated and often idiosyncratic. However, the theme which recurred most frequently in the forty-two African submissions[53] was that an official majority should be retained on the Legislative Council and that Africans should form fifty per cent of the unofficial side. Africans at that time feared that if colonial rule were to be relaxed too quickly, the minority communities rather than the Africans would acquire predominant control. The most detailed African submission came from the Dar-es-Salaam branch of the Tanganyika African Association. It asked that this distribution of seats (i.e. an official majority and one-half of the unofficials to be African) should be held constant for the next twelve years and that in the thirteenth year a common electoral roll should be introduced with a majority of the Council then being elected. The submission commented: 'Human beings are open to the temptation to experiment. Should you recommend an experiment, we wish to remember that you will recommend an experiment on over 7,000,000 Africans.'[54]

The Committee ignored these African objections. In 1951 it dutifully recommended to the Governor constitutional changes very similar to those proposed to it one and a half years previously by the Governor.[55] The

Committee's main recommendation in regard to the Legislative Council was that its membership should be increased to forty-three, twenty-one of these to be government appointees, twenty-one to be unofficials, with the Governor continuing as the chairman of the Council. The Committee recommended that the unofficial side should consist of seven representatives from each of the three racial communities.

However, neither the government nor the Committee was anxious to have these proposals implemented immediately. Both felt that multi-racialism should first be introduced at a lower level of government. Local government, they felt, was the main arena in which most Africans gained their political education. They were convinced that the future of Tanganyika required an acceptance by the African majority of the Asian and European minorities as partner communities within Tanganyika. They therefore concluded that the African must be educated to an acceptance of 'multiracialism' at the local government level as a prelude to constitutional advances at the centre.

The promotion of multiracial local government in the rural areas was a new idea in East Africa.[56] Such councils had not been mentioned in the terms of reference of the Constitutional Development Committee. Indeed Twining, who had asked the Committee to consider multiracial provincial and township councils, had said that 'rural local government must in practice be confined to the members of one race...it is not practicable to introduce non-native representation on to such councils'.[57] Nevertheless Twining did wish to introduce multiracial councils at some level between that of the central government and the Native Authorities. His memorandum to the Constitutional Development Committee argued:

> ...there is no doubt that the field of inter-racial cooperation is smoother and easier to plough at the local level than at central government level ...the establishment of these councils would help to ensure inter-racial cooperation at the level where it is at present lacking and affords facilities for the political education of the African in conjunction with the other races which is essential to the proper development of the territory.[58]

The government decided to create a two-tier local government system. The higher tier was to be made up of multiracial County Councils, each embracing several Districts. These County Councils were to be large enough to afford their own staffs, to control the disposition of important local revenues and to be responsible for extensive local government functions. The lower tier was to consist of Local Councils. These would be established at the District level and would replace the existing Native Authority Councils. The Local Councils were also to have their own revenues and functions, were to be African in composition and would not be subject to the control of the County Councils.

The Local Government Ordinance 1953 was an enabling act permitting the government to move forward with the creation of these Councils. It effected a revolution in local government policy. Only a few months previously Twining had lectured the Secretary of State on the necessity 'of encouraging development by evolutionary methods'. He had quoted with approval Sir Donald Cameron's view that 'the indigenous system which had its foundations in the hearts and minds of the people had to be molded to conform to modern ideas and higher standards but this could only be done by "enlisting the real force of the spirit of the people"', and he had concluded that 'nothing had yet been advanced to show the need for any radical departure from this basic principle'.[59] Yet in March 1952 Twining recommended to the Secretary of State a County Council system which would be totally unrelated to any traditional institution and was in no way a response to any felt need within the African community. In introducing the Local Government Bill the Minister of Local Government declared 'the underlying principle of the whole bill is inter-racial co-operation'.[60] This objective replaced the older preoccupation with the adaptation of tribal institutions. What now seemed essential was to ensure that the interdependence of the races was everywhere acknowledged and made explicit.

The first County Council was established in the Lake Province in 1955. It was intended to be the first of many. The Minister 'hoped and trusted' that five or six more would quickly follow, two in the Southern Highlands, one in Tanga, one in the Eastern Province, one in the Southern Province, and one uniting Kondoa, Singida and Mbulu. 'The possibilities are in fact almost limitless.'[61] The first Council, the South-East Lake County Council, was a complete failure. It embraced an area far too large for it to have any genuinely 'local' quality. Its operation was dominated by central government officers and there was little, if anything, to make Africans feel that somehow this was their local government. 'Few people in the Lake Province were aware of what it did, considering it, if they gave the matter any thought as "just another department of government".'[62] The African members of the County Council were in effect observers of a complex machinery which was kept in motion by the European members. They quickly lost whatever interest in it they might once have had.[63] Government officers wasted time and energy trying to work new and complicated institutions which served no useful administrative or political purpose.

The South-East Lake County Council was wound up in 1959. No new County Councils were started. There could hardly have been a more complete collapse of a project that had been heralded four years earlier as a creative experiment in multiracialism and as an important and essential stage in Tanganyika's constitutional development.[64]

The full measure of the government's determination to win African acquiescence to its multiracial policies then became apparent. Once it was clear that the County Council experiment was a failure, Twining led his administrative service in a determined effort to secure the introduction of multiracial councils at the District level. His earlier warnings that multiracialism was impossible at the District level were forgotten. By 1957, thirty District Councils had been persuaded to invite non-African observers to attend some, at least, of their Council meetings. The Local Government Ordinance was amended to permit the creation of multiracial District Councils to replace the Native Authority Councils as the local government authority in the Districts.

The word went out from Dar-es-Salaam that the Governor attached 'the greatest importance'[65] to securing the agreement of as many Native Authorities as possible to their 'conversion' into multiracial Councils. This conversion did not involve a significant immediate change in the powers, finances or functions of the Council. Nor did it increase its autonomy. What was important to Africans and to the government alike about the conversion of a Native Authority Council to a District Council was that it involved the appointment to the Council of a small number of non-Africans. Members of the provincial administration devoted much time and energy in 1957 and 1958 seeking to win African acquiescence to this symbolic acceptance of multiracialism. The Member for Local Government in 1957 hoped that it would be possible to convince the Native Authorities in at least thirty of the fifty-seven Districts to accept non-Africans into the new District Councils. He instructed the Provincial Commissioners 'to set themselves the immediate task of investigating the possibility of setting up councils in these areas as a matter of priority'.[66]

This effort to impose multiracialism at the District level, undertaken in the last few years of colonial rule, illustrates above all the strength of the commitment which Twining and others felt to multiracialism. The Asian and European populations in the rural districts were tiny, often no more than a few score Asian traders and a handful of European missionaries. The Native Authority Councils had always been totally African in composition. Many of these Native Authority Councils had evolved from earlier, purely traditional institutions. Colonial Office adviser Claude Wallis, who was invited to Tanganyika in 1955 to review the experience of the South-East Lake County Council, suggested that the government should not insist upon specially reserved seats for non-African members on the District Councils. He recommended that it be satisfied as long as the non-African was not by reason of race excluded from the Councils. This advice was not accepted. The Tanganyika government wanted the acceptance of non-African participation to be explicit and visible for all to see. The Minister of Local Government and Administration continued to insist right up until 1958 that no District Council could be established without the inclusion of a small number of non-Africans.[67]

These efforts illustrate the stubborn, entrenched commitment of the government to its own conception of what was in the best interests of Tanganyika. They illustrate that the government still had faith in the ability of District Officers to win African acceptance of policies which it alone defined. It is this aspect which in retrospect is the most revealing. There were few conceivable reasons why Africans should have been expected to agree to the reservation of seats for non-Africans in the District Councils. Whatever their position and background, Africans were bound to be suspicious of this move. The government's decision to press forward with the introduction of multiracial District Councils is above all a forceful expression of its confidence, even at that late date, in its ability to secure African cooperation with policies which it judged to be in their interest.

The government, in fact, was no longer able to secure widespread acquiescence in the rural areas to policies of its own design. The authority of its agents, the Native Authorities, had been seriously weakened by the government's reliance upon them to enforce land usage and related rules and orders. This prepared the ground for TANU. However, the hostility that had developed over the Native Authority rules and orders was not the immediate issue which TANU directly exploited as it moved into the rural areas. This hostility was a local phenomenon, repeated in a number of Districts, but in different configurations and with different overtones in each District. Moreover, TANU itself remained ambivalent towards these local protest movements. Although their leaders often became the local TANU activists, the national leadership of TANU never endorsed or encouraged resistance to the local development schemes. Nyerere and his colleagues at the national level of TANU were disturbed by vigorous and possibly violent local protests which they neither had initiated nor could control. They tended to accept uncritically the judgment of professionally qualified officers on such seemingly technical issues as the need for cattle-culling or tie-ridging. Wishing to behave 'responsibly' they therefore did not oppose measures which these officers said were necessary.

There was no such ambivalence in TANU over its opposition to 'multiracialism'. The national leaders saw that it was an application in Tanganyika of a policy which Britain was seeking to impose throughout East and Central Africa. They quickly sensed that the issue was, in fact, more fundamental than the timing of independence. If the British succeeded in their multiracial policies, the predominantly African composition of the population of Tanganyika would not be reflected by a similar African predominance in its political institutions. The African leaders therefore correctly saw their struggle against these policies as part of a common African struggle in East and Central Africa against British efforts to block the advent there of African majority rule. The attempt to impose 'multiracialism' at the District level dramatized this issue in terms immediately comprehensible to the rural masses. Opposition to multi-racialism became *the* cause in 1957 and 1958 which united the rural African and the educated and politically active town dweller. This issue aroused deep-rooted African fears that Tanganyika might yet be dominated by Asian and European minorities. The British effort to force 'multi-racialism' generated in turn an African sense of racial pride. Multiracialism was dismissed as 'mseta', a word used for the intermixing of inferior with superior quality grains. This issue more than any other single issue in the final years of colonial rule convinced Africans throughout Tanganyika to support TANU and to seek an early end to that rule.[68]

TANU grew in strength at a phenomenal rate. Nyerere did not begin an extensive tour of Tanganyika until the spring of 1955. He was joined at that time by Oscar Kambona as a full-time national organizer. Branches and sub-branches were rapidly formed in almost every District of the country. This occurred in some cases as a result of the initial organizational efforts by Nyerere and Kambona. More frequently it was a consequence of local initiative. TANU claimed a membership of 15,000 in July 1954. By September 1955, the party's estimated membership was between 40,000 and 45,000. In December 1956 Nyerere claimed over 100,000 members, and a year later, in a private letter, he estimated that the membership was between 150,000 and 200,000.[69] Joan Wicken, reporting in September 1957 on an extended tour of Tanganyika, wrote that over 200,000 membership cards had been issued.[70] TANU had, undeniably, become a major political force.

Direct government reaction to the rise of TANU

The image which most British officers had of their role in Tanganyika was one of a selfless paternalism exercised on behalf of Africans. However, paternalism does not easily accept nor understand the discontents of nationalists who suspect their motives, are angered by their assumption of superiority and appear to threaten much that they have laboriously developed. Many senior colonial administrators in Tanganyika were hostile to African nationalism. They were confident that their policies were in the colony's best interests. They felt that the great majority of Africans recognized this fact and, unless 'got at' by agitators from outside, favoured the continuation of British rule.* In May 1954, prior to the

* Twining continued to affirm this opinion of African nationalism after his retirement; in an address to the Royal Africa Society in October 1958 he said, 'TANU was not a home-grown spontaneous political combustion but the result of outside influences and pressures.' *East Africa and Rhodesia*, 35, 1771 (9 October 1958). In fairness the point should be repeated here that there were a significant number of British administrative officers, particularly at the District Commissioner level and lower, who did not at all take this view.

creation of TANU but in response to nationalist activities conducted in
the name of TAA, Twining made these scornful references to the nationalist leaders:

> My attention has been drawn to attempts which have been made in
> some parts of the territory by self-seeking individuals, usually men of
> straw, who, having appointed themselves as political leaders, have tried
> to stir up the people against their native authorities, and in some cases
> the Central Government, by exploiting local grievances real or
> imaginary...This cannot be allowed to continue and Government will
> not tolerate such activities which are contrary to the best interests of the
> people and are designed to damage, if not destroy, good government.
> Respect for authority, which is an inherent trait in the African character,
> must be preserved.[71]

As TANU grew in strength, government administrators found that
their jobs became increasingly political. They had to be ready to meet and
to rebut TANU criticism. They were in effect contesting with TANU
for the loyalty of the people. In June 1958, for example, a Provincial
Commissioner urged his District Commissioners to hold open political
meetings throughout their Districts. He noted that Nyerere was drawing
larger crowds than they were. However, he was sure that they could
reestablish the confidence of the people if they would check the tendency
whereby 'we are becoming a civil service before we have ceased in purpose
to be a colonial service'.[72] A confidential memorandum in April 1956
from the Minister of Local Government and Administration to District
Commissioners urged that every effort be made to develop viable village
councils. These would provide the means through which government
officers could press their case and win the trust of the people. They would
also serve to channel nationalism into local or tribal patriotism. The
Bahaya, the Chagga and the Hehe, three of the most tribally conscious
peoples of Tanganyika, were specifically cited by the Minister as examples
of what was to be encouraged.[73]

The government relied on more than the political skills of its officers
to contain African nationalism. Beginning in 1953 it introduced a series
of laws and regulations with which it harassed, though it could not
finally restrain, the growth of TANU. In 1953 the government ruled
that civil servants, including teachers, could not join any political movement. It was a blanket and categorical regulation which denied every civil
servant, whatever his position, the right not only to hold office or in some
other way to play an important role within a political movement, but
even to participate through party membership.[74] As a very high proportion
of educated Tanganyika Africans were in the civil service, this regulation
robbed the TAA and later TANU of the participation and leadership of
that most important stratum of the African community.

In 1954 the government introduced the Societies Ordinance[75] which required the formal registration of each branch of a society before it could legally be established. This gave the government a much tighter surveillance of all organizations and placed in its hands the power to refuse or to withdraw the registration of societies for failure to meet the rather demanding formal requirements of registration. Although the ordinance was worded to cover all societies, of the fifteen hundred associations which had been registered by 1955, the only societies which had been denied registration were in fact branches of TANU.[76] In 1955 the government also introduced the Incitement to Violence Act. George Bennett has commented that this Act 'made intercommunal attacks liable to penalty for sedition'. One clause was so drafted that TANU was seriously concerned lest it should prevent propaganda for an African state, especially because the onus of proving absence of hostile intent was put on the defence.[77]

Perhaps the most authoritarian innovation was the 1955 amendment to the Penal Code which made it an offence 'to print, publish or to an assembly make any statement likely to raise discontent amongst any of the inhabitants of the territory'.[78] In defending this amendment, the government offered a reply of a kind which is so frequently used whenever a government seriously infringes the rights of its subjects: 'The law-abiding citizen has nothing to fear from these provisions...but the evil-minded or mischief maker, I hope, has much to fear.'[79]

For three years TANU was an illegal organization throughout the Lake Province, which had been at that time the most politically active part of the country. The government had also been quick to ban branches whenever a local TANU official appeared to threaten public order or to undermine the authority of the chiefs. Typical offences which led to the banning of a branch were the usurping of judicial authority by a branch official, the refusal to acknowledge the jurisdiction of a local court and the encouragement of disobedience to lawful Native Authority orders.

In 1957, as a consequence of refusals to register branches and withdrawals of registration, TANU was unable to operate openly in ten Districts. As well, for a period of four months in the same year, Nyerere was not permitted to make any public speeches. The motivation behind these actions went beyond a legitimate concern for law and order. That motivation had been clearly stated by the Governor in the Legislative Council in May 1954: 'Government will not tolerate such activities which are contrary to the best interests of the people and are designed to damage, if not destroy, good government.'[80] At the very least it must be concluded that by 1957 the government was using every pretext to curb TANU's growth.[81]

A further aspect of the government's response to TANU was its belated effort to restore the chiefs to a position of authority and to employ them as a political counterweight to TANU. As TANU's strength grew in the rural areas, the government sought to build up again the status and the authority of the chiefs. To that end, it passed the African Chiefs (Special Powers) Act in 1957. This Act provided that even after the establishment of a District Council the chiefs in that District would continue to have the authority to issue rules and orders 'for all or any of the purposes for which from time to time native authorities may be empowered...under the provisions of the Native Authority Ordinance'.[82]

A second government initiative with the same objective was the creation of the Territorial Convention of Chiefs in 1957. The intention was to hold regular meetings of a representative group of chiefs on a territorial level. These chiefs would discuss government policies under ministerial guidance, and would in turn lead discussion on these policies at provincial meetings of chiefs. 'In this way, it is hoped to build up a solid body of rural opinion which this Government can use as a guide and to keep in closer touch with local affairs.'[83] Thus, after the decision had been taken to hold territorial elections and after TANU had become a major force throughout the territory, the government sought to revive the authority of the chiefs and to secure their loyalty more firmly to the colonial government.

Twining's opening speech to the first Territorial Convention of Chiefs was extraordinarily revealing. He reassured the chiefs that the British intended to remain in Tanganyika for a very long time. He extolled the chiefs as the leaders in Tanganyika. He was reported as saying 'that the tribe is the most important group in the territory and that its chief is its political and spiritual head...the tribal system is the very sheet anchor of the life of the African people in the territory and that the chiefs are an essential part of this system and are indeed, the bulwark of the territory... it is the duty of every servant of government to uphold the respect and honour due to the chiefs so that the people may clearly see that the government recognizes the importance and the dignity of the position which they hold.'[84]

Twining recognized that with the election soon to be held, the success of his policies required that TANU should be challenged electorally. He therefore encouraged a group of European-, Asian- and African-nominated members of the Legislative Council to establish the United Tanganyika Party (UTP). The UTP was led by Ivor Bayldon and was well financed by European and Asian businesses in Tanganyika. To try to secure for it some prominent African support, Twining decided that the ban on civil servants' participation in politics did not extend to the chiefs. A number of leading chiefs were therefore persuaded to lend their names to the UTP.

In 1956, when the UTP was founded, the government had not yet decided how the representative members of the Legislative Council should be elected. A common roll with high qualifications for the vote was at that time widely canvassed as appropriate to East and Central Africa. The rationale behind such a system was straightforward. The high qualifications would keep in balance the numbers of each racial community on the common roll. The fact that candidates would have to appeal to all of these voters would be a moderating influence. Moreover as each race could be counted upon not to vote for candidates that were known to be racists in their attitude towards it, the moderate candidates would thereby be further favoured. However, in Tanganyika, the African majority was so large that whatever qualifications were set, a large majority of the roll would be almost certain to be African. Kenneth MacKenzie had recommended, in consequence, that common roll elections were possible only in those few constituencies where in fact there might be some balance between the numbers of voters from each race.[85] He felt that a large majority of the unofficial members would have to be communally elected.

In the autumn of 1956 the government proposed that there should be common roll elections in three or four constituencies in 1958, with each constituency to elect one African, one Asian and one European member. It proposed that the voting qualification be set very high, the crucial qualification to be either an annual income of £200, Standard XII education, or employment in certain specified posts. The government suggested that after this election a committee of the new legislature would then consider how the remaining members should be selected.

At this point the dynamics of the government's own policies had their impact. The African members of the Legislative Council, though cautious men who owed their appointment to the Governor, felt that they could not endorse these qualifications. They were so high that they would have disenfranchised almost all Africans, including many in responsible positions. A Committee of the legislature was established to consider the question further. Inevitably the UTP dominated its unofficial side. The UTP then decided to try to strengthen its appeal to African voters by supporting a somewhat lower set of qualifications. The Committee therefore recommended, and the government accepted, that the alternative educational qualification be lowered to Standard VIII and that the alternative income qualification should be reduced to £150 per annum.[86]

These qualifications were still highly restrictive. Only 60,000 voters finally registered in a country of over nine million inhabitants. Shortly after this report was accepted, the government also decided that common roll elections would be held in all constituencies, fifteen members to be elected in five constituencies in 1958 and fifteen in the remaining five in 1959. These two decisions were later proven to have been a crucial turning point in Tanganyikan political development. Despite the high qualifications for the vote, African voters outnumbered voters of the other two races in almost all constituencies. This made it possible for African voters under TANU direction to control the elections for almost all of the other thirty seats, even though ten of them were reserved for Asian and ten for European candidates.

At the time, however, these two decisions were easily taken. The government had come to believe its own public relations handouts. It was confident that TANU represented only a detribalized minority and that the UTP would prove to be a major political force, rallying rural support for the government's multiracial policies.

The collapse of Twining's strategy 1958–9

By 1958 the strategy which had been followed by the government during the previous decade was in shambles. One component of that strategy, the promotion of rural development through an extensive use of Native Authority rules and orders, had been abandoned. The government began instead to concentrate its rural development efforts on extension work with the 'progressive farmer', the acquisitive, innovating few who were most receptive to modern farming practices.

The energy and effort put into the establishment of multiracial District Councils proved a hopeless endeavour. Within a few months of their creation four of the eleven Councils that had finally been established had to be disbanded because of sustained African opposition to them and each of the remaining was kept going only because of continuing pressure and insistence by the District administration.

The third component of the government's strategy to crumble was the government's reliance upon the chiefs as a political counterweight to TANU. As TANU grew in strength the chiefs were in an increasingly exposed position, losing the loyalty of their people because of the support the government insisted they give to unpopular policies, yet fearful to be too dependent upon the government because of the success of anti-colonial movements elsewhere in Africa. Many chiefs quietly tried to come to terms locally with TANU, without openly defying the government. TANU in turn was not adamantly hostile to them. Nyerere put this challenge to them:

> The chiefs' traditional place is the tribe. . .Since African nationalism is
> Tanganyika nationalism against British imperialism it cannot be
> regarded as a challenge to the chiefs unless the chiefs decided to side
> with the British and thus identify themselves with Imperialism. And
> that is the real question. Will the chiefs of Tanganyika identify
> themselves with Imperialism?[87]

The first major break came in 1958 when one of the leading chiefs, Chief Fundrikira, decided to run for the Legislative Council with TANU support. In June 1958, to the discomfort of the government and the UTP, the Territorial Convention of Chiefs endorsed this decision. They were unconvinced when assured that 'the Government intended to retain an official majority in the Legislative Council for a very considerable time'.[88] They were anxious rapidly to make their peace with TANU. At the last meeting of the Convention, on 7 March 1959, they unanimously endorsed a set of political and constitutional recommendations which were largely identical to TANU's demands and they asked that this be given wide publicity. Clearly, therefore, the chiefs were lost to the government as active political allies against TANU.

The September 1958 election saw the collapse of another element in the government's strategy. In March 1958, after a closely argued and strongly felt debate, the TANU Conference decided to take part in the multiracial elections. After nominating their five candidates for the five African seats to be elected in the first round, TANU leaders came to realize that they had it in their power to decide the results of the election of the five Asian and five European members. The electoral system was intended to favour a 'moderate' party such as the UTP. The government hoped that the UTP could win a substantial number of seats by winning most of the European and Asian votes and a portion of the African votes. However the system also permitted a well-organized African majority to defeat the UTP candidates by swinging its votes behind Asian and European candidates who opposed the UTP candidates. It was this second tactic which succeeded in the September 1958 elections. TANU or TANU-backed candidates won all fifteen seats. It was then so obvious that this pattern would be repeated on the second round of the elections in February 1959 that in only three of the fifteen seats were there second candidates to contest the seats against the TANU-supported candidates.

In October 1958, the Legislative Council met for the first time under Turnbull's chairmanship. In his opening address, he faced the implications of the election results. He announced basic policy changes relating to the two crucial aspects of his predecessor's multiracial policy. Concerning the multiracial District Councils he said:

> In the rural parts of the territory there has obviously been misunderstanding about District Councils and particularly about their composition. An essential prerequisite to their formation was acceptance of the principle that membership was not necessarily confined to members of any one race; and that any resident of the area, whatever the community to which he belonged, would be eligible to serve on such a council. This principle is not, however, a bar to the establishment of what may, in fact, be a purely African District Council; and in districts in which non-African interests are so united that the setting up of a purely African District Council would not be inconsistent with accepted local government principles the Government is ready to examine whether such a Council should not be established.[89]

He also made a careful but equally important statement on the equal representation of the three races on the unofficial side of the Legislative Council:

> A belief appears to exist amongst some people that a 'multi-racial' – or, as I would prefer to call it, and intend to call it, a 'non-racial' – policy will, in some way or other prevent the Africans of Tanganyika from reaching their full political stature and from playing their proper part in the government of this country. This is not so, and in view of the many statements that have been made about His Majesty's Government's intentions for the future of the territory I cannot understand why this misunderstanding should still persist.
>
> In terms of population the Africans are and always will be an overwhelming majority in Tanganyika and, as the country progresses, it is right and proper, as indeed it is natural and inevitable, that African participation both in the legislature and in the executive should steadily increase. It is not intended, and never has been intended, that parity should be a permanent feature of the Tanganyika scene. On the other hand it is intended, and always has been intended, that the fact that when self-government is eventually attained both the legislature and the government are likely to be predominantly African should in no way affect the security of the rights and interests of those minority communities who have made their homes in Tanganyika.[90]

These statements were hardly gracious or forthright acknowledgments of the legitimacy of TANU's opposition to the government's policies of multiracialism. Nevertheless they were clear. The British had abandoned their effort to impose their conception of multiracialism upon Tanganyika. Tanganyika was finally recognized by the British for what it transparently had always been, a predominantly African country. Ten years which might have been spent in developing institutions appropriate to that fact had been spent instead in the pursuit of a political strategy which stood no chance of winning African acceptance.

3: Shifting strategies 1958–61

TANU's cooperation with the government after October 1958

The announcement by Sir Richard Turnbull on 14 October 1958 that Tanganyika would develop as a primarily African state proved to be a decisive turning point in British policy in Tanganyika. Within thirty-eight months of this announcement Tanganyika achieved full and complete independence under African majority rule. At the time, however, this could not have been predicted. Turnbull's policy statement referred only to the abandonment of multiracialism. He did not comment upon the timing of Tanganyika's advance to independence. He did not intend that the decision to abandon 'multiracialism' should lead to an extremely rapid transfer of full power to elected Africans.

The announcement in October 1958 was a belated acceptance of political and racial realities which could no longer be denied following the electoral success of TANU in September 1958. The Governor anticipated that TANU would repeat this overwhelming victory in the second half of the general elections which were to be held in February 1959. He saw that he would then face a united opposition of elected members of all races who would be demanding the end of parity and the acceptance of an eventual African rule. He therefore quickly abandoned a policy which this united opposition rendered inappropriate and might very well have made unworkable.

Nyerere immediately grasped the importance of Turnbull's statement. The next day in the Legislative Council, Nyerere confirmed his full awareness of the victory which TANU had finally won:

> We have always waited, Sir, for the Governor of this country, even to indicate that it was government's policy that when self-government is eventually attained in this country that the Africans will have a predominant say in the affairs of the country. This statement we have been waiting for, a long time because it has implications, because once you have made this statement you remove the fears of the Africans.[1]

Nyerere did not then insist that all minority representation should be abolished. He would have been content to let this representation continue

until the minorities themselves felt that they did not need it.[2] Indeed he
welcomed that representation for this further reason: 'We must take even
greater care to avoid anything which might lead the majority of the
people of this country into thinking that the only men or women who
ought to represent them in this council, are those with a black skin,
because they would be thinking wrongly.'[3]

Nyerere was able to carry TANU with him in this matter. The TANU
submission to the Post-Elections Committee which was established in
1959[4] proposed, inter alia, seventy-nine elected seats of which thirteen
would be specially reserved for elected Asian members and six for elected
European members. Nyerere insisted upon this inclusion of specially
reserved seats for the minority so as to avoid any impression that Africans
were seeking to ignore or to overwhelm the interests of the non-Africans.[5]
Kawawa, Keto and the other TANU members of this Committee
accepted his lead on this issue and supported special minority representation for Europeans and Asians.

TANU's moderate and conciliatory policies after October 1958 extended
beyond the issue of minority representation. Under Nyerere's leadership
the Tanganyikan Elected Members' Organization (TEMO) adopted a
positive and constructive approach to government business in the Legislative Council. Beginning with the Legislative Council session in October
1958 the elected members, though 'in opposition', were remarkably
conciliatory towards the government. This is illustrated by their questions
in the legislature. They asked questions to secure more information about
governmental activities. Their questions were often highly local in their
reference. They were questions which were more typical of those asked by
backbench members of a government party in a well-established legislature
than by members of a nationalist movement in a colonial legislature.
Effective supplementary questions were rare. Even when the replies of the
Ministers were transparently evasive the Council rarely heard an angry
observation or a sarcastic rebuttal.

The few occasions when political passions were aroused indicate how
gently the elected members treated the British officials. On 9 December
1958, for example, Mwakangale inquired about the government's refusal
to permit Mr Kenayama Chiume to address a TANU meeting in Mbeya.
Chiume was a leading Malawi nationalist and a close colleague of Nyerere
and other TANU leaders in the Pan-African Freedom Movement for East
and Central Africa. This refusal was bound to irritate TANU enormously.
When the Chief Secretary was asked about it, he replied: 'The reason for
imposing the ban was that it was not considered to be compatible with the
maintenance of public order to permit the person named who has no direct
concern with political developments in Tanganyika to address such a
meeting.'[6] The reply illustrates that assumption of superiority which so
frequently offended but was so often present in the colonial relationship.

Mwakangale was unable swiftly to phrase a scathing supplementary question. He merely asked, 'Is the Chief Secretary aware of the fact that Mr. Chiume is an M.L.C. in Nyasaland and a leader of a registered party there?' When the Chief Secretary replied, 'Yes, and I am also aware of a great many other facts about him', Nyerere intervened: 'Is the Honourable Chief Secretary aware that the public of this country may be very resentful of the statement he has just made?'[7] It was neither a discourteous nor even a particularly sharp comment, but it stands out in the parliamentary debates of the period as one of the very few supplementary questions by elected members which revealed any element of anger or resentment.

A further illustration of this failure to use the parliamentary question period vigorously is provided by the questions which were asked concerning the future of St Michael's and St George's School, a very costly European secondary boarding school which had been built in 1956 as part of Governor Twining's effort to promote a permanent European community.* TANU rejected the whole policy of racially separate schools and regarded the particular expenditures on St Michael's and St George's School as wildly extravagant. During the 34th session of the Legislative Council (1958–9), Opposition members asked several questions on the integration of the schools and, more particularly, on the future of St Michael's and St George's School. Finally on 17 March 1959 the government made this policy statement on St Michael's and St George's School: 'When fully completed, and if a surplus is then available, children of other races will be eligible for admission to these schools provided their life style is compatible and their parents can afford the fees.'[8]

Few policy statements better illustrate the extent to which the understanding and the sympathies of even a comparatively liberal colonial regime are limited by its assumption of cultural superiority. From TANU's point of view everything about this reply was wrong; the school would remain primarily a European school; Africans would be admitted only to the extent that European students did not fill the school; the only Africans who would be admitted would be those who were able to pay the high fees and who had been brought up 'as Europeans'. It must have angered African members, yet it went unchallenged in the House.

TANU's willingness to cooperate with the British after October 1958 extended beyond the legislature to the country as a whole. Nyerere sought to bring the local branches of TANU under closer central control and to

---

* The money had come from the proceeds of the sale of German and Italian property which had been seized during the war. The Financial Secretary had defended this use of a significant part of these funds in these racist terms: 'I would suggest in the present case that the honourable member might possibly consider the source from which these funds came and I think if he gives full consideration to that point he will see nothing unfair in the proposed distribution.' Tanganyika, *Legislative Council Official Report*, 30th Session, vol. 1, col. 369, 18 May 1955.

halt the protests and mass agitation in which the local branches had participated with increasing frequency during the previous two years. In November 1958 Nyerere travelled to the Lake Province where some of the most severe disturbances associated with TANU had occurred in the previous months. Throughout this visit he took an extremely moderate line and greatly assisted the return of orderly administration.[9]

Nowhere was this more striking than in Geita District where the most serious unrest had occurred in 1958. The British appointed a new District Commissioner, Robert King, a particularly liberal and politically sensitive officer. TANU, in turn, appointed Ausosling Mahada as its new District Secretary, a man who was not from Geita and had not been involved in the earlier controversies. Mahada considered it an important part of his job to cooperate in reconstruction of local government in Geita, and thereby to consolidate TANU's victory over 'multiracialism'.[10] King, the District Commissioner, in an interview emphasized the effectiveness of the cooperation which he was receiving from the local TANU leadership in controlling racial hostility and in achieving the cooperation of the newly elected District Council. TANU controlled this Council. Only two of its members had been members of the discredited previous District Council. In the transformed atmosphere of Geita in 1959, swift progress was made in the reconstitution of the Council system and in the general reestablishment of more effective local administration. The administration made similar fresh starts in Kondoa, Manyoni and Pangani, in each case with TANU's cooperation.[11]

TANU's cooperation with the administration was general and widespread. The 1958 Annual Report for Tabora District, for example, comments that Chiefs Lugusha and Fundikira, two of the most prominent of the chiefs who were aligned with TANU, had been extremely helpful in encouraging the chiefs and their peoples to cooperate. The Provincial Commissioner of Tabora Province, Stubbings, reported in mid 1959 that he had been able to enlist the assistance of Provincial and District TANU officials in his efforts to wean local TANU branches away from negative and uncooperative agitation.[12] In Mwanza, African opposition to cattle inoculation was overcome by TANU. In Iringa, hostility to rabies control was halted. In many Districts local tax collections improved very significantly.

TANU's change of policy, or at least of manner and style, was thus very marked. However, TANU's cooperation with the government would not have lasted for long if the British had not conceded major constitutional advances. The Tabora conference in 1958 had declared that TANU would initiate a policy of 'positive action' if responsible government was not won by 1959. Nyerere had taken 'Madaraka 1959' (responsible government 1959) as the central slogan of his election campaign in September 1958. Both he and TANU were as deeply committed as ever to the early achievement of responsible government. However, as a tactician, Nyerere was moderate by instinct and by deliberate policy. Cooperation with the British after October 1958 was the latest expression of his judgment that the British would be more responsive to nationalists who cooperated positively than to a movement that was unrelievedly hostile. Nyerere's tactics had produced a victory on the issue of multiracialism. He was therefore able with comparative ease to win TANU support for the cooperation which he extended to the government after the October 1958 announcement.

British policy after October 1958

The abandonment of many of the policies which had been central to the government's political and economic strategies did not occasion a collapse of morale within the government service. The policies which were dropped had been foreign to the main historical traditions of the Tanganyika service. Officers who had joined that service knew of these traditions. They had originally chosen to belong to a service that had championed indirect rule and the paramountcy of African interests. Within the rank and file of the service these values had been dormant for years and had been overlain with other preoccupations. But they had not been extinguished. Many officers welcomed the changes in policy under Turnbull as a return to older traditions. They were glad to see the end of a reliance upon compulsion in their rural development policies. They welcomed with relief the abandonment of 'multiracialism', particularly at the District level. Most officers accepted the changes as a long-overdue facing of obvious realities.

Many officers by 1959 were in no doubt that the mood of the African majority could easily become one of sullen non-cooperation. Such a mood would have severely limited the effectiveness of those welfare and development policies which provided most officers with the main satisfactions of their work but which depended upon the active cooperation of the local people. That cooperation had already become much harder to win in the years 1956 to 1958. It had been restored after October 1958. In District after District, British officers were again able to secure popular participation in a wide range of government policies.[13]

Turnbull was not without a strategy to replace the strategy that had disintegrated over the previous year and a half. During the period from October 1958 to December 1959 the Tanganyika government belatedly sought to follow many of the policies that had been recommended to the West Coast Governors in 1947 by the Cohen group within the Colonial Office. Constitutional advances were conceded with sufficient rapidity to win the cooperation of the nationalists. However, the concessions stopped short of independence and left the British with a great deal of day-to-day power. It was hoped in this way to achieve a significant further period of colonial rule without the development of serious popular unrest. These final years of British rule could then be used, according to this strategy, to meet the special needs of the territory and to equip it for self-government. These needs, as the British identified them, were economic, political and administrative. In the economic realm the government continued to stress the expansion of primary exports. In the rural areas the emphasis shifted to a concentrated effort to help the progressive farmers, relying upon their example to stimulate others to follow improved agricultural practices. The government looked primarily to private foreign investors and to local non-African investors for the capital and the managerial and commercial skills which were needed for the further development of this colonial economy.

There was a further component to Turnbull's strategy. It involved an attempt to develop institutions which would check the growth of authoritarian rule by the central government after independence. This effort dominated the government's political and constitutional innovations in 1958 and 1959. Colonial rule in Tanganyika, as elsewhere, had been highly authoritarian. However, the British, though not doubting their own capacity to exercise absolute power without corruption, were opposed to the exercise of such power by others. They therefore concentrated their efforts in the final several years of their rule in Tanganyika on trying to build into the political institutions controls and limitations upon the power which their first African successors would inherit.

One major example of this was the energy which was devoted to the establishment of representative local councils in 1958 and 1959. The Tanganyika government thus took up with particular urgency the very policy which the Colonial Office had urged upon it ten years previously. A second illustration was the revival of interest within government circles in the possibility of a major decentralization of government in Tanganyika. In 1958 a Provincial Commissioner, E. G. Rowe, was released from other responsibilities to investigate how the government could best be decentralized. He proposed that the Provinces should become an important level of government with their own functions and sources of revenue and with a representative Council to which the Provincial government officers would be responsible. As his report was confidential within a service that was still almost entirely British he did not hide the political purposes behind such a radical set of reforms. The Provincial Assemblies, he said, would give Africans a chance to participate in the discussion of real problems rather than 'the empty shouting of exciting slogans'. The Assemblies would be 'a counter, entrenched in advance, to political irresponsibility and a bulwark against fragmentation into tribal units'. They would, by becoming jealous of Provincial interests, check the power of a national party. Finally, decentralization would take many administrative matters out of the jurisdiction of central government departments and thus 'protect them from the exuberance of the first political ministers'.[14]

Rowe's proposals were never implemented. The momentum of constitutional development was such as to rule out any innovations that would require any extensive delay. However, the British interest in local councils and in decentralization in 1958 illustrates their concern to diffuse the power which they had themselves carefully concentrated.

The officers promoting these various policies, without doubt, felt that they were seeking to protect the interests of the peasants under a future independent government. However the neo-colonial consequences of their policies are equally self-evident. Had their policies succeeded, the Tanzanian economy would be tied to the export trade and a rural middle class would have been created with a vested interest in the persistence of this policy. The modern sector of the economy outside of agriculture still would have been controlled by non-Africans and the capacity of the central government to act decisively in these and in other matters would have been limited.

It was still the intention of the British government during this fifteen-month period to retain authority over Tanganyika for a further significant period of time. This meant that there was still a very serious gap between TANU and the government. TANU was committed to achieving responsible government in 1959. Its cooperation with the government after October 1958 was tactical. It would have swiftly been replaced by a harassing antagonism had TANU not won major concessions by the end of 1959.

There was, however, no indication at the end of 1958 that Turnbull intended to move Tanganyika towards independence or towards responsible government nearly as rapidly as he was later to do. The evidence is to the contrary. For example, Turnbull, in December 1958, attempted to reassure the chiefs that the British intended to remain in Tanganyika for a further long period.[15] Turnbull's first public pronouncements on constitutional development were similarly cautious. He had inherited from Lord Twining a comparatively leisurely timetable for the next several rounds of political concessions. Twining had announced before the election that a Post-Elections Committee of the Legislative Council would be established to review 'all the implications of the development of the ministerial system' and to 'consider ways and means of improving the executive council and possibly replacing it by a council of ministers'.[16] The timetable which Twining had envisaged thus involved a new election in 1964 with the introduction of a minority of elected members onto the Executive Council only after that election. He had not intended any immediate increase in the participation by Tanganyikans on the Executive Council after the 1958–9 election. Neither had he intended that any elected members should be brought onto it.

After the TANU victories in the October 1958 and February 1959 elections, Turnbull recognized that it would be politic to replace the present unofficial members of the Executive Council by elected TANU members. To that extent, he wished to depart from the Twining timetable. Without that minimal concession, the relationship between the government and the newly elected legislature would surely have been extremely difficult. Turnbull therefore announced that he would not refer the reform of the Executive Council to the Post-Elections Committee. Instead, he indicated confidentially to Nyerere that he wished to proceed with the appointment of some elected Ministers after the second half of the elections in February 1959. That was, however, the only change which he envisaged in the 'Twining timetable'.

Constitutional issues after February 1959

After the elections, in February 1959, Turnbull discussed these appointments to the Executive Council with Nyerere. Turnbull sought to keep this concession minimal in character. He certainly did not wish to threaten official control of the Council of Ministers, as the reformed Executive Council was soon to be called.[17] Turnbull was also anxious that the appointment of the elected Ministers should not upset the ratio of 1 : 1 : 1 which had previously been adhered to in the appointments of the African, Asian and European unofficial members to the Executive Council.

Nyerere's reaction to Turnbull's confidential approach revealed the issues on which Nyerere was ready to compromise and the issues which he felt were too basic to permit compromise. He was willing to move somewhat more slowly towards responsible government than he was publicly demanding. He was willing to accept a minority of elected members on the Executive Council. Indeed he was willing initially to accept the appointment of only three elected Ministers. However, he refused to accede to Turnbull's initial insistence that one of these elected Ministers should be an African, one a European and one an Asian. He and his colleagues deplored this effort to attach racial conditions to the constitutional advances. Nyerere did not insist upon an official majority on the Executive Council. He did, however, insist that there should be no racial requirements attached to the appointment of the elected Ministers.

The detente which had developed since October 1958 between the TANU leaders and Turnbull nearly broke down on this issue. The crisis which followed, though occurring entirely within confidential discussions, generated more tension than any other issue throughout Tanganyika's transition to self-government. Turnbull, as a compromise, then sought agreement on the appointment of four rather than three Ministers, if it would be stipulated that two of these would be African, one European and one Asian. However, five was the minimum number acceptable to the

TANU leaders, for only with five elected Ministers, if there were to be one European and one Asian, could there also be an African majority.

Nyerere's bargaining position was much strengthened at this time by the unity of the thirty elected members of the Legislative Council whose full support in the Council he had very quickly won. Nyerere had been careful to ensure that the European and the Asian members had no cause to feel that they were treated as temporary or second-class members of the elected team.[18] The unity of the elected members held throughout the crisis. At one crucial stage in the confidential negotiations, Nyerere was joined by Derek Bryceson and Amir Jamal, the most prominent of the European and Asian elected members. Faced with this racially united front, Turnbull finally acquiesced and accepted the appointment of five elected Ministers, three to be African, one European and one Asian. Nyerere, in turn, agreed to recommend to TANU and to TEMO that they accept this offer.[19]

Nyerere's choice of the five elected members whom he proposed to Turnbull for appointment as Ministers further illustrated his concern to work cooperatively with the colonial government. After consulting with TEMO, itself an interesting indication of his concern to maintain the unity of elected members, Nyerere nominated the most experienced of the elected members. They were: Derek Bryceson, Chief Fundikira, George Kahama, Solomon Eliufoo and Amir Jamal. Bryceson was a Cambridge-educated ex-R.A.F. pilot who had come to Kenya to farm after the war and had then in 1951 moved to Tanganyika. He had been nominated to the Legislative Council by Twining in 1956 and had served briefly as an Assistant Minister of Labour in 1957–8. At an early date and at a time when he thereby aroused the hostility of many fellow Europeans in Tanganyika, Bryceson had made it clear that his sympathies were with the African nationalists. In 1958 he agreed to be a candidate opposing a leading United Tanganyika Party member and welcomed the support which TANU gave him in that election. After his election he was chosen by TEMO to be deputy leader of the Opposition.

Fundikira was a powerful chief in Tabora Province and was probably the most influential member of the Chiefs' Convention. He was a qualified and experienced agricultural officer and had been educated at Makerere College and at Cambridge University. Kahama had been manager of an important cooperative union from 1954 to 1959 and before that had studied for two years at Loughborough College, a cooperative college in Britain. Kahama had been nominated by Twining in 1957 to serve on the Legislative Council. Eliufoo was a Makerere College graduate who had also studied for two years in the United States. He had then been a secondary school teacher and was soon to replace Chief Marealle as the elected head of the Chagga. Jamal is a Tanganyikan-born Asian who had returned from university in India in 1943 to be active in a family business in Dar-es-Salaam. He was one of the very first Asians to identify himself fully with African nationalist aspirations.

None of these five men had been a close and active associate of Nyerere in the early years of TANU. Only one of them, Jamal, had had a good deal of political experience but it had been special and untypical, for it had been within the Asian community when he had sought to convince its members to align themselves with TANU. None of the new Ministers had active local political experience in TANU within the African community. Only Bryceson and Kahama had had any parliamentary or governmental experience and even in their cases, that experience had been brief. Nevertheless all five were able men who had already carried heavy and varied responsibilities. They were chosen because of this experience. They were also, racially and tribally, carefully representative. However, they were not representative of the various sections of the party. They did not reflect its varied moods, least of all its more emotional and populist temper. They were the five elected members who would be most competent within a Western bureaucratic structure and most likely to work effectively with a senior civil service which was still largely British.[20]

Despite this cooperation, Nyerere and TANU had in no way abandoned their demand for responsible government by 1959. The British may have regarded TANU as being in some sense on trial; but it is equally true to say that for TANU it was the British who were on trial. African cooperation would disappear and there would be vigorous TANU-led agitation if Turnbull's promised announcement was not forthcoming or if, when it came, it was equivocal on the issue of responsible government.

In the summer of 1959 Nyerere argued that Britain should, above all, 'avoid the dramatics'.[21] They should move swiftly to responsible government. This would assure that Africans would take over in a political atmosphere marked by the greatest possible amount of goodwill. The British would thus avoid the embitterment which would surely manifest itself if TANU were forced to seek independence through persistent mass agitation.[22]

Nyerere also argued that the interracial cooperation and the intertribal unity which TANU had generated and was sustaining were political and social assets of enormous value. They would be threatened if Africans came to feel that they would have to fight for their independence. Finally Nyerere pointed out that he was himself in an exposed position politically for he had used his influence and his authority in TANU to win an interim acceptance of the March 1959 proposals. His moderation was being used against him. In a very real sense, he claimed, the British owed it to TANU to give responsible government now. After all, if TANU had rejected the March offer and had initiated a program of positive action, the British would in fact now be talking responsible government but in a much-embittered atmosphere.

Arguments of this type were frequent during 1959. Kawawa for example said:

> There is no need to emphasize here that our people are now politically conscious and an ideal nation is being built in Tanganyika. Our unanimous demand for immediate responsible government is a realization of this fact. This development must be encouraged and this great spirit of nationalism which is already a strong feature of our lives must be utilized in building this country. We hoped that the Secretary of State and Her Majesty's government will not lose sight of this great opportunity.[23]

Nyerere ran a real political risk in seeking to hold TANU to moderate and cooperative policies in 1959. Any nationalist leader in a colonial setting who does not always voice his demands in the most categorical terms risks being labelled a stooge. Nyerere well recognized that he was no exception to this rule. He was gambling that the British would not overplay their hand and thereby force upon Tanganyika a period of embittered agitation.

It was still a genuine gamble in the summer of 1959. The speed of constitutional advance in Tanganyika was accelerating but Britain had not yet decided to pull out of Tanganyika as rapidly as it was soon to do. In March 1959 when Turnbull announced that five elected members would be appointed to the Executive Council, he avoided any commitment about an early responsible government. He merely said that he hoped that he would be able to make a further statement on the constitutional development of Tanganyika before the end of the year. He avoided any suggestion that the further statement would commit Tanganyika to the immediate introduction of responsible government:

> I hope at the same time to make an announcement concerning the next moves forward and to indicate the periods within which, provided the government of the territory had operated efficiently and peace and good order has been maintained, we can hope to accomplish these further steps in our constitutional program.[24]

In the same public statement in which he gave this undertaking, Turnbull announced that he would soon appoint the Post-Elections Committee. This involved no major breakthrough for TANU. Turnbull had had little choice but to proceed with the appointment of this Committee. It had after all been promised by Lord Twining several years previously. The most important task given to the Post-Elections Committee was to consider the composition of the unofficial side of the legislature, now that it had been decided that racial parity was to be abandoned. The terms of reference did not include the consideration of the possibility of an elected majority on either the Legislative Council or on the Council of Ministers.

Turnbull thus still hoped in March 1959 to be able to hold Tanganyika's advance towards independence to a moderate and deliberate pace.[25] The British decision to withdraw as rapidly as possible from Tanganyika dates therefore from some time after March 1959.

By December 1959, that decision had been taken. In that month, the Governor announced that the Secretary of State had accepted the recommendation that Tanganyika should move directly to an elected majority on its Legislative Council and that he had also accepted almost all of the major proposals of the Post-Elections Committee which were based upon that hypothesis. The number of elected members on the Legislative Council was therefore to be increased to seventy-one. Of these, fifty were to be elected for 'open seats', that is to say, seats which would be open to candidates of any race, while eleven seats wouuld be reserved for Asian and ten for European candidates. There would be no separate racial constituencies and no separate racial electoral rolls. Instead, Tanganyika was to be divided into fifty constituencies. Each of these constituencies was to elect one open member. Some of these fifty constituencies, however, would be two-member constituencies and a few would be three-member constituencies. In these two-member and three-member constituencies the second and third seats would be reserved for either an Asian or a European candidate. Thus a total of seventy-one members would be elected.

The franchise was to be significantly widened, increasing the number on the voters' roll from the 60,000 figure in 1959 to a possible total of over one million.[26] In each of the two- and three-member constituencies, all voters on the common roll, of whatever race, would cast a vote for a candidate for the open seat and would vote as well for a candidate for the racially reserved seat (or seats). The principle of a common roll was thus maintained. This was of great significance since Africans in every one of the fifty constituencies vastly outnumbered Asians and Europeans. The European and Asian members were thus to be elected by the voters on a common roll which in every individual case was bound to be predominantly African.

In the address to the Legislative Council on 15 December 1959 in which he presented the Secretary of State's decisions on the recommendations of the Post-Elections Committee, Turnbull at long last made the promised statement about the next stages in the constitutional progress of Tanganyika. Not even the flat and unemotional language of an Address from the Throne could hide the fact that a dramatic announcement was being made:

The Executive Government will be reformed after the general election
on the basis of an unofficial majority; that is to say the Council of
Ministers will be reconstituted in such a way that the numbers of

ministers selected from amongst the people of the territory will be greater than the number of ministers who are public officers.[27]

Tanganyika would therefore have responsible government after the September 1960 election. Turnbull had not only produced the announcement which he had promised by the end of the year; he had conceded all that Nyerere had demanded.

From responsible government to independence

The final advance to full self-government in Tanganyika was remarkably swift. It was not, however, uncontrolled or disorganized. Tanganyika went through each of the various stages of constitutional advance which have almost always marked the transition to independence in British colonies. The British had, however, clearly decided by December 1959 to transfer full power in Tanganyika as fast as was possible. Discussions on the details of the introduction of responsible government began in Dar-es-Salaam shortly after the December session of the Legislative Council. These went extremely smoothly and on 26 April 1960 the Chief Secretary announced the details of the changes to be made in the Council of Ministers after the election to be held in August 1960. These changes would involve the appointment of nine elected Ministers, a Chief Minister who would be the leader of the unofficial side, two civil service Ministers and a civil service Deputy Governor.

The election was held on 30 August 1960. TANU's victory was overwhelming. TANU candidates were unopposed in fifty-eight of the seventy-one seats. They lost only one of the remaining thirteen seats and that seat, Mbulu, was a special case.[28] Mtemvu, leading the racist African National Congress, ran in Bagomoyo constituency and polled sixty-seven votes, less than one per cent of the votes cast for the winning TANU candidate.

Immediately following the election, the Governor appointed Julius Nyerere as Chief Minister and, acting on his advice, he then appointed nine elected members as Ministers. In addition, three British officials served on the Council of Ministers, the Deputy-Governor, the Attorney-General and the Minister for Information Services. When Nyerere accepted the invitation to become Chief Minister and to form his first government, he identified full independence in 1961 as one of his major objectives. Discussions to that end began immediately. It immediately became clear that agreement would easily be reached. Iain MacLeod, the Colonial Secretary, broke precedent and accepted an invitation to come to Dar-es-Salaam for the final constitutional talks rather than insisting that they be held in London. These talks began in Dar-es-Salaam on 27 March 1961 and were concluded on 29 March. On that date it was announced that Tanganyika would acquire full internal self-government on 15 May 1961.[29]

Tanganyika's advance to independence had occurred at a prodigious pace. The result was a timetable for a transfer of power in Tanganyika which was so telescoped as to make it a quite different process from the transfer in most other British colonies.* Nigeria and Ceylon, for example, each had had a period of thirty-eight years between the year in which some members of the legislature were elected for the first time and the final achievement of independence. In Jamaica the equivalent period was seventy-eight years, and in the Gold Coast it was thirty-two years. In contrast to this there were a mere thirty-nine months between the first national elections in Tanganyika and 9 December 1961, the date on which Tanganyika became independent. Even more relevant is the fact that Nigeria had had nine years of responsible government before achieving independence, while Ghana had had six years, Ceylon seventeen years and Jamaica nine years. In contrast to these, the period of responsible government prior to independence in Tanganyika lasted only fifteen months.

Any full explanation of the timing and the manner of the British withdrawal in Tanganyika would have to give primary emphasis to the changing attitudes towards colonial rule in Britain, the increasing international opposition to colonialism and the close link between British policies in Tanganyika and her policies in Kenya, Uganda and Central Africa. There were, however, additional considerations which were specific to Tanganyika, which reinforced the more general arguments for a rapid British handover to a popular government in Tanganyika, and which explained many of the details of that handover.

Firstly there was the strength of TANU. TANU cannot claim so to have pressed the British that finally there was no alternative save independence. Nevertheless the elections of 1958 and 1959 did demonstrate that TANU had mass support throughout the whole country. In February and in early March of 1959 when the government briefly contemplated the possibility of ruling in the face of an organized TANU campaign of positive action, it recognized that it would have been very hard pressed indeed to maintain its authority. The enormous terrain, the widely scattered settlements, the poverty of the country and the comparative weakness of the police and the military forces were seen by government officials as decisive arguments against trying to rule Tanganyika with the mass of the people organized against them. TANU's potential for sustained and disrupting agitation had not yet been tested. But many were sure that it would have been very significant.

Moreover TANU's ability to embarrass the government rested upon more than the assured support which it commanded amongst the great

---

* So true was this that Nyerere pleaded at one point with impatient backbenchers that independence was coming every bit as fast as it was possible to arrange the details of an orderly transfer of power. Tanganyika, *Legislative Council Official Report*, 36th Session, vol. 1, cols. 389–90, 19 Oct. 1960.

mass of Tanganyikan Africans. Nyerere had succeeded in uniting in support of his leadership and in support of the political aspirations of TANU every one of the elected European and Asian members. Any British Secretary of State would also have been severely embarrassed if in 1959 he had sought to perpetuate British rule in Tanganyika in the face of this multiracial opposition.

The speedy transition to independence in Tanganyika should not be explained solely in terms of a Colonial Office which foresaw the difficulties of any alternative policy and which was in any case losing interest generally in its overseas responsibilities. At the end, rapid constitutional advancement in Tanganyika was optimistically and willingly promoted by many British officers in the hope that fuller advantage might thereby be taken of the racial harmony and the moderate political leadership which were such striking features of Tanganyika in the late 1950s. Time and again this harmony and this leadership were cited by British spokesmen as important reasons for Britain daring to move as fast as she did. Tanganyika was to be a British 'showpiece', a 'model', a 'pattern' of how the British can transfer powers smoothly and speedily in an African state.[30]

There was involved in this a policy decision of major importance. The British faced a problem in Tanganyika in 1959 which perhaps has its closest parallel in that which the Belgians faced in the Congo in the same year. Both the British and the Belgians recognized that these two large colonies could not begin to staff their own public services and that if independence was to wait until there was an adequate supply of trained local people there would have to be a further very long period of colonial rule. In Brussels as in London opinion had shifted markedly away from any such long-term continuing involvement. The Leopoldville riots in 1959 reminded the British in Tanganyika that they too would be hard pressed to meet a sustained nationalist challenge. The Belgians decided to move very rapidly to full independence, which was granted to the Congo in June 1960. They assumed that with power thus swiftly thrust upon the Congolese leaders they would recognize that they needed Belgian civil servants, police and army officers for many years to come. They hoped also that the swiftness with which independence had been conceded would generate a friendly and cooperative attitude towards Belgium which would make it possible for the Congolese leaders to accept a major dependency upon Belgium. Thus a long-term future for Belgian interests might in fact prove more, rather than less, likely if independence was rapidly conceded.

Although British interests in Tanganyika were vastly less than Belgian interests in the Congo, the British decision to leave Tanganyika was markedly similar to the Belgian decision in the Congo. It no longer seemed conceivable to continue British rule for a further long period nor wise to do so for a brief one. The administrative advantages of a further brief period of colonial rule might be real, but they would still be marginal. If these added years of British rule embittered relations between the nationalists and the British, the final result might well have been significantly less attractive for Britain. The antagonisms and animosities which would have resulted would have destroyed the confidence which the nationalists had in the goodwill of the British. They might also have shifted the political balance of power within TANU away from Nyerere and lessened seriously the acceptance of the Asian and European minorities which he had won from his African supporters.

Many British officers hoped that if independence were rapidly conceded the cooperation between the nationalists and the government which they had experienced since October 1958 would continue. They recognized the moderation of Nyerere's leadership. They had seen TANU check racialism and overcome opposition to agricultural and other developmental policies. They had noted the recognition which Nyerere and his colleagues gave to the continuing value of their contribution. They anticipated that independence would involve an alliance of nationalists and British officials with the detailed planning of policies remaining in British hands while its public pronouncement and its local promotion would become the responsibility of the nationalists. The British officers had not lost their confidence that they knew best what the country needed. All that they had come to recognize was that they needed help to win popular cooperation with their policies.

The decision to grant independence in 1961 did not involve any dramatic abandonment of the political strategy that had been followed after October 1958. It is much more accurately seen as a development or modification of that strategy than as proof of its collapse. Britain hoped that it had found in Tanganyika a political elite which would accept a continued major dependency upon Britain. The British gave up the idea that they could retain final authority for another decade in Tanganyika. They hoped that by that decision they would be able more effectively to secure a continuation of the economic policies initiated by the colonial government, a British predominance in the civil service for a long transitional period and, more generally, a continuing close association with Britain.

This was no secret British plan. It was not an act of subtle deception. It was an openly proclaimed strategy, a 'Grand Design' for Tanganyika in the phrase of Deputy-Governor John Fletcher-Cooke.[31] In expounding this 'Grand Design' to the Trusteeship Council[32] he stressed three main points: the need to retain as many British officers as possible, the importance of the economic contribution of the non-Africans, and the quality of Nyerere's leadership. He argued that Nyerere recognized the importance of the first two factors but he warned that:

It would be unwise to overlook the fact that there are Africans in Tanganyika who do not share Mr. Nyerere's philosophy. These Africans as I see it tend to allow themselves to be swayed by a purely emotional approach which leads them to follow a purely racial policy. I hope and believe, that Mr. Nyerere will be able to keep these disruptive elements in check . . .[33]

After December 1959 the British strategy rested on the assumption that they were handing over to nationalists who would make few changes to the major economic and social policies of the colonial government. They hoped that the energies that had been released by TANU would be channelled by TANU into support for the government's development policies. TANU's main contribution would thus be to mobilize support for a government that would still be largely run by British officers and to control the more radical and racist elements within the African community. They assumed that Nyerere would accept the need to retain as many British officers as possible and would rely upon them to shape the economic and social policies which the country needed. In the long run these officers would be replaced by Africans but only as fast as there were fully qualified Tanganyikans to replace them.

The British were, in effect, making a double gamble. They were gambling that Nyerere and his colleagues would choose to rely very heavily upon British officers after independence and that Nyerere would be able to control the more assertive nationalists within TANU. There was in these expectations more than the Belgian equation 'après l'indépendance = avant l'indépendance'.[34] There was the optimistic hope that, for Britain, 'after independence' would be superior to 'before independence'.

Part Two

Nyerere and the emergence of a
democratic and socialist strategy

4: Nyerere's political thought 1954–62

Nyerere's basic political values

In 1959, Nyerere brought to the consideration of government policies a profound belief in equality and, as a corollary to that belief, a faith also in democracy and in socialism. Indeed, he was propelled into political life by these values. They emerged from his own personal experience, his contemplation of the condition of his people and his religious faith. They emerged also from a rather eclectic reading in which classical liberalism and Fabian socialism were more prominent than Marxism, and from his reflections upon Tanganyikan and British political life as he observed them, reacted to them and selected from them. He had not worked out these values with others. He did not share them at first in any close way with a group within TANU. They were to an unusual degree personal to him. They were also to prove of abiding importance.

Not surprisingly, equality was the first of these three basic values which Nyerere expounded in detail. The most fundamental ground for his opposition to colonial rule was that it was, inherently and unavoidably, a denial of equality. When Nyerere argued the nationalists' case for independence he referred far more frequently to the indignity and the humiliation of being ruled by others than to any specific failings or injustices of colonial regimes. In December 1959, for example, he said:

> Our struggle has been, still is, and always will be a struggle for human
> rights. As a matter of principle we are opposed, and I hope we shall
> always be opposed, to one country ordering the affairs of another
> country against the wishes of the people of that other country. Equally
> we are opposed to the idea of a small minority in any country appoint-
> ing itself the masters of an unwilling majority. Our position is based on
> the belief in the equality of human beings, in their rights and their
> duties as human beings and in the equality of citizens in their rights
> and duties as citizens. We in Tanganyika believe, sir, that only a
> wicked man can make colour the criterion for human rights. Here we
> intend to build a country in which the colour of a person's skin or the

texture of his hair will be as irrelevant to his rights and his duties as a citizen as it is irrelevant to his value in the eyes of God.[1]

Affirmations of a belief in human equality appear frequently in the literature of colonial protest. They could in particular be expected in Tanganyika where African nationalists were opposing the imposition of a constitutional system which would give disproportionate power to non-Africans. Appeals to the principle of human equality were therefore much in evidence. In some circumstances this might suggest that such appeals were either contrived or shallow. This cannot be alleged of Nyerere's commitment to equality. Even before independence he was ready to battle African racists who wished to deny equal rights to Europeans or Asians. In September 1959, in an address to the Pan-African Freedom Movement of East and Central Africa, he argued for equal rights of all citizens of whatever race, in these uncompromising terms:

> Here we are, building up the sympathy of the outside world on the theme of human rights. We are telling the world that we are fighting for our rights as human beings. We gained the sympathy of friends all over the world – in Asia, in Europe, in America – people who recognize the justice of our demand for human rights. . .Are we going to turn round then, tomorrow after we have achieved independence and say, 'To hell with all this nonsense about human rights; we were only using that as a tactic to harness the sympathy of the naive'? Human nature is sometimes depraved I know but I don't believe it is depraved to that extent. I don't believe that the leaders of the people are going to behave as hypocrites to gain their ends, and then turn round and do exactly the things which they have been fighting against. I say again to my friends the non-Africans in East Africa, that when we say we want to establish the rights of individuals in our countries, irrespective of race, we mean it.[2]

In October 1961 Nyerere demonstrated the sincerity of his commitment to human equality. In that month the Tanganyika National Assembly debated government policy in regard to Tanganyikan citizenship.[3] The policy met very strong opposition from a group of backbench TANU members who wished to limit citizenship to Tanganyikan Africans. Nyerere's response was immediate and passionate:

> Discrimination against human beings because of their colour is exactly what we have been fighting against. This is what we formed TANU for and so soon, sir, so soon before even the 9th of December some of my friends have forgotten it. Now they are preaching discrimination, colour discrimination as a religion to us. And they stand like Hitlers and begin to glorify the race. We glorify human beings, sir, not colour. You know what happens when people begin to get drunk with power and glorify

their race, the Hitlers, that is what they do. You know where they lead the human race, the Verwoerds of South Africa, that is what they do. You know where they are leading the human race. These people are telling us to discriminate because of the 'special circumstances of Tanganyika'. This is exactly what Verwoerd says. 'The circumstances of South Africa are different.' This is the argument used by racialism. My friend talks as if it is perfectly all right to discriminate against the white, against the Indian, against the Arab, against the Chinaman. It is only wrong when you discriminate against a black man. Sir, what is the crime of the world today? It is the oppression of man by man. It is the treatment by those in power, of those who have no power as if they are goats and not human beings; that is the crime of this world; that is what we have been fighting against. . .this government has rejected, and rejected completely any idea that citizenship with the duties and the rights of citizens of this country are going to be based upon anything except loyalty to this country.[4]

A deep and abiding faith in democracy was the logical political corollary of his belief in human equality. Particularly in a society as sensitive to rule by others as a colonial society, a belief in equality carried the implication that all men had a right to share equally in their own governance. Nyerere opposed colonial rule on the grounds that it is always wrong for any group to rule others against their will:

Government belongs to all the people as a natural and inalienable possession, it is not the private property of a minority, however elite or wealthy or educated and whether uni-racial. Government is properly instituted among men not to secure the material or cultural advantages of the few, but to promote the rights and welfare of many. Therefore the many must inevitably be genuinely consulted, and the just powers of government derived from them. Government by representatives in whose selection most of the governed have no part is not rule but repression.[5]

Nyerere was as quick to reject any suggestion that an African elite should rule as he was to reject rule by a colonial elite. In December 1959 he demonstrated this with particular conviction when he argued against a qualitative franchise:

We don't see why wealth and education should be singled out as qualifications for either human rights or rights of citizenship. The educated are not necessarily more honest, or patriotic, or more selfless than the uneducated. . .They are not necessarily more wise. They don't necessarily have a greater love for their fellowmen. They don't always cause less mischief. . .History has shown very clearly that it is when the wealthy and the educated minority mistrusts the poor and the

uneducated majority that the menace of totalitarianism threatens a
state, not when the wealthy and educated minority trusts the majority.[6]

Several years later, in a pamphlet in which he presented the fullest
explanation of his ideas on democracy, Nyerere continued to argue for
democracy in terms of fundamental principles:

> Democracy, or government by the people, is a system based on theory –
> on reason – and can be defended rationally. Given that man is a rational
> being and that all men are equals, democracy – or government by
> discussion among equals – is indeed the only defensible form of
> government. . .The 'good' imperialist regards the colonial people as
> children whom it is his duty to teach. The native tyrant persuades
> himself of some 'divine' right by which he is called upon to lord it
> over his fellows. . .The moment either of them admits the equality of
> those he rules, his position is untenable.[7]

By 1957, Nyerere had come to a settled view of how to bring into
harmony his support for majority rule, which was a corollary of his commitment to democracy, and his concern to protect the rights of the Asian
and European minorities. He took the position which had in fact already
been applied to the Tanganyikan situation by a U.N. Visiting Mission,
that the rights of the minorities were individual rights – the right, for
example, to equal and fair treatment under the law – not community
rights to a share in political power that would deny the African majority
their right to rule. That point accepted, as we have seen, Nyerere would
himself have been perfectly content to continue some specially reserved
Asian and European seats as a reminder to the Africans that they had not
a monopoly of rights or of wisdom.

Nyerere never relaxed his uncompromising hostility to any form of
elite rule. He realized, however, that it was not enough merely to proclaim
his faith in democracy. He had to translate this fundamental commitment
into clear and precise ideas about the institutions which would realize
democracy in the particular setting of Tanganyika. This concern to clarify
his views on democracy began with an effort to resolve the apparent contradiction between his commitment to democracy and the fact that he was the
head of a government in what was *de facto* a single-party system. He
returned frequently to the question of whether a competitive party system
was essential to democracy, each time refining and developing further his
argument that one-party dominance was compatible with democracy.[8]

Nyerere was particularly concerned to establish in terms acceptable to
traditional Western democratic ideas, that TANU's dominant position did
not mean that Tanganyika was therefore an undemocratic state. This
Western orientation is suggested by the fact that these articles were almost
all written in English and were intended for non-African audiences. It is

borne out by several features of his most comprehensive piece on democracy, which he wrote at this time, the pamphlet *Democracy and the Party System*. This pamphlet was written for a National Executive Committee meeting of the party which was held in January 1963. Unlike the other articles to which reference has been made, this pamphlet was written for Africans. Nevertheless its whole tone suggests that Nyerere was still preoccupied with the criticisms which Western liberals might offer to the one-party state. The points which he chose to labour and the examples which he gave both demonstrate that he was still seeking to justify his contention that a competitive party system was not an essential prerequisite for democracy.

One section of the pamphlet demonstrates vividly that he was still casting his argument in Western liberal terms. His point in this section was to establish that party labels in Britain and other Western democratic countries were of little significance because Members of Parliament, once elected, claim to represent the interests of all of their constituents whatever their party allegiance. This is conceivable, Nyerere argued, only if party affiliations are comparatively unimportant. To dramatize this point he added, 'Try to imagine an 18th century Scottish covenanter politely listening to the problems of a group of Jacobites, and agreeing to "take the matter up on their behalf", and you will see what I mean!'[9] One might also try to imagine how members of the National Executive Committee of TANU would sort out the force of this illustration.

In these various articles on democracy, Nyerere was debating against himself rather than defending his ideas against Western liberal criticism. Nyerere had already absorbed much of the conventional wisdom of Western liberal democracy. He had not rejected these values. He was not discarding the ethical and political heritage which he had acquired from his church, his education and his reading. Rather he was examining the relevance to Africa of a number of constitutional arrangements which Western thinkers had long assumed were essential corollaries of these values. His difficulty arose from his belief that the traditional institutions of constitutional democracy were unworkable in tropical Africa. If there was to be democracy in Africa it would need to receive a different institutional expression than that normally associated with it. Nyerere's problem, in other words, was how to 'Africanize' democracy.

The starting point in this reappraisal of the meaning of democracy in Africa was a recognition of how vastly different and more difficult were the problems which faced the newly independent African states than those of established constitutional democracies.

The very success of the nationalist movement in raising the expectations of the people, the modern means of communication which put the American and the British worker in almost daily contact with the

African worker, the 20th century upsurge of the ordinary man and
woman – all these deprive the new African governments of those
advantages of time and ignorance which alleviated the growing pains
of modern society for the governments of older countries.

To the demands of the common man in Africa, intensified as they are
by the vivid contrast between his own lot and that of others in more
developed countries, add the lack of means at the disposal of the African
governments to meet these demands. The lack of men, the lack of
money, and above all the lack of time. To all this add the very nature
of the new countries themselves. They are usually countries without
natural unity. Their boundaries enclose those artificial units carved out
of Africa by grabbing Colonial powers without any consideration of
ethnic groups or geographical realities, so that these countries now
include within their borders tribal groups, which until the coming of
the European powers, have never been under one government.[10]

On several occasions Nyerere drew a close analogy between a wartime
coalition government in a constitutional democracy and the need for a
united effort in Tanganyika to achieve stable government and rapid
economic development. The 'war against poverty, ignorance and disease'
required a national effort similar to the effort needed to win a war against
an enemy power. A coalition government in time of national emergency
is not thought to be undemocratic; neither should rule by a dominant
nationalist movement in a newly independent African state. In such circumstances a *de facto* single-party system is a proper and genuinely
democratic response to a national crisis. It is the embodiment of a unified
national will to achieve goals which are endorsed throughout the society
but which would be unachievable if that community were to be deeply
divided by political controversy.

Nyerere made a further and somewhat different point in his effort to
clarify his views on democracy. On several occasions in 1960 Nyerere
noted that strong dominant parties would be likely in many African
states as an immediate consequence of the unity achieved in the struggle
for independence. This surely does not mean, he argued, that these
countries are not democratic. Democracy, he suggested, does not require
the presence of competing parties, it requires only the preservation of civil
and political liberties which would permit the appearance of rival parties.
Writing in June 1960 in the British weekly *Tribune*, he said:

The notion that democracy requires the existence of an organized
opposition to the government of the day is false. Democracy requires
only freedom for such an opposition, not the existence of it.

In the newly-independent countries it is most unlikely that there will
be a two-party system for many years. The nationalist movements are
going to be very powerful indeed; they will control the government

and organize local development in the economic and social sphere without there being any effective challenge to them from within – and any challenge from outside will only strengthen them. Development of a one-party government will in fact be the inevitable result of both the recent history and the environmental conditions. It will be a long time before any issues arise in the new countries on which it will be possible to build a real opposition organization. This will eventually happen and it will be brought about by a split in the nationalist organization.[11]

Nyerere found a further justification for the one-party state in the disruptive potential of criticism in countries such as Tanganyika which faced extraordinarily difficult problems. He accepted that the governments of these states must be ready on occasion to silence irresponsible critics whose activities might disrupt the unity of the country or undermine its efforts to achieve rapid development. In 1961 he wrote:

It is therefore the duty of the government to safeguard the unity of the country from irresponsible or vicious attempts to divide and weaken it, for without unity the fight against the enemies of freedom cannot be won. . .the irresponsible individuals I have mentioned have neither sincerity, conviction nor any policy at all save that of self-aggrandizement. They merely employ the catch-phrases copied from the political language of older, stabler countries, in order to engage the sympathy of the unthinking for their destructive tactics. Nor are the tactics they use those of a responsible democratic opposition. In such circumstances the government must deal firmly and promptly with the troublemakers. The country cannot afford, during those vital early years of its life to treat such people with the same degree of tolerance, which may be safely allowed in a long-established democracy.[12]

Each of these three arguments in defence of the democratic character of one-party rule in Tanganyika involves an implicit acceptance of a competitive party system as the normal and preferable form of democracy. Each involves an element of apology. This is most obviously true of the argument that social and economic conditions in Tanganyika do not permit the full exercise of the political freedoms. Similarly, the argument that democracy requires only that it be legally possible to organize an opposition party, or the argument that in a time of national crisis a single dominant party in fact reflects the democratic will of the people both admit by implication that a competitive party system is the more normal democratic arrangement.

Nyerere was not satisfied for long merely to argue in such terms. In his search for a settled view of the meaning and the form of democracy which would be appropriate to Tanganyika he came finally to a position which differs significantly from the liberal democratic view of constitutional democracy. In 1960 Nyerere began to develop the argument that the ideal democratic society was the small, closely integrated, self-governing community. In such a society the sovereign body can be an assembly of all citizens, and deep divisions would not develop to distract men from pursuing the good of all. The essence of democracy therefore is government by discussion amongst men and women who share a common life and who are agreed upon their common goals and their basic values. In such a society, men will be able, through discussions and without bitterness, to reach nearly unanimous decisions about governmental policies.

Once Nyerere had come to see democracy in these terms his central problem was to identify the institutions appropriate to a nation-state which would be likely to achieve a modern equivalent to such a decision-making process. By 1962 Nyerere was ready to argue that the nearest modern approximation to the ideal democratic community would be a society so well integrated that the vast majority of its people would see no need for any party organizations beyond that of a single national movement. In such a society there would be no need for a second party and no demand for it. The single party would be an expression of the underlying harmony of interests in the larger society. Within that party there might well be disagreements but these would be tactical debates on how to accomplish accepted common objectives. They would not lead to a separate party or to permanent factions within the single party. For Nyerere, articulate and active interest groups were far from being pre-requisites to effective democracy. They were in his view more likely to overwhelm the general interest in their scramble to promote their separate particular interests.

> In a society which is united, which is like a family, the only differences
> will be those between individuals; then that is the best starting point
> from which to reach the most mutually valuable compromise between
> the good of the individual and that of the community. Factionalism, on
> the other hand, is, by definition, self-interest. Therefore it is bound to
> be anti-social.[13]

In summary, the democratic society which Nyerere hoped to achieve in Tanganyika would have these four essential features: (1) it would be a closely united society in which no severe divisions existed to produce a demand for rival political parties; (2) there would be a single national movement open to all citizens and committed to the promotion of the common good; (3) there would be a sovereign national assembly whose members would be periodically and freely elected by all citizens;[14] and (4) within that national assembly, there would be as full an approximation as possible to government by discussion.

A faith in socialism constitutes the third basic element in Nyerere's political thought, though at this time he expressed it far less frequently than his belief in equality and in democracy. In the few references to socialism in Nyerere's writings of this period, there emerges a highly individual conception of the meaning which he attached to the concept. These references give very little evidence of any close or extensive reading of socialist literature. The socialism in which Nyerere believed owed little to Marxism or to European democratic socialism. There are parallels between his theories of socialism and the theories of some other socialists just as there are parallels between his democratic theory and the writings of Rousseau. But in each case these are parallels rather than derivatives.

Nyerere frequently presented his views on socialism as an expression of values which he felt to be the distinctive ethical core of a departing African traditional way of life. He saw the central challenge in terms of a need to preserve within the still wider society of the nation 'the same socialist attitude of mind which in the tribal days gave to every individual the security that comes of belonging to a widely extended family...It is therefore up to the people of Tanganyika to make sure that this socialist attitude of mind is not swamped by the temptation of personal gain or by the abuse of power by those in positions of authority.'[15]

Nyerere's commitment to socialism had at its core a concern with the moral quality of life. He rarely argued the case that socialism would bring major material advantages. 'Socialism', he wrote in 1962, 'like democracy is an attitude of mind...It has nothing to do with possession or non-possession of wealth.'[16] A socialist is a man who cares for his fellow men, who accepts that the proper and legitimate purpose of wealth is to provide for the welfare of mankind. A socialist society is a society of men with this attitude of mind. It is a society dominated by the spirit of *ujamaa*, of 'familyhood'.

Nyerere was in no doubt that some economic systems encourage and are compatible with *ujamaa* while others imbue their citizens with a spirit totally alien to it. Capitalism, Nyerere argued, was essentially alien to *ujamaa*, and he rejected it for that reason. Nyerere often expressed his views on capitalism in terms closely reminiscent of Roman Catholic social philosophy. He argued that wealth exists to provide for human needs and that no social and economic system is just which encourages selfishness and which permits severe inequalities in the distribution of wealth. By 1963 he was ready to argue in an interview that 'were he to have an entirely free hand government policy he would seek the complete elimination of private profit and would substitute cooperative methods of sharing the rewards of enterprise'.[17] Always the dominant consideration is moral, the effect upon the individual and the society; rarely is it economic, the impact upon the rate of growth.

The moral society in Nyerere's political thought

Nyerere's theories of socialism and democracy are intimately connected. They outline the economic and political systems of that just and harmonious society which is his ideal. The justice and harmony of this ideal society would not be the result of a balancing within that society of contending classes or factions each pursuing separate and partially conflicting interests. The goal was rather a society in which there would be a shared affection and a common life between all members of the society. In that ideal society the interest of the individual citizens and of the society would become identical. The responsibilities involved in membership in the society would have the same moral quality as the responsibilities that are derived now from membership in a family. The demands which this ideal society would make upon the individual would be moral in quality and would be accepted as an exercise of the individual's freedom not as a limitation upon that freedom.

To make this concept of a moral society central to his political theory, Nyerere had to make three basic assumptions. He had to assume, first, that a social order is possible in which there would be a fundamental moral harmony. Nyerere need not assume that there would be no conflicts within his ideal social order. It remains likely that the selfish interests of individuals will conflict with each other's and with society's interests. What the first assumption requires is the belief that the ultimate interests of each citizen would be in harmony in an ideal society and would therefore coincide with, indeed would constitute, the common good of the society.

> In human society the only rational distinction is between the individual
> and the community. Once that is recognized, it is fairly easy to
> distinguish between self-interest and the genuine good of the individual
> – which are two quite different things. The former may well conflict
> with the good of the community; the latter will not.[18]

A belief of this order is not subject to proof and Nyerere makes no attempts to provide such proof. Rather it is an axiom of his political thought. As such it is enormously important. Nyerere assumed that there is an objective common good which is rationally and easily discoverable by men who are not morally corrupt. He therefore tended to view politics as a search for the social and political institutions which would produce a government of uncorrupted men.

The second assumption necessary to Nyerere's theory of democracy was that most men, if not corrupted, would in fact wish to promote that common good. Without this faith in the goodwill of ordinary men, Nyerere would have had to rely upon a moral elite or to settle for a second-best balancing of interests which would avoid the worst abuses of power. With this faith in the goodwill of ordinary citizens Nyerere was able to assume that in societies in which men are not corrupted there could be popular elections which would produce a legislature whose members would seek the common good.

> We have got to have a little amount of faith, although I know that some members have been questioning the idea of faith. But, sir, democracy is a declaration of faith in human nature, the very thing we are struggling to safeguard here, the very idea of democracy is a declaration of faith in mankind. And every enemy of democracy is some person who somewhere has no faith in human beings. He doubts. He thinks he is all right, but other human beings are not all right.[19]

Other writers have already noted the close parallels between the political theories of African nationalists and those of Jean-Jacques Rousseau.[20] Nyerere's political thought, at least in these years, illustrates these parallels extremely well. Both Nyerere and Rousseau were seeking to define conditions under which man would remain free while yet living in society. Both could envisage that possibility only in societies of a very special nature. For Rousseau, man could be free only in small self-governing communities which were without sharp economic, religious or social divisions. In these societies, but only in them, Rousseau felt that a majority of citizens could be counted upon to recognize that the common good represented their own true interest. Nyerere also saw small and homogeneous societies as model democratic communities. Both recognized that the assumption that government policy in such societies would be based upon the common good rested finally upon a faith in the good heart of the ordinary citizen.

Finally, both Nyerere and Rousseau looked forward to the striking of a new balance between the individual and the community. The state would become a moral community. Its members would accept mutual responsibilities and pursue common ends. The conflict between their own interests and those of the state would be no greater than the conflict of their own individual interests and those of their family. Freedom would be maximized, not because the state would make very limited demands upon them but rather because the restraints and demands imposed by the state would be accepted by citizens as a necessary consequence of the pursuit of shared goals.

When at his most speculative and his most hopeful, Nyerere believed that Africa could solve the fundamental conflict between the individual and society and thus qualify for a role which was very close to his heart, 'the role of champion of personal freedom in the world today'.[21]

In writing about his ideal society, Nyerere occasionally referred to the Greek city-state as model. However, far more frequently, the traditional African village provided the model:

The traditional African society, whether it had a chief or not and many, like my own, did not, was a society of equals and it conducted its business through discussion. . .

'They talk until they agree.' That gives you the very essence of traditional African democracy. It is a rather clumsy way of conducting affairs, especially in a world as impatient for results as this of the twentieth century, but discussion is one essential factor of any democracy; and the African is expert at it. . .

In his traditional society the African has always been a free individual, very much a member of his community, but seeing no conflict between his own interests and those of his community. This is because the structure of his society was, in fact, a direct extension of the family. First you had the small family unit; this merged into a larger 'blood' family which, in its turn merged into the tribe.[22]

Nyerere made increasing use of these parallels in his public advocacy of his ideology. By giving his theories this African reference and claiming for them particular affinities with traditional African practices and values Nyerere succeeded in casting his theories of democracy and of socialism in terms which made them more immediately accessible to the members of TANU and to Tanganyikans more generally. This was not a cynical and opportunistic manoeuvre. Nyerere himself was engaged in a process of rediscovering his African identity. He continued to value the cultural and intellectual heritage which he had received from his church and from Britain. However, his own inner harmony, as well as his public effectiveness, required him to integrate these foreign values into an African whole. During the years 1959 to 1966 Nyerere strove to become a genuinely African thinker. He sought to cast his acquired values into African forms and to merge them with specifically African aspirations and convictions.

Nyerere began at this time to define Tanganyika's basic problem in terms of a need to achieve a modern and national equivalent to the close-knit traditional African community.

Here, then, I think is the problem; where does society or the state draw the boundary of its rights and obligations; and those of the individual. . . our problem is just this; how to get the benefits of European society – benefits that have been brought about by organization and based upon the individual – and yet retain Africa's own structure of society in which the individual is a member of a kind of fellowship?[23]

This 'discovery' of African origins for his theories of democracy and socialism was an important early landmark in Nyerere's transition from a young, anglicized intellectual to a profound African thinker.

The third assumption which was necessary if the concept of a moral society was to be treated as central to a political theory which would be relevant to the modern world was the assumption that modern societies can be created which are sufficiently united that antisocial factionalism will be a negligible factor. In such societies most men will normally and naturally associate their interests with those of the community. In their political actions they will, therefore, seek to further the community's interests.

Many argue that this vision, a national community of morally uncorrupted men who seek the common good as their own, is fundamentally misleading. Samuel Huntington, for example, has made this scathing indictment:

> The isolated family, clan, tribe, or village may achieve community with relatively little conscious effort. They are, in a sense, natural communities. As societies become larger in membership, more complicated in structure, and more diverse in activities, the achievement and maintenance of a high level of community becomes increasingly dependent upon political institutions. Men are, however, reluctant to give up the image of social harmony without political action. This was Rousseau's dream. It remains the dream of statesmen and soldiers who imagine that they can induce community in their societies without engaging in the labour of politics. . .This atavistic notion could only succeed if history were reversed, civilization undone, and the level of human organization reduced to family and hamlet. In simple societies community can exist without politics or at least without highly differentiated political institutions. In a complex society community is produced by political action and maintained by political institutions.[24]

It is worth being reminded of the assumptions normally made by theoreticians of constitutional democracy. They point out, as Huntington does, that economic development and the whole process of modernization greatly increase the diversification of activities within the society. The number of occupational and professional groups grows. The economic divisions within the society become more complex and more intense. In large political units with substantial populations, regional and local loyalties are the basis of additional subdivisions which economic development often aggravates and reinforces.

In these situations, they argue, the institutions of government must serve as an important integrating mechanism. There is no common good which embraces without conflict the interests of the members of a society. It is the task of political institutions to produce the working compromises which will achieve their tranquil coexistence. This does not rule out the importance of unifying general interests. There must still be 'common goods', that is to say valued institutions and objectives which are the subject of general accord. Without such accepted general interests the society cannot be harmoniously and peacefully governed. In particular, there needs to be agreement on how society takes legally enforceable decisions. Nevertheless, in modern societies many of the most important interests of the citizen and many of his most valued involvements are unrelated to the state. The lack of a natural harmony is not only due to conflicts that can be attributed to the selfishness of men. The legitimate individual aspirations of the citizens are not in total harmony. The political system has therefore a more limited and pragmatic task. It must sustain a social order within which men can pursue their individual and group interests; it must produce a government which sufficiently promotes accepted 'common goods' and reconciles the major groups within the society so that a large majority of the population are content to accept its rule and to live peacefully under it.

Nyerere's democratic society is altogether differently conceived. His ideal democracy is a society whose laws are based, not on the bargains which are struck between interest groups nor on the unifying aspirations of leaders, but on the deliberation of men who are each committed to the common good. It is a society which seeks to eliminate the divisive impact of voluntary associations, not one which views them as a vital element in the life of the community and an essential prerequisite to effective democracy. He had come to realize by 1962 that he was after a society different in its moral quality from the individualistic democracies of the West. He found the self-centred materialism of industrial societies morally repugnant. He wanted something superior for his own people. He believed that this was not an idle or impossible dream. Several rather different factors explain this optimism.

Firstly, in Nyerere's judgment, it was part of the living tradition of the great mass of Africans that they should merge their own interests with those of others and identify the common good as their own.

> In primitive African society this question of the limits of responsibility, as between the individual and the society in which he lives, was never very clearly defined. The traditional African community was a small one, and the African could not think of himself apart from his community. He was an individual; he had his wife – or wives and children, so he belonged to a family but the family merged into a larger 'blood' family which, itself merged again into the tribe. Thus he saw himself. all the time, as a member of a community – for his community was to him an extension of his family. He might have seen a conflict between himself and another individual member of the same community but with the community itself, never. One must not think that the African is therefore a natural 'communist'. He is not. To him the wage is his wage; the property is his property; but, his brother's need is his need – and he cannot ignore that need. He has not yet learned to ask, 'Am I my brother's keeper?' The African is not communistic in his thinking;

he is, if I may coin the expression 'communitary'. He is not a member of a 'commune' – some artificial unit of human being – but of a genuine community or brotherhood.[25]

The challenge therefore was to find an adequate modern expression for a 'communitarian' ethic which, in Nyerere's view, was still widespread in Africa.

Secondly, Tanganyika had experienced in TANU a national movement which did in fact unite most citizens in pursuit of a common goal. TANU was a modern movement and a supra-tribal national movement. Yet its members had been comparatively single-minded in their commitment to a 'common good', the achievement of independence. Moreover, the National Executive Committee of TANU, its Annual Conference and the Tanganyikan Elected Members Organization in Parliament were comparatively unstructured forums in which a good deal of free discussion of policy took place. Because of the underlying harmony of interests during the struggle for independence, there was in fact a tendency in these bodies to talk until unanimity or near unanimity was achieved. TANU, by its unity and its style of decision-making, seemed already to be a modern equivalent to the traditional political community as Nyerere saw it.

Nyerere finally argued that there were no sharply differentiated economic classes in African societies. A socialist society might therefore be achieved in Africa, not as a consequence of a class struggle in a deeply divided society but as the product of a well-managed transition from a classless traditional society to a modern socialist society. He began at this time to see the particular challenge facing Tanganyika in terms of its opportunity to achieve economic development without the intrusion of selfish individualism and the resultant class divisions which destroy social harmony.

These three factors, the vitality of African traditional values, the actual cohesion of TANU and the absence of classes within African communities, each reinforced Nyerere's conviction that Tanganyika could in fact achieve a national life that would approximate his vision of a moral society.

Freedom of association within Nyerere's political ideas

Many are likely to argue, as for example Glickman has argued,[26] that Nyerere's political theory has had severe anti-democratic implications, despite the importance within it of a rather special theory of democracy. These critics note that Nyerere was extremely hostile to the formation of organized groups within the society. 'The only socially defensible use of "we" is that which includes the whole society.'[27] He dismissed other political parties as undesirable factions. Although Nyerere advocated freedom of speech and government by discussion, he did not accept that the right to associate with men of like mind in a sustained pursuit of political objectives was an essential political freedom. This denial of the right of political association rested in part on a practical judgment that organized political divisions might destroy the still fragile unity of the newly independent Tanganyika. However it was also supported on theoretical grounds. Nyerere looked forward to an ideal democratic society in which there would be such an underlying harmony of interest that there would be no objective need for organized political factions. Tanganyika does not in fact constitute a close and harmoniously integrated society. To present such a society as an ideal could be to erect an ideological barrier to the development of values, attitudes and institutions which are necessary to the accomplishment of more modest and more pragmatic democratic goals.

A further set of questions remains to be examined in regard to the potentially undemocratic aspects of Nyerere's political thought during this period. Some have asked whether the emphasis on the African origins of his political values did not undermine his commitment to human equality. Glickman, for example, has argued that Nyerere makes the reconstruction of society depend upon the assertion of the uniqueness of African culture and that this is in conflict with his faith in human brotherhood. Glickman claims[28] that Nyerere's views on the traditional origins of his ideas on democracy and socialism involve him in a fundamental problem because Nyerere 'would also have us believe that these are peculiarly African traits, which non-Africans do not share and indeed avoid'.[29]

Despite the stress which Nyerere puts upon the moral significance of the economic and political institutions of traditional Africa, Glickman has pushed his argument too far. The society which Nyerere hoped to achieve was distinctly non-racial. There is no suggestion anywhere in Nyerere's writings that Africans are intrinsically different. There is minimal provision in his thought for the actual institutions of traditional Africa. Had he argued that there was a permanent and important role for tribal institutions, non-Africans would have been clearly relegated to a secondary and inferior position. It was the moral spirit of these traditional societies not their actual institutions which attracted Nyerere. He wished to revive that spirit in national institutions in which African and non-African alike would have equal rights.

The uniqueness of independent Africa in Nyerere's view lay in the fact that by historical chance its advance to socialism need not be violent. Traditional African societies embodied the values and social attitudes which were necessary to the achievement of a democratic and socialist society. Nyerere therefore hoped that Africa could make an easier and swifter transition to socialism than non-African states. The final socialist society, however, remains an ideal for all men. There is nothing in Nyerere's writing to suggest that he gave the slightest consideration to the proposition that because of their tribal past Africans alone had the social and moral capacities necessary for a socialist society.

Two cautionary points, however, must be made which lead somewhat back to Glickman's conclusions. Firstly, it is true that in Nyerere's own terms, non-African citizens, having a different cultural heritage from Africans, are not *initially* as ready for the transition to a socialist society. This is an unavoidable deduction from Nyerere's emphasis on the traditional roots of these values in African societies. Nyerere ignored this implication. He never suggested that Asian or European attitudes were a serious barrier to the achievement of a democratic socialist society. The African majority in Tanganyika was so overwhelming that the initial attitudes of Asians and Europeans were safely assumed to have but a marginal impact. African attitudes and values were bound to set the moral character of the political and economic institutions of Tanganyika.

The second point is, perhaps, more substantial. Nyerere viewed equality in individual terms. There is little room within Nyerere's thinking for organized groups within the society. The equality which a racially and culturally distinct minority normally seeks goes beyond individual equality. By 1959 the Asians in Tanganyika were no longer claiming any special and disproportionate political rights as a minority community. However, they did want something more than equal individual rights; at the very least, they wanted to exercise those individual rights in such a way that collectively they could remain a distinct and separate community. This meant that if the Asian minority was not to feel that it was being denied essential rights, Africans would have to concede to them the right to practice their own religions, to follow their own styles of life, to use their own languages, to have their own schools and to marry predominantly within their own communities.

Nyerere himself had no desire to intrude in matters such as these. In 1960, for example, he dealt brusquely with a backbench Member of Parliament who expressed the wish that Hindi programs should be dropped from the broadcasting programme of the Tanganyika Broadcasting Corporation. Nevertheless there is no solid intellectual ground in Nyerere's thought on which to defend the continued separate existence of organized and culturally distinct ethnic groups. The freedom which he sought for his fellow countrymen was the freedom which accompanied a full identification of the individual with the society. It was not the freedom of the individual or a group to follow an autonomous life. It is hard to find within his developing ideology the grounds on which to defend the rights of individuals or of minorities who did not wish to be fully integrated into the majority group. This point is not purely theoretical. It is directly relevant to the position of the Asian minority. It is relevant also to the position of African critics of TANU policies. In 1958, for example, Sheik Takadir, head of the Elders section of TANU, complained that there were too few

Muslims amongst the TANU candidates for Parliament. This complaint touched too sensitive an issue. He was read out of the party and ostracized by his former colleagues.[30] In 1959 when E. N. Kanyama, Secretary-General of the Tanganyika Railways African Union, supported a candidate other than the candidate receiving official TANU support for the reserved 'Asian' seat in the parliamentary election of February of that year, he was driven from his official post in the union and was even denied a continuing membership.[31] Chief Thomas Marealle, senior African collaborator with Lord Twining in the period of his governorship and paramount chief of the Chagga, failed to make his political peace in time with Nyerere and with TANU. He was rejected as paramount chief and faced such hostility that he had little choice but to live in seclusion and without any further involvement in public affairs. There is little in Nyerere's political ideas to check the vehemence with which TANU has tended to reject any who wish to be active in public affairs but who wish to remain outside of TANU.

Leadership and participation in Nyerere's thought 1959–62

During the several years after October 1958, Nyerere was very powerfully placed with TANU. He had led the party since its foundation. The tactics which had brought it so swiftly to power were his tactics. He had a close and sensitive rapport with ordinary Africans which no other TANU leader could rival. His style of leadership, modest, heavily dependent upon example, humour and simple allegories, fitted the popular mood better than the more flamboyant and more stridently anti-colonial style of some of his colleagues. Nevertheless Nyerere could not expect to have his own way on every issue. Even less could he expect his colleagues or the lower echelons of TANU rapidly to develop political convictions similar to his own basic values. There were widely shared political attitudes within TANU which were in fact incompatible with, or at least in partial conflict with, Nyerere's policies and values. An angry hostility towards Britain, a desire for self-advancement, a resentment towards the Asian minority, an opposition to the chiefs, all of these were part of the total complex of motivations that brought large numbers to their common decision to support TANU. After October 1958 and, even more, after TANU members became political Ministers in July 1959, the earlier unity that had been achieved around the single issue of responsible government was not so easily maintained. Nyerere's leadership was not challenged in any sustained and organized fashion. His position was far too unassailable for that. But there were eddies of discontent which had as their generating centre some of those earlier attitudes and aspirations which had been an integral part of the nationalist sentiments of many TANU members.

Many in TANU were less concerned than Nyerere about the possibly damaging consequences of a hasty departure of a large portion of the corps of British officers in the Tanganyikan government. Many did not share his antipathy towards anti-Asian prejudices nor his desire that Africans coming to power should not take over the high living standards enjoyed by their British predecessors. As a result, Nyerere often moved far ahead of TANU's rank and file, even on major issues. However, rarely, if ever, did he do this to the point of creating an unbridgeable divergence between himself and a majority of the people. Whenever such a divergence seemed to threaten, he would draw back, concede the minimum which popular opinion, at least as it was being voiced through TANU, was demanding and seek other ways to win popular acceptance of his views.

Any government leader with strong convictions is liable to be attracted by authoritarian short-cuts in moments when mass lethargy or, worse still, widespread self-seeking, seems to block the way ahead. Alternatively, he may so manipulate the people as to make its acceptance of his policies contrived and artificial and its participation in government instrumental rather than primary. He may at times be quick to dismiss honest disagreement as a product of either ignorance or self-seeking. His high-minded idealism may in fact provide a rationalization for actions and policies that are not a result of his idealism but of his or his colleagues' search for greater security in their exercise of power. Clearly there are both authoritarian risks and an authoritarian potential in the position taken by leaders such as Nyerere who are advocating a radical transformation of their societies.

Some commentators would push this point further. Glickman, for example, concluded that 'successful revolutionaries have understood, however, that as far as their followers were concerned, they had to force them to be free. Nyerere's emergent ideology creates no barriers to that conclusion.'[32]

This is, in regard to Nyerere's political ideas in the period to 1962, unjustified pessimism. There are many examples of political theorists who become so convinced of the validity of their own vision of a transformed society that they dismiss popular opposition as a product of the corrupting influence of the existing social and economic order. They are likely to decide that it is necessary initially to impose their vision upon those who, in their view, are 'morally insensitive', 'suffer from a false consciousness', are 'blind to their true interests' or 'absorbed in the selfish pursuit of individual gain' – the terminology differs from ideological authoritarian to ideological authoritarian but the phenomenon is a common one.

There were but few overtones of this in Nyerere's thought during these early years.[33] Three elements within his political ideas counterbalanced and offset any authoritarian potential that was present in his political and social convictions. Firstly, in his view, coercion was very largely ruled out by the nature of his objectives. The essence of his moral society lay in the moral attitudes of its citizens not in their outward compliance with codes of conduct nor in the increased efficiency of their economic activities. Coercion may sometimes secure these objectives. It rarely increases ethical awareness.

Nyerere's scepticism towards political dogmas provided a second check upon any authoritarian tendency in his political thought. Nyerere strongly opposed any suggestion that there was an elite which already knew in detail what was in a people's best interests. This is illustrated in the following paragraph in which he argued that the members of the legislature in a democratic one-party state must not be subject to party discipline in their debates:

> You cannot limit freedom of expression anywhere without a reason. People are not fools. . .We should have to convince them, and ourselves, that the party line they were compelled to support was so fundamentally right that any deviation from it would be tantamount to a crime against the 'people'. In other words, we should have to elevate policy decisions to a category of dogma. And once you yield to dogma you cannot allow freedom of opinion. You cannot have dogma without putting contrary ideas on the index.[34]

In the same year, 1962, he spoke on the same theme when opening Kivukoni College, the adult college which had been started by the party and was the main training centre for middle-rank officials. In this speech he avoided any suggestion that Kivukoni College should impart a party line. He rejected as arrogant any assumption that there had yet been discovered a perfect pattern for society. He called for a recognition of the central importance of intellectual freedom 'without which progress cannot be made'.[35]

A final strand in Nyerere's anti-elitism was his trust in the moral integrity of the ordinary African. The growing acquisitive individualism which was undermining traditional values was affecting in particular the very people who were most likely to be active in the nationalist movement. Aroused economic ambitions, education, the experience of town life and travel, all contributed simultaneously to the undermining of traditional values and to a heightened awareness of the indignities of colonial rule. It was implicit in Nyerere's writings that the politically active are more prone to selfish behaviour than the ordinary African whose pattern of life is still close to the purely traditional. He did not regard popular democratic controls as a control mechanism to be introduced only at a later date. They were important and necessary from the very beginning of independent rule.

These elements in Nyerere's thought do not entirely offset those which could be developed in an anti-democratic direction, but they provided strong restraints upon any such development.

Nyerere's perception of the state of his nation

Nyerere recognized that there was a real possibility of failure in the early years of independence. He anticipated that Africans would be demanding more welfare services and higher incomes and that unless significant economic progress was made there would be increasing discontent and unrest. If this should happen he foresaw that it would be harder and harder to control racial hostility towards the non-African minorities. Rapid economic development had to be achieved. It was essential to Tanganyika's stability and to her racial harmony. Nyerere argued this in the following terms:

> a complication in the social structure of Tanganyika...makes it imperative for us to raise the standard of living for the common people here in the shortest possible time. In this country, as in most other colonial or ex-colonial 'plural societies' of Africa, the economic divisions between rich and poor coincide almost exactly with the divisions between the races. Wherever extreme poverty exists beside a visibly high standard of living, there is the risk of bitterness; when the problem is linked with racial differences it is even more potentially dangerous than in a mono-racial society.
>
> At present the African can see that his quarrel is not with the non-African in his midst but with the colonial system itself. He does not allow his natural resentment against the humiliations of that system to degenerate into any sense of personal grievance against Asians or Europeans. But, when independence comes, we must tackle this economic complication quickly; if we cannot close the gap rapidly, so that the differences in economic status become less glaring and, above all, are freed from their former link with racial divisions, there is a possibility that the potential danger might become a reality and economic problems bring us back to the very race problem which we claim to have solved.[36]

Nyerere recognized that he and his colleagues were operating under extraordinary handicaps. Many objective features of Tanganyika's economy and of her government appeared to leave TANU no realistic alternative but to remain dependent upon the Western nations and particularly upon Britain in the first years of independence. Tanganyika was still extremely dependent upon a large number of highly trained expatriates. The administrative, professional and technical services of government and the officer corps of the police and the armed services were very largely staffed by British officers. Nyerere recognized that this dependence was vastly greater than the dependence of the West African states when they won their independence. Moreover this dependence could not be expected to decline swiftly. There were very few educated and experienced Africans who might replace the expatriate officers, and the educational system itself was still producing only a tiny number of qualified men.[37]

Nyerere frequently dwelt upon these hard facts in public speeches in these early years. He stressed that a rapid Africanization program in the civil service could have a disastrous impact upon government services. He could not envisage a major capital development program save one financed from foreign sources. He was not hopeful that foreign aid would be forthcoming in the quantity that was needed nor was he free of the fear that it would involve conditions which Tanganyika could not accept. But in 1959 he felt he had no choice but to seek foreign capital and in particular to seek it from countries such as Britain and the United States which seemed the most likely sources for technical assistance, for foreign private investment and for capital aid.

The enormous importance of these preoccupations in 1959 and 1960 is revealed by Nyerere's caution at that time over the issue of immediate independence. Until April 1960 Nyerere never demanded full and immediate independence for Tanganyika. It was, of course, always the objective but he never made immediate independence his central demand. At each stage Nyerere pressed for constitutional objectives which the British might conceivably be expected to concede. He thus focused African aspirations onto attainable goals. In 1954 he had been concerned to avoid an unofficial majority lest it include a majority of non-Africans. In 1956 he had advocated parity between African and non-African representatives, in 1957 he had pressed for an African majority on the unofficial side. In 1958 he had used his influence to assure that *Madaraka*, responsible government, rather than *Uhuru*, freedom, was TANU's immediate goal. This moderation was partially tactical. However at that time Nyerere was also genuinely cautious. He did not want Tanganyika to rush into full independence. This is borne out in particular in 1959 and in the first half of 1960. In that year and a half, there was a marked absence in Nyerere's public statements of any demand for immediate independence. In August 1959 for example he told the press that he was not pressing for full independence. 'In my talks with the Secretary of State I have not made any demands...In reference to TANU's case for independence I have not discussed target dates...We are impatient for responsible government. We are not impatient about independence. We want to handle the education of our people, economic development, improvement of communications and so on. When we are doing the job, independence can take care of itself.'[38]

In December 1959 he acclaimed the promise of responsible government in very fulsome terms:

Next year's Government will truly be a responsible Government, a Government responsible to the people of this country...

We welcome, sir, an end to the frustrations of the past, frustrations which were caused by the inevitable antagonism between the advocates of a New Order and the representatives of one which was dying. We welcome the advent of that New Order, the advent of full co-operation between the people of this country, their representatives, and the Civil Service, to bring about the birth of a new and a proud nation. We thank God Almighty who in his infinite wisdom has helped us to bring about these changes in peace and goodwill.[39]

In the same month Nyerere was asked about the timing of independence. He replied, 'The first steps towards representative government will come next September. The next stage will be the disappearance of the official members with reserved portfolios. The next and final stage will be independence. Before that we should like to achieve two things. First we must increase the economic momentum and secondly we must have a minimum proportion of local men in the civil service.'[40]

These quotations suggest that Nyerere briefly favoured a substantial period of responsible government similar to that of Nkrumah's government in the Gold Coast from 1951 to 1957. As long as Tanganyika formally remained a British territory there would be no major exodus of British colonial servants. A longer period of time would thereby be gained during which there would be no threat of administrative collapse and more Africans could be trained. Finally, in this period TANU could convince African nationalists to abandon the style of declamatory politics appropriate to the struggle for independence and acquire the disciplines which are required for major development effort:

To all intents and purposes. . .we are free already. What is freedom? It is the power we have to decide what is going to happen in Tanganyika and when it is going to happen and that power we have. All that remains is hard work. . .We have a fight ahead of us, a big fight ahead of us and at this stage it is no use; it is not part of our responsibility to spend sleepless nights planning or wondering how we are going to achieve our independence. We must spend our brains, we must spend our sleepless nights to see how we are going to give our people the water they need, to give them the schools they need, how we are going to give the people the health they require. It is easy to go about talking about Uhuru and arouse the people. . .We have to talk now of the road ahead of us. . .There is nobody now we can blame. We have been trained to blame. This is a colonial mind. This won't do.[41]

Nyerere did not persist in this effort to convince TANU to accept an extended period of responsible government. TANU's desire for independence was too strong. Even Nyerere could not have convinced the party to settle for less. In consequence he did not try. Nyerere's attitude in these months is easily oversimplified. His awareness of the difficulties which his government would face after independence explains his occasional willingness to have a somewhat extended period of responsible government. However, Nyerere also shared with his fellow Africans the conviction that their dignity as well as their progress demanded an early independence. He drew back from any real effort to convince TANU to accept something less than full independence. By April 1960 he had ceased to express any hesitations about early independence. He fully supported the TANU petition to the U.N. Visiting Mission in April 1960 which demanded independence in 1961.[42] He was ready by then to lead an independent Tanganyika.

A special role for Tanganyika in Africa

Nyerere's greatest hope at this time was that Tanganyika would prove that justice can be combined with democracy in the multiracial societies of East and Central Africa. He had rejected unequivocally the attempt to give the white and Asian minorities special political rights which were disproportionate to their numbers. He was equally determined that under African rule these minorities should not be singled out for special discrimination. At an early date, he saw that if this was to be avoided, it was essential that the minority races should support the aspirations of Africans for independence. In 1957 he wrote:

> Whether or not the non-Africans cooperate, that is the vital question. . .
> if freedom and independence is won with the willing cooperation of the
> immigrants, Tanganyika, our country, is bound to become a happy
> democracy and an example to the rest of Africa. If, on the other hand,
> freedom is won against the opposition, apparent or real, of the immigrant
> communities, democracy in this country will have to struggle against
> prejudices which could have been avoided, before this country can be
> what it ought to be.[43]

The wish had been granted. The absence of a white community of any significant size, the quality of Nyerere's leadership, the early vision of such outstanding non-Africans as Amir Jamal, Lady Chesham, Derek Bryceson and Al-Noor Kassum resulted in an achievement which was unique within the British colonies in East and Central Africa: prominent members of the minority communities supported the nationalist demand for the transfer of power to an elected majority without any entrenchment of special minority rights or privileges. In Nyerere's words:

> The lesson of Tanganyika must be learned correctly. The lesson is the
> trust of the immigrant minorities and the goodwill of the indigenous
> majority in this country. This is the lesson of this country. The minority

1. Nyerere (holding placard) after constitutional conference, April 1960.

2. Fourteen years later, President Nyerere relaxes at the day's end.

facing p. 86

3. Mao Tse-tung greets President Nyerere in Peking, June 1968.

4. Dar-es-Salaam, 1970; Nyerere welcomes President Kenneth Kaunda of Zambia.

5. Nyerere (on Land Rover) addressing an impromptu roadside meeting.

6. Dar-es-Salaam march in support of the Arusha Declaration, February 1967.

7. Nantira (Mara Region) *ujamaa* villagers in their tea nursery.

8. Carrying water to a building site in a Dodoma Region *ujamaa* village.

9. Wheat harvest from a 120-acre farm in a Sumbawanga *ujamaa* village.

10. Members of Nantira village in Mara Region building new houses.

11. Members of Parliament and Chamwino *ujamaa* villagers husking millet.

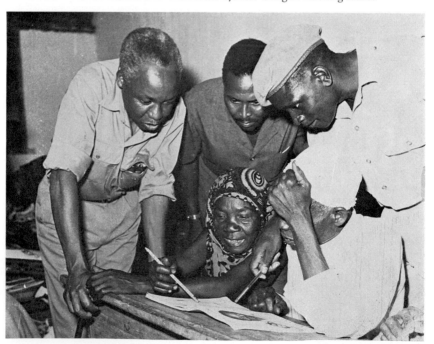

12. President Nyerere (left) calls on an adult literacy class.

13. Literacy classes adjacent to a family enclosure in Dodoma Region.

14. (Centre, left to right) Emperor Haile Selassie, Nyerere and the author at the University of Dar-es-Salaam site in 1964; in the background, a block of lecture rooms, part of a British government capital grant.

15. Rashidi Kawawa touring the Chinese-assisted Uhuru railway.

16. National Servicemen marching on the 21st anniversary of TANU, 7 July 1972.

facing p. 87

communities in this country, unlike the minority communities in other countries, have said, 'We will trust in the goodwill of the majority community in Tanganyika.' That is the big lesson, Sir, of this country,[44]

Our lesson must be learned by the diehards and reactionaries among the immigrants of Kenya, Rhodesia, Nyasaland and the rest. They are the ones that must learn that their only hope for security lies in trusting the goodwill of the majority. Unless those who have made their homes in Africa can forget the past, can abandon their false claims to be the heaven sent mentors of the African. . .then the example of Tanganyika will have been wasted.[45]

As soon as the predominantly African character of the political institutions in Tanganyika were assured Nyerere at once placed upon Africans the moral obligation to demonstrate to the non-Africans that their trust had been justified. He called his own people to greatness, seeking to establish it as a point of real national pride that the minorities would be treated generously and with full justice. In a radio broadcast which he made in September 1960, when he first became Chief Minister, he said:

We must learn to forget the arrogance and prejudices and also the irritations and humiliations of the past. . .I know the people of this country have already earned the admiration of millions of other people abroad through the way in which the struggle for freedom has been conducted. Militant nationalism has been combined with a smile and good humour. Temptation to violence and lawlessness as a means to independence has been resisted. The people of Tanganyika became fervent nationalists without becoming racialists. Colonialism was hated but the hatred did not spread to the peoples who represented colonialism. Bad laws were resented but there was no resort to lawlessness in order to remove them. This is maturity. I know this maturity has a firm foundation in our character as a people.[46]

Nyerere hoped that the example of Tanganyika would help to relieve the fears of the whites in Rhodesia and in South Africa concerning majority rule. He hoped Tanganyika could thus contribute in an important way to the resolution of the racial tensions that bedevilled the Rhodesias and South Africa.

The example we have set is worth much more than gold, and we will continue to show the world that it is possible for the people of different races to live together as one nation.[47]

We cannot afford to fail now for our progress will be watched from beyond our borders by those other countries whose human problems are still so tragically tangled. . .That must not be allowed to happen.

If it did, the tragedy would not be Tanganyika's alone. The diehards and reactionaries beyond our borders – the Doubting Thomases whom we are trying to convert – would point at us not as an 'example' but as an 'object lesson'. They would unscrupulously use that 'object lesson' as a tool to repair the breaches in the entrenched position of privilege, by blaming difficulties on 'democracy misapplied'.[48]

An important ingredient in Nyerere's hope that the example of Tanganyika would have a significant influence on Central Africa was his expectation that the British decision to grant independence in Tanganyika on the basis of majority rule marked a decisive triumph of the liberal over the imperialist tradition in British colonial policy. He was closer intellectually and personally to British critics of colonial rule than to any other group of intellectuals.[49]

Far from reacting negatively and with hostility to British traditions and values, he had drawn deeply from a major strand within these traditions and values. He acknowledged a continuing common cause with those in Britain who had sought to win British acceptance of majority rule in East and Central Africa.

Nyerere's dream that white attitudes in Rhodesia and in South Africa might be transformed by the example of Tanganyika, his hope that that example would strengthen British resolve to support majority rule in southern Africa, and his hard-headed assessment of the administrative and economic constraints to development in an independent Tanganyika all led to the same conclusion, that an independent Tanganyika should be very cautious in its internal policies and should work closely and harmoniously with Britain. This would at once reassure the minority communities of their long-term future in Tanganyika and help to convince Britain to repeat the 'Tanganyikan experiment' in Kenya and in the Rhodesias. These policies would increase the prospects of foreign aid. They would also lessen the risk of a major immediate exodus of British civil servants which would leave Tanganyika without the administrative talents and the technical and professional skills needed for a major development effort.

These considerations seemed compelling. Nyerere's ideas on socialism and on a one-party democracy remained, for the moment, intellectual exercises. In time their impact was to be very substantial. However in these years a different idea – that of encouraging Britain and the whites of southern Africa to a greater trust of African rule – and a different set of preoccupations – the overwhelming sense of a total lack of any realistic option – led Nyerere to the deliberate choice of a neo-colonial dependence upon Britain.

One final quotation will serve to illustrate how prominent were these two considerations in 1959 and 1960. In an unprepared statement in the

Legislative Council in October 1959, he defended in these terms his willingness to accept responsible government as a transitional stage:

> I am not sure, Sir, that the rest of Africa does not sometimes regard the people of Tanganyika as a bunch of stooges of colonialism; a bunch of fellows, who instead of asking for independence now, are perfectly happy with half-measures and compromise. Why Sir, have we elected to proceed in this way?. . .we are anxious to see that that process, which is an inevitable process, that this process does not create enmity between the people of this country and the people of Britain. This matter, Sir, of human relations is important. In fact it can be everything in life. . .
>
> We in Tanganyika want to demonstrate to the people of Britain, by the very methods that we are adopting to reach our independence, that we want nothing but lasting friendship between our two peoples. We are not doing this out of weakness, we do not regard this as a struggle between our people and the people of Britain; this is a development of historical process. . .We are doing it from a sincere desire to avoid the addition of bitterness to a world which already has too much bitterness. . .
>
> I have said before elsewhere that we, the people of Tanganyika would like to light a candle and put it on top of Mount Kilimanjaro which would shine beyond our borders giving hope where there was despair, love where there was hate, and dignity where before there was only humiliation. We pray the people of Britain, and our neighbours of all races, to look upon Tanganyika and what we are trying to do, not as an embarrassment, but as a ray of hope. We cannot, unlike other countries, send rockets to the moon, but we can send rockets of love and hope to all our fellow men wherever they may be.
>
> Last, Sir, but not least, we have a tremendous task ahead of us, a task which any under-developed country like Tanganyika must face. We want, as we have said, to wage a war against poverty, ignorance and disease and raise the standard of living of our people. We know that this task cannot be properly done without the willing co-operation of all our people and the harnessing of all the available brain and skill in Tanganyika. All these matters will depend upon the manner in which we achieve our independence. It is for this reason that we, the people of Tanganyika, have chosen to seek our independence in the manner in which we are doing.[50]

5: The operation and abandonment of a dependent relationship 1959–62

Introduction: the strategy of dependence

The argument has been developed in chapter 3 that the British expected that an independent Tanganyika would continue to accept a close and dependent relationship with Britain. The preceding chapter suggested that Nyerere had agreed that continued close association with Britain was necessary and that, despite some undercurrent of hostility to this policy, he had secured TANU's acquiescence to it.

There was thus broad agreement between TANU leaders and the senior British officials in Tanganyika about the political and economic strategy to be followed in Tanganyika. This strategy had these features:

1   The government of Tanganyika would be unable, for a good many years, to staff its civil service with Tanganyikans. It would have to retain the services of as many serving British officers as possible and be ready to continue to recruit expatriates for the civil service whenever it was clear that suitably trained and experienced Tanganyikans were not available.

2   Government policy would be under the overall control and direction of a political Cabinet. However, detailed policy preparation and implementation would fall very largely to the senior civil service, which would continue to be staffed predominantly by British officers. Thus both officers and the leaders of TANU expected no major change in government policies or in the way in which those policies were administered.

3   Rural economic development would be promoted by the continued encouragement of the progressive farmer, relying upon the example of his success to stimulate an increasingly active participation in the money economy by the majority of cultivators.

4   Tanganyika would continue to encourage private foreign investment and private local investment in the manufacturing and commercial sectors of the economy.

5   The European and Asian communities in Tanganyika would have an important contribution to make to the further development of Tanganyika. These communities had abandoned earlier claims to disproportionate political representation and to special rights and privileges as minority communities. Their members now needed assurance that they

could live in peace and without fear in Tanganyika and that their contribution to the economy was welcome and would be protected.

6 TANU's role in an independent Tanganyika would be twofold. The
party should check any popular expressions of racist hostility towards the
minority communities or towards Britain. Any serious outbreaks of
African racism would lead to expatriate resignations, declining foreign aid
and severe cuts in domestic and foreign private investments. It would also
end Tanganyika's dream to demonstrate that just rule under a majority
government was possible in East and Central Africa. Secondly, TANU
would mobilize popular support for government development policies,
converting the mass participation which it had secured in the independence
struggle into a government-directed, national development effort.

Nyerere had not expected that this strategy could be easily or soon abandoned. Nevertheless his resignation in January 1962, at a time when the
shortage of trained people had in no way yet abated, in fact marked the
end of this acceptance of a 'neo-colonial' relationship and the beginning
of a lengthy search for a development strategy which would not entail
a major reliance upon any foreign power.

This abrupt change in basic policy is explained by three consequences
of the dependence strategy, each of them essentially political and none of
them adequately anticipated. The close association with Britain involved
many more irritants both to the leadership and the rank and file of TANU
than had been expected. It intensified the strain and tension between the
top leadership and the middle-rank party activists. Finally, because government policies had been very largely devised by expatriate officials and were
still largely administered by them, it greatly increased the difficulty which
TANU faced in trying to transfer the mass support it had earlier received
to the support of these policies. These three factors, interacting with
ideological and personal considerations that were particular to Nyerere
himself, led in January 1962 to what was in effect a sudden abandonment
of the close and special relationship with Britain.

This chapter will illustrate the operation of the dependence strategy in
the period 1959–62, it will discuss the crisis which led finally to Nyerere's
resignation from the prime ministership on 24 January 1962 and it will
consider the main characteristics of the political strategy which then
emerged during the prime ministership of Rashidi Kawawa in 1962.

The dependence strategy in operation

Nothing was more influential in shaping the initial political strategy than
the realization that an independent Tanganyika would be incapable of
maintaining the level and standards of existing government services without a great deal of foreign assistance. Nyerere recognized that Tanganyika
was in a much more difficult position in this regard than the West African

colonies: 'In West Africa the Colonial Office made its policy clear from the beginning and a local service was trained in good time. Here events have suddenly begun to move so quickly that there simply are not enough local people with the necessary training available.'[1]

In 1959 there were 299 administrative officers serving in the government of Tanganyika. Only seven of these 299 officers were Tanganyikans. These seven had all been recently appointed. The first of these seven to be appointed, Dunstan Omari, had been appointed in 1955, and three others had followed between 1956 and 1959. Early in 1959 the final three were appointed and were then immediately sent to the United Kingdom for training. There were also a further 47 assistant administrative officers. These officers were Tanganyikans who were not graduates and who played a supporting and subordinate role within the provincial administration. They had first been recruited in 1955. They were, of course, soon to be one of the few sources of Tanganyikans with any experience at all in public administration.[2]

By June 1961 the situation was only marginally better. The assistant administrative officers, newly retitled Administrative Officers Class IV, now numbered 77. They were all Tanganyikans. There were 264 Class III officers of whom 16 were Tanganyikans. All 78 of the officers above that class, including the 6 Class I officers and the 21 staff-grade officers, were British. All Permanent Secretaries (the senior civil servant in each Ministry), all Principal Secretaries and all Principal Assistant Secretaries were expatriates. Every one of the Provincial Commissioners and 55 of the 57 District Commissioners were also British officers.[3]

This pattern was repeated in almost every Ministry. The Central Government Directory for September 1959 listed 115 senior government officers working in the Dar-es-Salaam area. Only 2 of these officers were African. There were only marginal improvements made to this pattern during the next two years. In September 1961, for example, there were still only 2 Africans amongst the 75 senior and middle-rank officers in the Treasury.[4]

The Ministries which were primarily involved in activities in the rural areas, such as the Departments of Health and of Agriculture, were also almost entirely dependent upon expatriates in those posts which required a full professional qualification. Thus, for example, in the Department of Agriculture all 15 of the senior agricultural field officers were expatriate as were 95 of the 124 agricultural field officers. In the Department of Health there were 157 medical officers and specialists. Fifty-six of these were local officers, but only 13 of these 56 Tanganyikans were African.[5]

Even in the field of education, the government was still heavily dependent upon foreigners. Of 616 government education officers in July 1961, most of whom were teachers, only 67 were African.[6] There were a further 75 education officers in the field of technical education, none of whom were African. At the end of March 1961, only 547 of the approximately 4,000 posts in the middle and higher salary scales were held by Africans.[7]

Not only within the civil service, but outside of it as well, there were very few Africans in occupations requiring professional or technical training. Tobias, in his 1962 report on high-level manpower needs in Tanganyika, identified 3,100 positions in the public and private sectors which required technical or professional qualifications. Of these, 1,300 were held by Africans. However, all but 200 of these were medical technicians, nurses or teachers. Table 1 illustrates how dependent Tanganyika was still upon foreigners for a great many professional skills which the country needed.

Table 1. *Employment in selected professions by race, 1962*

Profession	Total	African	Asian	European
Architects	11	0	2	9
Civil engineers	84	1	22	61
Mechanical engineers	52	0	6	46
Surveyors	94	1	1	92
Physicians	184	16	60	108
Lawyers	57	2	11	44
Veterinarians	45	9	1	35
Geologists	41	0	0	41
Zoologists	12	1	0	11

SOURCE: Tanganyika, *High-Level Manpower Requirements*, table no. 10, pp. 33–6.

The scarcity of Africans in these and similar employments was bound to continue for a long time. There was still only a small number of Tanganyikans graduating each year from the two university colleges in East Africa, Makerere University College, Uganda, and the Royal College, Nairobi. In 1958 there were 216 Tanganyikans at Makerere College, 200 of them African, and 26 at the Royal College, Nairobi, 7 of them African. Many of those enrolled were doing diploma rather than degree courses In 1959 the total output of Tanganyikan graduates from both institutions was only 12. Even by 1962 the number of Tanganyikans graduating from these two university colleges had only increased to 17.[8]

There were also large numbers of Tanganyikans studying overseas, but many of these were Asians, who might not return to Tanganyika. In 1959 it was estimated that 860 Tanganyikans were following courses overseas, a great many in technical or preparatory courses rather than in regular degree programs. Many of those who were taking courses which had a high priority for Tanganyika were Asian rather than African. Tobias reports that only 39 of the 241 Tanganyikans studying engineering abroad in 1962 were African. Similarly only 54 of the 139 Tanganyikans studying medicine were African.[9]

There was, therefore, no large body of Tanganyikans who were completing their university training and who would be returning to Tanganyika within the first several years of independence. Neither was there a substantial body of secondary school graduates available to begin professional or technical training. The secondary schools were the crucial educational bottleneck. It was estimated earlier in this study that there could not have been more than 2,000 Tanganyikans who had graduated from secondary school by 1960. Table 2 shows how tiny, still, was the number of the children able to find places in secondary schools.

Table 2. *School attendance by age groups*

Year		Lower primary	Upper primary	Secondary I–IV	Forms V and VI
1957	Population	895,000	792,000	720,000	338,000
	Enrollment	364,024	41,290	5,931	28
	Percentage	40.7	5.2	0.8	0.008
1962	Population	976,000	864,000	785,000	365,000
	Enrollment	443,799	75,936	13,690	485
	Percentage	45.5	8.8	1.7	0.1

SOURCE: These figures were prepared by the Ministry of Education for 'The Capital Development Programme of the University College, 1964–1967' (Dar-es-Salaam, 1963), p. 9.

In November 1960, there were 478 Africans enrolled in standard XII (secondary IV). Even this small enrollment was a good deal higher than it had been several years previously. In 1958, African enrollment in standard XII was only 174 students.[10]

The policy implications of these facts seemed at the time to be incontrovertible. Tanzania would have to accept a continuing important involvement by expatriates in her own governance and would have to find ways to secure that involvement.

TANU secured an elected majority on the Council of Ministers for the first time in September 1960. Nyerere then joined this Council for the first time and became Chief Minister. In making his appointments to the Council of Ministers he showed that he was primarily concerned to appoint men who could work effectively with British senior civil servants. He retained four of the five TANU Ministers from the previous Council of Ministers, all of them moderate and experienced men.[11] He brought onto the Council for the first time Rashidi Kawawa, Paul Bomani, Nsilo Swai and Oscar Kambona. Bomani was of the same mold as Eliufoo, Kahama and Fundikira, a politically moderate man with extensive administrative experience. Swai was a young graduate secondary teacher who thus represented or at least illustrated another element in TANU leadership at the time. Kawawa and Kambona were men of a different sort. They represented the new generation of nationalists which had given TANU its dynamism and its vigour in the late 1950s. Kawawa had been Secretary-General and then President of the Tanganyika Federation of Labour and Kambona had been the Secretary-General of TANU. Kawawa, in 1960, was only thirty-one years old and Kambona thirty-two. Nyerere thus did not ignore the more politicized wing of TANU. However, he hardly gave it a dominant position within the Cabinet.

Nyerere's most significant appointment confirms this judgment. This was his appointment of Sir Ernest Vasey as Minister of Finance. Vasey had been an extremely successful Minister of Finance in Kenya until 1956. He had justly earned the reputation of being a liberal with a strong sympathy for African political aspirations. In February 1960, on the invitation of Turnbull and with Nyerere's approval, Vasey came to Tanganyika to become Minister of Finance. In September 1960, Nyerere reappointed him to the same position, thereby demonstrating his concern to continue both the style and the policies of the previous government.

Vasey became extremely influential within Nyerere's government. He and the British officer who served as Nyerere's Permanent Secretary until January 1962, C. M. Meek, were largely responsible for the planning of the ministerial system which was established in April 1961 to replace the highly centralized Secretariat through which the colonial Governor had ruled the country. Almost all the major functions of government were made the direct administrative responsibility of one or other of the separate Ministries. The major coordinating and controlling functions within the government were given to the Minister of Finance. His schedule of responsibilities included financial policy, economic policy, development planning, economic relations, foreign aid, taxation, salary scales, the Establishment Division, and Organization and Methods Division. Very few functions were assigned directly to the Office of the Prime Minister.

The ministerial system, as it was introduced in 1960, was appropriate to the dependence strategy. Under these arrangements, policies and proposals were first worked out in detail within the separate Ministries, with the Minister of Finance exercising a supervisory role insofar as these proposals and policies had financial or staffing consequences. The expatriate civil service and Vasey himself were bound to play a very dominant role within this process. The Presidential input and the collective input of TANU would normally be felt only when the policy reached the Cabinet, that is to say only after it had already been given detailed form and content in a policy-making process dominated by expatriate civil servants. Had Nyerere wished to effect major policy changes in any field he would have had to exert his authority at a much earlier stage and in a much more sustained way than could easily be done within the ministerial system as it was introduced in Tanganyika.

A second feature of this ministerial system which reveals the dependence strategy in operation was the decision that the Ministry of Finance should be responsible for economic policy, foreign aid and development planning, as well as for financial policy and taxation. The higher ranks in the Treasury were still entirely filled by British officers and Vasey, the Minister, was neither an African nor a Tanganyikan. He was, moreover, conservative in economic matters and thoroughly Western-oriented. His appointment made good sense only within the terms of the strategy that Nyerere had chosen to follow. Vasey was *persona grata* with the major Western aid agencies and with the Western powers. Because he shared so many of their assumptions concerning the needs of countries like Tanganyika, he was able to negotiate effectively with them on Tanganyika's behalf. His views on the development policies that were needed did not differ essentially from the views of the responsible British officers within the Tanganyikan service, though his experience and his ability meant that he provided a thrust and leadership in their pursuit which might otherwise have been lacking.

The Three Year Development Plan which was produced in 1960 for the period 1961–4 demonstrates the dependence strategy in operation. The Plan was very largely a compilation of the individual capital programs of the separate Ministries which the Ministry of Finance then ordered and brought into line with its own expectations of the capital which would be available to government during this period.[12] The detailed preparatory work for the plan had been done by expatriate officers. The major policies embodied in the Plan were an amalgam of the separate policy recommendations of the individual Ministries, the report of a World Bank Mission and the views of the Ministry of Finance itself. There was no significant TANU contribution whatsoever during the preparation of the Plan. At no stage was a draft of the Development Plan or a statement on any of its underlined principles presented to any TANU body for discussion, let alone for approval. Even the completed document was not presented for formal endorsement to a TANU National Executive Committee meeting.

In this same year Nyerere and his party colleagues had prepared a new statement of TANU's aims and objectives which committed TANU to create a democratic and socialist state in Tanganyika. The Three Year Development Plan, far from being a first essay towards the realization of a socialist state, shows no evidence at all that these aims and objectives had had any impact upon it. Rural development was to be promoted primarily through projects which would encourage the individual enterprising peasant farmer to greater economic activity. Industrial and commercial investments were to come very largely from private investment both local and foreign. A public development corporation was proposed but it was seen primarily as a further technique to attract additional private capital.[13] The Plan recognized that this reliance upon private investment would mean that trade and business in Tanganyika would be very largely dominated by non-Africans. To achieve some African participation it proposed a special program of training and assistance for the aspiring African trader and businessman. Thus, in both the countryside and in the towns the Plan actively sought to promote an emergent African bourgeoisie.

This gap between Nyerere's developing ideology and the values implicit in the Three Year Development Plan was not an isolated occurrence. His more theoretical ideas on democracy also failed to have any influence upon the Independence Constitution. As early as 1960, Nyerere had questioned the 'suitability for Africa of the Anglo-Saxon form of democracy'.[14] For several years, he returned again and again to a discussion of the meaning of democracy in Africa. Yet he was content to accept an Independence Constitution which reflected in its every aspect British attitudes on how Tanganyika should be governed. He fully cooperated with the British during the last two years of colonial rule when they sought to install in Tanganyika a parliamentary system on the Westminster model.[15] The British, moreover, did not leave to chance how this system would run. They built into the Constitution a series of safeguards in regard to some of the key conventions of parliamentary government. The Constitution, for example, established a Civil Service Commission, a Police Service Commission, and a Judicial Service Commission and gave each of them wide executive responsibilities relating to appointments, promotions and dismissals. It also protected the autonomy of three important public offices – the Director of Public Prosecutions, the Attorney-General, and the Comptroller and Auditor-General.

Nyerere made every effort after becoming Chief Minister in September 1960 to win acceptance from his colleagues of the conventions which the Westminster model requires for its effective operation. His first Circular Letter as Chief Minister sought to define the relationship between the civil service, TANU, and the elected members of the legislature.[16] This letter was an excellent exposition of the traditional conventions of the parliamentary system. Nyerere was categorical that the civil service alone should be responsible for the implementation of government policy. Politicians were encouraged to help by giving further publicity to government measures and by conveying to the government reactions with specific policies. However, he went on to argue:

I would remind you that policy is decided by the central government and not by local party representatives. Political party organizations are not concerned with the execution or implementation of policy. . . Political parties and therefore members of Legislative Council, can certainly play their part in ensuring a good public reception for government policies. But I repeat that the responsibility for carrying out government policies lies with the civil service.[17]

On the eve of independence, he told TANU:

It is the job of the government to work out an overall plan and to check the direction in which we move just as the TANU National Executive in the past worked out the tactics of the struggle. . .In this TANU has a vital role to play. It is an organization of the people. Through it the people can and must express their desires and worries to the government. Through it the government can and must explain to the people what it is doing and why.[18]

This downgrading of the role and importance of TANU illustrates yet again the degree to which Nyerere and TANU accepted a dependence strategy and sought to develop institutional relationships in Tanganyika which would be most appropriate to that strategy. Nyerere held fast to this limited view of the role of TANU. There was no talk from Nyerere at this time of TANU representing the will of the nation or of TANU setting the policies which the legislature and the government would then implement. It has already been noted that many British colonial servants expected that they would continue very largely to shape government policies and that, with TANU with them rather than opposing them, they would be able more effectively to implement their policies. Nyerere's expectations at this time were identical: 'I firmly believe that the constitutional change which has just come about should make easier the work of civil servants in the field. The change should in itself remove many former causes of friction and misunderstanding.'[19]

Government policies towards the British officers

It was fundamental to the strategy being followed that an independent Tanganyika would in fact be able to retain the services of a great many of the British officials who had served in colonial Tanganyika. 'There is no group of local people', said Nyerere, 'so well able to hold a pistol at our heads. If the members of the civil service were suddenly to say that they were leaving they could cause more destruction than any other group.'[20]

To help reassure the serving British officers that their interests would not be threatened by an African government, TANU cooperated with arrangements which retained British control over the civil service right until the moment of full internal self-government, and which, thereafter, kept the civil service as free of political control as possible.[21]

Nyerere supported these arrangements: 'My colleagues and I also deter-mined actively to do everything we can to keep the civil service out of the political arena. Indeed, it is for this reason that we have warmly welcomed the establishment of a Public Service Commission.'[22]

Although this was a welcome reassurance to expatriates in the civil service, it did not touch their main worries. They were concerned about their salaries, the security of their pensions and the complex question of the compensation which they could expect to receive should they wish to leave or should the newly independent government decide that it no longer wished to employ them. The first two of these three factors were more easily handled than the third.

The first TANU government accepted that expatriate salaries in the East African governments had not kept up with salaries for comparable positions elsewhere in Africa or in Britain. It cooperated with an East African Salaries Commission and accepted its recommendations for major increases for all senior expatriate staff. The Tanganyika government also welcomed a British decision to assume itself the cost of the supple-mentary pay and allowances over and above the local salaries which would be paid to British-recruited expatriates.[23] There was nothing sinister or secret about these policies. They were public and they were welcomed by the East African governments. On 8 December 1960, on a motion moved by Nyerere, the Tanganyika Legislative Council noted 'with satisfaction and appreciation' the arrangements announced in Command Paper 1193.[24]

Discussions began early in 1961 about the pension rights of serving officers and about the compensation which they should receive in view of the achievement of independence. These were not easy discussions. The British were caught by the appeal of their own mythology of colonial rule. This mythology held that the British officers had always been serving the African peoples in the colonies. In their view, it was only right that a newly independent African state should accept full responsibility for all the obligations which the colonial government had already assumed to-wards its civil servants. Nyerere agreed to work within this mythology. The Tanganyikan government accepted responsibility for the pensions of the British officers and guaranteed their terms of service. Nyerere and his colleagues recognized that a small number of senior expatriates would need to be prematurely retired in order that Africans could replace them in a few highly sensitive positions. They accepted that compensation for loss of career should be paid to these officers. However, they felt that Tanganyika could hardly be obliged to compensate a civil servant for loss of career if in fact the Tanganyikan government wished that official to remain in Tanganyika and he refused to stay on.

It was this, the natural corollary of what Britain demanded of Tan-ganyika, which the serving officers could not accept. The British had been able to secure Nyerere's cooperation with their myth; it could not get the members of their own colonial service to do the same.[25] The officers insisted that employment in an independent African state was not the same as employment in the Colonial Service and they wanted compensation because of these differences. The British government finally supported them. It insisted that every British officer should receive compensation for loss of career whenever he chose to retire and without regard to whether he retired despite being requested by the Tanganyikan government to remain in its service. They had secured this from the West African governments and were adamant that Tanganyika do likewise. It was these arrangements which were finally embodied in the Public Officers Agreement of 1961 between Britain and Tanganyika.*

The arrangements in Tanganyika did succeed in providing most British officers with sufficient inducements to remain in Tanganyika. Over 1,200 of the 1,700 members of Her Majesty's Overseas Service agreed in 1960 to sign on for at least a further two years. A major and damaging exodus of British officers had thus been averted. However, the result was hardly ideal. In order to secure that objective the dice had to be loaded heavily in favour of the British officers. Young officers often decided to remain for a few years in order to accumulate larger final retirement benefits. Older officers who feared that they would not find satisfactory reemployment in Britain also tended to remain. Their compensation, having been frozen at its maximum level, would not be lessened if they stayed while their salary would likely be higher and their earned pension would be greater. Officers in mid career, however, those that is who might still have the most to contribute, had major personal incentives to resign which the inducements were unable fully to offset. These officers were of an age to feel that they should not delay their attempt to reestablish themselves in a new career especially as the generous compensation terms provided them with the capital which they would need to make the transition to a new career.

During the last months of colonial rule British officers and their wives

---

* It is hard to consider the details of this Agreement without being struck by the way in which each detailed feature worked to the benefit of the serving British officers. Maximum compensation was set at £12,000, and benefits were frozen for each officer at his maximum entitlement. An officer could thus remain in the employ of Tanzania until his normal retirement age and still receive the compensation which he would have received for loss of career had he been forcibly retired many years earlier. One other example illustrates that there was much more concern to assure that the compensation arrangements were 'fair' as between British officers than that they were 'fair' to Tanganyika. The Tanganyikans accepted a subterfuge by which British officers who secured a permanent appointment in the home civil service in Britain while they were still in the Tanganyika service would nevertheless be able to claim from Tanganyika major compensation payments for loss of career. See Tanganyika, 'Scheme of Retirement Benefits for Members of H.M.O.C.S. and Officers Designated Under the Overseas Service Aid Scheme', Staff Circular No. 4 of 1961 (Dar-es-Salaam, 1961).

were preoccupied with elaborate calculations of the comparative personal advantages to them of resigning or staying on in Tanganyika. It was not a simple exercise. Differing assumptions about the numbers of one's colleagues who would be resigning led to different assumptions about promotion prospects and, as compensation payments and pensions were related to final salaries, this in turn involved quite different estimates of the financial advantages of remaining. The exercise could therefore be constantly absorbing. This preoccupation with the calculation of personal advantage hardly generated amongst Africans or other expatriates exposed to it a high regard for the motivation of these officers.

These implications and consequences of the retirement scheme were not lost on Tanzanians. Nyerere and his colleagues understandably resented the lack of confidence in an independent Tanganyika which was at the root of the uncertainty of many of the expatriates. They were unhappy in particular that compensation should be paid to officers who chose to leave despite the fact that Tanganyika wished them to stay. Nyerere did not defend this save to say that it was part of the overall arrangements with Britain and that, as these were in Tanganyika's interests, they should accept the occasional displeasing feature within them. The most disappointing consequence of the retirement scheme was that the British officers who did remain in Tanganyika needed to make only a very tentative commitment to Tanganyika. They could at any time change their minds, take their retirement benefits, convert their pensions into capital sums and leave. Tanganyika was thus particularly exposed to fluctuations in the morale of the expatriates. The government had always to be solicitous of their mood if it was to avoid a sudden swing of expatriate feeling and a consequent rapid increase in the numbers choosing to leave. The pistol, in effect, was constantly at Nyerere's head.

Tanganyikan unease was further increased by the financial arrangements which the British insisted upon in regard to the pensions and the retirement benefits. The British government pressed Tanganyika to accept the pattern which had been set by the Nigerian and Gold Coast independence settlements. This involved the newly independent government rather than the British government accepting the financial responsibility for the lump-sum retirement benefits to which all British officers would acquire a continuing option, and for the capital-sum commutation of a portion of their accrued pensions on retirement. Although Britain gave loans and grants to Tanganyika to cover a large portion of the costs of these obligations, it was in Britain's interest to have them handled in this way rather than to assume direct responsibility for them. In this way, the assistance which Britain would pay to Tanganyika to help it meet these obligations could be presented as aid to a newly independent Tanganyika rather than as an unproductive internal British expenditure consequent upon the liquidation of the Empire.[26]

The TANU government accepted these financial agreements. It felt it had no reasonable alternative. It had judged that without the British ex-patriates there would be administrative chaos in Tanganyika. It therefore had to go along with the British to the full extent that they demanded. Nyerere and many of his colleagues also accepted these arrangements out of a trust in Britain's just intentions. They were confident that the British decisions to end multiracialism in Tanganyika and to grant independence were indicative of a basic and continuing liberal British commitment to development in East Africa. If Britain therefore wanted Tanganyika to accept these obligations they were confident in turn that Britain would include in the final independence settlement features which would offset these heavy obligations. An indication of the strength of this trust is the fact that Tanganyika accepted these obligations to the colonial civil ser-vants and announced them before the financial settlement with Britain had been negotiated.*

This explains the crisis in Tanganyika–British relations which then occurred in July 1961. Vasey, on the basis of his expectations of British assistance, had already presented to the Cabinet and to the National Assembly a Three Year Development Plan for Tanganyika which called for capital expenditures of £24m over the period 1961–4. Nineteen millions of these £24m were to come from external sources. Vasey noted that £4.5m should be obtainable from British Colonial Development and Welfare funds on projects for which commitments could be secured before independence. He hoped for a further £3m in grants from other sources and a final £11.5m in external loans. It was in this context that he said,

> Last, but by no means least, we know that we can look to Her Majesty's
> Government in the United Kingdom to assist in financing the Plan
> for we have the assurance of the Secretary of State in person that we
> shall not find Her Majesty's Government ungenerous. . .At London in
> June, we shall, in addition, seek to secure from Her Majesty's Govern-
> ment a promise of sufficient long-term loan finance to cover a consider-
> able part of our external borrowing.[27]

* Six years later, when relations with Britain had been strained for several years
  and British aid was negligible, Nyerere sought to renegotiate the division of these
  responsibilities, arguing that Tanganyika had accepted them in the understanding
  that Britain would provide aid to Tanganyika in other ways to offset these heavy
  expenditures. When Britain refused to accept the Tanzanian proposals
  Nyerere unilaterally abrogated the Public Officers Agreement and Tanzania
  ceased to accept any financial responsibility for pensions earned during the colonial
  period or for the compensation paid to officers whom Tanganyika wished to stay.
  The issue is outlined by Amir Jamal in his budget address in June 1967. Tanzania,
  *Speech by the Honourable the Minister for Finance Introducing the Estimates of
  Revenue and Expenditure, 1967/68 to the National Assembly, on 14th June, 1967*
  (Dar-es-Salaam, 1967), pp. 26–7.

In fact, in July 1961, Nyerere learned that Britain intended an independence settlement totalling only just over £10m. Of this amount, £4.5m was from Colonial Development and Welfare funds, as Vasey had anticipated in May. Three million pounds was a loan which could be used only for the commutation of pensions and the remainder consisted of a series of miscellaneous project loans under the Commonwealth Assistance Scheme. Hardly any of the settlement, as originally proposed, would have been available for the Three Year Development Plan.

Nyerere and his colleagues were bitterly disappointed. They had accepted the Public Officers Agreement on the understanding that there would be substantial developmental assistance to offset the financial responsibilities which Tanganyika assumed in this Agreement. Nyerere gave voice to his bitterness in London when he said:

> We were absolutely shocked when throughout all the discussions H.M.G. were pleading poverty. Tanganyika's friendship with Britain does not depend on money. If Britain were really too poor to help, I would ask my people to make sacrifices and not ask for money. It seems, however, that being moderate one does less well than less moderate people. If a revolution took place in Tanganyika, Britain would spend millions. Somehow, the balance of payments problem would disappear. Tanganyika's stability was used as an argument why we should not get financial help. . .The sole justification for keeping an expensive expatriate civil service in Tanganyika is that they can help in the development of the country. If the British Government are not prepared to produce the funds that Tanganyika has been led to expect, it would be embarrassing for both the Tanganyika Government and the individual civil servants, who genuinely want to help in the country's development.[28]

The British government finally agreed to increase the settlement. A £4m development grant and a £1m interest-free loan to cover the Tanganyikan portion of the retirement benefits were added to the earlier offer. It was hardly overwhelming but it did at least settle the immediate crisis and it permitted the Three Year Development Plan to go forward. However, the extended discussions about compensation and related benefits for the expatriate civil servants and the financial dénouement marked the beginning of a greater realism, if not of wisdom itself, in TANU's assessment of the implications for Tanganyika of a long-term dependence upon Britain.

Further strains in British–Tanganyikan relations

Nyerere's original choice of a dependence strategy rested upon three assumptions:

1 that a substantial portion of the serving British offcers would remain with an independent Tanganyikan government,

2 that Nyerere and his senior colleagues could win the acceptance of the party's middle-rank activists to this continued close association with Britain and

3 that TANU would be able to retain the mass support which it had mobilized for the struggle for independence.

The validity of the first assumption was far from assured. Tanganyika had entered upon a close and dependent relationship with Britain without thereby lessening significantly the risk of a major exodus of expatriate staff at a later date.

The second assumption was also quickly seen to be questionable. Nyerere and TANU came to realize that the maintenance of a large expatriate component within the government service involved social and political costs which they had not adequately anticipated. Part of the cost was emotional. Although Africans acquired constitutional power, the expatriate civil servants seemed to remain the dominant elite. The European clubs, which had been a central feature of colonial social life, relaxed their racially restrictive rules only slowly and nominally. The European nursery and primary schools resisted any major admission of Tanganyikan students. Government social events continued to be colonial in their style and manner. The Governor and his entourage were prominent at all official functions and European police officers were as numerous, as visible and as clearly in charge at these functions as ever they had been. These and many similar features of the general scene generated a discouragement and a sense of anticlimax amongst the rank and file of TANU.

There were further unanticipated costs which were particular to the political leaders. In 1961 the senior civil servants in every Ministry in Dar-es-Salaam were, almost to a man, British officers. They were moreover confident men, sure of the wisdom of their policies and the legitimacy of their presence. They did not look to their African Ministers for fresh policy initiatives. Rather they hoped the Ministers would generate popular and party support for policies which the civil service had already initiated. The British officers were members of an on-going government. It was the African Minister and not the British expatriate official who needed to be 'assimilated'.

This had important consequences. It was hard for many of the Tanganyikan Ministers to avoid a mounting irritation with what they regarded as an ingrained paternalism in the style and manner of their senior civil servants. This phenomenon is difficult to document. As it was extremely important, I shall illustrate it from personal memory. 'Oscar is like a son to me', said one senior civil servant of Oscar Kambona, his Minister. 'I try to guide him. I protect him from his own mistakes.' There was goodwill in these remarks but there was also a paternalism which Kambona surely noted and disliked.

The President or any Minister could of course overrule his senior civil servants. However, he would tend to do so only if he was either bold enough to issue orders without supporting arguments or patient and skillful enough to convince his senior advisers of the wisdom or the necessity of what he wanted. There was therefore a good deal of strain and tension within many Ministries which was uncongenial to the new Ministers and which they found difficult to manage. Much of this, no doubt, was an inevitable consequence of the initial contrast between their own experience and knowledge and that of their senior civil servants. But it was intensified by the fact that these senior civil servants were the very men who had previously exercised power over them as members of the colonial service.

This factor involved far more than a question of sensitivity and offended *amour propre*. In any area of policy the expatriate officers had already considered the issues and were already implementing the policies which they judged best. They therefore tended to regard most political initiatives as ill-conceived. They turned to TANU in general and to Nyerere in particular to hold to a minimum the unsettling impact of politics upon the on-going activities of the government. The point is not that the British officers blocked changes which Nyerere and his colleagues wished to introduce. It is, rather, that they convinced the leadership for too long to resist changes which were widely demanded and might have been expected swiftly to follow the achievement of responsible government. Moreover, when such changes had finally to be conceded their influence helped to assure that they were minimal in character. Two separate policy issues illustrate these difficulties. These issues are the Africanization of the civil service and the introduction of politically appointed Commissioners to replace the District and Provincial Commissioners who had, of course, been civil servants.

The Africanization of the civil service

The colonial government's policy had been to recruit locally whenever there was a likelihood that there would be qualified local candidates. However, because the output of highly trained Tanganyikans was still tiny and the formal educational qualifications for most middle and senior positions in the service were high, there were still only a very small number of Africans in the middle and senior ranks of the civil service in 1959.[29] The British administrators realized that there would be great pressure for a rapid introduction of many more Africans into the civil service. The government took some steps to increase the recruitment of African administrative officers. A training grade was introduced and an in-service training school for administrative officers was established. However, there was little sense of urgency in these reforms. The government continued to assume that Tanganyika should maintain the standards, the structure and the style of administration which had been introduced during the colonial period. The senior British administrators realized that there might be irresistible pressures for a faster rate of Africanization and that a mass exodus of expatriate officers was a possibility. This realization however did not lead to a crash program for the training of Africans for the civil service. Instead the British urged the political leaders to do all that they could to minimize these pressures.

Nyerere was responsive to these urgings. In part, this was but a further working out of the implications of the basic decision which he had taken that Tanganyika must strive to retain its expatriate civil servants. His caution over Africanization was reinforced by his recognition that no qualified Tanganyikan had a legitimate complaint about either his immediate or longer-run prospects within the government service. He also reacted critically to the personal self-seeking which was one aspect of the demand for a faster rate of Africanization. Moreover, there was in the popular pressure for Africanization a strong anti-Asian component which Nyerere found particularly antipathetic. These aspects explain why the main emphasis in Nyerere's public references to Africanization was on the need to resist the temptation to rush headlong into an indiscriminate program of Africanization.

Nyerere was unable to resist totally the demands from within TANU for increased Africanization. In October 1960 he defined the government's policy in terms of these three principles:

1. Every vacancy should if possible be filled by an appointment made locally and that resort should only be had to recruitment from outside of East Africa if no suitable candidate of any race can be found locally.

2. In the case of new appointments to the service, African candidates of Tanganyika should have prior claim to consideration...

3. Only if no suitable, qualified Tanganyika African candidate is available should other candidates be considered.[30]

Nyerere defended this preferential treatment for Africans by arguing that the racial composition of the civil service should in the long run broadly reflect that of the population of the country as a whole. However, he was clearly not too comfortable with this argument. He suggested that once Tanganyikan citizenship had been introduced the rights of each citizen, irrespective of race, would 'naturally include eligibility for appointment to any post in the civil service on grounds of equality'.[31] As there was to be a citizenship act within a year, there was no chance that the preferential recruitment of Tanganyikan Africans would be able significantly to alter the racial composition of the civil service before that time.

The pressures for Africanization continued unabated. Nyerere was unable to hold the line at these three principles. In December 1960 he announced that African officers would be given preference over non-African officers, Tanganyikan as well as expatriate, whenever a promotion post fell vacant.[32]

These concessions and the manner in which they were announced illustrate the dilemma which Nyerere could not avoid in his efforts to defuse the Africanization issue. Each concession came only after there had been much pressure for it from within TANU. Each was opposed by the senior expatriate officers. When each was announced, it was always linked with an explanation of the necessity, in any case, of retaining the service of the expatriates. These concessions therefore did not lessen the pressures within TANU for a more dramatic Africanization of the civil service.

Nyerere was receiving from another expatriate source quite different advice on these matters. The Ford Foundation had by this date already identified staff development and training as one of the most crucial of the tasks facing the independent African states. It had indicated to the Minister of Finance that it would be willing to advise in a general way on problems associated with the rapid development of an indigenous staff. Vasey took up this offer and formally requested this assistance. Two reports were produced, one in November 1960 and the second in May 1961.[33] The senior British officers were cautious and ambivalent about an emergency training program for Tanganyikans particularly when this was being proposed by Americans. They were anxious to protect the standards of the service and to avoid any action which might unsettle the expatriate officers. Thurston and Kingsley began from a quite different standpoint. On the basis of the experience of West African governments, they argued that 'no independent nation will, or can, long delay the nationalisation of its civil service and the problem is one of determining how one best produces an adequate administrative machine in time with the human material at hand. Fresh approaches are required.'[34]

Their emphasis was thus quite different from the conventional wisdom within the government at the time. The government had accepted the need to maintain the standards and structure of the civil service intact and, therefore, it had sought ways to limit the political pressures upon it for a more rapid Africanization. Thurston and Kingsley in contrast advised the government to accept the political reality that there would be rapid Africanization and to seek administrative ways to limit its damaging consequences. Their advice was not lost upon Nyerere. He had begun to shift his position towards that of Thurston and Kingsley.[35] However, Nyerere was not yet ready publicly to argue the case for a major Africanization program in these terms. He remained susceptible also to the concerns expressed to him by his British advisers. He was in consequence markedly ambivalent in regard to Africanization right up until his resignation in January 1962.

Reform of rural administration

Nyerere was strongly advised by his senior civil servants to retain the structure he had inherited for the administration of the rural areas. They wished the positions of Provincial and District Commissioners to continue to be held by civil servants. They favoured the development of a representative local government system with the retention of the chiefs and headmen as important agents of local administrative leadership and control. Nyerere at first took this advice. In October 1960, as we have seen, he decided to rule through the civil service and to limit severely the role of the party. He also sought to contain the pressure from within TANU to remove the chiefs from the local administration. On one occasion, in November 1960, he declared that 'if an instrument of government is doing its work properly there is no need to do away with it or to replace it. It would be madness to do away with it or to replace it. It would be madness to do away with the chiefs simply because in Europe they have a different system.'[36]

Nyerere could not sustain this position without amendment. For most TANU activists the struggle for independence had been a struggle against the chiefs and against the District and Provincial Commissioners. They had been the local representatives of British rule. They had been the authorities who had wielded power against TANU. Independence was likely to seem to mean very little if the pattern of local rule continued to be that of administrative officers ruling through the chiefs. In October 1961 Nyerere summed up his dilemma in this matter by describing what typically happened every time he visited a District headquarters:

> It is always a government affair. I am met by the provincial
> commissioner and by the district commissioner both of whom are likely
> to be colonial officers, the very men who TANU fought but a few
> years ago. I am introduced by them to the other government officers
> who are also usually expatriates. I am then introduced to the chiefs and
> to the officials of the native authority and again I am meeting men who
> either opposed TANU or who carefully stayed out of the political
> struggle. Then off to one side I notice a few chaps in torn green shirts
> wielding banners but looking somewhat forlorn.[37]

Nyerere was becoming sensitive to his failure to find an adequate and satisfying role for TANU. He was aware that the strategy which he was following was widening the gulf between himself and his Cabinet colleagues on the one hand and the rank and file of TANU on the other. Yet he could not easily convince his senior civil servants of the wisdom of any major reforms which would bring TANU and the government into a closer relationship at the district and provincial level. Indeed, he could not easily convince himself. He lacked any clear alternative to the traditional British view of the relationship between a political party and the civil service. He had accepted this view on first coming into office and, though increasingly discomforted by some of its consequences, he held back from any vigorous exposition and introduction of an alternative and more politicized system.

The two policy issues which have been briefly reviewed, the Africanization of the civil service and the politicization of rural administration, illustrate that the attitudes of the senior expatriate civil servants were an important barrier to politically necessary reforms and innovations. The British officers were not sabotaging policy. But too often they sought to dissuade Ministers from initiatives that made excellent political sense. Nyerere and his colleagues were inhibited from pursuing policies which TANU wanted because of the dominant role of the expatriates within the government. The second of the three assumptions that had eased the acceptance of the dependent strategy was therefore proving to be untrue. The third assumption, that TANU would retain its mass support, also began to look questionable.

Government policies offered very little to the party activist who had been a loyal party member during the years of political struggle. Few positions of prestige were opened to the party functionaries. They were isolated and disheartened by the failure of the first TANU government to reward them or, indeed, even to find for them a purposeful role in the soon-to-be-independent Tanganyika. The party, in consequence, atrophied. Its officials all sought the job security and the higher income of civil service positions. Those who were unsuccessful in that effort tended to be restless and disgruntled. The frustrated officials and the unrewarded activists sought their status and asserted their sense of their own importance by a continuing indulgence in the rhetoric of anti-colonialism, interspersed on occasion with a racist hostility to the Asian and European minorities.

Nyerere in consequence returned frequently to the need for party members to abandon the old themes:

> There are quite a few things which must be colonized before
> independence. . .but I venture to suggest that one of the most difficult
> things to decolonize is going to be the minds of some honourable
> members here. The colonial system has done such a good job on a few of
> them that I doubt if they believe that this is a people's government that
> they are addressing. . .There is nobody to fight. All are agreed that we
> must go ahead together just as quickly as ever we can. We must not waste
> our breath, waste any of our efforts which our country needs in other
> ways, in beating the air when there is nobody against whom to fight.[38]

There is the temptation, sir, to use a language which bears no relationship at all to the circumstances of Tanganyika in 1961, to this government. Well now, sir, I do accept some responsibility for that language because I had something to do with organising the opposition to the government – and all our training was done in opposition; all the speeches we were making were speeches in opposition; and the language, therefore, we learned, was the language of opposition. So I am not surprised that this language is still the language that is being used. Some people find it very difficult after dancing a certain step, to get out of it, even if the tune has changed.[39]

A profound disillusion occasionally intruded into Nyerere's references to the party. The self-seeking, the intrigue, the jockeying for office and for income were repugnant to him. In February 1960, he told a TANU conference,

I have seen TANU officials getting drunk with power and scheming to undermine one another. . .Too many big TANU officials seem to spend most of their time talking about their positions. To what sort of government would that lead when responsible government comes? You and I must reform because if we do not, we will be blamed by the 200 million in Africa. If we cannot reform, then we must destroy TANU because it will be of no use to this territory.[40]

Nyerere was insisting in these years upon an adherence to a set of policies which very few of his followers supported enthusiastically. Many no doubt, in their quiet moments, accepted their wisdom but few could feel enthusiastic about these policies and fewer still could arouse the enthusiasm of others for them. Nyerere was pressing his leadership to its limits as he strove to convince TANU to be moderate and to accept the inevitability of a close dependence upon Britain. He himself carried a very large part of the burden of defending the less popular aspects of this strategy. It was Nyerere who gave the major speeches on the need to retain the expatriates. He cautioned the Assembly continuously on the risks of a too-rapid Africanization. He toured the country calling for hard work, for maturity and for unity. There was not a major policy debate in the legislature in which Nyerere did not make an important speech. Many of his interventions sought to curb the excesses of those who argued for initiatives which would have been gratifying politically but which would have undermined the basic strategy being followed by the government.

Popular opposition to the government's policies received its sharpest expression in the labour unrest of 1960. This unrest was extensive and bitter and it had obvious political overtones.[41] Nearly one and a half million man-days were lost in that year through strikes and over twenty-five per cent of the total employed labour force were involved in these strikes. This unrest continued into 1961. The unions had grown rapidly during the previous several years. Their leadership was inexperienced and many had not yet accepted the discipline of collective bargaining. The political struggle for independence and the trade union struggle for improved working conditions were seen as aspects of a single endeavour. With the successes won in the political realm, economic expectations soared and a general erosion of discipline threatened the efficiency of many governmental services.

The trade union opposition and the parliamentary opposition to many of Nyerere's policies were closely interrelated. Several of the most outspoken parliamentary critics were also trade union leaders. Parliamentary and trade union critics attacked the government's Africanization policies. They criticized its efforts to integrate educational facilities. In each case, they accused the government of unnecessary caution. They argued that the government was unacceptably sensitive to the rights of the minority communities and was unduly concerned to retain the services of a large number of expatriates. Their criticisms often struck deeply responsive chords within TANU, unsettling many loyal supporters of Nyerere and causing him frequently to have to intervene directly in debates to re-establish the authority of the government.

Three debates in the National Assembly illustrate the extent to which there was a general restlessness within TANU. The first example is the debate on the Education Ordinance in 1961. This ordinance dismantled the separate school systems that the colonial government had supported for each of the races. It proposed their integration into a unified system within a short transitional period of three years. The ordinance was much more severe on the rights of the minority communities, as communities, to have their own state-supported school systems than would have been the policies recommended in 1959 by an interracial committee appointed by the government.[42] Nevertheless, most of the members of the National Assembly who spoke in the debate were impatient and critical. They did not particularly criticize the actual policies. They were irritated by the deliberate and moderate way in which the government was implementing its policies. Nyerere finally intervened with an impatience that had become typical of his responses to these critics:

> If anybody from outside Tanganyika was sitting up there and did not know what we were discussing here, he would not know from the speeches of some honourable members that we were discussing integration. He would think we were discussing a law which was intending to build racial schools in this country which is like talking about this racialism, this discrimination, this imperialism, and all this rubbish, when in fact, we were discussing the integration of the school system in Tanganyika.[43]

The second example is even more revealing. Despite the fact that the speed of constitutional advance in Tanganyika was extraordinarily fast, the desire within the party and within the legislature for a dramatic show of African authority was such that Nyerere had to intervene in October 1960 to convince the legislature to permit the government the few remaining months which it needed in order to negotiate and to execute an orderly transfer of power.[44]

In October 1961 the citizenship proposals of Nyerere's government provided an occasion for the most sustained expression of opposition to a major government policy. The government proposed that citizenship should be granted automatically to each adult person who was born in Tanganyika and one or both of whose parents had also been born in Tanganyika. Anyone born in Tanganyika of parents neither of whom were Tanganyikan-born was to be given two years to decide if he or she wished to be a Tanganyikan citizen. No one was to be permitted to become a citizen of Tanganyika who also retained citizenship of another country. The opposition to these proposals was essentially racist. Some critics wanted to withhold citizenship entirely from all non-Africans. Others would have required non-Africans, even if their parents had been born in Tanganyika, to apply on an individual basis for citizenship. All of the opponents of the government's proposals shared and expressed a profound suspicion of Asians and Europeans. All wanted citizenship to be available automatically only for Tanganyikan Africans.

The debate lasted two days. The critics dominated the first day and a half of debate, speaking forcefully and often intemperately against the proposals. Except for the able opening address by Kahama, the Minister of Home Affairs, those who spoke supporting the government proposals in this opening portion of the debate spoke briefly and made no attempt to reply to the racist appeals of the critics. Finally, in the middle of the second day, Nyerere delivered a blistering impromptu reply. 'The critics were', he said, 'potential Verwoerds...coming to this House, getting drunk with the atmosphere of the House and talking rubbish in this House hoping some people would clap for them.'[45] In angry despair he rejected their appeal to racial solidarity.[46]

Nyerere then, for the only time in his political career, declared that the government would resign if the citizenship proposals were rejected. Wambura immediately and courageously replied, 'We are also members representing the people just as well as the members of the Cabinet do. Now when certain matters are brought before this House, we have an equal right to discuss it without any fear.'[47] He directly challenged the government to hold a referendum on this issue. However, the anger and vigour of Nyerere's intervention and his threat of resignation stemmed the assault upon the citizenship proposals. Wambura's intervention was the last attack on the proposals during the debate and there followed then a series of speeches including three by prominent TANU leaders, Kawawa, Maswanya and Abedi, which supported the government's decision to avoid a racist definition of citizenship.

Nyerere easily carried the day. The citizenship proposals were endorsed by a substantial majority in the National Assembly. But Nyerere could not have been heartened by the fact that this victory had required his direct and angry intervention and the threat of his resignation.

The citizenship debate, far from clearing the air, only served to increase the frustrations within the party. These frustrations found expression, in particular, within TANU's Swahili political weekly, *Uhuru*, which first appeared in December 1961. Recurrently and with mounting intemperance *Uhuru*'s leading articles engaged in racist abuse of the minorities and demanded a style of government totally contradictory to the dependence strategy being followed. Two examples illustrate the bitter mood which was taking hold within a significant section of the party.

> An Imperialist does not give independence to a country until he has first planted the roots of confusion and chaos; until he has completed his schemes either for ruling the country secretly or for bringing about dissension that will cause the downfall of the government. . .The Imperialist is like a snake if he wants to bite you, first he will make you happy and speak sweet words to you. . .If Tanganyika wants to become strong, it must be on its guard against certain matters. We must look out for colonialists. . .we must avoid conciliatory ways. . .we must not be deceived by praise. . .constant statements that we should live happily with immigrants should be greatly reduced. . .
>
> Our enemies are still the same ones and several others have been added. All wealth is still in the hands of immigrants. All government offices and company offices are filled with English and Asian girls and old English and Asian men, some of whom are so old that I do not think they will be able to lift the thrones on which they sit in the offices of the people's government.[48]

Nyerere was discovering in the first fifteen months of office that he did not have an adequate political base for the political strategy which he had chosen to follow. There was no powerful and vigorous section of the society which directly associated its own interests with the maintenance of a close dependence upon Britain and with the continued pursuit of the policies of the colonial regime. The three sectors of a newly independent society which might be expected to provide influential support for such a strategy were each of little political significance in Tanzania. The professional and commercial bourgeoisie was not only comparatively small but, vastly more important, was almost entirely non-African. Far from providing a political base for a government pursuing this strategy, the existence of this bourgeoisie, racially and culturally so distinct from the

African majority, was itself a barrier to the general acceptance of the strategy.

Secondly, a traditional rural elite which has moved into the national politics has provided, in some African states, an alternative indigenous base for a government which has continued in a close and dependent relationship with its colonial rulers. The chiefs in Tanganyika, however, were too disorganized and too weak, and they had been too closely associated with the British as their subordinate agents, to be a national political force in 1960. The third possible social base for a government following a strategy of the type followed in Tanganyika from 1959 to 1962 was the civil service itself. In some African states, a largely Africanized civil service has been an influential lobby for the maintenance of a dependent relationship. However, in Tanganyika in 1962 the senior ranks of the civil service were still largely expatriate. African civil servants tended to see these British officers as a barrier to their own promotion. These Africans were therefore themselves a radicalizing factor, pressing for more rapid Africanization and thus seeking to undermine one important facet of the dependence strategy.

This lack of a political base meant that if Nyerere had persevered with the strategy which he had followed until 1962 he would have been hard pressed to retain his popular support and the general acceptance of his leadership within TANU. The tensions which were already visible within the party indicate that this support had begun to erode. Had Nyerere continued to pursue the political and administrative policies of his first year and a half of office, it can reasonably be assumed that he would have had to rely in a much more open fashion upon police and military forces which were themselves still very largely led by British officers, and he would have had to accept a falling away of colleagues and comrades with whom he had been in close association throughout the struggle for independence.

The abandonment of the strategy

These factors and developments predisposed Nyerere and his colleagues to consider a basic shift in the political strategy which they were following. However, when the shift did occur, it was not because of any direct consideration of these factors by Nyerere and TANU. The abandonment of the dependence strategy in 1962 was a consequence of a different decision, taken for reasons which were different from, though intimately related to, the developments discussed in the previous section. In January 1962 Nyerere decided to resign as Prime Minister in order to devote his full time to political work as President of TANU. This decision was not taken with the primary intention that it would then be followed by a series of government initiatives which would constitute a virtual abandonment of the earlier strategy. The decision to resign was a personal decision which cannot be understood without reference to his basic political and social values and, perhaps, to his personality as well.

Nyerere had not found it easy always to urge his people to be sensitive to the mood of the expatriates. He had an extraordinary capacity to work effectively with the British officers in his government. However, he was not one who sought their company by preference or who scorned the aspirations of ordinary Africans. Nyerere was in fact paying a high psychological price in constantly seeking to restrain his people from asserting their national and racial pride. That this was the case was revealed by his reaction to a series of incidents involving alleged indignities to Africans by individual Europeans which occurred immediately before and after independence.

The episodes themselves were slight. In early January 1962, the proprietor of an hotel in Dar-es-Salaam was deported after he had asked the Mayor of Dar-es-Salaam, his wife, Mrs Maswanya (the wife of a Minister) and Bibi Titi Mohamed, a prominent M.P., to leave the hotel after they had refused to order either food or drink. The owners of a small up-country hotel and a third European were deported for ejecting Jacob Namfua from the hotel after an argument had occurred when he had been refused service after dining hours. A Swiss engineer was deported after being accused by a Tanganyikan of placing an independence emblem upon his dog's collar and declaring that the dog was just as good as the people who were celebrating independence. The first of these episodes received publicity at the very time that the National Executive of TANU was meeting in Dar-es-Salaam. The hotel proprietor's reply was an apologetic statement that he had not recognized the members of the party whom he had asked to leave the hotel. Nyerere reacted in anger with an emotional statement which can only be explained, I think, as a consequence of the tension he had been under over the previous year as he battled within TANU for moderate non-racial policies.

> My patience and that of the government have been tried too far. Although there are many things it is impossible to give the people after independence, I am determined that they will at least achieve self-respect. For many years we Africans have suffered humiliations in our own country. We are not going to suffer them now. Neither can we allow Africans to be divided into categories of those who are entitled to respect and those who are not. The political position, wealth or birth of an African is utterly irrelevant to his right to respect and to the Government's determination that he shall get it. For many years I have advocated a policy of non-racialism. This remains my policy and that of the Government. But I will not allow this attitude to be exploited at the expense of the African community. . .This is not a government

elected simply to prevent the fury of the people from being directed against those who abuse the people. It is a government determined to stop these abuses.[49]

This was not a statement of a man reluctantly conceding the minimum necessary to irresistible pressures. Nyerere was finally rebelling against the need constantly to be guided by the importance of maintaining expatriate confidence in his government. His statement was not a minimal gesture in response to pressures which he deplored. Nyerere was permitting himself an angry demonstration that there was indeed a limit to what he and the government could tolerate.

A second aspect of the operation of government in these early years also distressed Nyerere. He was bothered by the degree to which the policies of the government and public confidence in the government were directly related to his own leadership. He made specific reference to this in his first press conference after his resignation. He admitted that this resignation might well affect the confidence of some expatriate civil servants, but these were men, he said, who had had confidence not in Tanganyika but in him. They were men, that is, 'who believed in a personal form of government'.[50] This factor related not only to expatriates but also to Africans. There was a real risk that his own prominent participation in so many of the politically unpalatable decisions permitted his colleagues to avoid any direct involvement themselves with these decisions.*

As opposition to government policies became more outspoken, the dilemma which it posed for Nyerere became more intense and unsettling. He could have resolved this dilemma by being either particularly firm with the critics or particularly conciliatory. He was inhibited from the former by his commitment to TANU as a major instrument of national unity. He had not yet moved sufficiently from his preoccupation with administrative efficiency easily to follow the latter path. Nyerere was later to show that he could act vigorously against political opponents whose influence he felt to be profoundly destructive. However, he was not ready to claim that he could act for the people's 'true interests' on an issue on which he did not have mass support. Nyerere's profound antipathy to ruling without the active support and involvement of the people was an important element in his decision to resign. He explained his resignation at the time in these terms:

I have taken this action and won the support of my colleagues for it after a long debate that has gone on for days because of our firm belief that this is the best way to achieve our new objective, the creation of a

---

* It was reported to me by one Cabinet Minister that Nyerere exclaimed, 'There, I told you. I was right to resign', when he heard Kawawa as Prime Minister defend a necessary but unpopular decision. It was a defence which previously would have been delivered by Nyerere himself.

country in which the people take a full and active part in the fight against poverty, ignorance and disease.

To achieve this purpose it is necessary to have an able elected government which has the full support and the cooperation of the people. This we have had and will have. It is also necessary to have a strong political organization active in every village which acts like a two-way all-weather road along which the purposes, plans of the government, can travel to the people the same time as the ideas, desires and misunderstandings of the people can travel direct to the government. This is the job of the new TANU.[51]

This statement has, understandably, led some commentators to argue that Nyerere resigned in order to build up the organizational strength of the party. This interpretation is misleading. Nyerere's concern was to check the development of an attitude of mind which suggested that the members of the government were distant and apart from the masses and that they had their own interests which were separate from those of the rank and file of the party and of ordinary persons. By resigning, Nyerere was going back to the people far more than he was returning to the party bureaucracy. He was not a politician who saw that his power would depend upon a strong party structure and who therefore resigned in order to build up that structure. He was a leader who returned to the party in order to renew his own relationship with the rank and file of the party and to find ways to involve them more intimately in the affairs of government and in the development of their country.

There was still another factor which contributed to Nyerere's decision to resign. It was, I believe, the most important factor. Nyerere's deepest commitment was to the development of a moral society in Tanganyika, an harmonious and just society in which the responsibilities of membership in the society have the same moral quality as the responsibilities which are now felt within a family. His experience of fifteen months in office had forced him to realize that there were real and early limits to his ability to use the power and authority of the office of the Prime Minister to influence men's social values or to change the institutions of society in advance of a transformation of the values of that society. More important still he sensed that the movement of ideas and values in his society was in a direction contrary to those that were necessary to the building of a democratic and socialist society. The unity and the commitment to the common good which he had seen as a central feature of TANU in the years of political struggle were being destroyed by the scramble of party members for status, income and personal power. Somehow party members must be led to see that the economic benefits of independence would not be immediate and certainly ought not to be seen in terms of personal advancement. There needed to be a recognition that the development of Tanganyika was now the responsibility of Tanganyikans and would be achieved only through sustained hard work.

Nyerere used a particular incident to dramatize the reason for his decision to resign.

> My problem in the party and the government was really a psychological
> one. My own psychology and that of the country. The problem was
> how to explain to people the difficulties. The first thing was merely the
> understanding of the responsibilities of change, of government instead
> of the easier responsibilities of opposition. The other thing is symbolized
> by the secretary of a branch who hammered a question at me. He asked
> me about the future of the party's functionaries, about their salaries,
> etc. Now the struggle was over, they should now have an assurance
> that their difficulties in these matters were over. I answered and knew
> my answer was not satisfactory. I said, 'We were seeking independence
> and we have it. It is no use asking what I get out of this.' I felt that
> this answer was not satisfactory because he could have said, 'You can
> say that but I am not in the same position.' I felt I was in a weak position
> to explain the difficulties of change as long as I was heading the govern-
> ment. Given my character and the facts of life, I could not explain
> these things while I was head of this government. I had to leave govern-
> ment to be an effective teacher. I went out to change the mood.[52]

Nyerere resigned to be a more effective teacher. He resigned in an effort to teach his people that a secure government job ought not to be the abiding ambition of TANU members, that success was not to be measured in such terms. The more he was drawn into the detailed responsibilities of government, the more he felt he was not doing his most important job. Nyerere chose in January 1962, not for the last time, to take a major and unexpected initiative in order to free himself sufficiently to become more involved directly with the development of values and attitudes of mind amongst his people which he saw as prerequisites to the building of a just and harmonious society in Tanganyika.

This interpretation of Nyerere's resignation, which emphasizes his concern to be more effective as a moral teacher rather than alleging an interest in building a strong party organization through which to consolidate his authority, is borne out by the use which he made of the year 1962. Nyerere made no attempt to create powerful party institutions at the national level. He made no effort to make the party a major participant in the formation and the direction of government policy. Nyerere and TANU had accepted that government policies were made within the machinery of government. He did not change this view during 1962. He neither widened the definition of the role of the party in policy-making nor strengthened its central institutions so that it would have the machinery and the party bureaucracy to permit it to define policies in detail. He did not totally ignore the activities of the government. However, he did not use the machinery of the party to exert whatever influence he wished to have on the government. Instead he acted through the Prime Minister and the other Ministers. On occasion, indeed, he attended Cabinet meetings in order to contribute to the discussion of specific issues. He thus accepted that government policies should continue to be made within the institutions of government.

Nyerere appears to have been equally unconcerned to strengthen the party organization at the local level. He spent a good deal of time travelling throughout Tanganyika, constantly meeting with local party officials, with rank-and-file party members and with ordinary citizens. In these travels he was not concerned to repair or to rebuild the party organization. There were no purges in the party and no restructuring of the party during this period. Instead, Nyerere was constantly the teacher urging party members to begin the long and arduous task of building a new Tanganyika.

In the early months of 1962, Nyerere wrote and published three important pamphlets.[53] These provide a good indication of what was paramount in his thinking during these months. The central message of these pamphlets was a simple one. It was that Africans must retain societies in which 'the people care for each other'. African society had had that moral quality but an aggressive acquisitiveness was now undermining these earlier values.

> Our first step, therefore, must be to educate ourselves; to regain our former attitude of mind. In our traditional African society, we were individuals within a community. We took care of the community and the community took care of us. We neither needed nor wished to exploit our fellow men...
>
> True socialism is an attitude of mind. It is therefore up to the people of Tanganyika – the peasants, the wage earners, the students, the leaders, all of us – to make sure that this socialist attitude of mind is not lost through the temptations to personal gain (or to abuse of positions of authority) which may come our way as individuals, or through the temptation to look on the good of the whole community, as of secondary importance to the interests of our own particular group.[54]

It is no exaggeration to say that central to Nyerere's political activity since then has been a search for ways to generate a socialist attitude of mind and to build a Tanganyika in which that attitude of mind would be sustained and reinforced. Nyerere did not yet have in 1962 a clear and detailed view of the policies which were needed to encourage such an attitude and to create such a society. He was still to experiment and to reflect a good deal more, before coming to settled conclusions on these questions. However, in 1962, he was ready nevertheless in these three pamphlets to identify these immediate policy priorities:

1 *'Parasitism' should not be permitted to develop.* He argued vigorously that exploitation is unjust and destroys the harmony and co-hesion of society. No one should be allowed to live off the labour of others. The immediate corollary of this proposition was that there should be no freehold land and that all land should be communally owned.

2 *The government must act to prevent the emergence of sharp income differences within Tanganyika. TANU na Raia* includes a sustained plea that Tanganyikans should not seek the high incomes which the Euro-peans had brought to the country. He foresaw that the Africanization of the civil service could easily mean merely the substitution of highly paid Africans for the highly paid expatriates. TANU, he said, intended to do away with the privileged positions of the Asian and European minorities. However, he insisted that this must mean more than merely the creation of a new privileged class of Africans.

3 *The party must arouse the people to greater effort on its own behalf.* 'We cannot let our people continue to live in poverty. We have to awaken them to more effort.'[55] This, however, did not lead Nyerere to make any claim on TANU's behalf that it already knew what the people wanted. Once again, Nyerere rejected that line of argument. 'The people themselves and only the people are the custodians of justice. To expect that the people's justice can be protected by leaders who do not share the same interest of the community is to take a wide chance. Of course, some-times, people have been lucky to get good leaders from outside their community. However, that is strictly good luck. Often it is the other way around and when that happens, it becomes extremely difficult to change these leaders.'[56] The party must therefore be a party of the people, its leaders living with the people, learning from them and helping the people to recognize that through common effort it can improve its liveli-hood.

4 *The party and particularly its leadership must remain open to criticism.* The whole of the pamphlet *Tujisahihishe* is a plea to party members to face reality fearlessly, to engage in the critical analysis of policies and social problems and to avoid seeking easy scapegoats for con-tinuing problems which can only be solved by hard work. The pamphlet urges party members to avoid personal factions, to stop being lazy and to be ready always to examine their own motives.

In 1962, Nyerere had thus shifted the main focus of his interest. He was no longer preoccupied with the problems of government and with the need to retain the expatriate civil servants. He had become concerned about the values and attitudes within the African community. He had come to feel that the most important contribution which he could make to the creation of a democratic and socialist Tanzania was to attempt to influence the values of his fellow countrymen. He decided that he would be able better to do this as President of TANU rather than as Prime Minister of

Tanganyika. For that reason, therefore, he resigned as Prime Minister on 23 January 1962.

The Kawawa interlude: January to December 1962

During the previous fifteen months Nyerere had been under increasing political pressure to use the powers of the government more vigorously and more dramatically to demonstrate that Africans were indeed now in control. He had yielded to these pressures only rarely and he did so with such evident reluctance that he won little political advantage from these concessions. Kawawa, in contrast, was much less prone to accept that administrative considerations should be more influential than political considerations. After he had become Prime Minister, the government was much less inhibited about overruling the civil service.

In 1962, therefore, policy changes took place which, by their nature and by the decisive manner in which they were executed, consolidated African support behind TANU. These changes *in toto* finally constituted an abandonment of the dependence strategy which the government, out of a fear of an expatriate exodus, had so far followed. If, as we have argued, the likely alternative to such changes was in fact a disintegration of TANU and a more open reliance upon the police and the military, then Nyerere's resignation and his replacement by Kawawa made possible, or at least greatly facilitated, political initiatives which were essential but which would have been difficult to accomplish under Nyerere's leadership. This interpretation of the consequences of his resignation was put to Nyerere in 1966. He commented in reply:

> Yes, it was not intended that way, but it is true. . .If I had remained in the Government, I would have resisted many things which Rashidi did successfully. My idea of efficiency is slightly more western and my emphasis would have been more on efficiency. Rashidi's emphasis was more on 'give the fellows a job and they will learn'. I do not think we would have done these things if I were in the government. As I was outside, we did two things: (a) Rashidi did some necessary things in government which I should not have done, and (b) in the meantime, I was handling the party.[57]

Kawawa was concerned to widen and to consolidate the political base of the newly independent government. This showed itself to a moderate degree in the appointments which he made to his first Cabinet. The solid group of experienced Tanzanian Ministers including Bomani, Bryceson, Fundikira, Kahama and Jamal were reappointed. However, Kawawa shifted the balance of influence within the Cabinet away from this group of Ministers and towards the more actively political wing of the Cabinet. Kambona and Lusinde each acquired more important positions, Kambona becoming Minister of Home Affairs and Lusinde, Minister of Local Government and Administration. Vasey was not reappointed to the Cabinet. Two of the three new Ministers, Kasambala and Maswanya, were men whose experience and claim to office were very largely political.[58] Kawawa also acted to lessen the very great concentration of economic and fiscal powers that had been consolidated in Vasey's Treasury,[59] thus opening up the discussion of economic questions to the more active involvement of other Ministers.

Kawawa appointed political activists to three of the first four parliamentary secretaryships which he created.[60] Mwanjisi had been the editor of *Uhuru* whose racist editorials had caused offence. Walwa was a party functionary who was close to Kambona. Kisenge had delivered two speeches during the previous year in the National Assembly – one on the need to get rid of the expatriates and the second on the advisability of excluding all foreign embassies from Tanganyika. The fourth newly appointed Parliamentary Secretary was Miss Lucy Lameck, an articulate, well-educated, and politically effective person. Three more of the vocal critics of the earlier policies, Barongo, Kundya and Mponji, were also made Parliamentary Secretaries before the end of the year.

The incorporation of party activists into the machinery of government was further pursued with the appointment of the first Regional Commissioners. Nyerere had indicated in October 1961 that he favoured the creation of political Regional Commissioners to replace the civil service Provincial Commissioners. Kawawa moved forward promptly with this. In February 1962 he appointed eleven Regional Commissioners. All were strong party men; most had been either TANU Provincial Secretaries or Chairmen. They included several who had been amongst the most persistent of the parliamentary critics of the government. This pattern was repeated later in 1962 when Kawawa appointed the first group of Area Commissioners. These appointments reflected a clearer appreciation of the magnitude of the task which TANU faced. They did not mean that a serious divergence of opinion had developed between Kawawa and Nyerere. Kawawa's appointments were a consequence of the same underlying recognition which had sent Nyerere back to the party. They both saw that they had to begin with political reality as it was.

A civil service, particularly one which included many expatriates, could not be the primary agency through which to promote a transformation of Tanganyikan society. A political instrument was needed and that instrument could only be TANU. Neither the rank and file nor the political activists in TANU could be ignored without destroying TANU. A deep harmony of purpose thus underlay the activities of Nyerere and Kawawa during 1962. Nyerere acted primarily to win the active cooperation of the rank and file and to deepen their understanding while Kawawa sought to check the alienation of the party activists.

The more widely based leadership which Kawawa assembled in 1962, though more representative than Nyerere's earlier Cabinet, was nevertheless still a political oligarchy, and a tough-minded oligarchy. A corollary of Kawawa's willingness to accommodate a wide range of opinion amongst those whom he appointed to public office was an hostility to any who remained outside the ruling oligarchy and challenged its leadership.[61]

The most serious challenge to the government came from those trade union leaders who opposed Kawawa, Kamaliza, Namfua and the other union leaders who had become active within TANU.[62] The issue which divided the two groups could be seen as an ideological conflict between those who believed that the unions should support the TANU government and concentrate on promoting production and those who wanted the unions to remain autonomous champions of the workers' immediate economic interests. However, the ideological issue was largely an adornment to a struggle for power between two rival groups of union leaders. As the Kawawa–Kamaliza faction had on its side the resources and power of the state, the outcome of the contest was never in much doubt. The pro-government faction used the whole range of techniques at its disposal, cooption, pressure, legal restrictions and, in January 1963, detention.[63] Tumbo, for example, was made High Commissioner in London, a most inappropriate appointment, and Kamaliza was made Minister of Labour in an early move to remove two of the main protagonists from the immediate scene of the controversy. In June 1962 three new Acts, the Trades Union Act, the Civil Service (Negotiating Machinery) Act and the Trades Disputes (Settlement) Act were introduced. The first of these strengthened the T.F.L. vis-à-vis the individual unions. The second banned participation by senior civil servants in trade unions and the third drastically limited the right to strike. These three Acts, followed in September by the Preventive Detention Act, were clear indications of the government's determination to limit factional opposition and to control economically disruptive trade union activity.

Paralleling this show of force, the government brought in several measures which were of real benefit to the rank and file of the trade unions. The most important was the introduction in January 1963 of a minimum wage of Shs.150 a month, a decision which not only caused a significant improvement in the wages of the poorest workers but also occasioned a more general upward revision of wage rates. As wages had also been increased in 1961, the result was a quite dramatic increase in African wage rates during the first three years of TANU rule. Average cash earnings rose from Shs.80 per month in 1960 to Shs.165 in 1963 (see table 3). In addition, the government required the payment of a lump-sum allowance to any worker dismissed without cause and it improved the law in regard to holidays with pay.[64]

Table 3. *Average cash earnings for African employees*[a]

Year	Shs. per month	Year	Shs. per month
1960	80	1962	122
1961	96	1963	165

[a] The 1960 figure is from Tanganyika, *Budget Survey, 1962–63* (Dar-es-Salaam, 1962), p. 16. The figures for 1961 to 1963 are from Tanzania, *Budget Survey, 1964–65* (Dar-es-Salaam, 1964), p. 9.

This adroit combination of progressive measures, cooption and tough-mindedness achieved its most immediate and obvious objectives. By 1963 the unions were no longer an open base for political opposition to the government and strikes were far less a threat to the economy.

Kawawa would not have had this success had he not also handled with great skill the explosive issue of the Africanization of the civil service. On this issue, he managed very largely to satisfy African criticisms of earlier Africanization policies without causing an immediate mass exodus of expatriates. He was greatly aided in this by the fact that there was already within the machinery of government the basis for an orderly pursuit of a more rapid Africanization of the civil service. Kawawa turned to the policies that had been recommended to the government eighteen months previously by Thurston and Kingsley. Moreover, because Nyerere had already begun to move in the same direction, Kawawa had in his immediate office a senior and experienced officer who could devise and implement an accelerated Africanization program which would not be destructively indiscriminate.[65]

There were four aspects to this program. The first was a much greater emphasis on in-service training in order to open up for many Africans much greater opportunities for advancement in the civil service. The second was a very careful effort to assure that the small numbers of young people who were completing secondary school would be distributed between jobs, training programs and university courses in numbers which reflected the country's priorities. The third was a subdivision into three of the complex responsibilities of the District Officers, those relating to judicial work, to local government and to central administration. This permitted educationally less qualified Africans to be trained either as magistrates, as local government officers or as administrative officers. The politically sensitive provincial administration could thus be Africanized much more rapidly than previously expected.

The fourth element to the Africanization program was the appointment of an Africanization Commission under the chairmanship of a strong party man, Saidi Maswanya. It was given the task of reviewing 'every

cadre and grade in the Civil Service with a view to ensuring that a satisfactory plan for complete Africanization exists'.[66] The overall figures on
the Africanization of the civil service show that there was not an over-
whelmingly rapid rundown of expatriates in the civil service. Nevertheless,
a basic change in emphasis had occurred. The emphasis was no longer on
the need to retain the British expatriates but was rather on the need to
train Africans.

Table 4. *Composition of middle and senior ranks of the civil service*[a]

1961	Africans	1,170	Non-Africans	3,282
1962	Africans	1,821	Non-Africans	2,902
1963	Citizens	2,782[b]	Non-citizens	2,642

[a] From Tanganyika, *Africanisation of the Civil Service, Annual Report 1963* (Dar-es-
Salaam, 1963), p. 2.
[b] These figures include some 300 Asian citizens.

Kawawa was more sensitive than Nyerere to the fact that there were
some posts to which it was politically very desirable to appoint Africans.
He dropped Meek as the Prime Minister's Principal Secretary within a
matter of days and quickly thereafter most Principal Secretaries were
African.[67] The most dramatic move came in regard to the police. A controversy between Kawawa and the British Commissioner of Police led
to the latter's dismissal, to the immediate Africanization of the posts of
Regional Police Commanders and to the decision to change dramatically
the racial balance within the police force as quickly as possible. At the
beginning of January 1961, all 12 Commissioners and Assistant Commissioners were British expatriates as were the 21 Senior Superintendents
and 51 of the 52 Superintendents. Even at the Assistant Superintendent
level African officers were in a minority, numbering only 27 in an
establishment of 157. This pattern continued until Kawawa became
Prime Minister. By January 1963, 86 of the 166 British officers had left.
A year later only 18 remained.[68]

Kawawa's greater responsiveness to the mood of the rank and file
showed itself also in April 1962 when he agreed, despite the direct intervention of Nyerere, that the government should be ready compulsorily to
retire non-African citizens in the civil service in order to make possible
the appointment or more rapid promotion of Africans. There is every
evidence that Africans were in fact advancing very rapidly within the
service and that Asian citizens in the civil service were not blocking
reasonable promotion prospects for Tanganyikan Africans. There is also
no evidence to suggest that any more than a very small number of Asian
citizens were in fact forced to resign to make room for African appointees.

The decision was therefore primarily a piece of bravado to appease racist elements within the party.

The main thrust of policy under Kawawa was nationalist and oligarchic, not radical or socialist. The Kawawa government sought to consolidate the authority of the ruling oligarchy and to limit the ability of its opponents to challenge that authority. It moved vigorously to remove individuals and symbols which were too reminiscent of the colonial period. It introduced a republican Constitution. It greatly expanded the employment opportunities for Africans in the middle and higher sections of the civil service. These actions were fairly typical expressions of the aspirations of a new political class, an African elite whose claim to status and power rested upon its political power rather than its economic power. The government of Tanganyika in 1962 was still a government without a consciously articulated ideology. It had not embraced Nyerere's egalitarian concerns nor did it seriously move in a socialist direction in its economic policies. The few measures which might seem to be 'neo-socialist', such as the abolition of freehold tenure and the promotion of cooperative retail stores, were more an expression of hostility towards the Asian and European minorities than deliberate first steps towards a socialist society.

Nevertheless, the Kawawa period is an important stage in the movement of ideas in Tanganyika from the acceptance of a major dependence upon Britain in 1960 to a strong commitment to socialism in 1967. By the end of 1962, TANU's political position was consolidated, a more assertively nationalist posture was adopted on many issues and the government was no longer gripped by an inhibiting fear of an expatriate exodus.

These were essential first steps towards a socialist Tanganyika. They were, equally, first steps towards authoritarian rule by a political elite. Nyerere's resignation had facilitated these first steps. However, his continued absence from the government would have made it more likely that these steps would lead to oligarchic rule rather than to a socialist democracy. Nyerere was already being called the Father of the Nation in 1962. He was in danger of becoming a beloved elder statesman before the age of forty, a moralizing oracle to whom homage was justly paid but whose maxims were increasingly ignored. His return to the party had accomplished its immediate purpose. The strains within the party and between the leaders and the people had been significantly lessened. However, his teachings had not made much impact upon his colleagues or upon the rank and file. If Nyerere was to continue to lead, he needed the prestige, the power and the authority of the Presidency.

On 9 December 1962, after an election in which he received an overwhelming majority,[69] he became the first President of the Republic of Tanganyika.

6: A loss of innocence 1963-8

Development strategy and foreign policy, an overview 1963-8

In the first years after the establishment of the republic, Tanzania's foreign policy and her development strategy were undeniably oriented towards the West. Tanzanian leaders used the rhetoric of non-alignment more frequently than they had previously, to demonstrate that Tanzania was not servilely dependent upon Britain and the United States. They took occasional initiatives such as the sending of a ministerial delegation to Moscow in 1964, the planning of a trip by Nyerere to India and China early in 1964, and the invitation to Chou En-lai to include Dar-es-Salaam in the itinerary of his African tour in 1965. However, the sources from which Tanzania expected to draw the great bulk of her foreign assistance, the countries from which she recruited her still numerous expatriate staff, the orientation of her educational system and of her army all demonstrated that in 1964 Tanzania still turned primarily to Britain and to other major Western powers for assistance and example.

The perception of international politics, at least as they related to Tanzania, which underlay this continuing close association with the Western states was described in these terms by Nyerere in August 1964:

> The world is divided into various conflicting groups, and each one of these groups is anxious for allies in Africa, and even more anxious that its opponent shall not find friends. In this field also we have, therefore, to think carefully and objectively about the implications of every move we make...The desire to help the United Republic in our economic struggle – even the desire for friendship with us – these things come second to what the other nation believes to be in its own interests. It is no use complaining about that; basically we ourselves adopt the same attitude. We have to recognize that some overseas nations will help us if they can, and if they do not believe that they will harm themselves while doing so; other nations will help us solely in the hope of some kind of return to themselves – whether this be diplomatic, political or economic.[1]

This statement was made by Nyerere on the occasion of the opening of the campus of the University College, Dar-es-Salaam. Much of the capital for that campus had come from British and American aid agencies. This context makes it clear that at that time Nyerere regarded Britain and the United States not as nations who would help Tanzania only if they could see a direct return to themselves, but rather as sympathetic countries that could be expected to help Tanzania as long as they did not thereby harm themselves. This assumption was an important ingredient of Tanzania's foreign policy and of her development strategy. They were thus at that time in substantial harmony one with the other.

Nyerere brought to the consideration of foreign affairs the same profound moral sense which he sought to apply to internal policies. In both areas he had not yet worked out in coherent detail the full implications of his basic values. However, on one important foreign policy issue his position was already unequivocal. He was committed to the achievement of freedom in the white-dominated regimes of southern Africa. He had already demonstrated that this commitment was not merely rhetorical. Under his instigation, the government had refused to allow any commercial aircraft to land in Tanganyika if they were on a flight destined for South Africa. It had introduced a boycott on the importation of South African goods. Nyerere himself had declared in 1960 that Tanganyika would not seek admission to the Commonwealth if the Republic of South Africa was readmitted and he had closed the Portuguese Consul-General's office in Dar-es-Salaam. These early indications of a determination to assist the liberation of southern Africa were not nationalist bravado. This commitment to majority rule in southern Africa was soon to become a major feature of Tanzania's foreign policy.

It will be recalled from chapter 4 that Nyerere had hoped that the decision by Britain to grant independence to Tanganyika marked a turning point in Britain's imperial relations with Africa which would make Britain a special friend of Tanzania and an ally in a common effort to bring independence and majority rule to the white-dominated countries to the south. As long as that faith held firm there was no apparent conflict between Tanzania's dependence upon British assistance and her commitment to freedom in southern Africa.

The basic congruence between Tanzania's development strategy and her foreign policy was shattered in the years 1963–6. A series of crises in Tanzania's relations with Britain and other Western countries compelled Nyerere and his colleagues to reassess their foreign policy. By 1967 Nyerere saw the world of international politics in a harsher and more sober light. By that date he had abandoned his earlier idealistic view of what might be expected of British policy in Africa. He saw with depressing clarity the conflicting motivations which were shaping the foreign policies of African states in ways that constantly jeopardized even a minimal inter-state cooperation within Africa. He realized how little influence Tanzania itself had in international affairs and how vulnerable she was. Nyerere's changing perception of these questions was a major factor contributing to his conviction by the end of 1966 that a very high priority must be given to the achievement in Tanzania of a democratic and socialist society. Central to the Arusha Declaration by which Nyerere launched Tanzania into its fresh commitment to socialist objectives was the proposition that Tanzania must become self-reliant. The loss of innocence in foreign affairs, it will be argued, was in turn a major cause of the importance which Nyerere was attaching to self-reliance. For these reasons a review of Tanzanian foreign policy and the major crises in Tanzania's relationships with other states is relevant to the purposes of this book. First, however, the extent and the persistent character of the dependence upon Britain must be demonstrated.

Tanzania's continued dependence: high-level manpower and development capital

The Five Year Plan for 1964–1969 expressed the aspiration that by 1980 Tanzania would be very largely free of any further need to recruit overseas.[2] This was a serious target, not a casual hope. The secondary school expansion and the growth of the University College, Dar-es-Salaam, were two of the very few sections of the first Five Year Plan which by 1969 had been totally realized. Within the government the rapid Africanization of the civil service remained an important preoccupation. The newly established Civil Service Training Centre each year provided a wide variety of courses which gradually raised the standards of competence within the middle ranks of the civil service. Most Ministries ran training courses at the post-secondary school level. Senior posts, particularly in the administration, were subdivided in order that the responsibilities of each of the newly created posts could be more narrowly defined and could therefore be entrusted to non-graduates who had received special courses of instruction directly related to the responsibilities of the new position.[3] The government, moreover, required that no vacancy could be filled by an expatriate unless the Principal Secretary of the Ministry concerned had certified that the post could not be filled locally, and, even then, only after the post had been advertised locally.

Over the two-year period 1963–5, the government took a series of decisions, many of them unpopular, which were designed to maximize the numbers of secondary school and university graduates available for government employment and to assure that their training reflected manpower priorities. The government held the expansion of primary school enrollment to the point where it only just kept up with the increase in the population of children of primary school age. It required all recipients of government bursaries, which in fact included almost all Tanzanian

Africans studying at university, to pledge themselves to work for the government for five years after graduation. Tanzanian entrants to the University of East Africa were distributed as between faculties in ratios that reflected the government's view of its relative need for their graduates. Thus for example fifty per cent of the students studying for a B.A. degree and eighty per cent of those doing a B.Sc. degree had to take education as one of their subjects in order that they could then become secondary school teachers. Finally the government sought to direct all secondary school and university graduates into government employment or into approved courses of further study. For the moment at least the government was so concerned to Africanize its own ranks as swiftly as possible that it allocated no graduates to the private sector.

Nevertheless throughout the decade of the 1960s the government of Tanzania had little real choice but to continue to employ substantial numbers of expatriates in the middle and senior ranks of the civil service. In 1961 there were over 3,200 non-Tanzanians in these ranks. By 1969, despite a decade of Africanization, there were still more than 1,500 non-Tanzanians in middle and senior positions within the regular and established ranks of the civil service.

Table 5. *Composition of the middle and senior ranks of the Tanzanian civil service, 1961–9[a]*

Citizenship	1961	1962	1963	1964	1965	1966	1967	1968	1969
Tanzanian	1,170	1,821	2,469	3,083	3,951	4,364	4,937	6,208	6,145
Non-Tanzanian	3,282	2,902	2,580	2,306	2,001	1,710	1,817	1,619	1,509
Total	4,452	4,723	5,049	5,389	5,962	6,074	6,754	7,827	7,654
% Tanzanians	26.1	35.5	48.9	57.2	66.3	71.8	73.1	79.3	80.3

[a] SOURCE: Tanzania, 'Annual Manpower Report to the President 1969' (Dar-es-Salaam, 1969), p. 27.

This table partly conceals the central importance of overseas recruitment for it does not give the number of government positions which were left vacant for long periods because there were neither local candidates nor available expatriates to fill them. In fact, year after year, a very significant number of middle and senior positions within the civil service were left unfilled. In the first year and a half of the First Five Year Plan, from July 1964 to December 1965, the Establishment Division sought to fill 512 vacancies overseas. In fact during this period only 103 expatriate appointments were made.[4] This pattern continued throughout 1966. In that year the government sought to fill 513 positions overseas but was in fact able to recruit for these positions only 213 expatriates.

The dependence upon aliens was, of course, much heavier in some

Ministries than in others. By September 1965, police officers, officials of the Ministry of Foreign Affairs and members of the administrative class were almost all African. In contrast there were many technical and professional cadres that were still very dependent upon aliens. There were, for example, 82 established posts for education officers, grades 1A and 1B, in the Secondary School Division of the Ministry of Education. Only 17 of these were held by citizens, with 41 non-citizens being employed and a further 24 posts being vacant. In the same year there were 451 secondary school teachers who were grade 2 officers. Only 41 of these were citizens. In the Ministry of Agriculture there were 29 established positions for veterinary officers. Ten of these officers were citizens, 10 non-citizens and 9 of the positions were unfilled. In the same Ministry there were established positions for 23 research officers, grades 1 and 2. Eleven of these were vacant while all the occupied posts were held by expatriates. In the Ministry of Communication and Works there were 57 established posts for executive engineers and quantity surveyors. Seventeen of these were unfilled and, of the remaining 40, only 3 were held by citizens. Finally in the Ministry of Health, there were 127 posts for medical officers. There were 30 Tanzanian citizens in these posts and 62 aliens with 35 vacancies.[5]

Figures such as these make it clear that the expatriate component was still extremely important in a number of technical and professional cadres within the civil service. They also demonstrate that qualified expatriates were very much in scarce supply. The government consistently was able to recruit far fewer expatriates than it needed and wanted. Unfilled vacancies in senior professional positions began to be recognized as one of the key limitations to the whole development effort.[6]

The conclusion is unavoidable that the Tanzanian government made major efforts to lessen its dependence upon alien civil servants, but that it judged, for good reasons, that their employment in substantial numbers continued to be essential to the maintenance and expansion of the public services, and that the difficulties in recruiting appropriate expatriates in sufficient numbers was an important limitation to the capacity of the public service to pursue even these development projects for which the finances were available.

The dependence upon expatriates was primarily a dependence upon the British. Throughout the whole period, no other country provided technical assistance personnel for Tanzania in anything like the same numbers as did the United Kingdom. This dependence was at its greatest, of course, in the first years of independence, because of the continuing presence in the Tanganyika civil service of large numbers of officers who had previously served in Tanganyika in the colonial service. Although their numbers gradually declined they nevertheless remained a significant group throughout most of the 1960s. In 1966 there were still more than 400

British officers on permanent and pensionable terms in the Tanzanian civil service and, even as late as June 1968, there were still 121 of these officers remaining in senior positions within Tanzania.[7]

The government of Tanzania made serious efforts to diversify the nationalities of the expatriates which it recruited. Nevertheless in these years the heavy dependence upon Britain was never really reversed. In the year 1963–4 there were over 1,200 British officers in regular civil service positions, a vastly greater number than that of any other foreign nationality. Most of the new recruits for regular established positions within the service continued still to be drawn from Great Britain. Over the three-and-a-half-year period from January 1962 to June 1966 the Establishment Division recruited 674 expatriates. Of these, 549 were from the United Kingdom.[8]

An analysis of the 205 expatriates who were listed in the senior staff directory of the Tanzanian government for May 1966 shows that 150 of these were British, 87 of whom were still on permanent terms. Eighteen of these 205 officers were provided by various United Nations agencies, and eight by the Ford Foundation. There were also fourteen Canadians, seven West Germans, six Israelis, two Americans and one Yugoslav. There was little let-up to this pattern. In 1966, for example, of the 213 new expatriates who joined the Tanzanian civil service, 135 were from the United Kingdom with the next largest national contingent being 31 from the U.A.R.[9] A full breakdown of expatriate recruitment by nationality for the four-year period from January 1962 to December 1965 is given in table 6.

Table 6. *Expatriates recruited by the Establishment Division January 1962–December 1965*

United Kingdom	516	Czechoslovakia	4
India	19	U.A.R.	3
U.S.A.	6	Netherlands	3
Yugoslavia	8	West Germany	1
Bulgaria	6	Jamaica	1
U.S.S.R.	5	Malaysia	1

SOURCE: The Central Establishment Division, communication to the author.

The continued prominence of British expatriates is explained by many factors. The language barrier itself automatically excluded anything but very occasional recruitment from most countries. There was often a preference for recruitment from Britain because it was felt that on balance a British officer tended to 'fit in' more easily than other expatriates. However, the most important reason was that the British Ministry of Overseas

Development was more effective in recruiting suitable expatriates in large numbers than were the other aid agencies. Moreover it provided generous support for British nationals who were recruited by the Tanzanian government in ways which were carefully worked out to cause a minimum of friction or offense.[10] In contrast to the British, most aid agencies tended to identify special activities which they wished to assist and to provide technical assistance personnel only in these areas. American personnel, for example, were concentrated in education, administrative training, community development and agriculture.[11] Neither the American A.I.D. nor any other aid agency was able to recruit and to provide financial assistance for the hundreds of expatriates needed still for regular civil service positions within the government of Tanzania. The Establishment

Table 7. *Tanzania government: Sources of external development funds 1961–5[a]* (*in thousands of shillings*)

	1961/2	1962/3	1963/4	1964/5	1961/2– 1964/5
Governments					
United Kingdom	61,620	93,720	22,680	23,900	201,920
U.S.A.	2,220	5,020	5,440	19,960	32,640
Federal Republic of Germany		2,540	16,400	7,220	26,160
Israel			700	8,460	9,160
China				5,980	5,980
Private trusts and charities					
British	120	160	880	800	1,960
American		1,420	1,940	760	4,120
Multilateral					
IDA			3,260	12,980	16,240
Refugee services			180		180
Nordic Council		260			260
Totals	63,960	103,120	51,480	80,060	298,620

[a] Calculated from tables in Tanzania, *Budget Survey 1965–66* (Dar-es-Salaam, 1966) and in the *Background to the Budget, An Economic Survey, 1966–67* and . . . *1967–68* (Dar-es-Salaam, 1966, 1967).

Division was bound to direct a high proportion of its requests for expatriate staff to the British Ministry of Overseas Development.[12]

The British government was also the source of by far the largest amount of external capital assistance received by Tanzania during the years 1961–1965. Table 7 presents an overall summary of the external funds received by the Tanzanian government for development purposes. These figures are not easily interpreted. They cover the external funds actually transferred to the Tanzanian Treasury for development purposes. They therefore do not include any estimate of the value of technical assistance personnel. They also exclude the value of any aid in kind such as military equipment, all loans to public corporations and all grants and loans to any East African governmental authority operation under the jurisdiction of the East African Common Services Organization.

Nevertheless, despite these qualifications, these figures demonstrate the degree to which British capital assistance predominated within the total capital aid received during these years. In the financial years 1961–5 over Shs.200m of the Shs.299m received from external sources by the Tanzanian Treasury as development revenues came from the British government. The next largest source, the American government, provided less than one-sixth the amount coming from the British government.

The foreign policy crises of 1964–6

British and other major Western powers thus provided almost all of the external capital assistance received by Tanzania in the period 1961–5. This might have been expected to reinforce and strengthen the Western orientation which was a general feature of Tanganyika's foreign policy in 1963. In fact, however, in the years which immediately followed, four interrelated issues brought Tanzania to a new perception of international politics and left in tatters the naive pro-Western assumptions and expectations of 1963.

The four issues which caused this 'loss of innocence' in foreign affairs were the continuing support given by the Western powers to the racist regimes in southern Africa, American and Belgian intervention in the Congo, the direct intrusion of cold-war politics following the union of Tanganyika and Zanzibar and the British failure to intervene in Rhodesia when its white-dominated regime unilaterally declared independence.[13]

The failure of the Western powers to support the liberation of southern Africa

Beginning in 1963 political refugees from southern Africa began to find their way to Dar-es-Salaam in increasing numbers. The African National Congress and the Pan-African Congress had been outlawed in South Africa in 1961 and their underground sections within South Africa had been uncovered and broken by late 1963. Many of those who had been able to escape gathered either in Dar-es-Salaam or London. In 1961 as well, the Southern Rhodesian government outlawed the main African nationalist movement, the Zimbabwe African People's Union, and its leaders congregated in Dar-es-Salaam. Mozambiquans had also begun crossing the border into Tanganyika in increasing numbers. By November 1964 they numbered more than 9,000. By then the Mozambique liberation movement, Frelimo, had been formed in Tanzania and had begun its long struggle for the liberation of Mozambique.

Nyerere permitted these political refugee groups to remain in Tanzania and to organize themselves for their continuing struggle. He and his colleagues strongly supported the establishment by the Organization of African Unity of an African Liberation Committee and offered the Committee accommodation and a secretariat in Dar-es-Salaam. In doing this they were doing no more than applying the position which Nyerere had stated to the United Nations General Assembly in December 1961: 'We who are free have absolutely no right to sit comfortably and counsel patience to those who do not yet enjoy their freedom.'[14]

Simultaneously with these developments, Nyerere tried to convince the Western powers that they should initiate a major international effort to use economic sanctions to convince Portugal to advance her African colonies towards independence and to win major reforms within South Africa. In May and June 1963, Nyerere went on his first official overseas visit since becoming President. He travelled to Washington, Ottawa and London. He used the occasion, in each case, primarily to speak not of Tanganyika's needs but of the urgent need for Western initiatives in regard to southern Africa. He stressed that the only alternative to such initiatives would be a long, arduous and embittering war. He was received politely in these capitals but he could strike no real response to his sense of the urgency and importance of this issue. In London, after the last of these meetings, he gave public voice to his frustration. 'If we do not find a peaceful solution', he said, 'our brethren in South Africa have absolutely no choice but to fight for it [independence] and we shall help them the best way we can... We say let us try sanctions. The only alternative is shooting and we do not want another Algeria...We are not challenging the existence of the white man on the African continent. But if the white man wants to remain in Africa to dominate then we are left with no choice but to fight.'[15] In November 1963, when Nyerere next visited Europe, he again called for a Western economic boycott of South Africa.[16]

The West, however, was unmoved. It became increasingly clear that if African rights in southern Africa were to be won, Africans would have to be ready themselves to fight for these rights. Nyerere had, therefore, at an early date to decide whether to permit the liberation movements which were organizing themselves in Tanzania to receive arms and training from those countries such as Algeria, the Soviet Union and China which were willing to help them. Many African states, though strongly condemning South African racism and Portuguese colonialism, had not wished to complicate their internal politics nor to compromise their relationships with the Western powers by facilitating such activities within their own country. Nyerere's answer, however, was never really in doubt. He would not engage in the moral gymnastics which would have been required simultaneously to condemn Portugal, South Africa and Rhodesia and then to obstruct the efforts of African nationalists to secure training and arms after they had turned in despair to armed struggle. He gave this permission, however, with a heavy heart. His preference remained very much for a peaceful and negotiated transition to majority rule in southern Africa which would be achieved with the active support of the Western powers.[17] However, as he had said in 1965, 'We can't fight with bows and arrows just to prove we are Africans. We will have to have modern arms. Presumably the West would not supply us with arms to fight the Portuguese. Therefore, we would have to get arms from the Communists.'[18]

This was, for Nyerere, part of the reality of African politics by 1965. The liberation movements were slow in building up their strength. The only states outside of Africa willing to help them were Communist countries. The Western countries, which at least in regard to the Portuguese territories were in a position to apply sufficient pressure to achieve major change peacefully, had no intention of doing so. This was particularly disillusioning for Nyerere. His commitment to the liberation of the African colonies was rooted in values which he had in part derived from the liberal political traditions of the West. More disheartening still, he foresaw that if the Western states failed to respond to their own fundamental values on this issue, there was the terrible prospect of a struggle in southern Africa which would not only be unnecessarily protracted and violent but would also be ideological and racial. He expressed this fear most fully in a speech in Canada in 1969 in these prophetic words:

> The freedom fighters use communist arms and are trained in communist countries because they have no choice. This is happening now and it will continue. And then South Africa and Portugal will proclaim to their allies this 'proof' that they are fighting communism. . .In the face of this kind of psychological pressure, I am afraid that western states would strengthen their support for the Southern African regimes. They would argue that for their own protection it was necessary to prevent Africa from falling into the hands of communists. . .And gradually this conflict will become the ideological conflict which at present it is not. At that point, because Africa does not look at things through cold war

spectacles, the nature of the conflict may change again; it may become a confrontation between the poor, coloured world and the rich white world.[19]

Nyerere has retained his faith that there is nothing inevitable about this prospect. He continues to believe, in his own words, 'that the basic philosophy of Western democracy has its own life and its own power and that the people's concept of freedom can triumph over their materialism.[20] But he has long since lost any easy expectation that the Western powers and the independent African states would be likely to share a common enterprise to bring justice to southern Africa without violence.

The intrusion of the cold war with the union of Tanganyika and Zanzibar

Zanzibar consists of two small islands lying some twenty-two miles off the coast of Tanganyika near Dar-es-Salaam. Its long and varied history is reflected in the racial composition of its peoples. Until 1964 the dominant class had been an Arab land-owning minority of some 35,000 who were the descendants of the rulers and traders who had made Zanzibar an important staging post in the movement of both slaves and trading commodities from the mainland to the Arabian Peninsula. The African population of Zanzibar numbers 270,000 and includes many who are members of tribes which have emerged out of an earlier absorption of Persian invaders by indigenous African Zanzibaris. Finally, there was until 1964 a further minority of some 30,000 Asians, a large majority of whom were traders, shopkeepers and clerical workers.

The politics of the island had been plagued by racial and economic tensions. These were intensified by historic memories of past oppression and by the fact that the racial and economic stratification largely reinforced each other. These tensions moreover had already taken on an international dimension. Even before independence a number of Zanzibar leaders had sought external support. The Arab-led Zanzibar Nationalist Party (Z.N.P.) had developed links with Egypt and with the Sudan, hoping that a politicized Islam would provide a basis for the unity of Zanzibar. This party also had a radical wing, led by Abdulrahman Mohammed Babu, which prodded the Z.N.P. to open an office in Cuba and to invite the People's Republic of China to open an embassy on Zanzibar. Babu himself had a modest retainer as a stringer for the Chinese News Agency. Just before independence this radical faction broke with the Z.N.P. to form the Umma Party (The Masses). The largest party was the Afro-Shirazi Party led by Abeid Karume. It was much divided by the frustrations of an electoral system which had twice given it a minority of seats despite the fact that it kept winning a majority of the popular vote. Its closest ties were with TANU and the mainland, though some of its leaders, and particularly Abdulla Kassim Hanga, had operating links with the Soviet Union.

When the British government decided in the early 1960s speedily to concede independence to Zanzibar, it negotiated the independence primarily with the leaders of the Zanzibar Nationalist Party. The British neither insisted upon a coalition which would include the Afro-Shirazi Party nor demand a reformed electoral system which would avoid the major anomalies which had twice in a row produced results which gave the Afro-Shirazi Party an absolute majority of the votes cast but only a minority of the seats. On 9 December 1963, Zanzibar became fully independent under a government dominated by the Z.N.P. and led by its leader, Ali Muhsin.

Earlier in this same year, Nyerere had warned the British government that if it gave power to the Arab-led minority Z.N.P. it would bequeath to Zanzibar an extremely unstable situation. Within five weeks of independence, while the leaders of the Umma Party and the Afro-Shirazi Party were still contemplating, and perhaps planning, separate revolutions of their own, the government was in fact overthrown by an uprising led by an unknown and untutored messianic African nationalist leader, John Okello. After a brief chaotic period of communal killing[21] Okello installed a revolutionary council under the leadership of Karume and including both Hanga and Babu.

The uprising in Zanzibar immediately attracted international attention. For both the Russians and the Chinese it meant a break in the largely inhospitable front presented to them by the independent African states. Within ten days the new regime was recognized by East Germany, China, the Soviet Union, Czechoslovakia, Cuba, North Vietnam, North Korea, Yugoslavia, Bulgaria and Albania. Many of these countries swiftly stepped in to assist the Revolutionary Council. China gave a £500,000 interest-free loan in convertible currency; the Soviet Union bought substantial quantities of cloves, Zanzibar's main export crop, and began to train the new Zanzibar army; the East Germans staffed the main hospital in Zanzibar, undertook a major slum-clearance project and provided a powerful radio transmitter. The Western powers, in contrast, although at first moving some forces closer to Zanzibar, decided not to intervene. However, they withheld recognition until late in February and withdrew many of their nationals.

A few months later, suddenly and without any prior announcement, Nyerere and Karume announced that they had signed an agreement of union between their two countries. On 24 April it was ratified by the National Assembly of Tanganyika. The union had been negotiated by Karume and Hanga on the one hand and, on Nyerere's behalf, by Kambona, aided by Roland Brown, the highly trusted English lawyer whom Nyerere had invited to be Tanganyika's Attorney-General in 1960.

Babu and the radical left had opposed the union and its sponsors had carefully brought it to the Revolutionary Council for ratification at a time when Babu was out of the country. The Communist left generally received the news of the union as a defeat.[22]

Colin Legum, in a report which was written following an interview with Nyerere, said that the union had been a brilliant manoeuvre to outwit the Babu faction which was seeking to move Zanzibar from a non-aligned position to a full orientation towards Communism.[23] Although this report was criticized in Dar-es-Salaam, it does seem likely that among the reasons why Nyerere favoured the union was a fear that Zanzibar might otherwise become a centre of Communist subversion directed towards the mainland governments.[24] However, Nyerere's commitment to the union had additional and deeper roots. There had long been close affinities between mainland Africans and the African majority on the islands. There had also been close links between TANU and the Afro-Shirazi Party. Moreover, the failure of Nyerere's initiatives in 1963 to achieve a political federation of the three East African countries, or of Tanganyika and Kenya left Nyerere somewhat isolated within East Africa. The union became, then, a test of his ability to make some advance towards larger political units.

The union, however, had its repercussions upon Tanzania's foreign policy. Tanzania became a contested arena in both the cold war and in the Sino-Soviet dispute. The prompt support given to the revolution by Communist countries had further increased the links between the Zanzibar leaders and these countries. The Soviet Union feared direct U.S. or U.S.-sponsored intervention in Zanzibar, while the U.S. Ambassador in Nairobi expressed concern that Zanzibar would become 'a staging base for political manoeuvres' on the African continent.[25] Nyerere was therefore propelled by the union into an effort to define a non-aligned foreign policy in terms which would be tenable in this new context of heightened entanglement within the cold war. This task was almost immediately made more difficult by two specific crises which were directly linked with the union.

The Democratic Republic of Germany had been the first country to recognize the new People's Republic of Zanzibar and the first to send an Ambassador to the islands. East Germany had also sent significant technical assistance by the time of the union and had pledged more aid. The East Germans immediately saw that they might lose the advantages which they had gained by Zanzibar's recognition. Karume, who had appreciated East Germany's early support, issued a statement on 6 May saying that 'the United Republic would continue to follow the foreign policies of Tanganyika and the People's Republic of Zanzibar unaltered and that the diplomatic relations which the People's Republic of Zanzibar had established with the GDR will continue to exist'.[26]

This formula, however, was not easily applied. The West German government at this time was determined to hold the line in Africa on the Halstein Doctrine. Any recognition of East Germany was therefore bound to have severe consequences on the relations between the Federal Republic and the recognizing government. In any case, Nyerere and his mainland colleagues had little sympathy politically with the Ulbricht regime in East Germany and did not want the union to involve them in a full recognition of the East German government. Moreover, West Germany had become an important source of technical and capital assistance for Tanganyika. Capital loans for a variety of projects concentrated largely in agriculture and in housing had totalled D.M. 45,000,000. Over fifty technical assistance experts and another fifty German volunteers were working in Tanganyika. Germany had undertaken the establishment, training, advising and equipping of an air wing and of a naval police force. Finally, the German government had contributed or pledged nearly D.M. 40,000,000 to education and health activities undertaken by one or other of a number of German voluntary agencies which were operating in Tanganyika.

Nyerere and his colleagues reacted adversely to pressure from the East German government that it be recognized by the United Republic, as it had been by the People's Democratic Republic of Zanzibar. Kambona, as Foreign Minister, tried to settle the issue in May 1964. After travelling to Bonn for discussions, he announced on 27 May 1964 that all countries which had had representation before the union in both Tanganyika and in Zanzibar would be permitted consulates in Zanzibar, but that the only embassies would be those in Dar-es-Salaam. This meant that the East German Embassy in Zanzibar would have to be demoted to the status of a trade delegation. The ruling was defied by both the East German government and by the Zanzibar authorities. Kambona's deadline of 30 June passed without his ruling being enforced. West Germany, in turn, made it increasingly clear that any recognition of East Germany would be an unfriendly act which would have adverse consequences on German–Tanzanian relations.

Ministers such as Bomani and Shaba, who had been particularly involved in the negotiations for West German assistance, were angry to see this being jeopardized. They were joined by others who resented Zanzibar's refusal to cooperate on this issue. In August the Ministry of Foreign Affairs issued a public statement which indirectly but categorically rejected the Zanzibar claims that East Germany had an embassy on the island. This statement said, 'The East German representation in Zanzibar cannot be an embassy since it is not accredited to the only sovereign government, that is, the Government of the United Republic.'[27] The result was a serious crisis within the Cabinet. At one time the East Germans nearly succeeded in changing the problem from being a German one into being a Tanganyika–Zanzibar issue.[28] Finally Nyerere prevailed upon Karume to accept the compromise that the East Germans would be allowed to open an 'unofficial' Consulate-General in Dar-es-Salaam, an arrangement which was widely believed at the time to have been suggested by the Bonn government about July 1964.[29] The compromise was then rejected by the West German government. There is no doubt that its officials strongly hinted that the flow of German aid would be adversely affected by any change which would favour the position of the Democratic Republic of Germany. They also suggested that the West German government would be willing to take up all of the East German aid projects should the East Germans react with hostility to a decision on this issue favourable to West Germany. Nyerere reacted angrily, resenting the elements of blackmail and bribery in these suggestions as well as their insensitivity to the fact that he had won from the Zanzibaris a major retreat from their original demand for the full recognition of East Germany. His patience finally snapped. On 19 February 1965, the official Gazette announced that the Democratic Republic of Germany would open a Consulate-General in Dar-es-Salaam, but this would not constitute official recognition. Bonn immediately recalled its naval and air training personnel and announced that there would be no new official aid unless Tanzania accepted a compromise.[30] Tanzania, in turn, ordered the withdrawal of all German technical assistance personnel. The most assiduous negotiations were necessary before German-supported volunteers and the German staff of German voluntary agencies were excused from this angry Tanzanian edict. The Tanzanian decision was explained to other African leaders in these terms:

> By withdrawing the military aid first and leaving the other form of aid for later action, the Germans hoped that this threat would make us change our decision. . .We decided to remove all doubt about our attitude to economic blackmail. The current position, therefore, is that Tanzania does not recognize East Germany: it recognizes West Germany and has an ambassador from Bonn in Dar es Salaam. Aid from East Germany continues to arrive in one part of the union; no aid comes from the West German government to any part of the union. This is a rather absurd way of demonstrating that our foreign and diplomatic policy has nothing to do with aid but for the present that is the position.[31]

At the same time as this crisis was developing, Zanzibar featured in a second foreign policy crisis. On 15 January 1965, the government of Tanzania announced that it was expelling two officials of the U.S. Embassy for subversive activities. They were Frank Carlucci, the U.S. Consul-General in Zanzibar, and Robert Gordon, the Deputy Chief of Mission in Dar-es-Salaam.[32] The incident quickly acquired a Gilbertian quality. Gordon and Carlucci appear to have had a telephone conversation over a public line in which they discussed their interest in having an American statement issued on the occasion of the first anniversary of the Zanzibar revolution. A statement merely from Carlucci himself, they felt, would not be sufficient to satisfy the Zanzibaris. 'Bigger guns' would be needed. An unskilled intelligence officer who monitored the call reported the suspicious phrase to his Zanzibar superiors. Immediately the fear was established. The two officers were planning a subversive operation for the anniversary of the revolution. Only the expulsion of the two Americans would satisfy Karume. There is no evidence which indicates that Nyerere did not believe the accusations but was forced to go along with the plan in order to placate Karume.[33]

One can nevertheless still suggest that if Nyerere had believed the accusations, it seems very likely that he would have proceeded in a much blunter fashion than he did. As it was, Nyerere refused to disclose the source or content of the intelligence report which he was accepting. He stressed that the subversion which he believed the two men were planning was a private conspiracy which did not involve either the United States Ambassador nor the United States government. He hoped as a result that the two officers might be withdrawn without any damage to Tanzanian–American relations. Although the American authorities recognized the goodwill behind this particular refinement, the United States could not go along with this subterfuge without doing severe damage to the reputations of the two officers involved. The United States then withdrew its Ambassador from Dar-es-Salaam. Tanzania in turn reciprocated by withdrawing its Ambassador in Washington. Relations with another Western power were thus in serious disarray by early 1965.

American and Belgian intervention in the Congo

The last of the U.N. troops which had been seeking to maintain the peace in the Congo left the Congo in June 1964. Sporadic rebellions broke out in several parts of that vast country, which the Congolese National Army was unable to contain. In July President Kasuvubu, in an assertion of authority that lacked any constitutional basis, dismissed the Prime Minister and appointed Moise Tshombe in his place. Tshombe was no ordinary African leader. With Belgian support and with the help of a white mercenary army, he had been able to maintain an independent Katanga for two and a half years. He is held responsible, accurately by most reports, for the murder of Patrice Lumumba, who had been delivered to the custody of the Katanga regime by the Congolese authorities. For a great many Africans, within the Congo and outside, Tshombe had become the epitome of the self-seeking adventurer who for personal gain becomes the agent for the reintrusion into Africa of colonial influence and control.

Once Tshombe had become Prime Minister in 1964 he again appealed to the same constellation of foreign interests which had supported him in the Katanga. He recruited mercenaries, in particular from South Africa, Rhodesia and Belgium, and he brought back many who had previously served him well. He turned also to the governments of the United States and of Belgium for support. They greatly increased their assistance, claiming that the Chinese Embassies in Burundi and in Congo-Brazzaville were aiding the rebels and that in contrast they were merely responding to requests from the constitutional government. The United States provided transport planes, trucks and arms and facilitated the recruitment in the United States of air pilots and other skilled mercenaries. The Belgians, in close liaison with the Americans, provided military support staff to augment the mercenaries and to train and lead the Congolese army.

This intervention was profoundly offensive to a great many African leaders. Tshombe was not the only African leader who had sought and had accepted Western military assistance. Indeed many had done so. Nevertheless, in their view Western assistance to Tshombe was inexcusable. With that aid Tshombe was attempting to check and then to reverse the advance of the rebels. Being sure of Belgian and American support he rejected the attempts of the Organization of African Unity to mediate between the Congolese government and the rebels. This whole episode, especially as it came at the same time as increasing direct U.S. military intervention in Vietnam and the American military operation in the Dominican Republic, confirmed for many African leaders the distressing fact that the Western powers would not hesitate to intervene in Africa whenever they felt it would advance their interests.

The OAU had condemned Tshombe and was attempting to secure a negotiated settlement between the warring parties in the Congo. Yet the United States and Belgian governments gave to Tshombe the help which he needed to stay in power. The parallel with Vietnam seemed close. Both the Chinese and the United States were intervening in Congolese affairs. The Chinese intervention, however, was indirect and involved the supplying of arms to men who were anxious to fight. The Americans, in contrast, were backing a regime which, though nominally constitutional, could maintain itself in power only by the recruitment of white mercenaries. The parallel was all the more disheartening in that the scale of intervention required for these purposes in the Congo was minimal. Such was the fragility of African states and the weakness of both their armies and the rebels' forces that a small number of white mercenaries, modestly equipped, were proving vastly more capable of determining the outcome of a political struggle in the Congo than was the Organization of African Unity itself.

Tshombe's mercenary-led and Western-assisted Congolese National Army (C.N.A.) soon began to regain control of areas which had recently been lost to the rebel forces. These forces then collected together in

Stanleyville, their 'capital', between 1,500 and 2,000 aliens, many of them missionaries and teachers. These captives were mainly Belgian though they included as well a significant number of Americans and other nationalities. They were held as hostages by the rebel forces in the hope that their presence would inhibit the C.N.A. from a direct assault on Stanleyville and that they might be used as barters to secure a favour-able political settlement. Their plight became a matter of major inter-national interest. As the C.N.A. advanced towards Stanleyville the fear grew that the hostages might well be murdered by undisciplined rebel forces in the last hours of their control of Stanleyville. The Belgians, with American assistance and British cooperation, then mounted a well-executed parachute drop on Stanleyville, rescuing all but sixty of the hostages. They then left Stanleyville, the whole operation taking only four days. Stanleyville was then quickly overrun by the C.N.A.

Few Western actions in Africa since 1960 have generated quite so swiftly such profound hostility as did this parachute operation. None illustrates better how rapidly distrust and suspicion can develop once a Western power openly uses its superior force to influence the politics of a major African state. For Belgium and the United States the parachute drop was a rescue operation which any sovereign state would try to effect if its nationals were threatened. It was done with the approval of the government of the Democratic Republic of the Congo. The Congolese National Army, no doubt, was aided by it. However, the Americans and the Belgians have always vigorously contended that the purpose of their operation was to rescue the hostages, not to aid the C.N.A.

A very wide range of African opinion viewed this operation in quite different terms. The force of the point that the Belgians and Americans were rescuing their own innocent nationals was for them much blunted by the fact that other nationals of these same countries were at the same time leading the attack on Stanleyville with the open assistance of the United States and Belgian governments. Africans were distressed and angered by the contrast which they saw between the disregard for African lives that they felt was a corollary of the American and Belgian military assistance to Tshombe and the West's concern for innocent civilians when those civilians happened to be white. African leaders resented the American and Belgian decision to bypass in an humiliating fashion the Organization of African Unity Committee, chaired by Kenyatta, which was trying to secure a cease-fire in Stanleyville at the very time of the parachute operation. They noted that the C.N.A. in fact benefited from the parachute drop and they suspected that that was indeed its purpose.[34] Nyerere, for example, referred to it as 'an action reminiscent of Pearl Harbor'.[35]

There then occurred a sad and perplexing episode in U.S.–Tanzanian relations which, one may safely assume, would have been much more easily handled and resolved but for the suspicion and distrust of U.S. motives which had developed in 1964 as a consequence of American intervention in the Congo. The incident was the celebrated American 'plot' to murder Nyerere and to subvert the government of Tanzania.[36] Early in November 1964, Mr Tibandebage, the Tanzanian Ambassador to the Congo, returned to Tanzania with photocopies of several documents purporting to be letters from an official of the U.S. Embassy in Leopold-ville to a mercenary offering him financial support to travel to South Africa in order to enlist others in a Portuguese-supported plot to over-throw Nyerere and his government. The timing was perhaps significant for a reply was expected any day from the U.S. government to an earlier request that it help with the training of the Zanzibar police. Nyerere, who was vacationing in north Tanzania, discussed the letters with Kambona, his Foreign Minister, and then turned them over to him for appropriate action. Kambona himself claims that Nyerere had said to him 'Let's handle this in an African way. Oscar, do you remember what you did as a school boy when a bully threatened you?' He reports that he then replied, 'I shouted as loud as I could.'[37] Whether or not on such advice from Nyerere, Kambona returned to Dar-es-Salaam and began to 'shout loudly'.

His first official statement, though making no reference to the United States, accused 'certain Western powers' of a plot to overthrow the government. However, the party newspaper, *The Nationalist*, which was at that time run by close associates of Kambona, printed the full text of the letters so that from the start the plot was identified as American. Very quickly, through his network of political contacts, Kambona had prompted into being a series of statements denouncing the plot as the latest example of American imperialism. All the liberation movements issued such state-ments. So also did President Ben Bella of Algeria, while the Ghanaian Foreign Minister travelled to Dar-es-Salaam to express his country's solidarity with Tanzania at this hour of crisis. Marches and demonstrations took place in Dar-es-Salaam and in other Tanzanian cities becoming with each passing day increasingly anti-American.

The American Ambassador immediately denounced the documents as forgeries. Many were easily convinced that this was true. The plot as outlined in the letters seemed more likely to be the product of an unskilled and simplistic forger than of the CIA. Nyerere returned to Dar-es-Salaam five days after the plot had been denounced to find that a massive demon-stration had been organized for him. He brilliantly defused the issue, dis-appointing Kambona and those of his colleagues who were hoping to keep politics at the level and pitch of the previous few days and leaving the thousands at the rally with nothing to do but quietly to return home. In this speech Nyerere sought to make it clear why he and Kambona had been ready to give credence to the possibility of an American plot to overthrow them. He discussed the West's fear of Communist influence in Zanzibar and in the Tanzanian army. He stressed Tanzania's commitment to aid Frelimo's struggle for Mozambiquan independence. He noted that only a month previously the Portuguese Foreign Minister had threatened to attack Tanzania and he added, 'Yet I did not hear any one of these sophisticated countries asking Salazar why he was threatening Tanzania.'[38] He assailed the African rulers in the Congo and in Malawi who were now ready 'to kiss Africa's enemies'. He then turned to the plot itself:

> In short, my countrymen, we are surrounded with difficulties. For a whole year we have been shaken with these difficulties. Now suddenly we get this news. The United States government is tired of seeing Dar es Salaam being used by the Chinese to the detriment of the Western countries and for the purpose of breaking the peace of Africa! And that their government has decided to put an end to this!...My brothers, we are not gods. We are human beings. We have been threatened too much in the past. What should we have done? It was only the other day that Portugal threatened us; and then today we get this news...Oscar made a big noise; and it became a problem. Suddenly other people were proclaiming openly that they were going to attack us. We cried out. If the news is untrue, fair enough: this will be the end of the whole thing and we shall be extremely happy. I shall be the first person to be delighted to know this. I have had a talk with the American Ambassador who has told me that the news was an utter lie...I told him that as they were the ones who knew about it, if they showed us that it was untrue then we would thank God – today being a Sunday...But during all this period of difficulty we have gone through, what else could we have done? We say that we do not know. The Americans say we have not shown them the evidence. We shall hand over to them the evidence so that they can see for themselves and explain to us the reason why the plot is untrue. We shall be happy and that will be the end of it all.[39]

The U.S. Ambassador was able quickly to produce a wide variety of detailed evidence that did indeed suggest that the letters were a forgery. There was, for example, no such person as John Blac, the name of the person who allegedly sent the letter, and the State Department's emblem on the letterhead was wrong in such observable details as the number of stars in the circle over the eagle's head and the angle of the eagle's beak. On 9 December 1964 Nyerere publicly announced that he had accepted the Americans' statements that the documents were false and that the government had replied that 'as far as it was concerned, it hoped the matter had now ended there'.[40] It was hardly a gracious or full apology but it was all that the American Ambassador was able to get, at least publicly. Nyerere, in private conversation with the Ambassador, is alleged to have 'all but' said that he did not believe the plot but that he could not openly say so without having to disown Kambona.[41] Whether this is true or not, the swift and uncritical denunciation of the plot, the immediate build-up of anti-American sentiments, the political limits which seemed to be set to any retraction of the Tanzanian allegations, all illustrate well the corroding and unsettling impact which the U.S. policies in regard to southern Africa and its intervention in the Congo had had upon American–Tanzanian relations.

The collapse of friendly relations with Britain

It was Britain, not the United States nor West Germany, which was the Western power with whom Tanzania had the closest relations and the most complex ties. As was argued in the previous chapter, the assumption that Britain was a particular ally and sympathetic friend of Tanzania was central to Tanzania's development strategy and to her foreign policy. Had that assumption been sustained, it would have offset the strains which had developed in Tanzania's relations with the United States and with Germany. It would have also provided a Western counterpart to the friendly relations which Tanzania was developing with China. However, this assumption was far from being sustained. Indeed, its total erosion was perhaps the most important aspect of that loss of innocence in international politics which Tanzania experienced during these years.

Tanzanians had never easily nor unanimously assumed that Tanzania had a special relationship with Britain. Britain had after all been their colonial ruler and, though the struggle for independence had been neither prolonged nor violent, TANU was an anti-colonial nationalist movement. Especially for those Ministers who had not become primarily absorbed in their governmental responsibilities, the powerful presence of a subordinate network of British expatriates within the civil service was a continuing irritation. At times the rhetoric of these Ministers revealed a profound antipathy towards Britain which was in open contradiction to the assumption that Britain was a special ally and close friend.[42]

For a great many Tanzanians including Nyerere the need still to be dependent upon Britain generated an emotional tension and strain which was a burden, however necessary the aid and however positive the other features of British-Tanzanian relations. These strains and tensions were very significantly increased by the humiliation of having to call upon Britain in January 1964 to put down an army mutiny. (This mutiny is discussed below, pp. 178–9.) The problems posed by this emotional undercurrent were not made easier by the style and presumption of British diplomats in Dar-es-Salaam. The heavy-handed paternalism which has already been commented upon as a feature of many of the British colonial civil servants in independent Tanzania reappeared in the attitude of many of the senior members of the British High Commission in the first years of independence. They assumed a relationship with Nyerere which gave the High Commissioner the right to offer advice to him whenever he was bothered by a Tanzanian initiative. Other Western diplomats tended also to acquire the same presumptions, so that by mid 1964 Nyerere had publicly to criticize them for the pressure they were seeking to apply upon him. That this was a matter of some importance is revealed by this angry public reference to Western criticisms when Tanzania accepted Chinese arms and instructors for the army:

> As I have told you, we asked for weapons from the Western countries. We have British, German, and Australian weapons here. We asked the Chinese to supply us with arms as well. The Chinese gave us weapons; but when they did so, we had created a problem! And a big problem too! We are grown up people, yet we will be questioned like children: 'Why do you ask for weapons from the Chinese?' From whom should we ask for weapons then? Yes, we asked for Chinese weapons and they gave them to us. After they had given the weapons to us we asked them to come to show us how to handle them. They sent seven Chinese to come to help us; and this still has become a problem! Towards a mere seven Chinese, people react as if there were 70,000 Chinese! And the seven Chinese are to stay for only six months! There was such a big row about this that I had to call a press conference and lash out like a madman. I am tired of being questioned about the Chinese.[43]

The strains and tensions which particularly affected British–Tanzanian relations might, however, have been managed but for the emergence of a fundamental and major disagreement between Tanzania and Britain over British policy towards Southern Rhodesia. When the Central African Federation collapsed and the African-controlled governments in Nyasaland and in Northern Rhodesia were promised early independence, the leaders of the white ruling minority in Southern Rhodesia were determined to win full independence for a white-dominated Southern Rhodesia. Britain in turn, though certainly in no mood to retain her nominal sovereignty over Southern Rhodesia, felt blocked at that time from giving independence to a government so obviously controlled by its small white minority.[44]

The governments of Tanzania, Zambia and other African states followed the negotiations between Britain and Southern Rhodesia anxiously and carefully. These African governments took a fundamentally moderate position. They did not call for an immediate adult franchise, for immediate independence under majority rule, or for a United Nations or African trusteeship to replace British colonial rule. They recognized the need for a significant transitional period. They accepted that Rhodesia posed very special problems for Britain as Britain had no military presence there nor any effective operating influence on Rhodesian legislation. Nyerere and Kaunda were ready, therefore, to accept a good many compromises as long as Britain would not give independence to Rhodesia while it was still under white minority rule. 'Our very minimum demand, below which we must not go, is independence for Rhodesia on the basis of majority rule. Independence by itself is not enough; independence – legal or otherwise – for Rhodesia before the African majority have the majority political power would mean the development of another South Africa.'[45]

The conflict between Nyerere and the British government first came to a head at the Commonwealth Conference in June 1965 when Nyerere sought to secure from Wilson the commitment that Britain would not give independence to Rhodesia without majority rule. When Wilson refused to agree to this, Nyerere in turn refused to sign the Commonwealth communiqué. It is small wonder that the incident generated intense feelings, for Wilson knew what Nyerere at that time did not know, namely that he, Wilson, had already given this crucial point away in his negotiations with Smith.[46]

The subsequent history of British–Rhodesian relations and of British–Tanzanian relations can be but briefly reviewed here. On 11 November 1965 the Rhodesian regime unilaterally declared its independence of Britain. On 20 November the United Nations Security Council called upon all states to do their utmost to break all economic relations with Southern Rhodesia. The resolution specifically encouraged the imposition of an embargo on oil. Britain at this time blocked the use of Chapter VII of the Charter under which economic sanctions could have been made legally obligatory. Britain also did not immediately impose an oil embargo. On 2 December the African Foreign Ministers meeting in Addis Ababa called upon Britain to 'crush' the Smith regime by 15 December. Nyerere, more out of anger that African leaders would pledge such actions and then casually ignore the pledge because it seemed tactically correct, led the minority of African states which then broke diplomatic relations with Britain after 15 December.[47] Britain in retaliation froze the £7.5m loan to Tanzania which had just been negotiated.

At Lagos in January 1966, with effective Canadian support, Wilson won acceptance by the Commonwealth Conference that sanctions should be given a chance to bring the Smith regime down before more direct action was contemplated. It was on this occasion that Wilson made his now famous judgment that sanctions would defeat the Smith regime 'within a matter of weeks, not months'. At the London Conference in 1966, Wilson was pressed by a large majority of the Conference to support the position that there should be no independence in Rhodesia before majority rule. He insisted, however, on one further effort to negotiate independence, promising that if that failed the 'British government...will not thereafter be prepared to submit to the British Parliament any settlement which involves independence before majority rule'.[48] These negotiations failed and in February 1967 Wilson dutifully informed the House of Commons that his government would honour the pledge which it had given to the Commonwealth Conference. However, in fact in 1968 there were fresh negotiations with Smith and, although Wilson was again ready to concede the reality of control to the white minority, the Smith regime finally rejected the British proposals.

If Nyerere's anger and disillusionment over British policy by that date is to be understood, it is important to recognize how far Britain had moved in its negotiations with Smith from the position which it had outlined to the Commonwealth Conference in 1966.

> After the illegal regime comes to an end a legal government will be appointed by the governor, who will form a broadly based representative administration and have authority over the police and the army. Britain will negotiate with this administrator a constitution directed to achieving majority rule, but will not consent to independence before majority rule unless the people of Rhodesia as a whole are shown to be in favour of it. The settlement will be submitted for acceptance to the people of Rhodesia by appropriate democratic means.[49]

In contrast to this position, by November 1971 Britain had conceded the following:

1   Independence would be granted many decades before there would be any chance of majority rule.

2   No interim, broadly based administration would be established.

3   Independence would be on the basis of the 1969 Constitution, an illegal and racist Constitution which is entirely the product of the Smith regime.

4   Smith and the other leaders of the rebellion would remain in power; the leaders of the African resistance would face terrorist and sedition charges if they returned to Rhodesia.

5   No meaningful safeguard was provided against retrogressive legislation.

6   The franchise and the constitutional amendment procedures would be such as to make it unreasonable to expect that an African majority would emerge in any foreseeable future.

It is small wonder that this estrangement grew more severe each year. Nevertheless, the Tanzanian government continued to honour its earlier agreement to pay the pensions of retired British officers, to permit these officers to commute their pensions on retirement, and to pay them sizable sums as compensation for loss of career whenever they chose to leave Tanzania. The pensions were paid each year as part of the regular government expenditures and the commutation and compensation payments were financed from British loans made explicitly for these purposes. By 1967–8

Shs.21m needed to be provided in the recurrent estimates for the pensions while the total amount borrowed by Tanzania for the commutation and compensation payments reached to nearly £9m. The repayment of these loans was to begin in 1968–9.

These arrangements were part of the Independence settlement. Nyerere and his colleagues had not been happy with these particular features but had accepted them as part of an overall arrangement which, in its other aspects, gave Tanzania compensating advantages. With the British refusal to proceed with the £7.5m loan for the Second Five Year Plan, Tanzania was thus left with the obligation to make major sterling payments to ex-members of the British colonial service and to begin to repay these very sizable capital loans without the continuation of the counterbalancing benefits which had been a feature of the initial agreement. Amir Jamal, as Minister of Finance, therefore proposed that Tanzania's obligation to these retired officers be limited to that portion of their service in Tanzania which followed 1 July 1961, the date at which the Public Service Commission assumed executive responsibilities for appointments to the civil service and therefore the date after which the British government no longer had any control over appointments to the Tanganyika civil service. Jamal proposed as well to make consequential adjustments to the commutation and compensation loans.*

It was hardly a propitious time for Tanzania to be seeking advantageous changes in any agreement already made with the British government. This was especially true in this case as a concession to Tanzania would almost immediately lead to demands from many other erstwhile colonies for similar concessions. Britain rejected the Tanzanian proposals. In June 1968 Jamal announced that Tanzania would unilaterally abrogate the earlier agreements and would accept obligations in regard to retired British civil servants only for their service following 1 July 1961. Britain in turn announced that no further technical assistance would be provided to Tanzania, no existing contracts of technical assistance personnel would be renewed at the end of their present tours of duty, and the £7.5m loan which had been frozen when diplomatic relations were broken would no longer be held in this form but would be returned to the Exchequer. The Tanzanian government went out of its way to reassure British expatriates in its service that its quarrel was not with them, and the British expatriates passed a resolution at a public meeting supporting the position of the

---

* The sums involved were substantial. When Tanzania unilaterally introduced them on 1 July 1968 the provision for pensions could be cut from Shs.21m to Shs.2.75m while the commutation and compensation loans which Tanzania continued to acknowledge were reduced from nearly £9m to £2.25m. For full details see Tanzania, *Speech by the Honourable the Minister for Finance Introducing the Estimates of Revenue and Expenditure, 1968–69 to the National Assembly, on 18th June, 1968* (Dar-es-Salaam, 1968), paras. 98–110.

Tanzanian government.* Nevertheless the estrangement between the two governments was clearly sharp and severe. Painfully and at real cost to itself, Tanzania had come to terms with the fact that no special ties and few common purposes united her to Britain.

Development strategy and foreign policy 1965

By 1965, the earlier underlying harmony between Tanzania's development strategy and her foreign policy had been shattered. Although in that year Tanzania was still drawing a large proportion of her capital development funds and her expatriate technical assistance personnel from Britain and from other Western sources, her relationships with Britain and Germany had so deteriorated that no further capital aid could be expected from these sources, while her relations with the United States had been marked by such recurring mistrust as to make any major dependency upon American aid most improbable. Her loss of innocence created an urgent need that Tanzania's foreign policy be redefined to take full account of the crises of the past two years and that her development strategy be brought into a realistic and close rapport with that policy.

Nyerere's changing perception of Tanzania's foreign relations

Under the impact of the dramatic events which had descended so furiously upon Tanzania's relations with each major Western power in turn, Nyerere had determined that Tanzania must stand by her principles and if necessary accept cuts in Western aid. He would not dilute his support for the liberation movements or accept a direct intervention by a major power in an African controversy. He refused to acquiesce in the use of development assistance by a major power as a bribe, or its withdrawal as a threat, to win African cooperation in a foreign policy matter of direct interest to that major power.

Nyerere's resolution in these matters was rooted in his nationalism. It was because he was profoundly an African nationalist that he would not ignore the oppression of his fellow Africans in southern Africa. It was because he was an African nationalist that he had been so offended by Western intervention to keep Tshombe in power in the Congo. It was because he was an African nationalist that he could not long tolerate the heavy-handed pressures from Germany over the question of an East German Consulate or from many Western powers over his acceptance of arms from China. These reactions were a product of a deeply felt nationalism rather than deductions from an intellectually perceived commitment

---

* The government of Tanzania was but several years ahead of a trend in its determination that Britain rather than Tanzania should carry those financial obligations that related to the colonial period. Two years later, in 1970, the British government in fact assumed this responsibility in regard to British officers who had served as colonial civil servants in any British territory overseas.

to socialism. Nyerere therefore moved from his Western-oriented posture of 1963 to a non-aligned position in 1967 rather than to a full incorporation within either of the two international socialist blocs.

A Marxian interpretation of Tanzania's relations with the Western powers was readily available in Tanzania by 1965. It was powerfully asserted by Premier Chou En-lai when he visited Tanzania in 1965.[50] It was repeated by the numerous visiting missions that came to Tanzania from China and North Korea. It was prominent in the party newspaper, *The Nationalist*,[51] and it provided the rhetoric for a few senior Ministers. It was popularized in two fortnightly papers that appeared in East Africa in 1964, *Pan Africa*, published in Kenya with a clear orientation to Soviet Marxism, and *Vigilance Africa*, published in Dar-es-Salaam with as clear an orientation towards Peking. Moreover, by 1966, Marxian analyses of Tanzanian affairs began to be developed with increasing skill by a group of academics at the University College, Dar-es-Salaam.[52]

The Marxian interpretation of Tanzania's foreign relations that was offered with varying rigour and consistency by these several different sources had these recurring themes:

1   The continuing poverty of the third world including Tanzania is fundamentally and primarily a result of its exploitation by the capitalist countries.

2   The central factor in world politics is the developing confrontation between the capitalist powers and the socialist peoples of the world or, as seen in the alternative Marxist view, between the industrialized and developed countries and the socialist peoples of Africa, Asia, and Latin America.

3   As political consciousness develops, the leaders of third world countries must either align themselves with the socialist powers and genuinely become socialists or face revolutionary action by their own people. The chances of the former are usually felt to be very slight, thus making the Tanzanian experience of particular theoretical interest.

4   Less regularly a feature of Marxist interpretations but still often prominent in radical analyses of African politics, is the Fanonist argument that a revolutionary struggle may be necessary to forge a socialist commitment strong enough to carry forward a full socialist transformation of the society. There is often expressed a regret that independence came to African states without violent struggle and that power was thus transferred to a party with little élan, less organizational strength and no socialist commitment. Arrighi and Saul, for example, argue not only that the liberation movements of southern Africa are the only hope for southern Africa (which seems increasingly to be true), but also that they are the main hope as well for the rest of Africa, for they alone are likely to be sufficiently committed and well organized to see through to victory a total socialist transformation of the continent.[53]

Nyerere did not support any of these four positions. He rejected (as do most Marxists) the fourth argument, above, that a violent overthrow of a colonial regime is preferable to a peaceful transfer of power. 'Our preference and that of every true African patriot has always been for peaceful methods of struggle.' The need to use force has been accepted by Nyerere but only when, as he said, 'the door of peaceful progress to freedom is slammed shut and bolted'.[54] This same point was repeated in another major speech two years later in which he directly rejected the suggestion that in the interests of a final socialist victory a violent struggle against colonialism is to be preferred:

> The right of a people to freedom from alien domination comes before socialism. . .There are some people who appear to believe that there is virtue in violence and that only if a freedom struggle is conducted by war and bloodshed can it lead to real liberation. I am not one of those people; the government of Tanzania does not accept this doctrine and nor do any of the other free African governments as far as I am aware. We know that war causes immense suffering, that it is usually the most innocent who are the chief victims and that the hatred and fear generated by war are dangerous to the very freedom and non-racialism it is our purpose to support.[55]

Nyerere also opposed the radical position that a socialist government must support and assist revolutionary African groups which are seeking to overthrow reactionary African governments. Nkrumah, for example, had been susceptible to this argument and had permitted the establishment in Ghana of Chinese-staffed training camps for revolutionaries from a number of neighbouring African states.[56] In contrast to this, Nyerere had been a strong supporter of the 1963 OAU resolution that African states must accept the integrity of the boundaries within Africa and must fully respect the sovereignty of all independent African states. Not all of his followers agreed with this and in 1963 Kambona had permitted, without Nyerere's knowledge, the arming and training of Malawi dissidents. However, Nyerere publicly rejected this, as soon as he learned of it. In a variety of ways and in many speeches he made the same basic point:

> We are not responsible for any other nation. We must accept the full implications of the existing separate sovereignty of all African states. . . We have to accept Africa as it is and not imagine that we have any more right to interfere with the internal affairs of others than they have to interfere in ours.[57]

Under the strain of the turbulent African politics of the years 1964–7, Nyerere modified this total ban in two important respects – 'Cooperation in the enslavement of our brothers in southern Africa must be excluded from our toleration' and 'Where a free African state is betraying the liberation of Africa...any African state has the right to protest.'[58] Even so, his purpose in these modifications was the extension of African freedom, not the promotion of socialism. He rejected any suggestion that African support for the liberation movements should be seen as part of a revolutionary pan-African socialist endeavour:

> What comes after freedom is an affair of the people of these territories... It is not for us to decide what sort of government they will have or what sort of system they will adopt. Tanzania must support the struggle for freedom in these areas regardless of the political philosophy of those who are conducting the struggle...Our own commitment to socialism in Tanzania is irrelevant to the right of the people of Mozambique (and the other areas) to choose their own government and their own political system...The support which is given to the freedom struggles by Tanzania...is neither a disguised form of new imperialism nor an evangelical mission for socialism...[59]

Thus in regard to both the liberation movements and the independent African states, Nyerere was firmly committed to a full acceptance of their right to shape their political and economic systems without interference or pressure from Tanzania or from any other African state.

A third fundamental difference between Nyerere's approach to international politics and that of Marxian commentators is that Nyerere did not seek to conclude from the conflicts which Tanzania had had with Britain, Germany and the United States that there was a fundamental conflict of interest between Tanzania and the Western countries.

> Tanzania has, over recent years, had so many quarrels with big powers which are part of the western bloc that it is useful for us to stress once again that we have no desire to be and no intention of being 'anti-West' in our foreign policies. We shall deal with each problem as it occurs and on its own merits. We shall neither move from particular quarrels with individual countries to a generalized hostility to members of a particular group nor to automatic support for those who happen to be for their own reasons quarrelling with the same nation.[60]

His most recurrent theme was that Tanzania wished to be friends with the nations of each of the major power blocs but that it was determined to remain separate from each bloc. He defined the issue succinctly in 1966. 'The choice before us really amounts to offering to all countries genuine friendship based on equality or becoming "reliable allies to certain large power groups and being more hostile to others".'[61] His own choice was never in doubt. 'We shall not allow any of our friendships to be exclusive; we shall not allow anyone to choose any of our friends or enemies for us.'

There were in this refusal to ally Tanzania with a socialist bloc a

number of components: a respect still for much in the Western democratic tradition, a suspicion of the motives of both blocs and a desire
stemming from his nationalism that Africa should be left alone to make
her way independently. These components can be illustrated by the
following quotations:

> Tanzania then finds herself faced with a divided world in which one
> side combines an economy based almost exclusively on public
> ownership of the means of production and a political system that
> severely curtails individual freedom and the other side combines a
> predominantly privately owned economic system with greater individual
> freedom and a degree of economic inequality which would be
> unacceptable to us. Tanzania's objectives, therefore, mean that she
> wants to adapt to her own needs some of the institutions from each side.
> Clearly she can best do this by having friendly relations with each
> side. . .[62]

> Our country is small. We have our difficulties trying to run our
> country. . .We need time. If people do not want to help us they should
> at least allow us time and we shall help ourselves.
>   We say that we are making friends with the Chinese and that
> friendship is quite manifest in Dar-es-Salaam. We are friends with the
> Americans. This friendship is clearly visible. . .The Chinese ought not
> to ask us why we make friends with the Americans. The U.S.A. ought
> not to ask us why we are making friends with the Chinese. Their
> quarrel is between themselves. It does not concern us. . .We are only
> asking the big nations to leave us alone so that we can rule
> ourselves.[63]

Nyerere thus rejected the Marxist overview of international politics.
Instead he advocated with skill and vigour what can best be described as
a policy of principled non-alignment. He wanted a non-aligned Tanzania
in order that Tanzania could find and express its own identity, pursue its
own development, speak for its own interests and judge according to its
own perception the requirements of international peace and justice.

Non-alignment and foreign aid: the search for new friends 1964–7

There are some commentators on Tanzanian affairs, mainly Western
Marxists, who would prefer to see Tanzania deny itself Western technical
and capital assistance and seek external assistance only from the socialist
countries. Many Tanzanians are rightly suspicious of the links which
Western aid reinforces between Tanzania and the major Western powers.
They know this capital assistance is likely to introduce inappropriate technologies, to stimulate consumer tastes that far exceed what is legitimate in

a country as poor as Tanzania and, generally, to reinforce a dependency which Tanzania is seeking to limit.

Although Tanzanian authorities have been increasingly sensitive to these adverse consequences of aid projects, they have not taken the position that Western aid was never to be accepted. When German and British capital assistance as well as technical assistance from German governmental agencies had been halted, Tanzania did not seek to generalize the controversies into a confrontation with Western capitalism. Instead special care was taken to try to assure that American and World Bank projects went forward smoothly and effectively. Moreover, in seeking sources of aid alternative to Britain and Germany, Tanzania turned first to a number of Western 'middle' powers with whom she already had cordial if underdeveloped links. These countries possessed the skills and the wealth which made it feasible for them to assist Tanzania. They were without the international or the African ambitions which might generate tensions between them and Tanzania. In 1964 after the army mutiny when Tanzania needed to train a new army almost *de novo*, in 1965 when Germany withdrew its air training program and in December 1965 when the British refused to proceed with the £7.5m loan that had already been negotiated, the Tanzanian government in each case sought emergency assistance from these middle powers. First Sweden and then Canada were asked to train the military. Canada accepted that undertaking and with the later withdrawal of the German air training program undertook as well to train the air wing to the Tanzania People's Defence Force. The Netherlands agreed to train the small naval force required for the coastal patrol which had been a West German undertaking. In December 1965, Sweden, Canada, the Netherlands and Denmark were all asked to help with the £2m worth of projects which had been initiated in anticipation of the British loan. Although this effort to secure emergency assistance from these powers was not successful, nevertheless by 1968 Tanzania was receiving technical and capital assistance from a much wider range of sources than had been true in 1964. In 1967 there were over twenty-five different national and international aid agencies with programs in Tanzania.

Canada, Sweden and the U.N. agencies illustrate this widening involvement. Canadian assistance developed rapidly during the period 1961–8 though it never reached a substantial figure. Its total cost to Canada in 1961–2 was a mere $24,000. In 1967–8 the total cost of the Canadian non-military aid program to Tanzania was $3.5m.[64]

In addition there was an important Canadian military mission which after 1965 was involved in the training of the Tanzanian People's Defence Force (TPDF) and of its air wing. This program was totally financed by the Canadian government and cost some $15m. Young Tanzanian officer cadets were trained in Canada in quite significant numbers. There were, for example, thirty-four members of the TPDF in Canada in 1966 as well as twenty Tanzanian air crew and ninety technicians. For five years a strong team of Canadian officers and senior non-commissioned officers, numbering at its peak nearly ninety men, played a most important role in the re-creation of an effective Tanzanian military force after the 1964 mutiny.[65]

Sweden was another middle power which responded positively to Tanzania's efforts to widen the sources of its technical assistance personnel. The major Swedish projects included Swedish participation in the Kibaha project, a combined secondary school, farmers' training centre and medical centre which was built, staffed and financed by the four Nordic countries, the Musoma Training Centre for child care, and a substantial rural water development program which began in late 1965 and by June 1967 entailed loan agreements totalling $7.4m. Swedish technical assistance personnel were involved on all of these projects. As well, in 1966 Sweden agreed to recruit and to finance up to fifty experts to occupy operational, managerial or executive posts in the Tanzanian government.[66]

In addition to such bilateral aid programs as these, Tanzania received technical assistance and capital support from many international agencies. Three International Development Association loans had been signed by 1971 to a total value of $23.6m. There were technical personnel from a number of U.N. agencies. This assistance, though very frequently involving lengthy delays and a greater than average gamble on Tanzania's part that the expert would in fact arrive and would have the competencies requested, nevertheless provided on the average over fifty experts a year during the period of the First Five Year Plan. In 1964 the three agencies most involved in Tanzania sent twenty-seven, eleven and thirteen experts respectively to Tanzania.[67]

Beginning in late 1963 Tanzania began to take more seriously the possibility of closer relations with the Soviet Union, the Communist countries of Eastern Europe and China. Even before the deterioration of her relations with the major Western powers, Tanzania had wanted to diversify her sources of technical and capital assistance. This rather general and not too pressing concern to demonstrate that Tanzania was not simply a dependent state acquired real urgency after the union with Zanzibar in April 1964. If Tanzania was not actively to gain the disfavour of both the Soviet Union and China she needed to dispel the view that the union had been effected in order to contain the developing Communist influence on Zanzibar. It was, therefore, a necessary political consequence of the union that Tanzania should make a special effort to develop cordial and closer relationships with the Communist countries.

This was not an uncongenial challenge. The Communist states were the major source of arms and of training for the various liberation movements whom Tanzania supported. This provided a further important reason, separate from a general attachment to the rhetoric of non-alignment and from the necessities resulting from the union, for Tanzania to seek to develop increased contact with the Communist countries.

In August 1964 the Second Vice-President, Rashidi Kawawa, led a delegation to Prague, Warsaw and Moscow. The delegation included two influential mainland Ministers, Kasambala and Swai, and, as well, Hanga, the Zanzibar Minister who was reputed to have the closest links with Moscow. The delegation appealed to the Soviet Union for assistance on ideological grounds, arguing, as Kawawa did in his speech on arrival, that 'it is important that changes be brought about or else neo-colonialism would stay. The British and the Americans are not ready to help in this respect because they are not prepared to destroy neo-colonialism.'[68] Their expectations, or at least their ambitions, were enormously high. They invited the Soviet Union to interest itself in the building of a railway to Zambia, in the exploitation of the iron and coal resources of southern Tanzania, in the establishment of a series of major state farms and in the building of several hydro-electric power plants. They also asked that the military assistance which the Soviet Union was giving to the Zanzibari army should be extended as well to include the Tanzanian army.

The Soviet authorities showed little interest in taking any advantage of this invitation to involve themselves in a major way in Tanzanian affairs. They did not follow up the suggestion of military assistance. They rejected out of hand any involvement in any major long-term projects such as the railway, the state farms or the iron and coal industry. They bluntly told the Tanzanians to concentrate instead upon light industries that would yield quick returns. Hanga himself commented in reply that 'it was disheartening that the Soviet Union, a socialist country, should be saying things that would normally be expected of a capitalist country' and he expressed disappointment over 'this doubt of the viability of some of the projects in the proposals'. The Soviet reply was to the point: 'Economic facts cannot be ignored. Every machine to this united republic is one less for the U.S.S.R.'[69]

The Soviet authorities then studied the Five Year Development Plan and identified within it eleven projects in which they were willing to take an interest. These were carefully chosen and were all worthwhile projects. They included some feasibility studies of major but still ill-defined projects such as the development of the iron and coal complex in southern Tanzania and the Kiwira River hydro-electric plant. They also included Soviet involvement in the development of a marine and fresh water fisheries industry, in the building of refrigeration plants in Tabora and Dodoma and in the construction and staffing of a technical college. In December 1964 a Soviet mission came to Dar-es-Salaam to discuss the proposals and to negotiate the terms of a possible Soviet loan in regard to them.

There is every evidence that the Tanzanian authorities tried hard to take advantage of this Soviet interest. However as they studied the details of the Soviet proposals it became clear to them that there would often be little advantage to Tanzania in going ahead with these projects along the lines suggested by the Soviet officials. The Soviet Union proposed a loan to Tanzania which would be repayable over twelve years and carry an annual interest charge of 2.5 per cent. The loan would be totally tied to the purchase of Soviet equipment for the approved projects and to the payment of Soviet personnel. There was no provision for a Soviet contribution to the local costs of any of these projects. All Soviet personnel involved in these projects would need to be fully paid by the Tanzanian government. The Soviet Union agreed to examine the possibility of increasing its imports from Tanzania so that Tanzania would have Soviet funds with which to repay the loan. However on that important issue it was unwilling to go beyond such an expression of goodwill. To cover the possibility that Tanzania might in fact not acquire through trade the Soviet funds necessary for the loan repayments, the Soviet Union required that Tanzania should set up a special convertible account of £1m from which the balance of the repayments could be made to the extent that Tanzania had not acquired a favourable balance of trade with the Soviet Union.

These were very stiff terms. Not only was the aid component within them slight but, as well, there were major risks that the assistance which would be provided would in fact not fit Tanzanian needs. The technical college for example would be to specifications set by Soviet experts rather than by the Tanzanian Ministry of Education. The Tanzanians sought to improve the terms of the proposed loans but made very little headway. Gradually, the negotiations slowed down until finally there was no activity at all. Nyerere, who remained anxious that there should be some Soviet involvement, then sent Amir Jamal to Moscow in May 1966 to do what he could to reactivate the negotiations. In May 1966 Jamal signed a loan agreement for 18m rubles (approximately Shs.140m). Although Jamal had won some minor improvements for Tanzania, the agreement was basically as it had been proposed by the Soviet Union in 1964. This loan agreement of 1966 had then to be supplemented by separate agreements in regard to each project. Many of the reasons for Tanzanian caution recurred in the discussions which followed. Tanzania, despite a political disposition to find ways to use Soviet assistance, found it very hard to do so. Three years later in June 1969 Tanzania had actually received loan funds to a total of Shs.1,974,127, a tiny fraction of the loan which had been approved in principle in 1966.[70]

Tanzania had very similar experiences with the East European countries. Despite Technical Co-operation and Educational Assistance Agreements with Poland, Czechoslovakia and Yugoslavia which included specific reference to a variety of projects, Tanzania did not in fact conclude any separate project agreements at all with either Poland or with Czecho-slovakia. In the case of Yugoslavia, there were several project agreements but the total funds received by June 1969 were Shs.568,963, again but a small fraction of the amounts which were theoretically possible under the earlier agreements.

Tanzania did not follow up these agreements. The negotiating teams from these countries appeared to the Tanzanians primarily as salesmen for the capital goods produced in their country. Although the East Europeans were ready to provide (at Tanzanian expense) experts who would prepare feasibility studies of the various capital projects in which they were interested, Tanzania hesitated to rely upon such studies, as they would be done by individuals from the very agencies which were anxious to pro-vide the capital goods which those projects would require. Moreover the terms offered were hardly such as to excite the Tanzanians. Yugoslavia, for example, offered loans with a three- to eight-year repayment period carry-ing interest charges at three per cent. The aid component in such a loan was sufficiently small that it might very well not offset the loss to Tan-zania which might be involved in the purchase of Yugoslavian capital goods without competitive tenders and without independent feasibility studies. There was also very little incentive to Tanzania to recruit technical assistance personnel from these countries. In the case of Polish and Czecho-slovakian personnel, Tanzania had to pay their total cost. The Polish arrangements involved the payment by Tanzania of the local salary for the position plus a twenty-five per cent gratuity, transportation and travel costs, free housing and free medical and dental services. The Czecho-slovakian arrangements involved the payment of monthly salaries and related expenses which the Czech negotiators estimated would cost an average of £300 a month, plus travel and housing.[71]

It is therefore no wonder that few East Europeans were recruited by Tanzania under these several technical assistance agreements. The Tan-zanian government had come to accept by 1968 that neither the Soviet Union nor Eastern Europe was a likely source of generous and imaginative international development assistance. The innocence which Tanzania was losing in these years was not only an innocence in regard to the policies of Great Britain and other Western governments. Many Tanzanians lost as well their naive expectations about the role which the Soviet Union would be willing to play in a socialist Tanzania.

Tanzania's experience with the People's Republic of China was markedly different from her experience with the Soviet Union and Eastern Europe. Nyerere's openness to China predated the union with Zanzibar. He had been, by basic and fundamental instinct, hostile to the efforts of the Western countries to keep China outside the international community. He had also accepted China as an important source of support for the libera-tion movements. Furthermore the union with Zanzibar provided Nyerere with the immediate necessity for a Tanzanian initiative relating to China to establish categorically his basic goodwill. In June 1964 Kawawa led a delegation to Peking which included Babu, the Zanzibari Minister who was closest to the Chinese. While there, Kawawa signed an agreement on Tanzania's behalf for a £10m loan. Superficially this loan was similar to the East European and Russian loan agreements of the same year. In each case, before any funds could actually be drawn they had to negotiate separate agreements relating to the specific projects which were to receive the assistance. However the differences between the Chinese loan and the loans offered by other Communist countries were far more important than this point of similarity. The Chinese loan could not be interpreted, as the Soviet, Czech and Polish credits certainly could be, as intended primarily to promote the export of capital goods. The Chinese loans were without interest charges and repayment was to be by ten annual payments beginning July 1975. Moreover China's own capital needs were such that any diversion to Tanzania involved a direct Chinese sacrifice. Whatever were her underlying policy objectives, there was no doubt that unlike the other Communist countries, China was ready to make a genuine sacrifice of resources to help Tanzania. As if to underline this fact, China also announced at this time a £1m grant, half in convertible currency and half in commodity credits, for development projects which would be jointly selected by the two governments. Finally, unlike the Soviet Union, China agreed to supply a quantity of arms for the Tanzanian army and to send instructors with the initial arms shipment. These arrived within several months of this undertaking.

The Chinese aid had many attractive features. The loan carried no interest charges. It could be used for local costs within the supported project, an arrangement which few aid agencies permitted to the full extent of the Chinese. Moreover, the Chinese technical assistance personnel who worked on the Chinese projects were vastly less costly to Tanzania than Western, Soviet or indeed even Tanzanian personnel would be. The members of the survey team, for example, which studied the Kidunda Dam received a monthly allowance which ranged between Shs.500 for skilled workers to Shs.580 for the engineer and the doctor on the team, with the leader of the team and his deputy each receiving Shs.615.

There were, nevertheless, real obstacles to an effective use of this Chinese offer of assistance. The Chinese wished to play a major role in selecting the projects which would be assisted. They did not hesitate to go outside of the Five Year Plan in their search for projects which they felt would be appropriate. They preferred to undertake a project entirely under their own management and to their own specifications, turning it over to the Tanzanian government only after it was entirely completed. The Tanzanians thus had very little control over the planning of a project or over the selection of the capital goods which would go into that project. Even the project's cost would only be settled after the project had been completed. Vastly more trust was thus required of Tanzania in going ahead with the Chinese project than was needed when accepting assistance from most Western bilateral or international aid agencies.

There was one further important difficulty. Although the Chinese agreed that their loans could provide funds to meet the local costs of their projects, this was to be done by their providing to Tanzania Chinese commodities which when sold would provide the funds to pay these local costs. The risks and dangers here are obvious. Tanzania imported very little from China in 1964. Her total Chinese imports in that year hardly exceeded $0.8m.[72] Tanzanian importers had very little idea what Chinese commodities could readily be marketed in Tanzania. To increase these imports in order to secure funds to meet local costs might involve importing goods which would be directly competitive with Tanzanian products or goods which might meet strong consumer resistance and remain largely unsold. There was thus a real risk than Tanzania might use up loan funds to acquire large stocks of unsaleable commodities.

Partly for these reasons, but more likely as well because the cultural revolution in China diverted Chinese energies and interests, the Chinese credit was initially slowly used. A high-power radio transmission station to broadcast southward was quickly agreed upon but other projects took shape more slowly. This changed by early 1966. A greater interest on the Chinese side in settling upon the projects to be supported was matched on the Tanzanian side by a much more purposeful effort. The various difficulties and problems involved in the use of the Chinese aid became problems which required solution rather than excuses for inaction.

Nyerere was determined that Tanzania should not prejudge Chinese aid adversely. He wanted Tanzania to fall into line with Chinese aid techniques just as, by and large, Tanzania accepts Western aid techniques when dealing with Western aid agencies. Nyerere had visited China in 1965. He had become deeply aware of two features of Chinese society, its frugal capacity for hard work and its egalitarian quality. He was not bothered by the cultural revolution. Indeed he appreciated that its underlying purpose was to check an emerging political and bureaucratic elitism.

> I must say that if you found it necessary to begin a cultural revolution, in order to make sure that the new generation would carry forward the banner of your revolution, then certainly we need one. We have seen in Tanzania how easy it is to pay lip service to the importance of socialism and the people, while in fact we behave like capitalists and petty dictators.[73]

By 1966 there was no dragging of feet by Tanzanian civil servants in regard to the Chinese aid. While perhaps not enamoured of the egalitarian aspect of the Chinese example, they were nevertheless very much in a frame of mind to make the Chinese aid 'work'. The crises with West Germany and with Britain had left them angry and determined to lessen their dependency upon these Western powers. The Chinese loan offered one way of offsetting this Western dependency. They therefore found ways rapidly to increase Chinese imports. These had risen from 0.6 per cent of Tanzanian imports in 1964 to 5.6 per cent in 1968. By 1966–7 the use of the £10m loan and the first £1m grant had been determined and the projects were being swiftly initiated. The major projects were a textile mill in Dar-es-Salaam, the Ruvu state farm, the Kidunda Dam, the radio transmission station, a farm implements factory in Dar-es-Salaam, a police training school in Moshi and an extensive village water supply project in southern Tanzania.

Even as these projects were being planned, the Chinese gave a further dramatic demonstration of their willingness and their capacity to assist Tanzania. In February 1965 China offered to consider building a rail line from Dar-es-Salaam to Lusaka. This was a project close to Kaunda's heart as it would enormously lessen Zambia's dependence upon Rhodesia. He had announced two years earlier that this railway was a political necessity for Zambia. In October 1964 the Zambian and Tanzanian governments had asked the World Bank, the African Development Bank and the governments of Britain, the United States, Japan and Russia to interest themselves in it. The World Bank had an assessment prepared of its prospects and concluded that it would not be economically viable.[74] A similar view was expressed in a report of a U.N. Economic Mission, headed by Dudley Seers[75] and also in a report of the U.S. Agency for International Development.

Despite the timeliness of the Chinese offer, Kaunda was very hesitant to accept it. He would have much preferred a Western-built and Western-financed line. Even as Nyerere proceeded with preliminary negotiations with the Chinese, Kaunda held back. A Chinese survey team in August 1965, for example, was not allowed into Zambia. For a while, Kaunda talked of the possibility of each country arranging for its section of the line independent of the other. Kaunda, with Nyerere's concurrence, invited an Anglo-Canadian team to do a feasibility study of the proposed line. Their report, published in 1966, was based upon a new assumption not made in the previous reports, that the railway would be used to carry almost all of Zambia's copper exports and most of her foreign trade. This report concluded that the economic prospects for the railroad were very good.[76] No offers of assistance with the railroad were forthcoming from Western sources. Meanwhile the unilateral Declaration of Independence by the Rhodesian white regime in November 1965 and the British failure adequately to respond to that seizure of power shifted opinion within the Zambian government towards accepting the Chinese offer. Early in 1967 Kaunda visited Peking, and in September 1967 a loan agreement relating to the railway was signed by representatives of the three governments.

The Chinese based their offer to a significant extent upon the Anglo-Canadian report. Many of its technical and engineering features are identical. It also used that report's estimates of cost as the basis of its own. The project itself was massive. It involved a single-line railroad, 1,858 km in length. Its construction was seen to require 89 million cubic metres of earth work and rock excavations and the building of 300 bridges and 19 tunnels. Its initial operation would require 102 diesel locomotives and 2,100 wagons.

The contract for the railroad was for £175m, of which £167m was a loan. The costs were to be shared by the two governments. The local costs, estimated at fifty-two per cent of the total, were to be met from the proceeds of the sale in Tanzania and Zambia of Chinese goods. These sums would form part of the £167m loan. The loan was interest-free with repayment to be in gold or in an acceptable third country currency. Repayment was to begin in 1981 and be completed twenty years later.[77]

In addition to this massive offer of assistance the Chinese acted swiftly in January 1966 to help Tanzania meet a more specific and immediate need. When Tanzania broke diplomatic relations with Britain in December 1965 Britain retaliated (as mentioned above) by freezing a £7.5m loan. Tanzania faced an immediate and specific crisis. All the details of this loan had already been negotiated with Britain and, with British approval, projects to the value of some £2m had already been initiated by Tanzania in anticipation of this loan. Tanzania thus found itself suddenly with some £2m worth of projects which had been initiated but for which it did not in fact have the necessary finance. Tanzania first sought a Western country which might be willing to take over these loan projects. None was interested. In June 1966 Paul Bomani, Minister of Finance, went to Peking and with comparative ease secured a £2m loan in convertible currency. China had thus helped Tanzania to extricate itself from a difficulty which had resulted from the break in diplomatic relations with Britain. At the same time, the Chinese offered to build, as a gift, several much-needed army barracks at a further estimated cost of £1.1m.

The Chinese contribution to Tanzania's development revenues was still surpassed in 1968–9 by the funds coming from the United States A.I.D. and from the International Development Association. However, the agreement to build the Tazara railway meant that China would very shortly become by far the largest single source of capital assistance to Tanzania. China also became at this time the main supplier of arms and equipment to the Tanzanian military. China had accepted responsibility for whatever additional specialized training might still be needed by the Tanzania People's Defence Force when the Canadian military and air training mission ended. Tanzania had thus developed a close and very substantial relationship with China which, by 1969, offset and more than offset the loss of British and German assistance.

These facts, along with Tanzanian–Chinese cooperation in assisting the liberation movements might well suggest that Tanzania was moving from a non-aligned position into a general alliance with China which, because of their comparative size, was bound to involve a significant dependence by Tanzania upon China. Certainly it is true that by 1968 Nyerere accepted that Tanzania had become an ally of the Communist powers in regard to the liberation of southern Africa. On that issue the policies of the Western powers had left Tanzania with no other option to this alliance save a humiliating acceptance of the permanence of racial oppression in southern Africa. However, Nyerere argued that this alliance was specific to this interest and had not compromised Tanzania's independence in regard to other foreign policy issues.[78]

A parallel point could also be made about Chinese capital and technical assistance. It was needed, it involved no unacceptable strings, it was not accompanied by any overbearing demands for Tanzanian backing for Chinese foreign policy objectives which Tanzania was unhappy to support. This developing close relationship with China would have been a contradiction of a policy of total disengagement from the major powers. However as each component of that relationship reflected specific Tanzanian interests it can fairly be seen as an expression of a positive non-aligned policy rather than a contradiction of it.

The extent and significance of external assistance for development 1965–9

The government of Tanzania became increasingly competent itself in raising local revenues for development purposes. In 1961/2 almost all of the capital budget came from external sources (Shs.143m out of total capital revenues of Shs.147m). In contrast to that dependence, in the four-year period 1964/5–1967/8 the public sector capital expenditures totalled Shs.1,082m of which only 34.5 per cent was from external sources. By the financial year 1968/9 the total development revenue for the year was Shs.460m, of which Shs.337m were from local sources.[79] Thus by 1968 the government of Tanzania was much more independent of external sources for its development revenues than it had been in 1962. This was clearly a desirable feature in the development strategy of a country which followed a non-aligned foreign policy.

However, as is clear from the preceding section, this did not at all mean that Tanzania decided to forgo foreign assistance or to seek it only from members of a socialist bloc. Table 9 compares the total capital development assistance by source for the period 1961/2–1964/5 with the annual amounts received for the years 1965/6–1968/9. These figures do not represent the total value of capital assistance received. They omit all

Table 8. *Tanzanian government – capital budget sources of funds* (*in millions of shillings*)

	1961/2	1962/3	1963/4	1964/5	1965/6	1966/7	1967/8	1968/9
External (loans and grants)	143.0	104.3	51.5	78.5	83.5	127.3	84.0	122.8
Internal (borrowing contribution for recurrent revenues, etc.)	3.8	9.1	93.8	125.3	146.4	167.1	260.1	337.7
Total	146.8	113.4	145.3	203.8	229.9	294.4	344.1	460.5

SOURCES: Tanzania, *Budget Survey 1965–66*, table 35; *Background to the Budget 1967–68*, table 67; *Economic Survey and Second Annual Plan 1970–71*, table 68.

military equipment, all capital loans to public corporations and all capital assistance which was made available directly to a project rather than being handled by the Tanzanian Treasury. Nevertheless, the table does demonstrate the very significant changes which had occurred in the pattern of capital assistance received by Tanzania. By 1968 Germany and Britain were no longer providing significant capital assistance. There was no overwhelming dependency on any one source. Instead by that date the four most important sources were the U.S.A., Sweden, the I.D.A. and China. It is a list which seems appropriate to a country seeking to be non-aligned in international politics.

It is not at all an easy matter even approximately to gain a clear impression of the actual worth to Tanzania of these external capital funds. The portion of these funds which were grants rather than loans declined significantly over the seven-year period 1961/2–1967/8, so that by 1967/8 under three per cent of the external capital was grant money (see table 10). The cost to Tanzania of the capital funds provided by loans varied enormously from one foreign loan to another. In most cases the loan charges were significantly less than the charges which Tanzania might have had to pay for such a loan were it extended on a strictly commercial basis and the repayment period was longer. The aid component in these cases was therefore significant. The aid component was likely to be highest of course in the case of those loans which carried no interest charges at all and for which there was an extended repayment period. Only if the loan had to be used to purchase equipment at prices that were not competitive would this not be the case. The various Chinese loans were all free of interest charges. The smaller Danish and Canadian loans were also free of interest charges. The aid component was high also

Table 9. *Tanzania treasury: external sources of development funds 1965–9 (in thousands of shillings)*

	1961/2–1964/5 total	1965/6	1966/7	1967/8	1968/9	1965/6–1968/9 total[a]
Governments						
United Kingdom	201,920	17,517	8,201	8,314		34,032
U.S.A.	32,640	29,956	17,395	24,841	55,278	127,479
Federal Republic of Germany	26,160	4,318	6,092	258	642	11,310
Israel	9,160	6,349	194			6,543
Sweden		1,593	3,361	7,943	20,803	33,691
Netherlands				753	1,949	2,702
China	5,980	19,091	51,279	3,796	1,725	75,891
Canada			665	2,283	10,458	13,406
Denmark					3,320	3,320
U.S.S.R.			46	494	a	530
Zambia			3,969	5,163		9,132
Private trusts and charities						
British	1,960	428	742	956	149	2,275
American	4,120	487	1,666	13	a	2,166
Multilateral						
IDA	16,240	18,699	30,213	30,091	42,453	121,456
UNESCO		4,020	500			4,520
Nordic Council	260					
Unidentified	180	210	1,400	1,947	11,429	14,986
Total	298,620	102,688	128,733	86,852	148,105	444,358

[a] Receipts from a number of sources including the U.S.S.R. and the American foundations were recorded differently in the 1968–9 appropriation accounts and so were no longer separately identifiable.
SOURCE: Calculated from the statements of development revenues and of unfunded debt for the year (revenue head 137) in Tanzania, *Appropriation Accounts of Tanzania for the Year 1965–6, . . .1966–7, . . .1967–8 and . . .1968–9*. These record funds received. The 1961/2–1964/5 figures are from Table 7 above, p. 133.

in the loans from the United States Agency for International Development, for its loans carried nominal interest charges, usually three-quarters of one per cent per year, and were to be repaid, usually, in sixty-one semi-annual installments. The International Development Association and the Swedish aid agency (S.I.D.A.) have also charged nominal interest rates. In contrast, some loans, which fortunately formed but a small proportion of

Table 10. *Tanzania government external capital funds: loans and grants*
(*in thousands of shillings*)

	1961/2	1962/3	1963/4	1964/5	1965/6	1966/7	1967/8
External loans	79,400	5,800	27,860	59,060	75,740	119,920	81,470
External grants	63,640	99,580	23,620	19,480	7,760	7,350	2,450

SOURCES: Tanzania, *Budget Survey 1965–66*, table 34; *Background to the Budget 1967–68*, table 67; and *Annual Economic Survey 1968* (*A Background to the 1969–70 Budget*) (Dar-es-Salaam, 1969), table 66.

the external funds for development, were little more than state-negotiated supplier credits for which Tanzania had to pay high interest charges. The Israeli loan to pay for the Israeli-built Kilimanjaro Hotel, for example, carried interest charges of six per cent while the interest charges on the loan to finance the purchase of the equipment for this hotel were set at one and one-half per cent higher than the going U.K. bank rate. The United Kingdom Commonwealth Assistance Loan for the Nyumba Ya Mungu Dam involved an interest rate of one-quarter of one per cent higher than the U.K. Treasury rate. Soviet and East European interest rates fell between these two limits, being set at from two and one-half to three per cent in most cases.

The ability of the Tanzanian government to use the borrowed funds to maximum advantage was limited by two features which recurred in most of the bilateral loan agreements. Most loans were tied in substantial part to the purchase of equipment, building materials, machinery and other commodities from the country which provided the loan.[80] Sweden and in some instances the Federal Republic of Germany extended loans to Tanzania which were fully 'untied', but they were the exception.

Foreign loans, moreover, were tied in a second important fashion. The typical bilateral loan has always been for specific purposes which were determined only after elaborate negotiation between the Tanzanian authorities and the officers of the aid agency concerned. As a result Tanzania has often had to accept loans for projects that were not of the highest priority but which Tanzania accepted because it was clear that these loan funds could not be obtained for other projects. For example, neither the Nordic Centre at Kibaha nor the Chinese-financed Friendship Textile Mill were in the Five Year Plan. Moreover their location near Dar-es-Salaam was in conflict with an established national policy to avoid such a concentration.

Nevertheless whatever discount one wishes to place upon the face value of the foreign capital assistance to Tanzania, it remains true that foreign capital assistance to the government of Tanzania throughout the period under review was substantial. The Tanzania government itself was never in doubt that it was of real value. Nyerere did not hold the radical position that Tanzania should not accept Western capital assistance. Where the integrity of his foreign policy demanded it, as in the crises with Britain and with Germany, he was ready to sacrifice their aid. But these sacrifices were specific to the individual dispute. There was no blanket rejection of Western aid. Rather, as we have seen, with each new crisis with a Western country, more care than ever was taken to minimize its wider consequences and to involve other Western states in Tanzania's developmental effort.

Foreign policy and development strategy 1967

In 1963 Tanzania's foreign policy and her development strategy had each assumed a close and special relationship with Britain. That harmony between foreign policy and development strategy was undermined in 1964 and 1965 when Tanzania first moved towards a non-aligned foreign policy, while continuing to assume a very heavy participation in her development by British and other Western agencies. By the beginning of 1967 the harmony between foreign policy and development strategy had been very largely restored. By that year, Britain was negotiating no new capital assistance to Tanzania. Instead capital funds for development were coming to Tanzania from a wide range of nations and locally raised capital had become a very significant component of the development revenues available to the government. These developments were appropriate to a non-alignment foreign policy. Indeed they were perhaps a prerequisite to it.*

Catherine Hoskyns, responding to the overall coherence of Tanzania's foreign relations, writes that 'what really distinguishes the Tanzanian experience from that of Guinea, Ghana and the Ivory Coast is the continued attempt to evolve a locally derived overall strategy for development and to see foreign relations primarily from the perspective of what helps or hinders the furtherance of this policy'.[81] This judgment exaggerates the influence of development considerations upon the formation of foreign policy during these years. Indeed influence may largely have flown in the

---

* One incongruity did continue through the whole of the period covered by this study. British expatriates continued to be an important element within the senior civil service. Tanzania still recruited expatriate civil servants in large numbers from Britain. But as this was almost the sole assistance being received from Britain, there being no new capital assistance since December 1965, this recruitment did not constitute a major dependency. This did not cease until June 1968. It came to an end then because Britain decided to stop all new technical assistance to Tanzania as a reaction to the crisis that came to a head in that month over the payment of pensions and compensation to British officers for their period of service in colonial Tanganyika. This issue is discussed above, pp. 150–1.

opposite direction. The controversies with Britain and Germany were a major impetus to the search for new sources of capital assistance. At a later stage, the commitment to non-alignment meant that a special importance was attached to increasing middle-power involvement in Tanzanian development and to maintaining U.S. involvement. Indeed it is truer to say that Tanzania sought Western and middle-power assistance because Tanzania was non-aligned than to say that she took a non-aligned position because of the importance of socialist and non-socialist aid to her development.

There is a further link between Tanzania's foreign relations and Tanzania's development strategy. The leaders of a country which accepts a dependent relationship with either a major capitalist state or a group of such states are unlikely to engage in independent thinking about their social, economic and political objectives. Instead the policies of a dependent state are likely to be imitative of those of the major power which is its international protector. The converse of this also tends to be true. A state which decides to avoid a close and general alliance with any major power thereby encourages and reinforces any predisposition within its leadership to radical and independent economic, social and political experimentation.

This, it will be argued, is what happened in Tanzania. During these same years in which Nyerere became convinced that Tanzania must follow a foreign policy of positive non-alignment, he also came to feel that there needed to be a major and radical redefinition of Tanzania's development objectives and of her strategy to pursue these objectives. These two developments in Nyerere's thinking were entirely compatible one with the other. The tendency towards non-alignment and the tendency towards socialism were mutually reinforcing. The developments in Tanzania's foreign relations were thus a contributing factor to the Arusha Declaration just as that recommitment to the achievement of a democratic and socialist society contributed to the determination to hold to a foreign policy of positive non-alignment.

7: The prelude to a socialist strategy 1963–7

Introduction: strategies and politics 1963–7

The government which President Nyerere returned to lead on 9 December 1962 was a sobered regime. The previous year had seen nationalist initiatives which were politically essential but which worried those Ministers who were sensitive to the difficulties which the government faced in maintaining an efficient public service. By the end of 1962, enough had been done by the government to lessen the pressures upon it to demonstrate its nationalist commitment. Their integrity as nationalists thus freshly reestablished, many Ministers were anxious now to concentrate upon the immediate tasks of managing successfully the business of government.

The policies of the government over the next four years are not easily categorized. They were not informed by an articulated ideology, as was to be the case from 1967 onwards. Neither, however, was the government inhibited as it had earlier been by a relentless assessment of its administrative limitations. Instead, from 1963 to 1967 there was a pragmatic willingness to pursue whatever policies appeared likely to promote development. The government made little systematic effort to relate these policies to any overall conception of long-term social, economic and political objectives.

The first statement of TANU's aims and objectives appeared in the 1954 TANU Constitution. It had no socialist content at all. Instead it accepted the capitalist character of the modern sectors of the economy and it sought merely to gain more advantages for Africans within that economy. The relevant clause in this constitutional statement of TANU's aims and objectives was the following:

To urge the government:
(1) to see that the producer gets the best price for his commodities and that consumers buy from the best markets,
(2) to help Africans establish small industries whenever possible and take an increasing share in owning and renting of big industries,
(3) to establish technical schools, training skilled African artisans,
(4) to establish a system of assisted farming and thus enable the

African farmer, either co-operatively or individually, to acquire
the modern methods of farming,

(5) to establish and enforce a minimum wage system to see that the
African gets a living wage and decent conditions of employment,

(6) to introduce compulsory and universal primary education for the
African child and to increase the introduction of secondary and
post-secondary education.[1]

In January 1962, the Constitution of TANU had to be revised as several
of its clauses referred to colonial situations and were no longer appropriate.
Nyerere took advantage of this to introduce a new statement of the party's
aims and objectives. The TANU Annual Conference accepted the new
Constitution and by doing so formally declared that its objectives included
the achievement of a democratic and socialist Tanzania. The relevant
section of the 1962 Constitution includes the following:

To establish a democratic and socialist form of government which would
be devoted to:

(a) consolidating national independence and insuring a decent
standard of living for every individual;

(b) giving equal opportunity to all men and women irrespective of
race, religion or status;

(c) to eliminate poverty, disease and ignorance by means of cooperation between citizens and their government;

(d) eradicating all types of injustice, intimidation, discrimination,
bribery and corruption.

To promote thoroughly the ways of increasing the wealth of this
country so as to help more people by:

(a) controlling collectively the means of producing national wealth
including the national resources such as land, air, water, power, transportation and the media for disseminating and receiving information;

(b) to promote to the highest level the possible co-operative functions
pertaining to the means of production, distribution and exchange;

(c) to encourage private enterprises which are run for the benefit of
the whole country.[2]

In 1965, the statement of TANU's aims and objectives was further
amended. This later version is more vigorously socialist than the 1962
statement.[3]

These socialist amendments to the TANU Constitution did not represent a settled view which had been arrived at by TANU after extensive
discussion. The 1962 amendment had been proposed to the conference by
Nyerere and was accepted with little discussion. The later amendment
was also adopted without debate. At the most, they can be said to reflect a

bias towards socialist rhetoric. The acceptance of these aims and objectives was not the culmination of a major educational effort within TANU to convert it into a socialist party. Rather it was an early stage in Nyerere's own efforts to win TANU to a genuine commitment to socialism.

The economic policies which the government pursued in these years were not socialist policies. The strategy which was followed was one of a tempered capitalism overseen by a socially responsible government. Agricultural development, for example, was provided primarily through the extension and improvement of small-holder peasant cultivation of cash crops. The government encouraged this in a variety of ways. It expanded its agricultural extension services. It promoted more effective commerce throughout the rural areas in the expectation that this would stimulate peasant interest in consumer goods and thereby generate greater productive efforts.[4] It sought ways to expand small-scale rural credit. In all of these efforts there was little or no concern for rural socialism. Even in the village resettlement schemes the individual initiative of the peasant, working for his own self-advancement on his own plot of land, was to be the main vehicle of agricultural development.

The commercial and industrial policies of the government were more ambivalent. Private and foreign investments were officially encouraged. There was however much emphasis on the growth of the cooperative movement both as a socially preferable way to organize the marketing and processing of agricultural produce and as a response to political pressures to limit the role of the Asian trader and middleman. Partly because of these racial overtones, there was always resistance within the government to any outspoken and vigorous encouragement of private investment. Nevertheless the main role which the government played in the manufacturing sector of the economy was to undertake the essential infrastructure investment which private investors would not undertake and to induce additional foreign and local private investments through jointly sponsored ventures. The First Five Year Plan anticipated that only £7m of the £40m which it hoped would be invested in the manufacturing sector of the economy would need to come from public sources. The Plan anticipated that the remainder would come from local and foreign private investors.[5]

The government relied upon taxation policies, joint ventures and the expansion of the cooperative movement to achieve a fair measure of equity in the distribution of the gains of the economic development. Income from company taxes nearly doubled in the first years of independence so that, despite the growth which occurred, the real value of retained profits fell by ten per cent between 1960 and 1963. Retained profits in 1965 were estimated as certainly not exceeding Shs.150m and as being more probably nearer to Shs.100m.[6]

From 1960/1 to 1967/8, Tanzania's Gross Domestic Product increased at an average rate of 5.9 per cent per annum, rising from Shs.3,701m to Shs.5,869m. Some 30 per cent of this increase was inflationary in character. The real annual growth rate over these eight years was thus 4.2 per cent.[7] As the rate of population increase was 2.7 per cent, the annual per capita increase in G.D.P. was thus only 1.5 per cent. This represents a greater economic achievement than these comparatively moderate figures suggest. Tanzania has been heavily dependent upon foreign trade, requiring overseas markets for her major crops such as coffee, sisal and cotton, and needing a very wide range of imported manufactured goods, machinery and transportation equipment. The terms of trade have moved against Tanzania. The unit cost of her imports increased by 17 per cent from 1960 to 1967 while, in contrast, the price of Tanzanian exports fell by 5 per cent. The export price of raw cotton in 1967 was 92.6 per cent of the 1960 price while the corresponding percentages for coffee and sisal fibre were 91.4 per cent and 66.7 per cent.[8] The net result of these diverging trends of export and import prices is that the index of the terms of trade in 1967 as compared to 1960 stood at 82.[9] Despite the dampening effect of such adverse trends, Tanzania was able, nevertheless, to maintain a growth rate at constant prices of 4.2 per cent.

Primary responsibility for this achievement lies with the ordinary peasant farmers. They continued to expand their output of the major export crops to an extent which more than offset the adverse effect of falling international prices. The contribution of the agricultural sector to G.D.P., in consequence, rose from Shs.935m in 1960–2 to Shs.1,334m in 1967.[10] Table 11 shows the crop production figures for the major

Table 11. *Tanzania major export crops (in millions of shillings)*

	1962		1965		1967	
Crop	Quantity	Export value	Quantity	Export value	Quantity	Export value
Cotton bales (000)	190[a]	153	369	244	393	251
Coffee (132-lb bags)	435.5	132	472.5	172	743.4	237
Cashew nuts (000 tons)	59	46.7	63.7	82.5	69.8	92.2
Tea (million lb)	9.5	32	12.5	29	15.8	43
Tobacco, flue-cured (million lb)	2.5		8.6	19.5	10.1	14
Tobacco, fire-cured (million lb)	1.3		2.7		7.0	
Pyrethrum (million lb)	2.5[a]	5.1	8.1	20.8	11.9	29.2
Sisal (000 long tons)	214	315	214.2	286	216.6	201

[a] 1960–2 average.

SOURCE: Tanzania, *Tanzania Second Five Year Plan for Economic and Social Development, July 1, 1969–June 30, 1974*, vol. 1 (Dar-es-Salaam, 1969), pp. 44–8.

agricultural export crops. Government policies, of course, contributed to
the achievement which it records. Nevertheless the most important single
factor which explains it is the increasing effort put into agricultural production by thousands of individual peasants.

Tanzania achieved modest success in its efforts to develop a manufacturing sector during these same years. A substantial start was made in
the local manufacturing of substitutes for imported textile, beer, cement,
cigarettes and soap. The value of the import of each of these items was
lower in 1967 than it had been in 1960. Some progress as well was made
in the processing for export of several of Tanzania's primary products.
Table 12 indicates the expansion which took place in several of the fastest-
growing industries. The net value of the output of manufacturing in-

Table 12. *Production in selected industries*

Industry	Unit	1963	1965	1967	1969
Beer	000 gal	1,962	2,673	5,120	7,290
Textiles	000 sq yd	6,225	12,126	17,338	55,326
Cigarettes	million	1,144	1,869	2,044	2,366
Paints	000 gal	95	163	275	353
Sisal twine	000 tons	—	6	15	18

SOURCES: Tanzania, *Background to the Budget 1968–69*, table 46, p. 62 and *Economic
Survey and Second Annual Plan 1970–71*, table 61, p. 71.

dustries in constant prices rose on average by ten per cent a year over the
period 1960–7, thus growing at more than double the overall growth
rate of the G.D.P. The value of imported consumer goods in current
prices, in contrast, increased on the average between 1962 and 1967 by
only 1.7 per cent, with the value of imported intermediate goods and
imported capital goods increasing at annual rates of 14.5 per cent and
13.5 per cent respectively.

These developments suggest that some structural changes were taking
place. However these changes were not such as to have dramatic consequences. Even by 1969 industrial production was responsible for only
7 per cent of the G.D.P.[11] As table 13 indicates, Tanzania's heavy dependency upon agriculture continued to be the most prominent characteristic of
the Tanzanian economy. Agriculture was still the source of more than 50
per cent of the G.D.P., it provided 80 per cent of Tanzania's exports, and
well over 90 per cent of the population secured their livelihood from it.

The activities of the Tanzanian government over these four years
cannot be told solely in terms of its development strategy and the success
and failures of its various economic initiatives. Much that the government

Table 13. *Tanzania Gross Domestic Product by sector contribution*
(*constant 1960 prices in million shillings*)

Sector	1960–2	1965	1967
Agriculture	935	1,210	1,334
Mining	105	115	117
Manufacturing	124	178	227
Construction	52	67	79
Transport	76	97	119
Public utilities	21	26	35
Commerce	416	548	598
Rent	75	90	97
Other services	143	152	170
Total G.D.P.	1,947	2,483	2,776

SOURCE: Tanzania, *Annual Economic Survey 1968*, table 3, p. 6.

did was not at all the product of a concern for development. It had continuously to cope with the unexpected and to contend with insistent
political pressures. Indeed, a rhythm can be traced throughout these years
which distinguishes those periods in which the development requirements
of the country were the major preoccupation of the government and those
other periods in which foreign policy issues or internal political difficulties dominated its counsels.

In 1963, the first year of Nyerere's Presidency, government leaders
were able to devote a good deal of their time to development projects.
Only one external issue at that time required their attention over long
periods of time. That issue was the complex set of questions relating to a
possible East African Federation and to the future of the East African
Common Market and the East African Common Services Organization.
Nyerere had long favoured a full political federation of the three East
African countries. However by late July 1963 he had realized that neither
of the other East African leaders, Obote and Kenyatta, was anxious or
able to bring his country into such a federation.* For the next two years

---

* The dating of this recognition is important for an understanding of the politics of
this question. Ali Mazrui has argued that Nyerere was primarily to blame for the
failure of the move towards an East African Federation. His main evidence,
however, relates to initiatives which were taken after July 1963. (See his article
'Tanzania versus East Africa', *Journal of Commonwealth Political Studies*, III, 3
(November 1965), 209–25.) By the reading suggested here, these initiatives are a
result of the fact that Nyerere had seen by then that the federation was in fact not
going to be introduced. They were thus the result of the failure of the federation
movement rather than its cause.

at least, relationships were strained within the East African community, largely because of Tanzania's efforts to secure a fairer distribution of the benefits of the common market. The various ramifications of these issues recurrently required the sustained attention not only of such Ministers and officials as Kahama, Swai, Jamal, Kassum and Brown but also of Nyerere himself.[12]

Despite this major issue, development questions were the central focus of government preoccupations during 1963. Special emphasis was given in particular to four activities. The first of these, the village settlement scheme, was given prominence by Nyerere in his Presidential inaugural address to the National Assembly in December 1962. He announced at that time that a major effort would be made to transform the countryside by convincing peasant cultivators who had traditionally lived in comparative isolation upon their scattered holdings, to move into villages and to begin to work together in closer cooperation.[13] A second activity to which senior members of the government devoted a good deal of effort was the attempt, which was largely successful, to secure from overseas sources the capital support which was needed for a major expansion of Tanzania's secondary schools and of the University College, Dar-es-Salaam. Thirdly, the President and a few senior Ministers hoped to achieve through careful economic planning a closer integration of governmental activities, a more effective mobilization of financial resources for development purposes and a clear and more systematic identification of priorities as between the different possible major projects. A fourth preoccupation of Nyerere and his colleagues in 1963 was the cooperative movement. Under his leadership, government and party officials throughout the country promoted the rapid expansion of marketing cooperatives. As a result total membership in agricultural marketing cooperatives rose by over twenty-five per cent in the course of the year, rising from 361,000 members in December 1962 to 453,000 members a year later.[14]

In the years 1964 and 1965 diverse and unexpected issues unrelated to development became more and more prominent. In January 1964, the two battalions of the Tanzanian army mutinied in what appears to have been little more than a soldiers' strike for more pay and for the rapid replacement of British officers by Tanzanians. During the five days of uncertainty and irresolute leadership which followed the mutiny, the fragility of the power base of Nyerere's government was painfully revealed. In the two days immediately after the mutiny, Nyerere and Kawawa went into hiding and Kambona bravely stepped in to provide what control and leadership he could in a very difficult situation. He had no choice but to concede major pay increases to the troops and to send the British officers in the Tanzanian army back to Britain. Yet the troops remained undisciplined. They refused to return their arms to the central stores at their camp. Numbers of them continued to move about freely in the streets of Dar-es-Salaam in battle dress, bearing their guns in an intimidating if still casual manner. Inevitably popular anxiety slowly developed. It was indeed one of those situations in which power lay in the streets waiting to be picked up. On the fifth morning after the mutiny, in response to a request from the Tanzanian government, a group of sixty British marines landed by parachute and helicopter and order was quickly restored in the capital.

The government's inability to handle this situation, the total absence of any capacity within TANU to mobilize mass support which might have contained the mutiny and the fact that the political leaders had so dramatically to be dependent again upon the British were humiliating lessons for the government. It disbanded the two mutinous battalions and began from scratch to build a new national army. It also invited the Organization of African Unity to meet in Dar-es-Salaam in February 1964 in order to hear the Tanzanian explanation of why the British had been asked to intervene and to receive its appeal for African troops to replace the British troops until an Tanzanian force had been trained. These consequences of the mutiny inevitably required the attention and the time of Nyerere, Kawawa and other senior members of the government.[15]

For the next eighteen months, events did not permit the government of Tanzania to give to development questions the concentrated attention which they had received in 1963. The revolution in Zanzibar had occurred immediately preceding the army mutiny. It was during the difficult aftermath of the mutiny that Nyerere and a few close political associates succeeded in arranging the union of Zanzibar and Tanganyika.[16] The final inauguration of the union on 24 April 1964 was, however, but the beginning of a major Presidential preoccupation with Zanzibari matters. Nyerere had made substantial concessions to Zanzibar to achieve the union. Although the population of the island was only three per cent of the population of the mainland, Zanzibar received very substantial representation in the political institutions of the newly created united republic. Karume, the President of Zanzibar, became the First Vice-President of the United Republic, five Zanzibari political leaders were made Ministers in the government of the United Republic and up to 52 Zanzibaris were to become members of the National Assembly. (These included all members of the Revolutionary Council up to a total of 32, plus 20 Zanzibaris, nominated by Nyerere.) Despite these concessions, Nyerere gained very little control over Zanzibari affairs. The government of Zanzibar retained a number of responsibilities which might have been expected to be transferred to the new central government. For example, Zanzibar retained control over its own army and over immigration and emigration. The Tanzanian authorities also did not gain control over the very large foreign reserves which Zanzibar had carefully sequestered in a London branch of a Soviet bank. Moreover, Karume and the Revolutionary Council showed every sign of being unresponsive to policy suggestions from the mainland. Nyerere was unable to assure even minimal adherence to government policies on the island.

There were many dramatic examples of the existence of major differences between the mainland government and the government of Zanzibar. The Revolutionary Council, for example, passed a decree in March 1964 which empowered the President to acquire any property without the payment of compensation whenever it appeared to him that it was in the national interests to do so.[17] Under this decree, members of the Revolutionary Council helped themselves indiscriminately and without payment of compensation to the property of a great many Arab and Asian citizens.[18] In their rejection of compensation, their racist motivation and their corrupt purposes, the expropriations were at variance with the values and the policies of the Tanzanian government.

Early Tanzanian expectations that Zanzibari cooperation with the mainland would quickly grow closer proved unfounded. It had been expected that the Afro-Shirazi Party and TANU would merge to form a single party for the whole of the United Republic. The initial constitutional arrangement of the union which had been hastily prepared was embodied in a Constitution deliberately entitled an Interim Constitution. The Revolutionary Council of Zanzibar, however, was unwilling to engage in any further constitutional discussions as its members feared these might further delimit its powers. As a result, the union had had to continue to operate within the framework of the Interim Constitution. Another example of the inability of the Tanzanian government to win the cooperation of the Revolutionary Council came with Nyerere's presentation to Parliament of the First Five Year Development Plan. When presenting the Plan, Nyerere announced that he intended 'to initiate a similar development planning operation for Zanzibar. The plan thus prepared would become an integral part of the union plan just as the document before you will be.'[19] Nyerere in fact was unable to take any such initiative. The Revolutionary Council, instead, accepted several East German economists who, with an absolute minimum of cooperation with the mainland, prepared a five-year plan for Zanzibar. This plan was never presented to the National Assembly even though a great many of its portions covered areas which were legally under the jurisdiction of that Assembly.

Tanzanian concern about Zanzibar was further heightened by frequent rumours of killings and other serious abuses of power by those in authority on the island. The Zanzibaris, moreover, kept a very tight control on the movement of people between the mainland and the island thus further increasing the general unease in Dar-es-Salaam. In 1964 the mainland police authorities were so concerned about the situation upon the island that they prevailed upon Nyerere to postpone his first official visit to Zanzibar. Babu, the senior Zanzibari Minister in the government of Tanzania, made his home in Dar-es-Salaam and, for reasons of personal safety, gave up returning to the island. That these and similar fears were not extravagant was distressingly revealed in 1965 when Othman Shariff, a prominent Zanzibari whom Nyerere had appointed as the Tanzanian Ambassador to Washington, was detained on the island. Shariff had been active in Zanzibari politics and had earlier fallen out of favour with Karume. Although there were no charges raised against Shariff and no malpractices suggested, Nyerere had to intervene several times before he was able to secure his release and his return to the mainland. Nyerere then, to protect him further, invited him to be a personal guest at the State House. It was a clear gesture of support for Shariff and a rebuke to the Revolutionary Council, but it hardly suggests that Nyerere was acting from a position of strength in his dealings with Zanzibar.*

The affairs of Zanzibar must thus be counted, along with the aftermath of the army mutiny, as major new preoccupations of the government of Tanzania. Moreover it was just at this time that the Tanzanian government had also to cope with that series of crises in its relations with the United States, with Germany and with Britain which were studied in some detail in the last chapter. The net result of these events, internal and external, was that for over a year and a half, the Tanzanian government was no longer in charge of its own priorities. It was, instead, having to react in an increasingly harassed fashion to activities and to initiatives which were not at all of its own design.

Under the pressure of these events, neither the President nor his colleagues were able to give to the shaping and guiding of economic policies the energy and time which they needed. The Five Year Plan, which had been of central interest to the President for at least the preceding six months was not followed by any sustained developmental effort based upon it. The Plan was rapidly of very little significance in the identification of those projects which were being presented to potential sources of capital assistance. Planning as an on-going process within the government hardly took place at all. After the introduction of the Five Year Plan, Nyerere set up a particularly unworkable structure to implement it. He appointed three Ministers of State to head a Directorate of Economic Planning and delegated extensive powers to these Ministers in the hope that this would ensure the vigorous pursuit of the Plan's objectives. However, Presidential powers cannot be easily exercised by anyone save the President and

* The situation did not improve, as the tragic dénouement involving Shariff reveals. In October 1969, while Nyerere was out of Tanzania, though probably with his acquiescence, Shariff was arrested in southern Tanzania where he worked as a veterinary officer and was returned to the island. He was then murdered by the authorities without even a semblance of a trial.

Ministries can hardly be run efficiently or cordially by three rival Ministers. This structure rapidly proved to be unworkable yet the international tensions which gripped Tanzania at that time left no one with the energy or patience to diagnose the problem or to reorganize the structure. At the political level, the Economic Committee of the Cabinet, created especially to provide the on-going coordination of policy which effective planning required, was in fact never called into session by the President. There could hardly have been a more dramatic indication of the degree to which other preoccupations had thrust developmental considerations into the background.[20]

In this general atmosphere it was perhaps inevitable that the coordination of policies should at times be severely inadequate. In November 1964, for example, the rights of occupancy of twenty-one foreign-owned farms in the Arusha region were revoked and the British officer, who was the senior land officer in the region, was deported. This was done without any discussion within the Cabinet and without consultation with the Minister of Agriculture or with other of the Ministers most likely to be affected. These actions caused a minor crisis in Tanzania's relations with Britain. In calmer times it could no doubt have been easily handled. However, at this time it provided but another occasion for the government to demonstrate its declining capacity to take decisions in a careful and considered fashion.

This deterioration in the cohesion of the leadership provided by the Tanzanian government was checked by the end of 1965 and by 1966 the government was again able to concentrate much of its energies on developmental matters. Three interrelated factors explain this impressive ability of Nyerere's government to regain its equilibrium. Firstly, the elections in October 1965 did much to restore the political confidence of the government. Ministers and Members of Parliament renewed their rapport with their constituencies or were replaced by the others in whom the people had more confidence. Secondly, with each additional year of experience the senior African civil servants became increasingly more self-confident. In the early years immediately after independence they were, in a sense, doubly intimidated. They were intimidated by the major responsibilities into which they were suddenly thrust and they were intimidated also, in some cases, by their political Ministers with whom they found it difficult to work out an effective relationship. However, by 1965 the senior African civil servants were far more confident. They had real accomplishments to their credit. They recognized the importance of the role which they were playing in the government and they had developed a significant esprit de corps. Their cohesion and their sense of purpose were important stabilizing factors in a political and governmental situation which was often quite unsettled.

The third factor which helped to stabilize the political scene by early

1966 has already been discussed. The strained relations which had developed first with the Federal Republic of Germany and then with Britain were at first severely divisive. Many Cabinet Ministers and senior civil servants were distressed by the probable impact upon the foreign assistance which Tanzania was receiving from these major powers. However, when West Germany rejected the Tanzanian compromise relating to the East German Consulate, and when Britain froze a £7.5m grant following the break in diplomatic relations between Tanzania and Britain, opinion within government circles consolidated behind Nyerere in a way which was not only much more assertively nationalist but was also concerned effectively to promote Tanzanian development despite the loss of German and British assistance.

This revived and development-oriented sense of purpose quickly had its impact upon government policies. In 1966, the government subjected major areas of its developmental activities to a close critical reassessment. This began when Nyerere in effect turned the whole Cabinet into a seminar on development. In 1965, he had recognized that the government's developmental efforts had very largely lost their impetus. Unable to see how a group of senior Tanzanians could be spared to assess this situation, he invited a particularly able team of British experts to review the appropriateness of Tanzania's developmental policies.[21] Beginning early in 1966, session after session of the newly revived Economic Committee of the Cabinet was given over to a Ministry-by-Ministry review of the comments of the British Economic Mission. It was the most sustained consideration ever given at the political level to the economic policies of the government. This review quickly had its dramatic consequences. The village resettlement schemes which had been a central feature of government policy in 1963 were halted and were publicly acknowledged as having failed. The cooperative movement and the trade union movement, two major institutions with which the government was closely associated, were made the subject of separate public inquiries which in turn produced reports which were severely critical.[22] The government had already acted vigorously in regard to economic planning. A Ministry of Economic Affairs and Development Planning was created in October 1965. Bomani, the previous Minister of Finance, was made its Minister and Amir Jamal became Minister of Finance. The government had thus made a determined effort to correct an institutional failure which had contributed to the general collapse of economic planning in 1964 and 1965. There seemed every reason in 1966 to assume that economic development had again become a central preoccupation of the government of Tanzania and that government policies would again be shaped by the development strategy that had been dominant in the period 1963–5.

This was not to be the case. In January 1967, at Arusha, Nyerere won the backing of the National Executive Committee of TANU for a major policy statement which committed it to the achievement of a socialist society in Tanzania. The previous chapter discussed a number of developments in Tanzania's relations with foreign states which contributed to a greater Tanzanian sensitivity to the risks of dependency upon the major Western powers and to a general predisposition towards a more radical stance. However that interest in greater Tanzanian self-reliance and that predisposition towards radicalism are not adequate in themselves to explain the commitment to socialism which came with the Arusha Declaration of 1967. The explanation for that commitment must be sought in large part in Nyerere's perception of several basic tendencies within Tanzanian society and in his reactions to them. These tendencies were the persistent inclination within the political leadership towards authoritarian rule and the emergence of significant social and economic stratification within the African population of Tanzania. Nyerere's recognition of these developments made 1966 a year of crisis for him. This authoritarian tendency and this emergence of economic classes threatened the development in Tanzania of that democratic and socialist society which, however absorbed he was in the immediate preoccupations of government, remained Nyerere's long-term objective for his country. They are therefore essential components to any explanation of the commitment to socialism into which Nyerere led Tanzania in 1967. They are also essential to an understanding of the political strategy by which Nyerere hoped to lead Tanzania through its transition to socialism.

A tendency towards oligarchy

A convincing case can be made that Tanzania has needed an occasional exercise of authoritarian power in order to preserve the stability of the whole society and to maintain its continuing economic development. Nyerere himself has argued this case. In an extraordinarily honest address at the opening of the new campus of the University College, Dar-es-Salaam, in 1964 he said:

> To suspend the rule of law under any circumstance is to leave open the
> possibility of the grossest injustices being perpetrated. Yet, knowing
> these things, I have still supported the introduction of a law which gives
> the government the power to detain people without trial. I have myself
> signed detention orders. I've done these things as an inevitable part of
> my responsibilities as President of the Republic. For even on so
> important and fundamental an issue as this, other principles conflict.
> Our Union has neither the long tradition of nationhood nor the strong
> physical means of national security which other countries take for
> granted. While the vast majority of the people give full and active
> support to their country and its government, a handful of individuals

can still put our nation into jeopardy and reduce to ashes the efforts of millions.[23]

Admittedly this type of argument is pure intellectual quicksand. It can easily conceal an oligarch's determination to hold onto power. However, whatever weight one wishes to give to arguments such as these, the tendency in Tanzania to restrict the autonomy of major institutions and to limit the political rights of the opponents of those in power cannot be explained solely or even primarily in such terms. The political leaders who came to power in 1961 have tended to take a proprietary view of governmental authority. They have been suspicious of critics and quick to rely upon force rather than persuasion. Many factors explain why they have been prone to authoritarian rule. The colonial regime was the only governmental system which they had actually themselves experienced. The constitutional democratic system within which they now exercised power was not well established and the rules of the game which were relevant to it were neither universally accepted nor even well understood. Moreover TANU was a nationalist movement which in the popular view had spoken for the nation against its colonial rulers. Those who opposed TANU could thus easily be viewed as having placed themselves outside the ranks of their own nation and their opposition could easily be felt to be disloyal rather than merely wrong-headed.

These general elements in the political culture of the new political class were reinforced by powerful considerations of self-interest. The political leaders of TANU had, after all, won independence for Tanzania. They had, themselves, long been without secure employment or regular incomes. They had now become the inheritors of the colonial regime. Political office was very likely the only way in which many of them were able to earn a significant income. Few had professional or technical skills which would have made them easily employable within the government service and there was no large private sector capable of absorbing them in any number. For many, therefore, a loss of political office would have meant an eventual return to peasant farming. It is small wonder that many TANU leaders tended to jump rather swiftly to the view that critics of TANU ought to be restrained.

The existence of an incipient authoritarianism was demonstrated in 1962 with the passing of the Preventive Detention Act.[24] This Act is a particularly illiberal piece of legislation. Under it, the President can detain anyone whenever he is satisfied that the person to be detained is a danger to peace and good order or is acting in a manner prejudicial to the defence of the country or the security of the state. The President may also detain anyone if he is satisfied that this is necessary to prevent that person from becoming a danger to peace and good order, to the defence or to the security of Tanganyika.[25] The Act includes none of the safeguards which are sometimes introduced into Acts such as this in order to lessen the risk of flagrant abuses of the power to detain. The period of detention is unlimited rather than specified. There is no requirement that the names of those detained should be made public. Judicial review of the exercise of the power of detention is carefully excluded and there is no alternative appeal procedure. The Act provides that the detained person shall be informed of the ground for his detention and that he shall be permitted to make representation to the Minister of Home Affairs concerning it. However the detainee has no access to counsel and he has no right to appear in person before the Minister, to face his accusers or to call witnesses. Moreover the requirement that he must be informed of the grounds for his detention has lost whatever significance it might have had, by the tendency for it to be met merely by the simple statement that the Minister is satisfied that there are satisfactory grounds for that detention. Finally, in May 1963, the regulations issued under the Act required that the Minister must give his approval in writing before a detainee can receive a visitor and before he can write or receive any letters. The regulations also deny the detainee the right extended to other prisoners to be visited by ministers of religion and to be visited by relatives when ill.[26]

The Act was soon used. In 1963, the government secured the co-operation of the Kenyan police in what amounted to the kidnapping of one of the few outspoken Tanzanian critics of the TANU leadership. Christopher Tumbo, a trade union leader and Member of Parliament, had left Tanzania in 1962 in order to avoid detention. He lived in Mombasa, Kenya, and from there issued occasional critical comments on Tanzanian affairs. At the most he was but a minor irritant. Yet, on the instigation of the Tanzanian authorities, the Kenyan police picked him up and transported him to a Tanzanian border post where he was immediately arrested and detained. He remained in detention for just over four years.

Preventive detention was given its most extensive use in January 1964. During the week of uncertainty which followed the army mutiny a number of trade union leaders, along with other opponents of the Tanzanian leadership, sought to organize a conspiracy against the regime. Once the mutiny had been brought under control and at a time when the British troops were still in Dar-es-Salaam, the government detained over five hundred persons throughout Tanzania. These included those who were suspected of being involved in the conspiracy but their numbers extended far beyond the original conspirators to include a great many who were regarded by their Regional or Area Commissioners as being politically discontented.

Nyerere has recurrently used his authority to release detainees so that there has not been any gradual increase over time in the numbers being held in detention. Rather the use of preventive detention has waxed and waned in direct correlation with fluctuations in the tranquillity of the political scene.

The Preventive Detention Act was not the only authoritarian instrument available to the government for the disciplining and the restraining of its critics. By using powers which had originally been enacted during the colonial period, the government was able, without trial, to restrict to a remote part of the country any critic who it felt was a threat to peace and good order. This power was used, for example, in 1963 to silence Victor Mkello, who was President of both the Plantation Workers' Association and the Tanganyikan Federation of Labour. Chief David Kidaha Makwaia, perhaps the ablest and the most prominent of the chiefs who had represented Africans in the colonial legislature in the late 1940s, was also restricted to a distant and inaccessible District in late 1962 along with his brother Chief Hussein, when their Regional Commissioner was unable to cope with the challenge to his authority which the Makwaias posed and symbolized.[27] In 1963 Chief Lukamba II in Bukoba was similarly deported for several months when he came into direct conflict with Peter Walwa, the Regional Commissioner.

Regional and Area Commissioners were given the power to arrest and to hold in detention for a period up to forty-eight hours anyone whom they suspected of being guilty of a crime. This power, initially, was a modest extension to the powers of the police. The Act required that anyone so detained had to be presented on charge before a magistrate within forty-eight hours. This power quickly became in practice a right on the part of the Commissioners to detain anyone without having to show real cause, as long as they were held for a period less than forty-eight hours. By 1965, the purpose of this particular provision had been totally reinterpreted. In that year, the Second Vice-President urged the Regional Commissioners to restrict their use of the forty-eight-hour preventive detention to political detentions, leaving criminal arrests to the police.

A tendency towards authoritarianism can be discerned as well in the support given to the introduction in Tanzania of a single-party system. The idea that every self-respecting nationalist movement should establish itself as a single-party regime was widespread in tropical Africa in the years 1962–4. The rationalizations for this were many. Competitive party systems were divisive and wasteful. They were an unnecessary part of the neo-colonial heritage. A single-party system was more attuned to African values and African ways and would be more likely to maintain the unity of African countries and to promote their development.

Nevertheless an important part of the support for single-party rule stemmed from the reluctance of some members of the political class to accept any challenge to their newly won political power. In Tanzania the several tiny parties which appeared in 1962 were harassed out of existence, their leaders deported or detained and their right to register and to hold meetings severely restricted. When Nyerere first suggested that there could be competitive elections within a single-party system there was little support for the idea within the leadership ranks of TANU. Kambona, who was then the Secretary-General of the party and a strong supporter of a single-party system, argued publicly that Tanganyika did not need any elections. Many leaders supported the introduction of a single-party system because they assumed it would assure their continued enjoyment of high office. It is small wonder that they opposed Nyerere's suggestion which, while it would provide for a one-party system, would nevertheless open up the possibility that those presently in high office might be un-seated through democratic elections.

The introduction of preventive detention, the forty-eight-hour detention power of the Regional and Area Commissioners and much of the support given to the idea of a single-party system all illustrate a tendency to regard criticism as disloyal. Nyerere has always argued that this authoritarian tendency will only be checked when the people themselves shake off that submissive and fearful attitude towards those in power which has continued to be a feature of the political culture of Tanzania.[28] This has been an important and prominent theme in Nyerere's popular speeches. In his volume *Freedom and Socialism*, Nyerere reproduces an impromptu speech which he gave on Mafia Island in February 1966.[29] It is a simple, humorous but effective call to the people to overcome their fear of authority and to be ready to press for their rights against their leaders. To be submissive, he said, is a bad habit:

> This is your country. We tell you every day that this is your country and that you have freedom of speech. If you do not accept your responsibility for this country I shall claim ownership of it. Any country must be looked after by people. If you do not like to accept the responsibility of looking after this country, I shall get a few clever people and together we will declare this country to be our property. . .If we do not remove fear from our people and if you do not abolish the two classes of masters and servants from our society clever people will emerge from among us to take the place of the Europeans, Indians and Arabs. These clever people will continue to exploit our fear for their own benefit. And we leaders can become the clever people. . .This is going to happen if you do not remove fear from your minds. You will even lose your property. Suddenly you will discover that your area commissioner has a farm of 3,000 acres. You will be surprised to hear that even Julius has a 3,000 acre farm.[30]

It is not enough merely to exhort the people to assume responsibility for their own affairs. The people must be provided with institutions which facilitate this popular participation in ways which bring the leaders and the people into a relationship which is creative and positive rather than divisive and alienating. The need to find democratic institutions which would be appropriate to Tanzania was a continuing preoccupation of Nyerere during the years 1963 to 1966.

The search for appropriate democratic controls: NUTA and the Cooperative Union

In the first years of independence a genuine fear of the destructive capabilities of the trade-union movement and an authoritarian impatience towards criticism resulted in the unions being brought under the direct control of the political leadership. Nyerere's government in 1963 continued the determined efforts of its predecessor to bring the trade unions under closer control. A strike of plantation workers early in 1963 was broken by restricting several union leaders to a remote village. Kamaliza, the Minister of Labour, then sought unsuccessfully to convince the Tanganyika Federation of Labour to disband so that the individual unions could be merged directly into the Ministry. Disagreements continued to arise between the unions and the government. The unions maintained their opposition to the compulsory arbitration provisions of the 1962 Trades Disputes (Settlement) Act. They also attacked Nyerere's announcement in January 1964 that preference in appointments to the civil service and in promotions within it would no longer be given to African over non-African citizens.

The government followed the activities of its trade union critics with some anxiety. This anxiety increased with the army mutiny of January 1964 when the government became highly sensitive to potential threats of internal subversion. Immediately after the mutiny, some two hundred trade union leaders were amongst the five hundred people who were detained in a disorganized and hasty effort to block any chance of a political upheaval. At the same time, Tandau, the Acting Secretary-General of the T.F.L., yielded to government pressure and disbanded the Federation. In the same month, February 1964, the National Union of Tanganyika Workers Act was passed. Under this Act a single national union, the National Union of Tanganyika Workers (NUTA), was created. From its inception NUTA was closely integrated into TANU. Its Secretary-General was appointed by the President of Tanzania. It was formally affiliated to TANU and it was represented on the various governing councils within TANU. Its objects included the obligation 'to promote the policies of TANU and to encourage its members to join TANU'.[31]

There was an important element of cooption involved in these new arrangements. The trade union leaders who cooperated secured greater personal job security and higher salaries. Because the new Act introduced both the union shop and the check-off, total membership and union revenues were much larger than previously. The union leaders moreover were no longer on the periphery of the ruling oligarchy, vacillating between opposing it or aspiring to it. Instead they had secure positions within it.

In a further effort to assure that NUTA would cooperate actively with TANU, Nyerere appointed Kamaliza, the Minister of Labour, as the first Secretary-General of NUTA. Officials of the disbanded unions were often incorporated into NUTA's hierarchy, though the senior officials who were in detention were replaced by others, many of whom were old associates of Kamaliza from the period when he had been head of the Tanganyika General Workers Union.[32] The government had thus acted in the immediate aftermath of a national crisis and at a time when many union leaders were in prison to disband the autonomous trade unions and to create a new movement that would be much more closely under its control.

Nyerere offered no opposition to these developments. He had never favoured separately organized interest groups. He hoped for structures which would provide for mass participation in ways that would not be divisive but rather would encourage individuals to work cooperatively for the common good. The establishment of NUTA fitted his conception of democracy. It was for him more than the extension of government control over the trade union movement. It was also a new beginning. It represented a deliberate break with liberal and pluralist preconceptions of the role of trade unions. NUTA's official objectives, far from giving prominence to securing the maximum possible wage increases for its members, suggest merely that it is 'to consult with the government on all matters concerning a national wage policy'.[33] However, the hope behind the Act went beyond the wish to assure that the unions did not upset the national wage policy. There was also a vision that the workers, far from being alienated by this loss of autonomy, would be drawn more actively into wider and more responsible activities as trade unionists and would be actively integrated through TANU into a common Tanzanian society.

NUTA was given representation within TANU. NUTA, moreover, was required by its first official rules to spend sixty per cent of its substantial income on social welfare activities or to transfer funds to that total to a new Workers' Development Corporation.[34] In the same year, the government required that workers' committees be established in all establishments in which ten or more NUTA members were employed. These committees were to share with employers the enforcement of discipline and were to concern themselves with efficiency and with productivity. The new structures thus opened up the possibility of a meaningful involvment of workers and their representatives in discussion and decision-making relating to a far wider range of matters of direct interest to them, at both the level of the plant and at the level of the nation, than they had in fact enjoyed when their unions were autonomous.

These however were possibilities only. NUTA did not have the administrative or managerial skills to make a success of the Workers' Development Corporation. It did not have a sufficient number of committed organizers to see to it that the workers' committees were established and that they served as more than instruments for the control of workers. Its responsibility in regard to wage increases was largely preempted by the government's decision in 1966 to hold wage increases to a maximum of 5 per cent per annum. NUTA in fact quickly lost whatever trust and confidence the workers had in it. On 26 April 1966 when Nyerere told a meeting of workers that he would establish a commission to investigate NUTA, the announcement was cheered.

The Commission reported that NUTA was indeed in sorry shape. It presented a portrait of NUTA as unpopular, ineffective, out of touch with its rank and file and corrupt.[35] Nyerere and the government did not abandon their efforts to achieve genuine workers' participation within structures which were closely integrated into the party and the government.[36] However, the Report of the Commission indicates that this participation was still minimal. The more immediate reality was the elimination of independent trade unions and the incorporation of a trade union bureaucracy into the political ruling class.

The cooperative movement was another of the major institutions which became more closely associated with TANU in the period 1962–7. The two movements had been intimately connected throughout the whole of their history. Both were expressions of the determination of Africans to be free of exploitation and domination by foreigners. Both gave ambitious and able Africans more substantial opportunities to lead their people than were available to them in other institutions. After independence the government and TANU conducted a major drive to introduce marketing cooperatives in Districts where they had not yet been organized and to increase their membership in the Districts where they were already established. The results were dramatic. The numbers of societies rose from 857 in 1960 to 1,533 in 1966, with the total quantity of produce handled by the cooperatives increasing from 145,000 tons in 1960 to 496,000 tons in 1965.[37]

Although there had not been the same conflict and strain between the cooperatives and TANU as there had been between the trade unions and TANU, the relationships which emerged were nevertheless very similar. Proposals from more pluralist-minded Ministers never carried the day. Derek Bryceson, while Minister of Agriculture, urged the creation of a genuine Farmers' Union which would be separate from TANU and from the government and would speak for the interests of the peasants. However, he could never win much support for the proposal. Paul Bomani, a Minister whose public career had begun in the Victoria Federation of Cooperative Unions, fought a long battle to protect the cooperative unions from being converted into control agencies through which the government extracted economic surplus from the countryside for governmental development expenditures. He succeeded in killing that particular proposal, which had originated in a rather doctrinaire paper by Babu in 1965.[38] However, he and others could not secure a hands-off policy towards the cooperative unions. Not only was there a general ideological bias against it and a reluctance in TANU to permit important African interests to organize autonomously of the party, but as well, the unions had become too important to the economy for the government to leave them alone. As part of its campaign to increase African participation in the economy, the government had given the cooperatives a monopoly in the purchase from growers of the most important peasant-grown export crops. A breakdown in the marketing of a major crop would have immediate political and economic consequences. The efficiency and the honesty of these operations became a matter of unavoidable importance to TANU and to the government. Moreover, many of the unions had accumulated large reserves. The government was bound to be concerned that these funds should be used for high-priority development investments.[39]

As a result of these several factors every effort was made to bring the cooperative unions closely into line with TANU and with the government. The separate unions were brought into a government-sponsored national union, the Cooperative Union of Tanzania (C.U.P.). The unions were subjected to a variety of controls designed to assure their efficiency and honesty; the leadership of the unions was integrated politically into the ruling hierarchy, with the C.U.P. being represented on the National Executive Committee of TANU. While the new structure permitted and indeed encouraged participation, it was participation within institutions which were closely integrated into a national system which was dominated by TANU and the government. As in the case of the trade unions, the democratic provisions and the bureaucratic controls worked but fitfully. By 1966 the government recognized that the new structures were not providing an effective check upon the officers and committee members of the cooperative societies and unions. Nyerere therefore appointed an important commission of inquiry into the cooperative movement. This commission was so distressed by what it discovered that before publishing its final report, it submitted two confidential interim reports to the government on specific unions that seemed urgently to require corrective action. The second of these interim reports revealed 'abysmal' faults in the operation of the Victoria Federation of Cooperative Unions at every level – the federation itself, the nineteen member unions and the five hundred or more primary societies.[40] Committee members owning buses and construction companies were awarded contracts by the Federation without tenders. Senior officials employed close relatives on the staff. Financial controls were extremely inadequate and payrolls were grossly inflated. The unions received far higher fees than could be justified by their limited services. The controls exercised by the Registrar of Co-operative Societies in Dar-es-Salaam were totally inadequate. His instruc-tions were ignored, his advice unheeded and the public criticisms in his annual reports without impact. An accountant's report suggested that Shs.2.8m could have been saved for growers if the Victoria Federation had maintained a reasonable level of efficiency and honesty. The Com-mission's recommendations in regard to the Victoria Federation were drastic. It called for dismissal of the Federation's General Manager and of all committeemen in the Federation and in each of the nineteen unions. The more general published report was hardly less critical. It identified major administrative weaknesses at every level within the movement and it stressed the growth of grower discontent.[41]

Nyerere thus had to face the fact in 1966 that the integration of the cooperative movement and the trade unions into the national 'party-state' had consequences quite opposite from those intended. In theory the leaders of both movements were to have become an integral part of the TANU leadership while also remaining democratically responsible to their mass membership. This, it was hoped, would draw their members into the dis-cussion of a wider range of issues and would increase the democratic component within the political system. Conversely, however, these arrangements were intended as well to result in the loyal acceptance and implementation of any major national decision once it had been taken.

In fact however neither the democratic nor the centralist aspects of this exercise in democratic centralism had worked well. The cooperatives and the trade unions had not become efficient instruments for the promotion of national policies. This was obvious on even the most fundamental issues. NUTA, for example, was not an effective proponent of the government's policy that wage increases should not exceed the expected five per cent annual increase in national productivity. Similarly the policies of the co-operative unions did not easily fall into line with national priorities in such matters as the price they paid to growers and the investment of their substantial surpluses. It was also the case that there had not been any significant increase in the participation of workers and peasants in the management of their own affairs through these movements. The partici-patory elements in their structures were easily circumscribed or easily dominated by locally powerful individuals. The idea that public officials should be responsible to the rank and file was still but weakly held. As a result, both of these movements lost much of their popular legitimacy. They were in danger of being widely regarded as impositions upon workers and peasants rather than as structures through which they could participate in the discussion and control of matters closely related to their interests.

It may well be suggested that this section has unfairly tested the

Tanzanian political system against a model which the Tanzanians have themselves rejected. This has not been its intention. Tanzania does not aspire to be a liberal constitutional democracy. Tanzania is searching for new institutional forms of mass participation and democratic control which will be more appropriate to its needs and more expressive of its communal values. However in addition to this search for new structures there have also been strong oligarchic and authoritarian tendencies. It is obfuscating to present the developments discussed in this section solely as a search for a Tanzanian way or as the introduction of a socialist discipline. Whatever the longer-term democratic potential of the new structures which are discussed in this section, their immediate consequences have been to consolidate power in the hands of the present leaders, to silence their critics and to lessen the autonomy of previously independent institutions.

The search for appropriate democratic controls: representative local governments

Local government was in particular disarray in 1962. The older colonial framework of local rule, the Native Authorities, was clearly inappropriate, while the modern local government system represented by the District Councils seemed discredited because of the efforts from 1955 to 1959 to secure a protected representation in the Councils for the minority races. The government in 1962 quickly took the major decisions which were required to remove the various uncertainties that affected local government. The Native Authority system was abandoned. The chiefs as chiefs lost their official powers and responsibilities in the administrative and legal systems of rural Tanzania.[42] The Kawawa government decided not to construct *de novo* a system of rural administration. Instead, Kawawa replaced the Native Authorities by District Councils under the 1953 Local Government Ordinance. That law, freed of the particular use made of it by the Twining administration, provided for the establishment of elected District Councils which would exercise important local powers under the close supervision of the central government.[43]

The District Councils were formally responsible for such important local services as primary education and rural dispensaries. They also had significant sources of tax revenues. By 1966 their total recurrent expenditures were Shs.194.4m. Shs.110.4m of this was raised by various local rates and Shs.46.2m was covered by central government grants-in-aid, and the balance came from other sources.

The rural local authorities needed to be closely supervised to avoid severe breakdowns in these important services. This had often to extend to the preparation of their estimates, the control of their finances and the organization of their deliberations. There never was any question of allowing the Districts wide autonomy in the running of these services. The

Table 14. *Revenue and expenditures of rural authorities 1966*
(*in million shillings*)

Revenues		Expenditures	
Taxation		Education	104.3
Personal rate	83.7	Health	20.4
Produce cess	21.6	Roads, etc.	6.4
Cattle rate	4.6	Agriculture, veterinary,	
Property tax	0.5	water, etc.	7.9
	110.4		
Administrative revenues	28.2	Administrative and other	55.4
Miscellaneous	7.7		
Grants-in-aid			
Education	43.4		
Other	2.8		
Reduction in reserves	1.9		
Total	194.4		194.4

SOURCE: S. B. Skottan, 'Report on Local Government Taxation in Tanzania' (Washington, D.C., 1969), p. 11.

local government services were too important and the sums involved too large for any responsible national government to permit gross negligence to continue for long. Nor in any case could it be assumed that the processes of democratic control would eventually correct major failings by local authorities. It was much more likely that the causes and the possible correctives of these failings would elude the Councils, with the whole experience being, for them, more alienating than educational.

The central government had extensive controls over the local authorities. The Minister of Local Government had to approve their by-laws. He also formally appointed all elected members to the Council so that he could veto any individual election merely by refusing to make the appointments. Finally the Minister had the authority to issue instructions to the Councils concerning many aspects of their responsibilities, while the Regional Commissioners were in a position to influence the shaping of the Councils' estimates, as the estimates were not valid until approved by the Regional Commissioner.

The central government was also able, or should have been able, to guide and influence the development of the local governments in many important indirect ways. The District Councils did not have senior staff of their own in such fields as agriculture, health and education. They had no alternative but to rely upon central government officers for advice and for administrative control over local government activities. The Councils, for example, employed 2,892 subordinate staff in their health services in 1967, 555 in their veterinary services, 236 in agriculture and 220 in forestry.[44] They paid the salaries of these staff members but relied upon central government officers to organize and direct their work. Thus in every District the District Medical, Education, Agricultural and Veterinary Officers were intimately involved in Council affairs and able to exert a significant influence. As well there was a Ministry of Local Government to keep a watchful eye on the local authorities and to champion the cause of local government within the central government. There were officers of this Ministry in many Districts who were intended to work closely and cooperatively with the local authorities. The government, finally, used matching grants to encourage particular local services in which it was especially interested and it ran a Local Government Training Centre to raise the level of competence of the senior and middle-rank staff of the Councils.

These controls and influences were very extensive. Nevertheless, the long-term objective remained the creation of autonomous and representative local governments. That this autonomy was not yet a reality does not detract from the importance of this objective. The services were done in the name of the local authorities. The intention and expectation was that gradually the authorities would be able to perform these services without close supervision. The government kept alive the ideal that even in a state ruled by a popular national movement, local communities ought themselves to be responsible for an important range of local services.

The District Councils were established in 1962, at the very time when there was a sharp reduction in the number of experienced expatriate District Officers. These new local authorities received far less assistance at first than they needed. As a result many of them were in serious financial and administrative disarray in 1963. There were, moreover, unresolved political questions relating to the relationship between the local TANU branch and the elected Councils. TANU dominated the first elections to all of the District Councils. TANU candidates in fact won almost all of the seats without even a contest. In 1962, of the 923 seats to be filled by election, only 15 were contested.[45] However, in the following year the hold of the local TANU leadership in the Councils was challenged in several major Districts, including Bukoba, Mwanza and Kilimanjaro by Council members who decided to be partly independent of the local party.[46] Party leaders at the local level saw these independents as a serious threat. One Regional Commissioner complained, 'They are damaging to the prestige of our party, TANU. Without party discipline no council government or any of us can survive and the building of our nation would be in peril.'⁴⁷ The Regional Commissioner of Bukoba refused to appoint the elected Councillors whom he knew to be opposed to TANU directions. He threatened ominously that some deportations might be necessary and he asked that schoolteachers, being the most independent-minded of the Councillors, should be refused permission to stand for elections to the Council. Nyerere, after some hesitation, agreed to the deportation of Chief Lukamba and three others in a show of strength to reassert TANU's authority in Bukoba.

These and similar tensions, along with the many administrative inadequacies of the new local authorities, led some within the government to question the validity of autonomous representative local governments as an ideal in a Tanzania ruled by TANU. The issues were brilliantly put in an exchange between two senior administrators, Joseph Namata, Secretary to the Cabinet, and Frederick Burengelo, Principal Secretary to the Ministry of Local Government. They are worth extensive quotation. Namata wrote:

> The most pressing needs of our government are to forge or maintain the political unity of the nation and to force the pace of economic development. The councils have got a very important role to play in meeting these needs and they can only do so if they keep politically in step with the central government. . .Experience has shown that since the Area Commissioners have no statutory powers under the Local Government Ordinance but yet, in addition to being the central government representative at the district level they perform similar functions to the district councils. Such a situation. . .has resulted in many cases in making it impossible for the Area Commissioner to obtain cooperation from the councils. It is therefore considered that. . .the Area Commissioner should be made ex officio Chairman of the district councils. This is not considered a retrograde step to take. The Government should not at this stage of the development of local authorities make too much play with the idea of local autonomy. Guided democracy is necessary.⁴⁸

Burengelo in his reply first outlined the rapidity of the recent changes in the local government structures, stressing that some confusion and decline in their performance was inevitable. He then continued:

> This state of affairs has now created a situation whereby the local government system is in a position where it does not command the full trust of the central government. . .There are two alternatives: to take away all the powers which have been conferred in the councils and make them advisory to the central government or to concentrate on training not only the staff to man the councils but also the councillors themselves. The first of these is retrograde and reminiscent of colonial rule.⁴⁹

The particular issue in this exchange was resolved along lines nearer to Burengelo's position than to Namata's. The government introduced a law which gave the Minister the power to name an Area Commissioner as Chairman of a Council, should he judge it to be necessary. However, it was not mandatory. Indeed the threat itself proved sufficient and the power was never used. More important, however, was the fact that an autonomous and representative local government remained the model and the goal. Although the government sometimes assumed a very close direction of a local government's activity, it did so in ways which did not contradict the formal responsibility of the Councils for these services. Thus, for example, although the Local Education Authorities were carefully regulated and the District Education Officers played a major role in them, they were nevertheless, in law, committees of their District Councils. Similarly the District Development Committees which were set up in every District in 1963 under the chairmanship of the Area Commissioner to coordinate the development activities of the central government departments and the local authorities, were established as committees of the District Councils.

Simultaneously with these developments, many in TANU came to the view that the ideal of autonomous local authorities was out of harmony with the emerging ideology of a democratic one-party state. They saw the local Councils as rivals to the local branch of TANU. There was, as the Commission on the One-Party State commented, 'considerable confusion between the role of TANU and that of the local Authorities'.[50] The Commission did not seek to resolve this confusion by recommending that the District conference of TANU replace the District Council. It did however seek to bring their structures closer together. It recommended that the District Executive Committee of TANU should be ex officio members of the District Council. Neither the government nor the party accepted this particular recommendation. Instead, in 1966 the government introduced a series of reforms which closely integrated the party and the local authorities. At the village level the institutions of each were totally merged, with village development committees being established whose members would be the TANU cell-leaders in the ward. At the District level, elections were introduced which were very similar to the national electoral system. Candidates present themselves, the branch annual conference votes its preference as between them and the District Executive Committee of TANU then selects which two of these candidates will be presented to the electorate on the ballot. A further integrating measure was the decision that the District Chairman of TANU should become the Chairman of the District Council. Finally, all elected Councillors were to be members of the party's annual District conference.[51] Under these changes, the local governments continued to be recognizably separate structures. Moreover, local elections became much more frequent than previously, though within a system that assured TANU control. An effort had clearly been made to make representative local government and one-party rule compatible one with the other, along lines similar to the way in which a reconciliation had been sought in the previous year between a representative legislature and a single-party system.

This reconciliation at the District level collapsed within a few years. Although this collapse takes us beyond the years being considered in this book, it illuminates the problem of participation in a one-party system as it was emerging in the years 1965 7. In 1971 the Tanzanian government decided totally to scrap the local governments. All local services are now run by the appropriate central government department. In each District a District Development and Planning Committee coordinates and plans all local services.

The reasons for this dramatic change in policy are largely administrative rather than political. The local government system had certainly provided every opportunity for the central government to control the development of local government in any way it wished. But the controls were complex and they required continuous and careful detailed attention by civil servants who were committed to the development of autonomous local governments. The civil service however was greatly overextended. The promotion of local government gradually lost what priority it once had had as an objective of policy. For example, the cadre of local government officers was quickly raided for personnel for other tasks. By 1965 the local government officers were abolished altogether as a special cadre, far sooner than the efficiency of the local authorities justified. The Ministry of Local Government was severely understaffed. It could neither review closely the affairs of the local governments nor effectively protect their interests against encroachments by other Ministries. As a result the controls which were theoretically ample were in fact not well used. Maladministration and financial inefficiencies were neither quickly spotted nor effectively checked. By 1965, in area after area of local government activity, the only answer seemed to be a central government takeover.

An example may help to explain the process just described. By 1968 perhaps the most glaring example of the failure of the local authorities was felt to be in the field of primary education. District Council after District Council had gravely overextended its school building program and had acquired soaring recurrent expenditures on education. These first threatened all other local services and finally endangered the solvency of the Councils themselves. Yet the central government and the party had always had ample powers to check this. The Regional Commissioner could have vetoed expenditures at any time and he could have insisted upon a more careful planning of the financial resources of the Council. The Ministry of Education could have used its control over the supply of teachers to secure a more manageable development. The party in theory could have used its control of the Council to correct these abuses as they emerged. All of these controls existed. None of them were used. By 1968, as a result of overspending on education, many Councils were near to bankruptcy and the central government had to take over responsibility for the payment of all teachers. Similar gross administrative inadequacies led to a gradual takeover by the Regional Road Authorities of all responsibility for local roads and to a full takeover of responsibility for rural health services by the Ministry of Health. When finally the collection of local rates also became increasingly inefficient, the total takeover of local government seemed the only reasonable response to a situation that had been allowed to deteriorate for far too long.[52]

Nyerere's reaction to these developments is illuminating. He tried to save local government. As recently as 1967 he had stressed that autonomous and democratic local government was an integral part of his vision of a socialist Tanzania.[53] His inclination was to keep the local governments going despite their present inadequacies. However, he finally came to the view that the whole structure was an obstacle to the achievement of an effective relationship between the agents of the central government and the local representatives of the people. Instead therefore of trying any longer to keep alive the complex local government system, he began to experiment with new structures which might produce a more fruitful relationship between central initiators of change and local representatives.

This search for new structures was a factor in the creation in 1968 of the Regional Development Committees. Each year the government since that date has given sizable funds for local development projects which are chosen by these Committees. This search contributed also to the major decentralization of government which Nyerere began actively to consider in 1968 and which he introduced in 1972.[54] The new institutions with which he proposed to replace the local authorities were the District Development Councils and District Development and Planning Committees. Each Council, he announced, would consist of the elected members of the old District Council plus the District Officers of the government development Ministries. The Committee, which will be the executive body, consists of these Officers and some ten elected members of the Council under the chairmanship of the Area Commissioner. The Council and the Development and Planning Committee concern themselves with the whole range of government development activities in the District. Elected members are thus able to discuss a wider range of government activities than they could on the District Councils, but it will be within structures in which their role is advisory and in which there is no suggestion that a locally elected council should ever have autonomous responsibilities for local services.

Government policy in regard to local government has thus evolved in a direction very similar to that taken by policy towards political opposition groups and towards the trade unions and the cooperative movement. The independence of each of these has been thoroughly undermined in the interest of efficiency, of a greater social cohesion and of a more unified and sustained leadership from TANU. The effort has then been made to achieve a closely integrated national political system in which socialist leadership through TANU and the central government can be combined with a meaningful degree of popular participation. In regard to local government, the more immediate result which must be acknowledged has been the destruction of institutions which contributed a pluralistic element to the political scene and which offered some check to oligarchic tendencies at the centre. As in the case of the reforms relating to the trade unions and the cooperatives, the centralizing consequences of these changes and their authoritarian potential are immediately apparent, while the possibility of increased popular participation within a more closely integrated national political system remains has been created but is still to be realized.

This is not to conclude that the result is in some way less democratic. It cannot be essential to the democratic character of a country's institutions that it struggle on with a local government system, a trade union movement and a cooperative movement that have severe structural faults, are grossly inefficient and bring into prominence narrow and parochial aspirations that threaten the accomplishment of national objectives under national leaders who have every bit as much claim to be representative leaders as have the leaders of the trade unions, the cooperatives and the local governments.

Two observations however can be made. The failure as yet to make a reality of popular participation in these once more-autonomous institutions has widened the gap between the reality of Tanzanian politics and Nyerere's vision of a truly democratic society as a self-governing community of equals who share a harmonious and closely integrated common life, for democracy conceived in these terms requires above all the active involvement of citizens in structures that directly affect their daily life. Finally, these developments relating to local government, to the trade unions and to the cooperatives mean that the democratic character of the Tanzanian political system depends, in large part, upon the reality of the popular participation and the democratic control that are achieved within the national political institutions.

The search for appropriate democratic controls: the democratic one-party state

The most important innovation which can be attributed primarily to Nyerere during the years 1963 to 1967 was the democratic one-party state Constitution which was introduced in Tanganyika in July 1965. By mid 1962, Nyerere had come to the firm view that democracy did not require a competitive party system. His vision of a democratic society was not that of the pluralist, constitutional democracy of Western democratic theory. Rather the ideal democratic society was the self-governing community of equals in which each accepts a moral responsibility for the welfare of his fellows. Democratic self-government in this intimate communal sense is most easily conceived as feasible in small communities. Nyerere felt that many traditional African communities were democratic societies in this sense. The contemporary challenge as Nyerere saw it was to find an equivalent for democracy of the sort experienced in those traditional societies which would be appropriate to a modern nation-state. His answer, it will be recalled, was a Legislative Assembly of representatives, chosen by local communities, who would then take their decisions as lawmakers after thorough discussion. Nyerere's ideal was thus a government by men of goodwill who are trusted by their fellow citizens and are electorally responsible to them.[55]

This view was in many ways closer to a no-party system than to a one-party system. The party would be coterminal with the nation. All citizens would be involved in selecting their representatives and the selection procedures would be such as to exclude the influence of factions and the exploitation of ethnic, religious and similar divisive group identities. Nyerere recognized that, even in such circumstances, decisions in a National Assembly might be influenced by narrow and selfish interests. Nevertheless, he felt that a constitutional system should be organized on the presumption that individuals would in fact cooperate and that elected representatives would pursue the public good. This he hoped would encourage and strengthen the development of standards of public morality which such a system requires. There is room in this conception of democracy for leadership by example, explanation and exhortation, but no room at all for any vanguard which claimed that it could perceive the people's true interests better than the people itself and that therefore it should rule on the people's behalf.[56]

Nyerere came to these convictions about democracy in Tanzania at the same time as the oligarchic tendencies within TANU were manifesting themselves in a demand that TANU should be made the sole legal political party in the country. In a brilliant and sustained exercise in democratic leadership, Nyerere succeeded in converting this demand into a welcome acceptance of a new Constitution which, while introducing a one-party state, also assured very significant popular electoral participation within that system.

In January 1963 Nyerere announced that he would appoint a commission to advise the government on how it could best introduce a democratic one-party state in Tanzania. The Commission was appointed a year later.[57] Nyerere took great care in the terms of reference which he gave to the Commission. The Commission was instructed that the one-party state should be established in the context of what Nyerere called 'our national ethic'.[58] He proceeded then to define this national ethic. It was an un-compromising affirmation of the nation's commitment to individual liberty, social justice, democratic participation and racial equality. He also defined for the Commission a comprehensive set of questions which it was instructed to consider. These were a detailed elaboration in question form of the implications of his basic instruction to the Commission that Tanganyika was to establish 'a free, democratic and stable one party state'.[59] The questions reveal an acute awareness of the dilemmas involved in seeking to establish TANU as the only legal national political move-ment in Tanganyika while yet maintaining democratic participation in the politics of the country. The emphasis is very much on the arrangements within a one-party state which would be necessary 'for the full expression of the people's will...[and] the untrammelled free choice of the people as regards to both their President and their Representatives in the Legis-lature'.[60] Nyerere even asks the Commission 'How can freedom of the people to form pressure groups for particular purposes be insured?'[61] There is no reference in these questions to any of the problems which would have required answers if the objective had been to establish a state run by a socialist vanguard party. This is hardly surprising. Nyerere's concern was how to avoid an elite or vanguard party while nevertheless creating a single-party system. He was therefore after ways to maximize popular electoral participation in a one-party system.

Nyerere selected the members of the Commission extremely carefully. The Commission was chaired by Kawawa and included four other African Members of Parlament, including Oscar Kambona, the Secretary-General of TANU. The other members were an Asian and a European Member of Parliament, four senior African civil servants and Roland Brown, the trusted expatriate Attorney-General. One of the civil servants, Amon Nsekela, was named by the President to serve as Secretary to the Commission. Nyerere had not excluded those in the party who had wanted an oligarchic pattern of rule but he had been careful to establish a Commission which would not be dominated by them. He encouraged the Commission to invite public submissions and to tour the country in order to hold public meetings. Even after its appointment he kept a close watch on its proceedings through continuing informal contact, particularly with Kawawa and Nsekela.

Nyerere had thus endeavoured to assure that the Commission would produce recommendations for a one-party state which would be of the sort which he wanted. Oscar Kambona, perhaps the most openly authoritarian of the TANU leaders, quickly found that he had been thoroughly out-manoeuvred. He stopped attending the Commission meetings and did not sign the final report.[62]

The Commission did not in fact follow every one of Nyerere's instructions to it. For example, it did not consider Nyerere's question of how citizens could be assured the right to form pressure groups. It also recommended a system of elections for the President which was a serious retreat from that 'untrammelled free choice' which Nyerere had asked for. Nevertheless, to a very significant extent the report of the Commission and the Constitution which was based upon it were a shrewd and highly original effort to build a political system which would reflect Nyerere's conception of a form of democracy appropriate to Tanzania.

Nyerere was able to achieve this for reasons that extend beyond the tactical skill with which he guided the One-Party Commission. The more fundamental reason was that he reflected popular attitudes on the one-party state a good deal more accurately than did those of his colleagues who favoured a more authoritarian single-party system. Within the rank and file of the party and in the country more generally there was little interest in entrenching the leadership of TANU as a ruling oligarchy. This was quickly borne out by the evidence submitted to the Commission as it toured the country hearing witnesses and receiving memoranda.[63] There was widespread support for the proposition that TANU should be the sole political movement in Tanzania. Factions and alternative parties were deplored because they threatened the unity of Tanzania. However, alongside this conviction was an equally widespread belief that there should be effective democratic checks on those exercising power. There was no support for the idea of rule by an ideological elite. The only limits to popular participation which were accepted and supported were the minimal limits necessary to preserve a continuing central role for TANU as the national movement. The reasons for supporting the one-party state were nationalist rather than socialist. TANU was seen as representing the nation. All men of goodwill should therefore be able to join TANU. No barrier should exist to their membership. The Commission itself made this point in these terms:

> The principles of TANU as set out in Article 2 of the TANU Constitution, do not contain any narrow ideological formulations which might change with time and circumstance. They are a broad statement of political faith. We believe they carry the support of the vast majority of the people of Tanganyika and must strike a responsive chord in men of good will in every civilized country in the world. A party based upon these principles and requiring adherence to them as a condition of membership would be open to all but an insignificant minority of our citizens and would, we believe, be a truly national movement.[64]

This affirmation, of course, conceals a real difficulty. The Commission recommended that the government enforce and perpetuate by law a dominance which TANU had so far earned for itself. However the point that is relevant to the argument here is that the Commission found widespread support for what were in fact the three essential components of Nyerere's position, namely that TANU should rule as a single party, that it should be open to all men of goodwill and that there should be effective democratic controls exercised over the government created by it. Although Nyerere and the Commission were highly innovative in the arrangements which they proposed for a democratic one-party state, their fundamental objectives were very close to popular aspirations. Nyerere was thus acting in this matter very much as a democratic leader. He was in harmony with the popular will. He was defining it more sharply, prescribing what institutions it would require and then acting astutely to secure their introduction. This representative quality of his leadership helps to explain why he was effective in winning TANU's support for a one-party system which was very significantly different from the initial authoritarian ideas of many in leadership positions in TANU at the time.

The actual constitutional arrangements which were introduced need to be only briefly summarized here.[65] They are an original effort to construct a democratic Constitution which would reflect a communitarian view of democracy rather than an individualist and pluralist view, to use rather inadequate labels to identify the distinction between Nyerere's democratic values on the one hand and those of the main Western tradition of constitutional democracy on the other. The main features of the Tanzania electoral system which permit Tanzania to be called a democratic one-party state are the following:

1 Anyone may be nominated to be a candidate for election to the National Assembly if he or she is a member of TANU and has the support of twenty-five electors.

2 TANU is not a closed and ideologically exclusive party. Membership is open to anyone willing to accept the aims and objectives of TANU, a requirement that has excluded very, very few from party membership.

3 In each District the Annual District Conference, a comparatively large and representative party meeting, interviews all the candidates in each constituency within the District and votes its preference as amongst them.

4 The National Executive Committee of TANU then decides which two of the nominated candidates in each constituency will in fact be presented to the electorate as candidates. In the first election Nyerere introduced the further important rule that the NEC would only upset the ranking of candidates which had been done by an Annual District Conference when the NEC agreed that there were compelling reasons why one or other of the top two names should not be put to the electorate.

5 The electorate campaign which then follows operates within a set of rules designed to assure as fair a contest as possible. No candidate may spend any money on his own campaign. All election meetings are

organized by the District Executive Committee of the party and each meeting is addressed by both candidates in the constituency. No candidate can claim that he is supported by any prominent TANU leader and no one may campaign in any constituency on behalf of a candidate other than the candidate himself. No tribal language may be used in electioneering and no appeal may be made to issues of race, tribe or religion. A three-man supervisory team of TANU elders from outside the region attends all the election meetings to assure that these rules are obeyed.

This electoral system goes a long way to provide an Assembly of individuals who have been selected for their personal characteristics in an election which excludes organized factions and which minimizes selfish and divisive appeals. At every stage the system reflects Nyerere's particular vision of a communitarian democracy. This is true even of the decision to include several other categories of members in the National Assembly. In addition to the elected members there were, in 1966, 14 National Assembly members elected by the Assembly itself from amongst a list of nominees submitted to it by major national institutions such as NUTA, the Co-operative Union, the Tanganyika African Parents Association, and the University of Dar-es-Salaam. There were also 17 members nominated by the President directly, 7 of them Zanzibaris and 10 from the mainland. All 20 Regional Commissioners (including the three Zanzibari members) were members along with the 17 members of the Zanzibar Revolutionary Council.[66]

The Zanzibari members were *sui generis*. However the other members reflect a view of the National Assembly as being not so much representative of a sovereign people but as representing a well-integrated nation. Once an assembly is regarded in those terms, new categories of members can be added who, though not elected, would be able to contribute positively to the work of the assembly. This was the logic behind the appointment of the non-elected members. The ten Presidential nominees and the ten national members were expected to bring to Parliament special abilities and a breadth of vision which might otherwise be lacking. The Regional Commissioners, in turn, were seen as 'a link between the government, the party and the people...with an important role to play in Parliament'.[67] A final indication of the influence of Nyerere's views was the decision of the National Executive Committee to refuse to consider as a candidate for one of the ten national members anyone who was an officer in the institution nominating him. The national members were not to be representative of special interests. They were to be men and women who would be particularly well equipped to provide a national perspective in Parliamentary debates.

The first election under this Constitution took place in October 1965. There were 803 candidates for the 107 elected seats. In 6 constituencies only one candidate was nominated and in a further 4 only two were nominated. There were thus 97 constituencies in which there were more than two candidates and for which therefore the NEC had to select the two candidates for the final election. The NEC set aside either the first or the second choice of the District conferences in only 16 cases. The whole process resulted in a significant replacement of Members of Parliament. Twenty-seven sitting members chose not to seek reelection. Thirteen members including 3 junior Ministers either failed to rank first or second in the District conference vote or were rejected by the NEC. Finally the election itself eliminated a further 17 Members of Parliament including 2 Ministers and 6 junior Ministers. Eighty-six of the 107 elected members of the 1965 National Assembly were therefore new to it.

The 1965 Constitution thus provided for meaningful democratic participation. The people were given constitutional means to express their discontent towards those in power and the people used it. Those who had lost popular confidence were replaced by new members in whom the people had confidence. The regime had thus found a way to open up its leadership to those within TANU's rank and file who were politically able and ambitious and who could revitalize the party's links with the people. All this happened without any undermining of TANU's position. Indeed this increased capacity to respond to democratic pressures must have further consolidated TANU's status as the national political movement.

Two further features of the elections under the 1965 Constitution should be noted. They are very unlikely to produce a vigorous national debate on a major national issue. As factions and national campaigning are both ruled out, there is no easy way by which most constituencies can see their choice of a member as expressing a decision upon a major policy issue. The elections are not intended to have such a consequence. They are not designed to provide a means whereby popular sovereignty can be expressed directly upon major issues. They are designed to assure that each constituency chooses its representative without the intrusion upon it of outside pressures. These representatives are then to discuss and to decide upon the major national issues. They are not the cyphers through which a sovereign people records its decision.

A further consequence of this electoral system is that it is a barrier to certain types of socialist mobilization. It is not appropriate nor suitable for a mobilization effort that seeks to organize the masses against any indigenous class enemies. The underlying assumption of the system is that the nation is harmonious and united and that the elections involve the choice of trusted individuals who will then legislate on the nation's behalf. Its ideological implications are nationalist and populist rather than Marxist.

It is however too soon to draw conclusions about the longer-term consequences of the Tanzanian democratic one-party system. In its early manifestation as well as in its original purposes it was intended to provide and did provide an effective popular check upon authoritarian tendencies within the TANU leadership. However, the electoral system could easily be adapted to a more authoritarian style of leadership. If TANU were to become a vanguard party whose members must meet rigorous ideological tests, the whole character of the elections would change. Those who could become candidates would be much more narrowly circumscribed and in consequence so also would the people's choice. The election might continue to be a useful technique whereby the party seeks to engage the commitment of the masses, but they would no longer provide anything like the same degree of meaningful popular participation. The democratic features in the Constitution could be very significantly nullified if the President and the NEC were to use their powers to control the electoral process rather than to make a reality of its democratic features. Potential candidates could be dissuaded from running, and the local party machinery could be used to influence voting at the District conference. The NEC could ignore District conference rankings much more frequently. It could, for example, drop popular candidates whom it disliked. It could manipulate the ballot in order to favour a candidate whom it preferred. It could, for example, select for the final ballot in a constituency the candidate which it supported along with a second candidate whom the NEC knew to be one of the least popular of those nominated.

These particular possible developments have so far been avoided in Tanzania. Nevertheless, for a different reason, it must be concluded that the elections have been less significant than they might have been as a check upon the oligarchic tendency within the Tanzanian political leadership. The importance of the elections in providing such a check depends in large part upon the importance of the National Assembly within the Tanzanian political system. The Assembly, however, has never established itself as a vigorous and fearless legislature.

The first Parliament, which sat from 1960 to 1965, was cautious, indeed timid in its exercise of its sovereign responsibilities.[68] In almost all cases government bills received but a superficial scrutiny. They were frequently and unnecessarily introduced under certificates of urgency which permit bills to pass through the first, second and third readings in a single day without the bill even having been previously published before the date of the debate. Many other bills also went through their three stages on the same day. Motions of adjournment were rarely used for general and critical debates, amendments were seldom introduced, parliamentary questions were rarely pressed to the point of embarrassment and sensitive issues and whole areas of policy, such as the military and foreign affairs, tended to be completely ignored save for speeches which were little more than affirmations of support. Parliament did not have the prestige or status that would have enabled it to assert itself against the TANU leadership. There were clearly present, as Hopkins comments, latent political norms that dictated that delicate and controversial issues are best avoided or commented upon only in a constructive manner'.[69]

For a brief period after the 1965 elections, it looked as if Parliament might become more assertive. Nyerere had hoped for a National Assembly which would engage in open and vigorous debate. The vision was still that of an Assembly of trusted men who would reach their decisions after thorough discussion. He welcomed the Commission's recommendation that the Assembly improve its competence by establishing a series of standing committees. In opening the new Parliament he said that there would be no party whips. In 1965, many of the newly elected members came to the Assembly with an enhanced sense of its importance. As a result there were a number of debates in the first several years after the election in which the government was more sharply criticized than it had been since the more vigorous debates of the 1960–1 period. The issues chosen for this criticism suggest that the Members of Parliament were representing popular opinion. They criticized the purchase of an additional seventeen Mercedes-Benz cars for Regional Commissioners after a Presidential order that the government should not purchase any car whose price exceeded £900. They opposed the introduction of substantial ex-gratia payments to Ministers in lieu of pensions. Several members vigorously criticized a heavy-handed and insensitive assertion of government authority by the Regional Commissioner in Bukoba in the promotion of socialist villages there.

These criticisms were more than the party leadership in the National Assembly wished to tolerate. Nyerere's ability to generate a more tolerant attitude towards parliamentary critics was limited because he was not himself a member of the Assembly. It was the party leaders in the Assembly who interacted with these backbench critics and who, in fact, defined the limits of their right to comment and to question. The backbenchers were ill-matched for this interaction. The electoral system had been designed to assure that they did not come as representatives of any outside organization or group. They had no political support wider than their own constituency following to back them in any assertion of the rights of Parliament as against the government. They were therefore easily routed. In October 1968, despite an effort by Nyerere to protect them, the NEC expelled seven of the most active of the Members of Parliament along with two other Members, Oscar Kambona and E. Anangisye, whose expulsion had different and more justified causes.[70] These expulsions had as their intended consequence that these men lost their seats in Parliament. It was a decisive indication of the weakness of Parliament as an instrument to control the political leadership.

There is a further important dimension to the failure of the National Assembly to establish itself in a central position within the Tanzanian political system. The Assembly lost out not only to the government leaders, but to the party as well. Gradually over the period 1960 to 1968, the

National Executive Committee of TANU increased its authority, prestige and political importance until by 1967 it had replaced the National Assembly as the paramount representative political institution in Tanzania. This had not been part of the original intention of the TANU leaders. They had initially sought to work the parliamentary institutions very much according to the assumptions and conventions that have been traditionally appropriate for a constitutional democracy on the Westminster model.[71] There were, in particular, frequent official statements of support for the sovereignty of Parliament.[72] These were not pro-forma statements. They reflected the fact that the leaders of TANU had focused their interests and energies upon the running of the government. The senior leaders became Ministers, many others became, or hoped to become, Members of Parliament and others still sought well-paid government jobs. As a result, after independence TANU lost to the government or to political offices almost all of its abler administrators. No effort was made to maintain, let alone to augment the competence of the party. It is hard to exaggerate the disorganization and incompetence that existed in the central offices of the party by 1965. These offices did not receive regular payments of fees from branches. There had been no approved annual estimates for the previous two years. There were no staff records, no established salary scales and no system of regular reporting from the branches to the central offices. This in turn increased the tendency of the leaders to rely very largely upon the machinery of government. Very quickly the Cabinet, the Ministries and Parliament, far more than the party, were central to their interests and involvements. Effective decision-making very largely took place, in consequence, within the structures of the government rather than of the party.

Despite the severe decline in the administrative competence of TANU, the two major representative party assemblies, the National Conference and the National Executive Committee, continued to meet.[73] The Conference met annually for a few days a year until 1965 and since then has met biennially. Its membership now includes two elected representatives from each branch, all TANU Regional and District chairmen, all Members of Parliament and all members of the NEC. It is thus well representative of the rank and file of the party and of its middle-rank cadre. However, it is a large body. Its membership now exceeds fifteen hundred persons. It meets infrequently and for only a few days. It is chaired by Nyerere and is run in a casual fashion which encourages frank comment but does little to equip the Conference to take a lead itself in identifying issues and in defining positions. In these circumstances, the Conference has not been a policy-initiating body nor even a body which deliberates in a systematic way upon the major policies of the TANU government. Instead the National Conference has been a ratifying body whose support increases the legitimacy of the government and provides an occasional opportunity for the government to inform itself of the reaction to its policies of the party and, hopefully, of the populace as well.

The National Executive Committee is a smaller body whose members include both elected individuals and important party officers. The Regional Commissioners in their capacity as Regional Party Secretaries are members, as are the three or four senior TANU leaders who are the party's national officeholders. The major representative component of the NEC are the Members of the National Executive (the MNEs) who are elected by the Conference to represent each of the Regions, and the Regional chairmen of TANU. The NEC includes the members of the Central Committee,* and senior officers or delegates from the major organizations affiliated to TANU.

There are significant differences between the representatives that are chosen to be members of the National Assembly and those who are MNEs or Regional chairmen of TANU. Many of the MPs are well-educated men and women, often with a wide experience in public affairs.[74] They included a large number who have had no particular status in TANU. Cliffe estimates that seventy-four per cent of the winning candidates in 1965 were 'merely card holding members' and that only twenty of the winning candidates had joined TANU in the first two years of its existence.[75] Until 1965 MPs had to be literate in English. If they are to be at all effective they have to be able to deal knowledgeably with complex financial, legal and administrative matters. As the Ministers of the government are very largely appointed from their ranks, the natural ambition of the more enterprising of the MPs is to be appointed to a Cabinet post. Thus not only the Ministers but those MPs who aspire to be Ministers have an incentive to take a national viewpoint rather than a parochial one on important issues.

The elected MNEs and the Regional chairmen of TANU are a different type of politician. In most cases they have had many years of political activity at the local and District level. They often speak little or no English and their formal education has been significantly less than the MPs. Information available on 10 of the 17 MNEs in 1968 shows that none of them had completed secondary school and 6 had had little or no primary education. Of the 13 Regional chairmen on whom information could be obtained, one had been to a teacher-training college and one to a middle school. Of the other 11, 3 had had no schooling and the remaining 8 had had but a limited number of years at primary school.

---

* The Central Committee, despite the associations of its name, was throughout this period deliberately kept a casual and minor committee by Nyerere. Its members were nominated by him and were a miscellaneous group of TANU elders and loyalists from the Dar-es-Salaam area. It was little more than a housekeeping committee. It was in no sense a central policy-planning body. Only recently has it become a powerful and more representative body.

Almost all of these 23 men and women had been members of TANU for many years. A majority of them had joined within the first two years after TANU had been formed. They had typically held a series of lesser elected positions within TANU in their areas before becoming MNEs or Regional chairmen. They were significantly older on the average than the MPs. Not one of these 23 members of the NEC was under thirty-five years of age while over half the MPs were.[76]

The NEC meets regularly four times a year and it is a manageable size. It might have become, from the beginning, a major policy-initiating body. However, it was not organized for the purpose. The Central Committee did not generate a flow of carefully prepared policy proposals and the party bureaucracy was incapable of doing this. The NEC did not create its own well-organized committee system. It therefore could not itself produce a wide range of policies. There was usually no advanced circulation of an agenda and little if any circulation of preparatory papers prior to its meetings. The NEC occasionally was seized of an issue which might then result in governmental action. However the NEC was in no way a rival to the Cabinet as a policy-initiating or policy-deciding body. The NEC's role in these regards was merely supplementary to the institutions of government.

Nevertheless the NEC was important politically. It provided Nyerere and the TANU leadership with a valued means whereby they could keep in touch with the middle-rank leaders in the party. It was also a supplementary channel through which local political discontents and restlessness might be made known to the national leaders. It is fair to say that the meetings of the NEC tended to be orchestrated by Nyerere to maximize these advantages. His opening speech often provided the main topic which would then dominate the NEC's discussions. He thus used the NEC to win party endorsement for his ideas and to gain directly a feel of popular reactions to these ideas. He chaired the meetings in a relaxed fashion which kept the discussions open and frank. In a society in which parliamentary discussion was none too vigorous, the newspapers were controlled or extremely timid and the upward flow within the bureaucracy of honest reporting on local reactions was halting at best, an institution able to fulfill these functions was an important political institution. However the NEC was rarely, during these years, an initiator of policies or an effective supervisor of government. These roles remained very largely with the Cabinet and Parliament.

This distribution of functions between the institutions of government and the party seemed at first to be reasonable and appropriate. However, it was not maintained. Instead, there was a shift in the comparative importance of the Cabinet and Parliament on the one hand and the NEC on the other, until, by 1967, the NEC was unquestionably the most important of these institutions.[77] There were a number of interrelated reasons for this shift. Firstly, the Cabinet failed to maintain its central position. In 1962 the Cabinet was a collection of men who were of political importance in their own right. Some Ministers such as Bomani, Kahama and Kawawa had had leading positions in either the cooperative or the trade union movements. Some were leaders of powerful tribes, as were Fundikira and Eliufoo. Some, such as Kambona, had proven rhetorical skills which made them a power in the party. The Cabinet was therefore a group of leaders whom it was of real political value to keep united. Whatever the constitutional provisions, it made good political sense to regard the Cabinet as the central policy-initiating body.

This political factor gradually became less significant. Cabinet Ministers who had had a strong institutional base for their political influence in 1960 found it was of declining importance as these organizations were brought under closer government control. Many Ministers became so involved in their departmental responsibilities that by 1965 they were no longer the independent political force they had been in 1960. As a result, a full Cabinet discussion was often no longer the most effective way for Nyerere to sound opinion upon a complex and potentially divisive political issue. By 1967 he had taken a significant number of major policy decisions without any Cabinet discussion. These included the ending of discrimination against non-African citizens in the civil service in 1964, the breaking of diplomatic relations with Britain in 1965 and the introduction of the one-party system. More recently neither the Arusha Declaration nor the two major policy papers on education and on rural development which followed it were preceded by any Cabinet discussions.

Parallel to this, the National Assembly failed to emerge as the unchallengeably dominant representative institution in the country. Its origins, its style and its procedures all kept it distant from the rural masses. It was not helped by the fact that Nyerere did not add the prestige and status of his presence to the Assembly nor make the effort directly to aid the Assembly to establish itself in fact as the sovereign institution which it was in law. The National Conference and the NEC were often more appropriate forums for the discussion of new policies, particularly when these policies depended upon their effective promotion by the party and the active cooperation of the masses. Nyerere therefore began to choose with each new policy which was the best arena in which to present it. By 1967 many major political policies were being brought to the NEC first rather than to Parliament. This was true, for example, of the Second Five Year Plan, the Arusha Declaration and the decision to promote socialist villages (*ujamaa vijijini*).

TANU, despite the declining competence of its central organization, was more important in the popular view and in its own conception of its role, than the early emphasis on the sovereignty of Parliament allowed. Its sense of its own special claims as *the* national movement merged with the

oligarchic aspirations of some of its leaders to generate the powerful demand, already discussed, for a one-party state. Once the force of that
demand had been conceded, a redefinition in the relationship of the
Assembly and the NEC and National Conference was inevitable. In 1965
the NEC acquired powers and a status equivalent to those of the National
Assembly. It was given the power to summons witnesses and to require the
production of documents, and its members were to receive the same
salaries and privileges as Members of Parliament.[78] The Presidential
Commission on the Democratic One Party State sought to define their
different roles in these terms:

> The role of the National Assembly and that of the NEC are essentially
> different. The NEC is concerned with the formulation of the broad
> lines of policy. It is the soul and conscience of the Party. . .The National
> Assembly, on the other hand, is primarily concerned with the more
> detailed task of giving effect to Government policy through appropriate
> legislative measures and exercising vigilant control over all aspects of
> Government expenditure.[79]

Briefly after the 1965 election some MPs sought to reassert the
supremacy of Parliament vis-à-vis the party. This issue was as important
an aspect of the controversy that led to the expulsion of the nine MPs in
October 1968 as was their challenge to the TANU leaders in Parliament.
Their expulsion settled this issue. The institutions of TANU from then
on were accepted as superior to those of the government. Kawawa made
this point in the Assembly in 1966 arguing 'that TANU is more
supreme than the government and that the government as such is the
people's instrument for administration'.[80] He made the same point two
years later, saying with reference to TANU and the Afro-Shirazi Party:
'These are the institutions which are leading this country. It is these institutions which initiate and decide on this country's policies. This Assembly
and the Revolutionary Council in Zanzibar merely assist the Government
in implementing the policies of these two Parties.'[81]

This view of the National Assembly as an assisting and implementing
agency is a far cry from the initial conception of Parliament as a modern
equivalent to the elders sitting under a tree discussing matters until agreement is reached. If the institutions of the party were to become as representative and as open as the Assembly, it could be argued that despite the
decline in the position of the Assembly, the NEC and the Assembly together will assure effective democratic participation and control. However,
the immediate consequence of the declining vigour of Parliament and the
rising stature of the NEC has been significantly to lessen the importance
of the elections as providing a democratic control upon the oligarchic tendencies within the leadership. There has been a shift away from a representative institution whose members have been elected by the whole

people in well-run elections, whose debates are public and whose rules of procedure assure that the leaders remain answerable to it, towards an institution whose members are selected in a more casual manner by a much less numerous electorate, whose meetings are closed and whose open style of debate does not depend upon well-established procedures but upon the inclination of Nyerere as its chairman.

The reality of popular participation and democratic controls in Tanzania will thus depend increasingly upon their reality within not only Parliament but even more within the institutions of the party. That issue, by 1967, had yet to be tackled in any systematic way. It was at that time not a critical issue. Nyerere might have been content to leave it for a while to its own dynamics but for the appearance of a far more important dimension to this whole question, the emergence of class stratification within the African population of Tanzania and a widening economic gap between the rural and urban areas. These developments not only directly challenged Nyerere's basic values but seemed likely as well to reinforce the oligarchic tendency within TANU and to permit those in power to transform themselves into a self-perpetuating political class.

Economic stratification and class formation in Tanzania

Despite the central importance of agriculture in the economy of Tanzania, the peasant gained little from the annual growth rate of 4.2 per cent which had been achieved between 1960 and 1968. Declining world prices and a high rate of population increase very largely offset the impressive increases which were achieved in the cultivation of cotton, coffee, tea and other cash crops. The Treasury reported in 1967 that 'even with 1966's successful crop results it appears likely that rural per capita purchasing power is not more than 5 per cent above 1961'.[82] Even this very modest gain was more than offset by tax increases. On the average therefore peasant disposable income did not increase at all during the first six years of independence.*

The urban working class fared much better. The gap between urban and rural incomes began to widen soon after independence. In 1962 the

---

* The marketing boards and the cooperative societies each involved heavy deductions from the limited money which the peasants received for their crops. Tanzania, *Report of the Presidential Special Committee of Inquiry into Cooperative Movement and Marketing Boards* estimates that the average coffee farmer in Kilimanjaro paid 64.1% of his gross proceeds in production costs, 6.3% export tax, 4.7% in development levy, 3.8% in cesses, 6.9% in union and society levies and 7.7% in marketing board deductions (Appendix B, p. 63). The British Economic Mission produced similar figures to show, for example, that the total deductions from the price per 100 bags of maize produced by members of the Iringa Farmers Co-operative Union were almost 50% of the price paid to the farmer for his maize. ('Report of the British Economic Mission', ch. 11.)

government appointed a special Minimum Wage Commissioner to report upon urban wage levels. The Commissioner, Donald Chesworth, a British socialist, did not concern himself with the contrasts between urban and rural incomes. He concentrated upon the needs of urban workers and upon the merits of a higher wage level which would encourage workers to settle permanently in the towns. He recommended very significant increases in the minimum wages.[83] These recommendations were quickly accepted. They resulted in a twenty-seven per cent increase in the wage level in 1963. Urban wages continued to rise in each of the subsequent years. The government supported important increases in the sisal industry in 1964 and approved a twenty per cent rise in the minimum wage in Dar-es-Salaam in September 1965. As a result by 1966 wage levels were eighty per cent higher than in 1960, an increase which, in constant prices, amounted to a sixty-five per cent rise. It is a fair observation to suggest, as does Colin Leys, that one of the central policies of the government at this time was the utilization of the national surplus to buy the support of the urban workers.[84]

In addition to this widening gap between rural and urban incomes, significant class differences were developing within the rural and urban communities. In almost any area in which there had been peasant cash-crop cultivation some economic differentiation was probably inevitable. Over time, differences in the responsiveness of peasants to the initial opportunity to grow cash crops as well as differences in the size and productivity of their landholdings, their access to investible funds, their willingness to invest and the availability to them of casual labour for employment in 'peak' periods, were very likely to generate income differentials. These differences might at first be short-lived, for a prosperous farm would often be divided by the sons of the farmer who had developed it, on his death. However, as economic aspirations increased and new sources of income were introduced into the rural areas, cultural patterns changed. Families became smaller and inheritance patterns shifted. As a result, class stratification in the rural areas tended to become more prominent and more severe.[85]

The rural stratification which was occurring in Tanzania did not take place in defiance of government policies. The opening up of new areas, the promotion of new cash crops, the extension of agricultural credit, the work of the agricultural extension officers and the constant official exhortation to greater effort all tended to increase income differentials within the ranks of the peasantry. The economically successful farmer had responded to TANU's exhortations and the advice of the extension officers. Far from being a likely target of their censure and criticism, he was more likely to be an integral part of the leadership group within his community.[86]

Only rarely did the more successful farmers earn incomes approaching those of middle-rank or senior civil servants. Van Velzen reports, for example, that the most prosperous farmers in Rungwe District would be unlikely to earn a net income as high as the wages of the lowest-paid functionary in the civil service. Ruthenburg, in his study of a subdivision of Kilimanjaro, estimates that the coffee and banana farm of a size equal to the arithmetic mean of all farms in the area (2.2 acres) would yield a net annual income of Shs.1,323. As holdings ranged from one acre to four acres in size, the highest income would be unlikely to exceed Shs.2,200.[87] Sizable African capitalist farms have primarily appeared only in the comparatively few areas which have been newly opened by individual farmers and in which a new cash crop is being cultivated.[88] In most areas, however, agricultural development has not yet produced severe income differentials. Gottlieb's study shows that in the rural areas 'the decisive differentiation occurs by reason of the escalation of incomes arising outside farming operations proper'.[89] He also establishes that there has not yet emerged to any significant extent either a class of farmers that regularly employ others on their land or a class of farm workers that regularly work on the land of others for their livelihood. Gottlieb calculates that in 1967, out of a total of over five million Africans gainfully employed in agriculture, only 13,400 of these employed farm workers regularly and only 1,600 of them were employed by these African farmers.[90]

Nevertheless, in many rural areas, leadership, particularly in the co-operatives, in local government and in TANU, had increasingly been exercised by the economically more successful African farmers. Their economic activity, though motivated by a desire for personal gain, was also directly in response to the advice of both TANU and the government. They could understandably regard themselves as loyal TANU members. Yet for Nyerere and for others who had not lost sight of the long-term goal of a socialist and egalitarian society, there were problems in a pattern of rural growth which brought the wealthier and more successful farmers into prominence within the very institution on which they would in particular have to depend for the promotion of socialist and egalitarian objectives.[91]

An equally important feature of the class stratification which occurred in Tanzania in the 1960s was the emergence for the first time of a class of men and women who were employed in the modern sector of the economy and who earned incomes which were very significantly higher than those of African workers and peasants. This class hardly existed in 1960. Nevertheless, it was clear at that date that such a class was about to be created, for Africans would soon be replacing Europeans in the middle and senior ranks of the civil service. Nyerere anticipated the class consequences of this development as early as 1959. He took the position at that early date that African civil servants and politicians would have to accept that their salary scales should reflect local realities rather than imported British conceptions of what were suitable salaries.

We are not going to enter the government to make money. We are condemned to serve, condemned to wage war against poverty, disease and ignorance. I warn our future civil servants that they must think in terms of our country and not compare themselves with anyone outside this country. We are not going to get into power by promising fat salaries. We shall slash the salaries of local people; if necessary we shall slash them hard.[92]

As a move towards this end, in 1961 Nyerere appointed a salaries commission under the chairmanship of A. L. Adu, a senior Ghanaian civil servant. He asked it to devise 'a salary structure for the local civil service consonant with the general economic circumstances of the country'.[93]

The Commission's report and its reception by the civil service and by TANU illustrate how difficult it has been for Nyerere to implement any policy which was a product of his own deep convictions but which was not widely supported within the government or the party. Adu and his fellow commissioners produced a very competent report. However they were not fired by Nyerere's dominant concern for a more egalitarian society. In assessing the levels of remuneration which would be fair to the middle and senior ranks of the civil service they examined trends in the costs of living, family budgets and patterns of expenditures for these income groups and they studied rates of pay for comparable employment outside the government service. They recommended significant increases for the subordinate staff within the civil service. They rejected any cutting of the higher salary scales, arguing that 'it was advisable to relate the maximum salaries to such salaries as may be applicable for comparable posts in the adjoining territories or in commerce or in industry within Tanganyika'.[94] The government accepted the Commission's recommendations with only minor amendments. The result was that the salaries of subordinate staff were increased by twenty-eight per cent, with the starting salaries for unskilled staff increasing from Shs.107.50 per month to Shs.132. The recommendations as accepted added £1,100,000 to the government's wage bill.[95]

There had been no support in TANU or in the Cabinet for a radical egalitarian assault upon the middle and upper salary levels. When the report was discussed in Parliament almost all the speeches called upon the government to extend additional benefits to one or another category of civil servants. It was left to Nyerere to remind Parliament that it was the rural peasant, with a per capita income of under £20, who would have to pay the salary increases. His speech at the end of the debate amounted to a lament that TANU had not the moral conviction and courage to press for a more egalitarian wage and salary structure. He noted that the World Bank report had said that the Tanganyikan government could not expect to raise its revenues by more than £1,000,000. He went on to argue that if there was a person on the moon and he had taken the World Bank Report...and then taken the recommendations of the government and put them side by side, he would say 'this government!' An intelligent mission tells us that they cannot raise their revenue by more than £1,000,000 and they are handing all this £1,000,000 to their civil service. They must be in serious love with their civil service.[96]

Except for special increases to teachers and to police in 1964, salary scales for middle and upper levels within the civil service were not increased at all during the whole of the period covered by this study. However, as these were years of rapid promotion for Africans, there were many more highly paid Africans in 1967 than there had been in 1962. In 1962 there were 3,100 professional, administrative and technical jobs in Tanganyika. Only 1,300 of these were held by Africans. Eleven hundred of these 1,300 were teachers, medical technicians or nurses.[97] There were thus fewer than 200 Africans in all the other administrative, professional, technical jobs. In 1963 only 7,500 Africans, 0.08 per cent of the population, earned more than Shs.500 a month.[98] These numbers increased rapidly in the 1960s. By 1968 there were 10,200 Tanzanians in professional, administrative and technical occupations. By 1970, in contrast to the 7,500 Africans earning salaries of more than Shs.500 a month in 1963, there were over 37,400 Africans earning such incomes, including 11,500 who earned more than Shs.1,000 a month.

Africans in administrative, professional and technical positions in the civil service or in private employment were not the only ones to benefit directly and immediately as a result of independence. TANU politicians were also anxious to ensure that they too received high salaries. The salaries paid to the first thirty elected members of the Legislative Council had been £700 a year plus a variety of supplementary allowances. This was clearly a salary which took account of the fact that one-third of these members were Europeans and one-third were Asians. In 1961, in anticipation of an enlarged National Assembly most of whose members would be African, a committee of the Legislative Council considered afresh the question of the emoluments for Members of Parliament. The Committee made no pretence of assessing what ought to be the ratio between the income of elected members and the average income of their electors. Instead it took into account 'the emoluments which existed with regard to other Parliaments in the Commonwealth'. It was guided, it said, by the principle enunciated by Lloyd George in 1911 that members should be enabled 'to live comfortable and honourably but not luxuriously'.[99] The Committee recommended that members of the National Assembly receive an annual salary of Shs.14,000 a year plus a constituency allowance of Shs.6,000. The government accepted this recommendation. By so doing the political

Table 15. *High- and middle-level employment 1968–9*

	Citizens	Non-citizens	Total	Vacancies
I. University level				
Science/Maths-based	446	1,491	1,937	326
Arts-based	966	1,177	2,143	285
Total[a]	1,403	2,673	4,076	613
II. Sub-professional	8,797	2,146	10,943	668
III. Secondary school requirement[b]				
Skilled office	18,074	2,256	20,330	2,415
Skilled manual	7,412	1,341	8,753	192
Total	25,486	3,597	29,083	2,607

[a] Totals are as given in the source.
[b] Many of these posts were, however, filled by individuals without a secondary school certificate. The terminology used in the report is that these are jobs 'requiring a secondary school education for adequate performance of the full array of tasks involved'.
SOURCE: Tanzania, *Tanzania Second Five Year Plan, 1969–74*, vol. IV, tables 4, 5, 6.

Table 16. *African higher incomes 1964 and 1970*

	1964	1970
Exceeding Shs.100 per month		
A. Enterprise sector	2,246	6,707
B. Public sector	—	4,890
Total	2,246	11,597
Between Shs.500 and 999 per month		
A. Enterprise sector	7,269	11,148
B. Public sector	—	14,762
Total	7,269	25,910

SOURCE: Tanzania, *Survey of Employment and Earnings, Tanzania, 1970* (Dar-es-Salaam, 1972).

leaders of TANU made apparent their determination to take over the standards of living which had been set by their colonial rulers.

There continued to be pressure from within TANU to secure a greater number of highly paid political posts. Nyerere and the government made a number of important concessions to these pressures. The creation of Regional and Area Commissioners and the appointment of an increasing number of Parliamentary Secretaries each involved an increase in the number of political figures appointed to highly paid positions. In 1965 this number was very significantly increased when the government agreed to pay each member of the National Executive Committee of TANU a salary equal to that received by Members of Parliament.

By 1967 there was real class stratification within Tanzanian society. The Tanzanian government was hardly a government of working people and peasants. It was a government of politicians and civil servants whose incomes, although modest in Western or international terms, were nevertheless vastly higher than the incomes earned by ordinary Tanzanians. Some commentators have seized upon these facts as being of central importance to an understanding of the politics of independent Tanzania. They identify the civil service in particular as the new class enemy of the workers and peasants of Tanzania.[100] They fear that until its members have been severely humbled, the prospects of progressive change are slight. Arguments of this sort are oversimplified and unrealistic. In the period under study the African bureaucracy and the political leaders in Tanzania had not become a narrowly selfish oligarchy. They were not primarily concerned with the advancement of narrow class interests. There was, for example, no upward revision of the salary scales for middle and upper civil servants after 1961 despite the steady rise in their cost of living.[101] A continuing nationalist commitment, sustained professional standards, democratic pressures from within TANU, the leadership of Nyerere and the comparative weakness still of this elite as a socioeconomic class all checked the emergence of a crass and self-seeking oligarchic rule. It is wrong to argue as if the only alternatives were corrupt government by a 'parasitic political-bureaucratic bourgeoisie, the ally of imperialism'[102] or selfless rule by a vanguard whose members are committed to a socialist ideology and who share a common life with ordinary workers and peasants. These are not the alternatives between which African states have had somehow to choose. They are rather the two extremes of a spectrum which contains the whole variety of options which are theoretically open to these states. The Tanzanian political and bureaucratic leadership in the years under study was close to neither of these extremes. Its members were an elite. They enjoyed incomes very significantly higher than the average income of most Tanzanians. However their incomes were not being extracted from a resisting society which rejected their legitimacy. These salaries were part of an income and salary structure which was not challenged within the society. Moreover these salaries were approved by a government which was still widely popular. As a result, the politicians and civil servants had no reason to feel either guilty towards or threatened by ordinary citizens. They were able still to respond to a variety of professional, nationalist, democratic and ideological considerations and motives which, to varying degrees, operate to keep governments reasonably committed to the public good.

An example may help to establish the point which is being made. There is hardly an activity of government in which the African middle class is likely to be more directly and personally interested than the allocation of places in the secondary schools. It was crucially important for any primary school leaver to gain entry to a secondary school. However, by 1967 only one in eleven primary school leavers could do this. In 1967, for example, there were 6,635 students admitted to secondary schools in contrast to over 60,000 students who had finished primary school in that year.[103] A secondary school certificate was a virtual *laissez-passer* either to university or to a middle-level position. A student who failed to get into secondary school would be most unlikely ever to be able to earn a 'middle class' income. None knew this fact better than the members of the African middle class. They were bound to be very anxious that their children should secure secondary school places. If, therefore, the civil service were well on the way to becoming a self-perpetuating oligarchy, this tendency would reveal itself at an early stage in a serious intrusion of nepotism and corruption in the allocation of secondary school places.

One commentator indeed suggested in 1968 that 'there is already evidence that the selection of secondary schools is being tampered with. It would appear that the trend towards an educated oligarchy is well underway.'[104] An investigation made in 1969 to test the validity of this judgment suggests that it was, at that date at least, unjustified.[105] In response to the increasing pressure for secondary school places, a much more carefully controlled selection process was introduced in 1965. Under that process, each Region was allocated a share of form-one places in the residential secondary schools in Tanzania in proportion to the number of primary VII places in its government-assisted schools. This meant that the wealthier Districts, which had been able on their own to finance numbers of unassisted primary schools, did not receive an additional share of form-one places because of the graduates from these unassisted schools. This greatly helped to check any projection into the allocation of secondary school places of the advantages which wealthier Districts had secured for themselves in regard to primary places. The places in each of the secondary schools were awarded through a complicated system which was carefully designed to minimize the risk of favouritism. The key body in this process was a regional selection committee whose membership included primary school headmasters, school inspectors, TANU representatives and representatives of the Tanganyika African Parents Association. Even these committees, of course, may occasionally have succumbed to pressures from local leaders who wished to secure secondary school places for children who might not have received them in a truly competitive allocation. However, a system in which a widely representative committee takes the key decisions is less likely to become corrupt than one in which these decisions are made by individual bureaucrats, politicians or headmasters. This new allocation process was introduced by the Ministry of Education. Thus on an issue which was one of particular importance to members of the ruling strata, the bureaucracy acted not as the champion of its selfish interest but rather as the defender of the public good. Personal idealism, professional ethics, political leadership and democratic responsibility had combined to avert a potential abuse of power.

There were still important inequalities in the distribution of secondary school places. Children of literate parents had the nearly unavoidable advantages they always have in any system which does not positively favour children of workers and peasants. Moreover, the incorporation of a number of Asian non-residential secondary schools into the public school system in 1963 and 1964 meant that the ratio of primary VII to form-one places in the towns was lower than in rural areas. As these schools were day schools, their students had to be drawn from the towns and, in consequence, children in Dar-es-Salaam and in the other major towns in Tanzania had significantly greater opportunities to gain places in secondary schools than did children living in rural areas. This discrepancy worked to the advantage of the bureaucracy, for a high proportion of them lived in these favoured towns. Nevertheless the Ministry of Education sought to eliminate this feature by locating many of its new secondary schools in the less-favoured rural areas. On this issue as well, therefore, the Ministry followed policies which deliberately sought to promote the public good rather than to advance the self-interest of those exercising governmental power.

There were three decisions in which the Ministry of Education can fairly be said to have responded to political pressures. In 1963 and 1964, Tanzanian Asian candidates for secondary school places, particularly in Dar-es-Salaam, were proportionately much more successful than were African candidates. This caused a good deal of critical comment from the African community and, in response to it, the Ministry of Education quietly decided to give African students in the urban areas a clear preference over Asian candidates be they non-citizen or alien.*

Class interest appears to have influenced two further decisions. In 1965,

* This was defended to me by officials of the Ministry of Education in June 1966 as being necessary to avoid a much more severe and uncontrolled outbreak of anti-Asian sentiment, which, they felt, would surely occur if Asians continued to be as successful as they had been in securing secondary school positions.

the decision was taken that within a two-year period the teaching language in the primary schools should be changed to Swahili. However, a few fee-paying English-language primary schools were permitted to continue in the major towns. These schools were intended particularly for the children of expatriates. Nevertheless African parents who were able to pay their fees could send their children to these schools as well. This was defended on the grounds that it would be socially and education-ally undesirable to have 'all-white' primary schools in Tanzania. However, it is fair to suggest that a further reason for this decision was the interest which many prominent Africans had to secure for their children the advantages which they felt they would gain from attending a school in which the teaching language was English. The government also con-tinued to run one residential secondary school (Ilyunga Secondary School) separately from the regular school system. Ilyunga had been a 'white' secondary school. The government decided to continue it as a fee-paying secondary school in order that it could offer expatriates the option of secondary school education for their children within Tanzania. This meant, in addition, that members of the African bourgeoisie whose children failed to secure a place in a regular secondary school had the option of sending their children to Ilyunga as fee-paying students.[106] Finally, the government took a more lenient view of private secondary schools, which began to appear in significant numbers to serve the needs of the children of wealthy parents who failed to secure a place in a state school.

There have thus been some developments in education in which the interests of the African middle class have been particularly catered for. However, as yet, these developments have been secondary if not marginal in character. The continuation for a few years of Ilyunga and the decision to permit an increased number of private fee-paying secondary schools can more reasonably be viewed as the creation of safety valves to protect the public school system from the full and direct impact of pressures from influential middle-class parents than as the beginning of a serious erosion of the impartiality of that system.

This long digression on educational policy is intended to illustrate that the civil service has continued to have the capacity and the will to serve the public interest rather than narrowly to pursue its own class interest. Our conclusions concerning the emergence of an urban African middle class are rather complex. By 1967, very largely because of the Africanization of the civil service, there was for the first time a significant class of Africans in public life and in the public service who were exceedingly well paid in Tanzanian terms, though only modestly rewarded in comparison to salary levels elsewhere in Africa. These men and women had not become an aggressive ruling oligarchy which used its power primarily to protect and promote its own selfish interests. They were not using the instruments of power in any serious and sustained way to perpetuate themselves as a ruling class or to advance their interests in ways which seriously offended the values and expectations of the wider Tanzanian society. They were loyal members of TANU. They were still responsive to the various influences and pressures which operate to keep public services reasonably efficient and free of corruption. Nevertheless they did constitute an economic elite with aspirations, with a standard of living and with a style of life which set them apart from their ordinary fellow Tanzanians.

Tanzania was thus following a pattern of development which, in one fundamental way, was very similar to that of almost all third-world countries. Tanzania had created a modern elite, rewarded its members at levels far above the incomes of ordinary citizens and then relied upon that elite to promote the further development of the country and to ensure that more and more of the citizens benefited from that development. An alternative to this pattern existed in theory alone. That alternative would have involved the maintenance of a society in which the leaders and the masses remained fundamentally members of the same economic class, a society that is in which no severe income differentials divided the bureaucracy and politicians on the one hand and the people on the other, a society in which the benefits of growth were equally shared. Tanzania did not have this option. Tanzania inherited a salary structure in which there were wide income differentials between the lowest wage and the highest salary. Tanzania's continued employment of expatriates, its easy contact with neighbouring states whose leaders and senior civil servants enjoyed what can reasonably be called an international bourgeois standard of living, and the desire of individuals with special skills and talents to work for the advancement of their own economic interests, all were barriers to the introduction of any radical change in this inherited salary structure. Moreover, there was no radical egalitarian ideology with a widespread influence in Tanzania nor a party committed to such an ideology which was powerful enough to enforce this alternative pattern of development. Nyerere, whatever his personal values, had no real alternative initially but to accept the wide income differentials which were a feature of the salary structures inherited by TANU and to hope to lessen them gradually.

In February 1963, Nyerere gave expression to his conviction that the inherited structure was unjust, and to his recognition that nevertheless these injustices could be alleviated only gradually:

> We are committed to a philosophy of African socialism and basic to this is the principle of human equality. One of our concerns, therefore, must be to prevent the growth of a class structure in our society. . .our inheritance and our needs put us in great danger in this respect. The great shortage of highly educated skilled persons to run and operate the new industries, modern farms, civil service and co-operative societies

has meant that such persons receive salaries and conditions of service which are often better than those in the highly developed societies of Europe. At the same time the vast mass of our people exist at subsistence level. We have in other words developed an income structure in our society which is inconsistent with our declared aim of social equality... the wide gap in income levels leads almost automatically to artificial social divisions and to the growth of social attitudes which deny the equality of man...The only way to avoid the growth of these unhealthy attitudes is to reduce these incredible income differentials.

The important question, of course, is how can we deal with these income inequalities given the present facts of our economic life...First, and obviously, we must energetically pursue policies which will increase the amount of wealth produced in this country...Secondly and equally important we must prevent the present position from solidifying into a class structure and we must not allow the present income differentials to become sacrosanct. All of our emphasis must be on improving wages and conditions at the bottom of the economic scale.[107]

By 1966, the difficulties and the limitations of this approach had become more apparent. During the years 1961 to 1966 thousands of Africans had moved into the more highly paid positions within government. The class stratification which had largely been along racial lines in 1960 was thus an African phenomenon by 1966. It was therefore more threatening to the diffusion of socialist values in Tanzania than it had earlier been. The main African beneficiaries of the inequalities within the social system were the bureaucracy and the leadership within the party. These were the very strata whose oligarchic tendencies posed a continuing threat to Tanzanian democracy. They were also the major instruments on which Nyerere would have to depend to promote greater equality. Nyerere did not see any way in 1966 to break free from these contradictions. However, his greater recognition of the threat they posed to the eventual achievement of a democratic and socialist Tanzania were important factors contributing to that commitment to socialism into which he led TANU in 1967.

8: The commitment to socialism 1967–8

Nyerere and the Arusha Declaration

A number of features of the Tanzanian scene in 1967, when viewed in retrospect, suggest that a variety of economic and social problems in Tanzania were to become more severe. Tanzania was likely to face a persistent balance-of-payments problem which would require economic controls and a social discipline that had not yet been necessary. The rate of economic growth in the rural areas was likely to fall because further expansion in output would largely have to come from improved agricultural practices rather than increases in the areas under cash-crop cultivation. Further industrialization would also be more difficult to achieve as not a great deal of additional import-substitute manufacturing was feasible.

Despite these prospects, popular demands upon the economy were certain to increase rapidly. Pressure from the urban working force would not abate. Moreover, the primary and secondary schools were sending into the labour market each year an increasing and substantial number of young men and women whose job and income expectations would be impossible to meet. The peasants had benefited very little, if at all, from the economic growth that had taken place since independence so that widespread disillusion and discouragement seemed almost inevitable.

These various prospects had not escaped the attention of the government. The problem of the school leavers had already been widely discussed. The Turner Report[1] had made the government aware that much of the benefits of development so far had accrued to the small minority of the population who lived in the urban areas. The Treasury was paying increasing attention to the balance-of-payments problem while it and several other Ministries had succeeded in generating an awareness in government of the fact that Tanzania was likely soon to reach a plateau in regard to agricultural production and manufacturing. Nevertheless, these developments were not so pressing as to suggest that immediate and radical changes were needed in the development strategy of the government.[2] Nor did they incontrovertibly point towards a need for major socialist initiatives. Even less were there important sections of the working class, the peasantry or the intelligentsia who were demanding a socialist reconstruction of Tanzanian society.

The rhetoric of socialism was common in the English-language daily newspaper owned by TANU, the *Nationalist,* and in the public speeches of a few political figures. It had gained in credibility from the foreign policy crises of 1965 and, as well, had a continuing appeal to those in TANU who still harboured animosities towards Asians and Europeans. There were, finally, a few scholars at the university and at Kivukoni College, almost all of them expatriates, who had begun to develop a Marxian analysis of Tanzanian affairs.[3] They were soon joined by a number of younger African scholars whose writings, along with their own, now form an influential body of Marxian analysis of Tanzanian affairs. However, in the years in question here, 1965–7, their immediate influence in Tanzanian affairs was negligible.

The few pronouncements on socialism and self-reliance which were made at this time by TANU or by related organizations reveal that their grasp of socialism was still shallow and their commitment to it casual. NUTA (National Union of Tanganyika Workers), for example, had passed occasional resolutions which called for socialist initiatives by the government. However, when Kamaliza, the Secretary-General of NUTA, spoke of the policies NUTA was advocating, he identified the sale of shares by companies to their workers as a socialist measure to increase workers' participation.[4] At about the same time, the TANU NEC called for a national lottery as its main contribution to a discussion of how to achieve self-reliance. It is understandable that Nyerere has commented on several occasions that there were very, very few socialists in Tanzania in 1967.[5]

The conclusion is unavoidable. There were no policy imperatives which were widely seen to require socialism nor a radicalized petty bourgeoisie which was providing an influential application of Marxian analysis to Tanzanian affairs. There were no substantial political or class demands for socialist initiatives. Without Nyerere, Tanzanian socialism would have been most unlikely to become a major force in these years. As well, without his leadership, the strategy which was followed in the pursuit of socialism, at least as that strategy was initially defined, would also have been much different.

Nyerere has always sought to hold in creative tension his role as a visionary leader and his role as a head of government. In the years 1963–6 he had not seen these two roles as being at all in conflict. If government were to be severely inefficient or if the economy were to fail to progress, he felt that his chances of winning Tanzanian acceptance of the values of a democratic and socialist society would be slim indeed. By 1966 he saw these two roles as being still more intimately interconnected.

Nyerere had continued to define the long-term objectives of his government in terms of providing a national environment in which the older communal values would receive a modern expression compatible with economic progress.⁶ However, he now saw this task as being more urgent than he had previously recognized. Communal values were being rapidly eroded under the impact of an acquisitive individualism which was generated by economic development, the example of wealthier countries and a host of other aspects of the rapid processes of change in Tanzania. There would soon no longer be any widespread acceptance of communal values on which to build a modern socialist society. In 1966 he wrote:

> It is essential, therefore, that we in Tanzania. . .should deliberately fight the intensification of the attitude which would eventually nullify our social need for human dignity and equality.

> The traditional order is dying. The question which has yet to be answered is what will be built on our past and, in consequence, what kind of society will eventually replace the traditional one. Choices which involve clashes of principle must therefore be answered in the light of the kind of society we want to create, for our priorities now will affect the attitudes and institutions of the future. We must look ahead and try to gauge the effects of our decisions in 20 years' time.⁷

The interrelatedness of his roles as a visionary teacher and as a head of government was thus all the more intimate by 1966. Yet he had also come to the view in 1966, as he later expressed it, that 'although some economic progress was being made, and although we were still talking in terms of a socialist objective, the nation was in fact drifting without any sense of direction. . .on balance we were drifting away from our basic socialist goals of human equality, human dignity and government by the whole people'.⁸ Thus, during a period in which Nyerere was particularly absorbed with immediate government affairs, he grew aware that the government's handling of these affairs seemed little influenced by the long-term policy objectives which it nominally professed.

There are close parallels between the position in which Nyerere felt himself by the end of 1966 and the position which he had felt himself to be in five years earlier. In each case he was at the end of a period in which he had primarily concentrated upon the immediate problems of government. In 1966 as in late 1961, he had come to the view that unless he could in some way break out from these preoccupations, he would not be able to promote the fundamental developments and changes in Tanzania to which he remained profoundly committed. In 1962 he resigned from the prime ministership and returned to his people as 'Mwalimu'. In 1967, he 'broke out' in a different way. He did not leave the Tanzanian government but rather he shifted the emphasis of his own activities as President. He began to lead TANU and the Tanzanian government in the immediate pursuit of major socialist objectives. He made the transition to socialism in Tanzania his central concern.

This difference between Nyerere's actions in 1967 and his resignation in 1962 can be explained by the fact that in 1966 Nyerere had identified government policies and attitudes as important contributing causes of the trend away from communal values. It would have been no answer to withdraw to become again the 'full-time' Mwalimu. Not only had something to be done, but it had to be done within government and the party. The immediate policies of government had to be brought more into harmony with the long-term objective of building a socialist Tanzania.

Certainly in the years 1965 and 1966 many government and party policies with which Nyerere had been particularly associated had floundered. The village settlement schemes were halted. The Five Year Plan had led neither to a sustained and integrated development effort nor to any increased flow of external aid. The cooperative and trade union movements were in serious difficulties and there was but slight realization of the possibilities for mass participation which their structures in theory offered. Government concessions to urban workers and a general bias in favour of the towns in the distribution of social services had resulted in the small urban population of Tanzania garnering much of the benefits of the economic growth that had been accomplished since independence.

Nyerere had also come to the view that the government's agricultural development policies were intensifying capitalistic motivations within Tanzania. The Ministry of Agriculture had concentrated upon assisting those farmers with the initiative, the resources and the land to respond to the opportunities of cash-crop cultivation. 'Our feet', he wrote in 1967, 'are on the wrong path and if we continue to encourage or even to help the development of agricultural capitalism we shall never become a socialist state.'[9]

He had similar misgivings about the investment policies of the National Development Corporation. This public corporation had been established in 1965 to manage a variety of publicly owned companies and to be the agent for the investment of public funds in the manufacturing, mining and commercial sectors of the economy. The N.D.C.'s capital funds were limited. It had sought to use these funds in ways which would associate with them as much additional private investment as possible, both domestic and foreign. As a result the N.D.C. favoured joint ventures in which its participation was as minimal as possible. Nyerere reacted strongly against this policy. Early in 1966 he instructed the N.D.C. not to seek an indiscriminate maximization of private investment. He called upon it to be the agency through which the government would gradually acquire majority control in key areas of the economy.[10]

Nyerere's concern in 1966 about the longer-term implications of governmental activities extended beyond the consequences of specific policies such as these. He had come gradually to the view that several attitudes within the ranks of the leadership were contributing in a fundamental fashion to that drift 'away from our basic goals of human equality, human dignity and government by the whole people' which he had observed. The first of these attitudes was the view that Tanzania could only develop economically if she received major and sustained foreign capital assistance. The second was a self-seeking acquisitiveness and an elitism which he sensed were becoming more prominent within the values of his political colleagues and of the senior civil service.

The Arusha Declaration is a direct consequence of Nyerere's concern over these two attitudes. He attached the greatest importance within the Declaration to the section on self-reliance, which was his counterattack on an overreliance upon aid, and to the section on the leadership rules which sought to check capitalist practices by political leaders and senior civil servants.[11]

The Arusha Declaration contains other sections as well. It begins with a brief exposition of the meaning of socialism in terms of an absence of exploitation, the public control of the major means of production and exchange, democratic government and a leadership that believes in socialism and practices it. There is a brief eleven-line section calling for greater care by the NEC to assure that party members accept 'the faith, the objects, and the rules and regulations of the party'.[12] The Declaration has been extensively discussed and analyzed since 1966.[13] There is already a substantial and varied literature on Tanzanian socialism since 1967. There can be disagreements about which sections of the Declaration will prove historically the most important and different emphases have been given which reflect, amongst other things, the differing ideological sympathies of the commentators. However, it does seem incontrovertible that the sections to which Nyerere attached the greatest importance were those on self-reliance and on leadership.

The emphasis on self-reliance was a direct conclusion drawn from the wisdom and scepticism concerning the motives of the major Western powers which Tanzania had acquired as a result of the foreign policy crises during 1964 and 1965. Despite these new insights, many in the government and outside it, too, had continued to think of economic development as something which could not happen without foreign capital. When a development need was discussed, attention would still be focused on which foreign government or international aid agency might be willing to finance it. After the Five Year Plan had been prepared and approved, for example, Ministers discussed (and squabbled about) how best to secure external capital assistance for it rather than how best themselves to promote its implementation. 'There is in Tanzania a fantastic amount of talk about getting money from outside. Our government and different groups of our leaders never stop thinking about methods of getting finance from abroad.'[14] This would have been offered and accepted as praise in 1964. After the 1964–5 crises it was strong criticism.

Tanzanians might have believed in 1962, or even in 1964, that they could rely upon foreign aid for their development. However by 1966 they had lost, or should have lost, their innocence about international politics. Capital aid in the dimensions which Tanzania needs will not be forthcoming from foreign sources. 'The donors are not our relatives nor charitable institutions', Nyerere told the special TANU Conference[15] called to consider the Declaration. Moreover, even if foreign capital assistance of the order needed for Tanzanian development could be secured, Tanzanians had come to recognize that an overreliance upon foreign aid exposes a country to donor pressures which can seriously undermine its capacity for independent action. Yet, complained Nyerere, far too many of his political colleagues and far too many civil servants could not conceive of a development effort save in terms of attracting foreign aid. This preoccupation with 'money, money, money' as he called it, had become a major inhibition which blocked the Tanzanian leadership from taking primary responsibility themselves for their own development.[16]

Self-reliance was a call to Tanzanians to concentrate their energies and efforts upon what they can do with their own resources. Nyerere did not rule out foreign aid, far from it, but he wanted it to be regarded as supplementary to a national development effort. It was a call for self-respect. It was a call for greater realism about international politics. 'Self-reliance' was thus an understandable development from a number of ideas, values and attitudes that had long been present in Tanzanian politics. It is intimately linked with nationalism, with a concern for African dignity, with the earlier TANU call for 'Uhuru na Kazi' (freedom and work) and with a foreign policy of positive non-alignment.

Nyerere's second fundamental worry can be bluntly expressed. He saw the beginnings of capitalist motivations amongst the leaders of the government and the party. He recognized that if their values and their commitment to the public good were undermined by an acquisitive individualism, whatever policies were pursued the prospects for a genuinely egalitarian socialism in Tanzania would be very slim indeed. This unease had always been with Nyerere. Even before independence he had been distressed by the transparent self-interest displayed by TANU activists in the scramble for positions.[17] In the years since independence the Office of the President had recurrently to deal with personal self-seeking in high places that ranged between the highly questionable and the indefensible. A High Commissioner ignored financial regulations and ordered an official Austin Princess motor-car which he felt the dignity of his office required. A junior Minister spent public funds to rent herself a Jaguar for a holiday weekend while in Britain. A Minister drew a generous daily living allowance while on a foreign trip, even though his expenses were fully met by the host government. Ministers and junior Ministers persistently sought new perquisites additional to their salaries. The Minister of Regional Administration ignored a Presidential instruction and ordered seventeen Mercedes-Benz for the Regional Commissioners. Ministers sought a gratuity of twenty-five per cent of their total salaries because they had no job security. The issues were often minor, even petty, but they revealed an acquisitiveness that was discouraging to Nyerere. 'Enough! I do not want to see this file again', was his angry, perhaps even desperate minute in regard to one of the minor ministerial abuses of office.[18]

The attitudes and values of those in privileged positions in Tanzania became a major topic of public discussion in October 1966. Earlier that year the government had made it compulsory for all post-secondary school students to spend two years in the National Service, a para-military corps.[19] This requirement was seen as a healthy corrective to the socially exclusive character of their education, a repayment to the state for part of the cost of their education and a reminder to them of the poverty of most of their fellow citizens.

The scheme itself was hardly oppressive. The students were to spend five months under canvas in military training. They would then work in their regular jobs but would continue to be members of the National Service for a further eighteen months. During these months they would receive approximately forty per cent (tax free) of the regular salaries of these positions, the balance being a saving to the state.[20] Student reactions were bitter. They alone were being singled out for compulsory service. They had come through a highly competitive educational process and now, for two years, they were to be denied the full rewards they had expected. Moreover they were being denied these rewards by political leaders whose formal education was often much poorer than theirs and who had not themselves made any similar sacrifice. The tactics of the students and their estimation of their influence revealed a breathtaking ignorance of Tanzanian politics. They directly challenged the honesty of Kawawa. They paraded to State House in their academic gowns carrying their protest signs in English. They threatened non-compliance with the law. They talked ominously of situations in other countries where students had brought governments down. Their manifesto ended with the words 'Unless the attitude of our leaders changes, we shall not accept National Service. Let our bodies be taken but our souls will remain outside the scheme. And the battle between the political elite and the educated elite will perpetually continue.'[21]

Nyerere and Kawawa each met student leaders on several occasions in an effort to win their acceptance of national service. This patient reception only heightened the students' sense of their own importance. Their next move then was to organize a march of nearly four hundred students to State House for an open-air confrontation with the whole Cabinet. At this confrontation Nyerere began quietly, his manner suggesting that he still hoped to conciliate the students. However, as the meeting proceeded, his anger grew, until his despair tumbled forth in a near-incoherent rage:

> I accept your ultimatum. I shall take nobody, not a single person into the National Service whose spirit is not in it. I am not going to take there, I am not going to take. It's not a prison. So make your choice. I'm not going, I'm not going, I'm not going to spend public money to educate anybody who says National Service is a prison. . .
>
> All of us, me and you, we belong to a single class of exploiters. Is this what the citizens of this country worked for? Is this what we fought for, the men of this country fought for? In order to maintain a top level of exploiters. . .You are demanding a pound of flesh; everybody is demanding a pound of flesh except the poor peasant. What kind of a country are we building?[22]

Nyerere announced in this impromptu, angry speech that he would cut his own salary by twenty per cent and that he would see that ministerial salaries were also cut. He concluded with the unplanned decision 'Send them home.'* All of the students present, including most of the graduating class of the university, were then sent to their home Districts.

It was an angry, impetuous gesture. It was also illegal for Nyerere did not have the power to expel students from the university and while he did have the legal power to rusticate individuals, he had not followed the legally prescribed forms. This mass expulsion had a traumatic impact upon the university and the nation. Moreover Nyerere did not easily or swiftly shift his position. It was more than five months later before finally he yielded to petitions from the university and resolutions from the National Assembly asking that he permit the students to return to their classrooms.

The episode had touched an old unease within Nyerere. In 1961 he had reluctantly agreed to continue salary scales for the senior ranks of the civil service and for Members of Parliament and Ministers which he felt were far too high for a country as poor as Tanzania. By 1966 he had come to feel afresh the wisdom of his earlier concern. The salaries permitted a style of life that separated the leaders and civil servants from ordinary people. They were an important reason why government was becoming less responsive to the needs of the great majority of the people. They made much less likely any real acceptance of equality. They divided the society, generating amongst the masses aspirations that could not be met and

---

* David Martin, a newspaper man who was present, told me (June 1968) that Nyerere's senior officials did not in fact know whether Nyerere meant by 'home' the university of their home Districts.

amongst the fortunate few, a contempt for the ordinary citizen. When Nyerere announced that he would cut his own salary by twenty per cent and would have other high government salaries cut as well, he said, 'These damn salaries. These are the salaries which build this kind of attitude in the educated people...All of us, we belong to a single class of exploiters.'[23]

At the same time as this issue reached its height, a parallel issue also became a matter of public debate. By 1966 there were signs that some senior politicians and civil servants were beginning to engage in private, capitalist activities in addition to their government jobs. The opportunities for this were not enormous. Large-scale market gardening or the cultivation of fruit and flowers for air export to Europe did not offer the same exciting opportunities which they did in Nairobi. Company directorships were not nearly as numerous or as available in Dar-es-Salaam. The most evident activity of this sort which had begun to develop in Tanzania was the building of substantial houses in Dar-es-Salaam, which would then be rented to a foreign Embassy or to an international corporation. This was not illegal but it can be assumed that a Minister would find it easier than would less prominent individuals to raise the money to build such houses and to find the tenants willing to pay a high rent. Moreover activities such as this inevitably distract a Minister's attention from his government responsibilities and eliminate any serious commitment on his part to the introduction of socialism in Tanzania. Changes in civil service regulations relating to housing loans had halted the spread of this practice amongst senior civil servants. However, action was still needed to stop Ministers from building houses for rental. Nyerere and Kawawa decided to handle this by an NEC resolution.

That Ministers should be building houses for rent was for Nyerere the latest of a series of reminders that he and his government had allowed an increasing intrusion of values and attitudes which were the antithesis of the socialist society which Nyerere was determined to build. He decided, therefore, to ask the NEC to apply to anyone in a leadership role a far wider range of prohibitions than merely a prohibition upon the building of houses for rental. He decided to seek NEC support for a set of leadership rules which would prohibit anyone in a middle- or senior-rank position in either government or the party from each of the following activities: (1) holding shares in a private company; (2) being a director of a private company; (3) receiving more than one salary; (4) owning one or more houses which are rented to others; (5) employing others to work for him.[24]

Nyerere attached enormous importance to the acceptance of these rules. The parallel is not at all with the enforcement, say, of civil service regulations against minor infractions. The parallel is, rather, with antisocial conduct which a society decides to make illegal. In Nyerere's judgment, living off the labour of others is exploitation. It is morally wrong. The five activities which he wished to deny to all leaders in Tanzania were the main opportunities to exploit which were open to Tanzanians. They each represent conduct which Nyerere regards as morally wrong. Each is an activity which would not occur in any fully socialist society. At the least, Nyerere argued, Tanzania should not permit its leaders to engage in any of these forms of exploitation.

Nyerere was attempting something that was the very opposite of an effort to change the values and behaviour of a society by moral exhortation and legal coercion. He was acting on the belief which he had long affirmed, that traditional African values were communal and that these values were still a reality for most Tanzanians. The rules were an attempt to provide a modern and relevant application of these values. He did not see the leadership rules as the imposition of a morality which was not accepted. They were the enforcement of an ethic that was still part of the values of the society. It was an ethic that was being rapidly replaced in the towns, amongst the leaders and within the civil service by an aggressive acquisitive individualism. Nevertheless, even in these groups he hoped that the older values could still be tapped so that they too would accept the ethical validity of the rules. He stressed that the abuses which the rules would prohibit had only just begun to appear. He was reminding leaders what was expected of them rather than trying radically to change the conduct of large numbers. Nyerere developed this point at a press conference in these terms:

> I think the chances are that all leaders will surrender their personal
> possessions and remain leaders. The atmosphere in Tanzania is
> extremely difficult for them to do otherwise. It is almost untenable for
> a leader to prefer personal possessions to leadership. And in any case
> they haven't got very far. . .what some of them have done is to whet the
> appetite a little bit. One little house – when you built the first house then
> your intention was to live in it yourself, and then suddenly you said,
> 'why not rent it out?' And now you are making plans for a second
> one. This is not good but it is the temptation we have stopped. It was
> really a lot more temptation than fulfillment. . .This was the right time.
> Had we delayed, you would discover two years from now that our
> leadership has become rather entrenched in the accumulation of personal
> property.[25]

The leadership rules were thus as much a product of concerns and values that had long motivated Nyerere as was the doctrine of self-reliance. Indeed, to a remarkable extent, these two central portions of the Arusha Declaration are little more than an application of the ideas which Nyerere had developed in the several pamphlets which he had published in 1962.[26] It is understandable that he reacted with particular sharpness to suggestions that the Declaration was an application in Tanzania of foreign ideas. 'There is no African Marx in this country. We are a bunch of pragmatists in this country. We have no Bible', he said in March 1967, when commenting on the intellectual origins of the Declaration. 'We need no Mao Tse-tung to tell me the difference between Uzanaki [the rural area where he was born] and Msasani [the locale of his lovely though modest seaside villa outside of Dar-es-Salaam].'[27]

The Declaration and its immediate consequences

Nyerere, in consultation in particular with Kawawa, decided to seek the support of the National Executive Committee of TANU for these two important policies. They recognized, as Nyerere later put it, that they needed a peg for these proposals, a theme which would bring them together in a coherent fashion. The answer was to present both as related aspects of a more determined pursuit of socialism.[28]

This was more than a tactical decision. They realized that in self-reliance and in the leadership rules they had identified two very essential components of a socialist strategy for Tanzania. They had come to these two central policies out of their judgment of Tanzanian needs. Those decisions taken, they recognized that they were in fact giving a sharper and more immediate focus to the general but ill-defined affirmations of a commitment to socialism that had been a feature of TANU rhetoric since at least 1961.[29]

Once it was decided that socialism would be the 'peg' on which he would hang the doctrine of self-reliance and the leadership rules, Nyerere had no hesitation in adding to the resolutions which he planned to put to the NEC a call upon the government to take further steps towards bringing all the major means of production and exchange under public control, and a call to the party to instruct party members in the party's ideology. These were but simple corollaries of the decision to present their main proposals as part of an overall move towards socialism. The President's opening statement to the NEC thus urged TANU to commit itself afresh to socialism. He proposed, as the immediate and major expression of this new commitment, that the NEC endorse the leadership rules and the doctrine of self-reliance and that it affirm its recognition of the importance of the public ownership of the major means of production and exchange and of socialist education in the party.

To understand how Nyerere came to these recommendations is not, however, to understand why they were accepted. No leader, not even one in the commanding political position occupied by Nyerere in 1967, can secure a major change in the direction of government policies, can convince a political and government elite to accept restricting limitations on their acquisition of wealth, and can win a national movement to a fresh ideological commitment unless much has happened to predispose the government, the party and his immediate senior political colleagues to accept what he proposes. There had, after all, been socialist initiatives before by Nyerere. He had secured a socialist content to the aims and objects of TANU in 1961 and had had these reinforced in 1965. He had published *Ujamaa, The Basis of African Socialism* in 1962. These had not had any noticeable impact on government policy. Nor indeed had Nyerere expected any extraordinary reaction to his presentation to the NEC in January 1967.[30]

Yet the reception given to Nyerere's presentation and the immediate follow-up to the Arusha meetings were, by any standards, extraordinary. There was a great deal of unease and discontent about the leadership rules. The whole discussion was dominated by this issue.[31] Time and again, members expressed their unhappiness over these restrictions on their income-earning activities.

In contrast, the nationalization issue proved extremely popular at the NEC meeting. There was great political pressure that the nationalizations should be immediate and considerable. The closest parallel was the Africanization issue in 1962. The requirements of stability in each case might have seemed to call for caution but nationalist rhetoric demanded action. As had happened in 1961 over Africanization, so in this case also a nationalist momentum developed which would have been very difficult to contain without some major governmental response. Unlike January 1962, Nyerere did not step aside this time. Instead he seized the issue and he used it. At a single, hurriedly called Saturday Cabinet meeting on 6 February 1967, Nyerere sought Cabinet approval for a substantial number of nationalizations. The approval was easily secured. The Cabinet had been as infected as any by the surge of self-confident nationalism that the idea of taking over the major non-African firms had released.

Beginning on the following Monday morning Nyerere announced these nationalizations in daily batches to large popular demonstrations that were each day organized by major national organizations associated with TANU, including the army and the national service. By the end of the week the newly nationalized firms included all the private banks, the major food processors, the National Insurance Corporation and eight major foreign export trading companies. In addition Nyerere had identified six major manufacturing companies in which the government would acquire majority shareholding and had announced its intention to take a controlling interest in the sisal industry. All of this occurred without any detailed planning by the relevant Ministries, without any full Cabinet discussion based upon a detailed briefing and without any proper legal preparation. Nyerere was capitalizing upon a surge of political consciousness in order to advance Tanzania towards socialism far faster than he had expected to do even two weeks previously.

Nyerere then brought the nationalizations to a halt and immediately concentrated upon winning a real acceptance of the leadership rules. A number of compromises quickly proved to be politically necessary. Two of these were major. Leaders were allowed to transfer the ownership of property to a trust which they could set up in the name of their children. This meant that investments in property whose purpose was to provide for the future needs of a leader's children were again permissible. The second compromise limited the ban on the employment of labour to workers who were employed on a permanent and full-time basis. This permitted many leaders in the rural areas who were also substantial farmers to continue to employ casual labour in periods of peak-labour need.

These were compromises, not total reversals. In the prevailing mood of enthusiasm for the Declaration, there was no chance that the leadership requirements could be overturned. They were endorsed by the TANU Special Conference in March. They were incorporated into the civil service regulations and were required as well of all the various categories of party leaders mentioned in the Declaration. Compliance may not have been perfect but neither was it grossly inadequate. The socialist morality embodied in the Declaration became an important component of the political culture of Tanzania. From that time on, the effective transition to a democratic and socialist society became a central preoccupation of the government.

One returns therefore to the observation made a few pages earlier. No leader can secure such major changes as these unless a great deal has occurred which prepared the party and the government for these initiatives. What are the events and forces which explain the acceptance of the Arusha Declaration and the sustained and vigorous effort since 1967 to move Tanzania towards socialism?

The first factor to consider is the one to which Nyerere made special reference, as has already been indicated. Nyerere has argued that there is a close affinity between traditional communal values and socialism. The masses at least would therefore understand his initiatives and respond positively to them for they had not yet been corrupted by the individualism that had come to Tanzania with colonial rule. Politicians, civil servants and urban dwellers generally might be less enthusiastic but they were not yet so distant from their traditional values as not to acknowledge the moral legitimacy of the restrictions being placed upon them.

This proposition is very hard to assess. There is however some *prima facie* evidence that there is real substance to this argument. Most members of the NEC and of Parliament were likely to be affected by the leadership rules or, at the least, were likely to be aspirants to positions in which they would be affected. All reports of their discussions suggest that while they were unhappy about the rules, even distressed by them, they did not have a sense of outrage that the rules were unjust and unfair. This perhaps illustrates that they accepted the moral legitimacy of the rules. It is reasonable, though unprovable, to suggest that this can be explained by the basic identity between the values underlying these rules and a traditional ethic whose claims upon them still had some force.

It is also worth considering whether this was not reinforced by a parallel acceptance of TANU's claim upon them. The party had not lost its integrity or its idealism. In its earlier years a high level of personal sacrifice had been common amongst its leaders. The leadership rules were also an appeal to the leaders to return to the older values that had once marked their conduct of TANU's affairs. Perhaps the analogy that is most illuminating is with a religious revival. TANU was being called by Nyerere back to a faith which it still affirmed but practiced with declining frequency. Nyerere therefore struck deeply responsive chords within TANU and within Tanzanian society. It is that deep response which is the first factor to note in any explanation of the acceptance of the Declaration.

Two other, more mundane factors further facilitated that acceptance. First, most of the individuals who were affected by the nationalizations were Asians and Europeans. The nationalizations were, therefore, popular for a range of reasons that went far beyond their socialist purposes. As they were part of a cluster of policies that Nyerere had linked together in the Declaration, the other policies in that cluster benefited politically from the popularity of the nationalizations. The leadership rules and the nationalizations had not been deliberately linked to achieve this end. Nevertheless the acceptability of the leadership rules, which largely affected Africans, was greatly aided by the nationalizations, which largely affected Asians and Europeans.[32]

The second factor which facilitated the acceptance of the Declaration was that socialism was already part of the rhetoric of one element within the party, namely the 'political Ministers' and their associates. They acclaimed it publicly even before Nyerere had launched it officially or even released it to the press. It was they, through their control of the *Nationalist*, who immediately gave it a great deal of sympathetic publicity. Indeed it was the *Nationalist* and *Uhuru* which first coined the term 'the Arusha Declaration' for the resolutions and accompanying exposition which had been approved by the NEC. The Declaration thus had its political champions from the very first day.

The poverty and underdevelopment of Tanzania were themselves a further important factor which eased the acceptance of the Declaration. An African entrepreneurial class hardly existed. Rural stratification, save in a few Districts, had not produced a strong class of substantial African farmers who could form a class alliance with the urban salary-earning African bourgeoisie. The officer corps of the army was still unsettled and insecure as a consequence of the mutiny and the post-mutiny army reforms. Thus the economic and social classes which might have been expected to oppose socialist measures were economically and politically weaker than their counterparts in many African states.

An explanation is also needed for the acceptance of the nationalizations by the senior civil service. Whatever force one concedes to the first factor discussed above the senior civil servants might have been expected, nevertheless, to oppose the nationalizations. This was in fact not the case. The senior civil service had become increasingly self-confident, particularly in regard to its overall management of the Tanzanian economy. The senior officials and Ministers of the Treasury and the Ministry of Economic Affairs and Development Planning had begun actively to consider and indeed to take a variety of stronger initiatives. Reginald Green reports that

> From 1964, the independent government has pursued a more comprehensive and activist policy of parastatal expansion, not simply to fill gaps in private investment, but to secure a stake in banking, insurance, import–export trade, wholesale commerce, and manufacturing and to transform electric power from a partially to a fully publicly-owned sector.[33]

There was, therefore, a group of highly able senior civil servants as well as a number of 'administrator-Ministers' such as Jamal and Bomani who were intellectually ready to support the nationalizations. They were much more ready to intervene in the economy than they had been a few years earlier. They were very uneasy about the hasty and unprepared way in which the nationalizations were done but they were not basically hostile to them. They greeted the proposals as Nyerere later recalled 'not with horror but with concern'.[34]

The government's reception of the Declaration was also aided by that general radicalization of opinion which had followed the foreign policy crises of late 1964 and early 1965. In an African state that lacks an African entrepreneurial and investing class, there is obviously a very close link between nationalism and nationalization. If Tanzania was to be more self-reliant, if she was to control her own economic destiny to a greater extent, then nationalization was in fact the only way. 'Our purpose', said Nyerere, 'was thus primarily a nationalist purpose...The only way in which nationalist control of the economy can be achieved is through the economic institutions of socialism.'[35] For this important reason as well, the senior civil service did not fight the nationalizations but instead worked hard to maximize the advantages that might be gained from them for Tanzania.*

---

* Shivji extends this general point beyond the credible and into the realm of radical mythology when he suggests that the bureaucratic bourgeoisie sought through the nationalizations to bring the economy under its control for its own class interests and for the protection of the interests of international capitalism with whom this bourgeoisie remains intimately linked. Nationalization in his view was thus but an alternative, equally nefarious, to the development of an African *(cont.)*

There was one final important factor which affected the reception given to the Arusha Declaration by the bureaucracy. This was the appearance by 1967 of political discontent on a fairly widespread basis. This discontent was still diffuse and received little organized expression. Nevertheless, the 1965 election had shown the strength of popular opposition to those leaders who were judged to have grown proud and selfish. The bureaucracy was less likely by 1967 to ignore this discontent than they might earlier have been. The army mutiny of 1964 had revealed how fragile was the whole structure of government and authority. The several coups in Nigeria, Ghana and other West African countries reminded those in power of how easy it is in African states to sweep aside a civilian regime which has lost the support of the people.

These reminders might, of course, merely have generated an intensified anomie within the ruling group increasing the urgency with which its individual members sought to advance their own narrow self-interest. However, in Tanzania, the continued reality of TANU as a national movement, the moral quality of Nyerere's leadership, the continued strength of his rapport with ordinary Tanzanians, and the comparative integrity and capacity of the government meant that people could conceive as feasible the further response of a committed endeavour to advance the welfare of the whole society. This meant, more specifically, that those with political and governmental power responded positively to Nyerere's call for a collective endeavour to achieve a socialist transformation of Tanzanian society.[36]

Nyerere commented shortly after the Arusha Declaration that he felt the timing of the Declaration had been right. He meant by this not only that within a few years those in power would have come to be so interested in personal property and wealth that socialist initiatives would then have been more strongly opposed by them. He meant as well, and perhaps primarily, that by 1967 the validity of the socialist initiatives was recognized within the leadership of TANU and the government, whereas in 1962 it would not have been. At that earlier date almost everyone accepted that the Africanization of the civil service should mean that Africans would begin to earn much higher salaries. Nyerere could interest no one in his idea that salaries in the middle and upper ranks of the service should be cut. These salaries, rather than just the positions and responsibilities that went with them, were part of the fruits of the nationalist victory. Nationalists were in no mood to consider the need for restraints upon their

(*cont.*) bourgeoisie which associated directly with the foreign corporations in order similarly to advance their common interests. In this interpretation Nyerere becomes the agent of the bourgeoisie, and the Arusha Declaration, far from being a product of nationalist and socialist concerns, was a selfish, class-motivated intervention manipulated into being by the bureaucratic bourgeoisie. 'The Class Struggle Continues' (Dar-es-Salaam, 1973).

incomes and their income-earning activities. In March 1967 Nyerere said of this matter, 'In 1961 they would not have understood. In 1962 they would not have understood. It is clear now.'[37] A greater realism about Tanzanian political development and about the security of their own positions had helped to increase the willingness of the senior civil service to accept the Arusha Declaration and to cooperate loyalty with its implementation.

Nyerere's strategy for the transition to socialism

'Socialism', said Nyerere in 1962, 'is an attitude of mind.'[38] This was still his point of view in 1967.[39] Some social arrangements and some economic institutions encourage and support the development of socialist attitudes and others arouse and reinforce selfish ambitions that are their antithesis. Nevertheless the essence of socialism does not lie in the character of institutions. 'The essence of socialism is the practical acceptance of human equality.'[40] 'The equality of man may or may not be susceptible to scientific proof. But its acceptance as a basic assumption of life in society is the core and essence of socialism.'[41]

Socialist equality for Nyerere is equality of a special sort. His view of equality does not stress the autonomy and independence of the individual and his right to pursue his own welfare as he wishes. Rather it is a view of equality which recognizes that the lives of men in society are closely and irrevocably interdependent. Men differ in their skills, their strength and their intelligence. It is Nyerere's conviction that these differences, by themselves, cannot be the basis of wide income differentials. Large differences between the incomes of some and the income of the majority are evidence that an exploitative relationship has been established.[42] A socialist society, therefore, is one 'in which all have a gradually increasing basic level of natural welfare before any individual lives in luxury'. 'Socialism as a system is in fact the organization of men's inequalities to serve their equality.'[43]

For Nyerere, this equality should primarily be a consequence and an expression of the felt values of the society. A socialist society is a closely integrated, harmonious society guided by love and sharing, to use the terms he used in 1966 to identify its central characteristics.[44] Africa is thus to create a new synthesis of the individual and society, a synthesis free of the selfish individualism of modern Western societies. Africa can hope to do this because of the continued vitality of traditional communitarian values. Africa's task is to find a way to utilize modern technology selectively so as to advance the welfare of her people while also building social and economic institutions which will express in modern and national terms the socialist values of traditional African societies.

A further essential ingredient of a socialist society for Nyerere is that it is a democratic society. Democracy is an unavoidable corollary of Nyerere's belief in equality. There is no equality when a few, however identified, rule over a majority to whom the few are not responsible. Nyerere felt as strongly in 1967 as he had in 1962 that autocratic rule by either a colonial power or an indigenous elite is a profound denial of man's equality and is incompatible with socialism. A society cannot be socialist if it is not 'governed by the people themselves through their freely elected representatives'.[45]

Finally, there continued to be room in Nyerere's political values for an emphasis also on personal liberty. His socialist society involved the striking of a new balance between the individual and society which would emphasize social duties and communal relationships rather than individual rights. Nevertheless Nyerere recognized that there would continue to be areas of human endeavour in which an individual's activity had little bearing upon the life of others. In these areas a socialist society would scrupulously recognize the freedom of the individual.[46]

Nyerere, writing in summary of his socialist faith in 1968, said 'one will not recognize or define a socialist society by its institutions or its statements but by its fundamental characteristics of equality, cooperation and freedom'.[47] He could easily have written this in 1962. Indeed, the same is true of all the Nyerere quotations on socialism in the preceding several pages. Nyerere's vision of a transformed Tanzanian society was fundamentally the same in 1967 as it had been in 1962.

Nyerere's views on the transition to socialism had developed but they had not fundamentally changed. In 1968 he wrote that the transition to socialism 'depends upon the growth of socialist understanding and socialist attitudes amongst the people. In particular it depends upon the speed and success with which the concepts of human equality and the people's sovereignty are accepted by the society and the leadership in the society.'[48] This too might well have been written in 1962. However, there are two features of Nyerere's view in 1968 of the transition to socialism which distinguish it from his earlier view. First, the trends in Tanzanian society which he felt would soon greatly increase the strength of the opposition to socialism led him to a greater sense of urgency about the need seriously to set in train the transition to socialism. Second, in 1967 he had a much clearer perception of the initiatives the government should take to achieve an effective transition to socialism.

This new perception of the transition to socialism owed much, of course, to the character of the socialist society which Nyerere finally hoped to achieve. It was however very much shaped as well by his understanding of the political realities of Tanzania in 1967. It has been Nyerere's ideas on the transition to socialism rather than his vision of a transformed Tanzania which have had a direct and major impact upon policy and politics in the years since 1967. Tanzania's pursuit of socialism since the

Arusha Declaration is a subject for other books by other writers. However, as Nyerere's ideas on the strategy to be followed are a product of the period reviewed in this volume, perhaps they are an appropriate final section for this study.

Nyerere's strategy for the transition to socialism can be examined under four headings, the promotion of greater equality, the maintenance of Tanzanian self-reliance, the creation of a socialist environment and the enhancement of democratic participation.

The promotion of equality

The most important single conclusion concerning the transition to socialism which Nyerere had come to by 1967 was that it required greater equality. Nyerere had seen Tanzanian leaders move farther away from basic socialist values under the impact of high incomes or the prospect of high incomes. TANU was as affected by this intrusion of acquisitive individualism as was the government itself. The NEC and Parliament for example were each as unhappy over the leadership rules as was the civil service. Nyerere was driven to recognize that once severe income differentials appear in a society, elections, by themselves, either within the party or for the National Assembly, may not provide an adequate means to make the political leaders responsive to the needs of the poor. 'There is no problem with the people. They support us completely. My problem is with the leaders', Nyerere told the 1967 TANU Conference.[49]

By 1967 Nyerere viewed the wide income differentials in Tanzania between the masses and those in middle and senior ranks in government and the party as a major immediate obstacle to an effective socialist strategy. The high incomes earned by a few arouse envy and generate hostilities that are socially divisive. They cause ordinary peasants and workers to concentrate upon the private accumulation of wealth as the primary way to improve their livelihood. This not only undermines communal values, it also is profoundly misleading for, in fact, 'the goal of individual wealth is an unrealistic goal'[50] in a country as poor as Tanzania.

In 1967, at the height of the excitement following the Arusha Declaration, Nyerere told a gathering, 'Some countries believed they could only develop by having a middle class and they measured progress by the number of people in the middle class. We shall be a nation of equals.'[51] That was the ideal, that was the target: a Tanzania which would develop as a nation of equals, sharing fairly amongst the whole people the benefits of whatever economic development is achieved. The strategic question was how to move to that situation from a present in which the bureaucracy and the political leaders constitute an elite whose level of income is vastly superior to the income of ordinary citizens.

One answer to this question which recurs in Marxian writings on

Tanzania is that Nyerere ought rapidly and thoroughly to have subdued 'the politico-bureaucratic bourgeoise' or indeed even to have replaced it.[52] It is argued that Nyerere ought to have sought more vigorously to mobilize the workers and peasants and to heighten their class consciousness so as to secure a political base for the proposed assault upon the bourgeoisie. This objective in turn would have required that Nyerere bypass most of those in senior positions in the party and the government as both these structures were badly infected by capitalist aspirations. He would have had to build up a new ruling cadre of ideologically committed men and women drawn from the radicalized section of the petty bourgeoisie, that is to say from the very group which has advocated this strategy.

This strategy was in fact advocated by one member of the special TANU Conference in March 1967. Kassela-Bantu, one of the small number of articulate Marxists in TANU, proposed a radical program of action: severe salary cuts, nationalization of all property, the use of the TANU youth league rather than the government or the party to promote and enforce the policies, and the rapid development of an ideologically committed vanguard.[53]

Nyerere immediately rejected this strategy. 'It would make us adventurists and opportunists not revolutionaries', he said. 'We cannot go "full-speed" into socialism. Where are the leaders for "full-speed" socialism?'[54] He returned to this question again. The Arusha Declaration was not, he said, an attempt immediately to be socialist. 'It was, rather, an attempt to remove capitalist tendencies and interests in our leaders.' Or again, 'the Declaration is an attempt to cultivate our leaders to a socialist program'.[55]

Nyerere's whole inclination was to preserve the unity of TANU and Tanzania and to advocate that Tanzania advance as a united society towards socialism. Moreover he was convinced that Tanzanians must be prepared to work harder for a better future and he was hostile to those who seemed to suggest to the people that their poverty was primarily somebody else's fault: 'It is not part of a Tanzanian leader's duty simply to encourage people in envy or to turn that envy into hostility or hatred against others.'[56]

The argument presented in the previous section to explain Nyerere's confidence that the leaders would accept the Arusha Declaration is relevant also to his feeling that Tanzania can move peacefully and as a united society towards socialism. The bureaucracy and the political leaders were not so far removed from the lives and values of ordinary Africans that they were not responsive to socialist ethics. If these leaders were not too much abused or their incomes too suddenly and too drastically slashed they could still be 'won over' to a socialist commitment. It was ideas of this nature that underlay the belief that the leaders could be 'cultivated to a socialist program'.

Political realism also compelled Nyerere to reject the radical strategy. Nyerere felt that there was no possible basis for the immediate imposition of radical egalitarian policies. He did not have the popular support nor the cadres to enforce such policies. Moreover, in his judgment the country could not do without the skills, the experience and the education of those in the middle and upper ranks of the party and the government. A total assault on their privileges would have severely alienated them before they could be replaced. Tanzania had no choice but to follow an evolutionary path.

> We shall become a socialist self-reliant society through our growth. We cannot afford the destruction of the economic instruments we now have nor a reduction in our present output. The steps by which we move forward must take account of these things. Our change will be effected almost entirely by the emphasis of our new development.[57]

A few months later he made the same point. 'We must equalize income as we make our total wealth grow.'[58] Nyerere had thus taken the hard-headed decision that a major initiative to redistribute incomes would be more disruptive to the economy and to the polity of Tanzania than they could be expected to bear. Svendsen, who was to be the Economic Adviser to President Nyerere, commented:

> Social and economic efforts must have a fair chance to bring results. The worst enemy of any socialist policy is bad economic performance. It will not help a group of political leaders, a party or a country that there is a high level of political consciousness if this does not also mean economic results in the form of a better life for the population.[59]

Thus, despite his conviction that wide income differentials constitute a major barrier to the achievement of socialism, Nyerere decided that Tanzania had no choice but to follow an evolutionary policy. That policy has not been a sham. Salary scales for middle and upper level have been held without upward revision for a thirteen-year period while there has been a series of increases in the minimum wage and in the lower wage scales more generally.* As well, personal income taxation has increased significantly in the higher brackets, and a variety of fringe benefits such as heavily subsidized housing, car loans and particularly long vacations have been abolished or cut. As a result, the ratio of the purchasing power after direct taxation of the top civil service salaries compared to the minimum wage has fallen from an estimated 80 : 1 in 1960 to 16 : 1 in 1971 and

* Finally, in 1974, modest overall increases were granted to offset, but only partially, the results of an expected significant rise in the cost of living. Even these overall increases were weighted in favour of the lowest income groups, as they gave a Shs.100 increase in the minimum wage per month but put a Shs.300 ceiling on the maximum increases in the highest brackets.

to 11:1 in 1974.[60] This is still a sizable ratio, but the fall in this ratio over a thirteen-year period is dramatic, especially as it has entailed a fall in real income for many senior civil servants.[61]

This strategy involves an effort to walk a narrow path between a too-vigorous equalizing policy which would undermine morale and produce declining efficiency if not more forthright obstruction, and a too-timid policy which might result in an entrenched and self-perpetuating new political and bureaucratic class. There is clearly a risk that in fact this narrow path does not exist and that the strategy will generate discontent and declining morale in the civil service and spark a downward spiral of inefficiency, lethargy and corruption. For this reason a strong and popular TANU is important both as a check to any political expression of elite discontent and also to provide an overall climate of opinion in the society which would in turn influence the mood of potentially restless TANU leaders, government officials or army officers. For the same reason a whole range of questions relating to administrative organization, personnel policies and managerial practices become singularly important as they are variables which influence the morale, the commitment and the efficiency of the civil service.*

The strategy which TANU has followed since 1967 in pursuit of a more egalitarian society has its obvious risks. However the original decision still seems defensible. These risks are less than those involved either in permitting the full entrenchment of a bureaucratic and political elite or in a strategy which would have sought to move much more rapidly to a more egalitarian society at a time when Nyerere lacked the political base for such a policy and when such a policy might have generated widespread and severe discontent amongst a strata of society whose skills and whose cooperation were still essential to effective government and continued economic development.

The maintenance of national self-reliance

National self-reliance was not in itself a socialist objective. It was primarily a product of nationalist sentiments. Nevertheless it had important consequences for Tanzania's transition to socialism. It provided a major part of the argument for the nationalizations in February 1967. These socialist measures were done, Nyerere himself has said, primarily for nationalist reasons:

* One consequence of the strength of Marxian scholars in the social science department at the university and Kivukoni College is that these questions receive scant attention in much of the work being done in the social sciences in Tanzania. Whatever the validity of their analysis of the international and class aspects of Tanzanian underdevelopment their work does not encourage attention to that immediate threat to Tanzanian socialism, which continues to be serious and which Svendsen identified seven years ago, the threat of inefficiency and economic failure.

I do not think that there is any free state in Africa where there is sufficient local capital, or a sufficient number of local entrepreneurs for locally based capitalism to dominate the economy. . .A capitalistic economy means a foreign dominated economy. These are the facts of Africa's situation. The only way in which national control of the economy can be achieved is through the economic institutions of socialism.[62]

There was, and is, a further corollary to Nyerere's call to self-reliance which is of central importance. This is the belief that Tanzanians do in fact have it within their own power to act upon some at least of the major obstacles to their own development. The call to self-reliance is in some ways the reverse of a call to Tanzanians to see their poverty as a consequence of imperialism or neo-colonialism and to seek therefore to overcome it by participation in an international socialist effort to defeat international capitalism. This sort of language is almost totally absent from Nyerere's exposition of self-reliance. Certainly the motivation behind self-reliance involves a determination that Africans will no longer be oppressed or humiliated. However the call is for Tanzanians to stand on their own, rather than to join sides in any international struggle. He explicitly rejected the argument that the people should be mobilized politically by arousing in them a sense that they are exploited and oppressed.

In particular, at this stage in our history we should not be trying to blame particular groups or individuals for things which are not to our liking or not to the liking of the people. The exploiters, who are now apparently so beloved by our leaders that they spend all their time talking about them are a negligible factor in our development now.[63]

A commitment to self-reliance could only make sense on the assumption that Tanzanians can in fact significantly advance their own development by their own efforts. Svendsen made this point at the time in these terms:

But the privileged in Tanzania are few – a tiny part of the whole population – and not much can be gained by redistributing income and wealth. . .The narrow base of the economy is the main reason for the low living standards. Some people earn too high incomes, there are adverse trends in the prices of foreign trade etc., but there is only one real explanation of the existing poverty – too low production. Low income per capita is due to low production per man. It is the purpose of the policy of self-reliance to dispel any illusions in this connection.[64]

The nationalist component to the concern for self-reliance contributed also to the maintenance of a foreign policy of positive non-alignment. Nyerere after 1967 had no more desire to see Tanzania attached to any major power bloc than he had before that date. He made the point in a press interview in 1968 in these terms:

The big Communist states are as likely to indulge in attempts to
infiltrate societies as the big capitalist states. The major difference which
I see at the moment is that the eastern powers are not used to controlling
Africans...They don't assume they have the right to 'give us advice'
in the same way as some of the large western powers do...The real
truth is that capitalism is by nature expansionist. Communism is on the
other hand evangelical...and Africa has some experience of the things
that can follow evangelism.[65]

Some commentators have read into the Tanzanian doctrine of self-
reliance an opting out of trade relations with Western countries.[66] This
reading of Tanzanian self-reliance cannot be sustained and was, indeed,
directly rejected by Nyerere. 'Self reliance', he said, 'does not imply
isolationism...it is not the same thing as saying we shall not trade with
other people.'[67]

Small, poor countries, such as Tanzania, have no choice but to bargain
as best they can for the skills and the technologies which they need:

We have no alternative. The world supply of disinterested altruists and
unconditional aid is very small indeed and however self-reliant we try
to be in our economies and our development we are up against the fact
that progress out of poverty has everywhere throughout history required
some injection of capital or expertise. Even the largest states of the
world have used outside resources; small ones have to use more. It
becomes a question of how far we will go and what kind of compromises
we will make. We cannot refuse to make any. For our own people will
refuse to accept poverty without hope of change. We must have
economic development or we have no political stability; and without
political stability we have no political independence either, but become
playthings of any other nation which desires to intervene in our affairs.[68]

Perhaps the clearest indication of Nyerere's personal belief in positive
non-alignment was revealed when Chinese assistance to Tanzania was
rapidly becoming more substantial than any bilateral assistance from a
major Western power and was involving China in a number of activities,
such as the equipping and training of the army, which at the very least
have the potential to upset Tanzania's non-alignment. At the very time
that this became clear, Nyerere reaffirmed in three successive major
speeches and in many minor ones his commitment to non-alignment. It is
fair to suggest that it was because of the increasing links with China that
he stressed that Tanzania was determined to remain outside of the major
power blocs. Nyerere was careful in these various reaffirmations of non-
alignment to avoid the suggestion that non-alignment meant merely
staying outside of the U.S.A. and the Soviet power groupings. Such an
interpretation of non-alignment would have opened the way to an actual
alignment with China against the U.S.A. and the Soviet Union. Nyerere

avoided that particular path. He urged TANU in October 1967 'to persist in our attempt to follow a policy of non-alignment in the ideological and power quarrels of the world, committing ourselves to no great power alliance'.[69] In his speech to the preparatory conference of non-aligned countries in 1970 he identified China as one of the three major powers involved in 'the Power Game'.[70] In 1968 in Peking, he made it clear in discreet but definite terms that Tanzania did not intend to enter a general alliance with China.[71]

There can be no doubt that at the time of the Arusha Declaration and in the several years immediately thereafter, despite the closer links with China, the estrangement with Britain and Germany, and the suspicion of American policies, non-alignment continued to be central to the view of Tanzania's place in international politics which Nyerere was urging upon his fellow countrymen, and a key component of Tanzania's foreign policy. It was also totally compatible with and partly an expression of Tanzania's concern to maintain and enhance its self-reliance.

The creation of a socialist environment

It had been implicit in Nyerere's position in 1962 that when modern socialist institutions were introduced in Tanzania they would be quickly accepted and supported by a large majority of the population. This followed from his conviction that traditional communal values were still widely influential and were, in their essence, socialist. The point has already been made that by 1967 Nyerere felt that acquisitive individualism was rapidly undermining the force of these traditional values.

This judgment explains many of Nyerere's socialist initiatives since that date. Nyerere sensed an urgent need to create a more socialist environment in order thereby to check the otherwise growing influence of selfish individualism and to draw people towards socialist values.

The importance which Nyerere attached to creating institutions in which socialist attitudes might develop and socialist relationships be established shows itself in a number of important initiatives which he has taken in recent years. These have included the creation of works councils and workers' committees in all sectors of the economy and a major decentralization of government.[72] These initiatives are similar in purpose to Nyerere's earlier interest in democratic participation in the cooperative unions and in the trade unions. The workers' committees, the works councils, and the District and regional planning and development committees created under the decentralization program – as was also true with the earlier initiatives in regard to the cooperative movement and the trade unions – each hopes to achieve meaningful mass participation within structures that will encourage broader and more responsible attitudes and will aid the development of social relationships and a work ethic that is more appropriate to a socialist society.

These various socialist initiatives all involved socialist measures which were likely to be widely popular. However, once Nyerere had become convinced that acquisitive individualism threatened to be widely prevalent in Tanzania, he had to come to terms with the possibility that some basic socialist initiatives might, at least initially, be opposed by a majority of the people. Glickman, writing on the basis of research conducted in 1962, had concluded that Nyerere's thought at that time offered few barriers to the authoritarian conclusion that 'men must be forced to be free'. In chapter 4 I rejected this judgment, arguing that Nyerere's scepticism towards elites and the character of his ideal society were powerful and sufficient restraints upon any authoritarian potential in his thought.[73] The logic of his position by 1967 might seem to have pushed him towards a more authoritarian stance. He had clearer and surer ideas of what he felt was necessary and desirable for Tanzania. He also was admitting the possibility that the people's communal values had been corrupted so that many might not initially recognize that a socialist initiative was in their interest. Was Glickman's judgment therefore more premature than wrong? Was Nyerere by 1967 ready to accept coercion as a necessary feature of the transition to socialism?

Nyerere did not take this position in 1967 and has not since assumed it. His thought continues to exhibit the same tension as previously between what might be called its leadership strand and its democratic strand. Nyerere does not rule out, and indeed on occasion he has ordered, government actions which are unpopular but which he feels are very evidently necessary. For any moral person in a position of authority, this is, in fact, an unavoidable duty. Whatever one's commitment to democracy, most people would surely accept that a political leader cannot take the position that a government on every occasion must only do that which it knows will be immediately acceptable to its people. Indeed, in Nyerere's case it is arguable that one feature of the popular confidence in him was a recognition that occasionally the popular will ought to be defied and the judgment that the people have in Nyerere someone whom they are content to have exercising that power.

What then restrained Nyerere from a fully self-confident assertion that he and his government would use what force was necessary to establish the institutions of a socialist society? Why did he not accept that coercion might be necessary at first to overcome the consequences of a corrupting individualism, while expecting that as people lived under the new institutions they would gradually return to socialist ethics and free themselves of capitalist motivations?*

* Saul, in his interesting study of the Tanzanian political system, in effect attributes this view to Nyerere. He 'assumes' that Nyerere sees electoral participation and central control as two techniques available to a 'benevolent leadership' to move Tanzania along the path to socialism. He suggests that, to the extent that the

I do not believe that this has been the position taken by Nyerere. He has rejected it, in lesser part because he has recognized that neither the government nor TANU has the power to impose socialism on a reluctant people. He has also recognized that an intensification of central control often intensifies and entrenches opposition to a policy rather than overcoming the initial hurdles to its acceptance.[74] However, his rejection is far more than merely tactical. He has remained powerfully sceptical of the morality of this whole line of argument. He has never made the assumption that his socialism is objectively or scientifically correct.[75] What authoritarian potential there may be in his commitment to socialism has not been reinforced and rationalized by this particular reassuring assumption. He has been as impatient with such pretensions in recent years as he had been ten years previously. For example he told a TANU Conference in 1967, 'The delegates here come from the people and are responsible to them. It is impossible for us at this meeting to take over their responsibilities or to act as if we had some God-given right to force goals of our choosing upon the people.'[76] Two years later he told Parliament: 'Nor can we lead a country as if it were a Church with the priests and bishops choosing and rejecting each other as leaders without the believers having any chance to choose or to throw out their leaders.'[77]

Nyerere continued to recognize that the establishment of socialist institutions does not assure the triumph of socialist values. A state which has fully nationalized its industries and its trade can as easily be a tyranny as a capitalist state. Nyerere rejects the idea that the achievement of socialism might be a two-stage affair, the first part of which can be done by an elite. For him it has always been an unacceptable paradox to suggest that the people might need to be coerced into a socialist society. 'A people cannot be developed: they can only develop themselves.'[78] Nyerere's rejection of an authoritarian imposition of socialism thus rested finally and perhaps most fundamentally upon a profoundly felt conviction that in statesmanship no great thing can be accomplished without the people.

These ideas had their immediate relevance. The most important socialist initiative since 1967 has been the sustained effort of the government and TANU to convince the peasants throughout the country to move from their scattered homesteads into socialist villages, *ujamaa vijijini*. Nyerere had been long convinced that rural Tanzania would develop slowly and haltingly as long as its peasants did not live in villages. He anticipated far-reaching advantages from villagization, to use the clumsy term then current. It would be much easier for the government and TANU to reach the peasants once they lived in villages. Only then could it be feasible to

party becomes more tightly ideological and its leadership more firmly committed to socialism, there will be a correspondingly increased justification for a greater degree of authoritarian rule and for a lessening of the democratic component in the electoral system. Saul, 'The Nature of Tanzania's Political System', Part 1, p. 123.

hope that schools, water supplies, dispensaries, agricultural and veterinary services and political education could reach all the people. Moreover peasants living in villages would be able to employ a range of modern agricultural practices that are uneconomic on widely scattered and disorganized holdings. The driving force behind these considerations was a nationalist concern to move rural Tanzania into the modern world in order that the peasants might share in its advantages and be full participants in the newly independent state.

These considerations continued to be important after 1967. However, by that date another consideration, more strictly socialist in character, became important. Nyerere had come to fear that peasant cultivation of cash crops on individual holdings was, in his words, 'the wrong path'. It encouraged an individual acquisitiveness that it could not satisfy, it undermined communal values and it led to class stratification and the creation of a landless rural proletariat. The peasants must therefore be urged not only to live in villages but also to farm communally. Only in this way could economic growth come to the rural areas in ways compatible with 'traditional concepts of human equality'. Only in this way could Tanzania 'build up the countryside in such a way that our people have a better standard of living while living together on terms of equality and fraternity'.[79]

Nyerere has succeeded in making the introduction of *ujamaa* villages the most important single policy of his government and of TANU since 1967. His reason for doing this is straightforward. 'The vast majority of our people will continue to spend their lives in the rural areas and continue to work on the land...If our rural life is not based on the principles of socialism our country will not be socialist regardless of our commercial and political arrangements.'[80]

Here if anywhere, the temptation has been great to advocate a two-phase transition to socialism. In the first phase the party and the government would impose the institutions which would check the development of personal acquisitiveness and would channel development aspirations towards communal targets. Then would follow the second phase in which the people, no longer corrupted, would welcome and support the socialist institutions. Nyerere has resisted the temptation of an authoritarian first phase. He has insisted that the establishment of *ujamaa* villages must be done with the full and active cooperation of the peasants. 'Viable socialist communities can only be established with willing members.'[81] This has been a recurrent, indeed an insistent, theme in his many speeches on the *ujamaa* villages. Despite the evident strength of acquisitive individualism in the countryside and the great importance he has attached to the *ujamaa* villages, he has not yielded to the attraction of an authoritarian shortcut to socialism.

Nyerere has also refused to accept the Marxists' recommendation that

he generate class antagonism amongst the peasants against their economically more active and more successful fellow peasants in order then to build
the villages on the basis of a class-conscious poorer peasantry. He has
recognized that the unease about the *ujamau* villages extends beyond the
so-called 'Kulak' class. Moreover he is no more anxious on this issue than
on any other to create deep divisions or to build a new society upon a
deliberately generated envy. He has therefore taken two steps backwards.
He has come to accept that the small-scale farmer working on his own
land is not incompatible with socialism, though he hopes that in time he
will merge his land with others in a cooperative endeavour. He is ready
in this issue to go more slowly. However, he has simultaneously insisted
that strong pressures be applied to get the peasants to live in villages.[82]
This, he feels, is such a basic requirement of progress that some coercion
may be justified to overcome initial opposition to it. His motive here is
primarily nationalist not socialist. It issues from a nationalist's conviction
that his country must develop. The coercion which Nyerere appears to
accept here is an expression of an impatient nationalism not a coercive
socialism. This does not make the use of coercion any less risky or any
more attractive. The efforts of impatient nationalists to effect rapid social
transformation in the rural areas, particularly if some of them still exhibit
a general inclination to authoritarian rule, may prove as difficult as the
efforts of an impatient colonialism in the 1950s to coerce the peasants into
agricultural practices which it judged to be in their interests. Nevertheless
it does appear to be the case that despite this readiness to use coercion to
bring the peasants into villages, it has still remained Nyerere's view that
the creation of a socialist environment, which is an important component
of Nyerere's strategy for the transition to socialism, must still be accomplished with the support and cooperation of the people. This continues
to be his conviction even as regards socialist farming. The balance between
the leadership strand and the democratic strand in his thought has thus
been sustained in that area of policy in which it was, perhaps, most
severely strained.[83]

The enhancement of democratic participation

It will be argued in this section that increasing democratic participation
is the final essential component to Nyerere's strategy for the transition to
socialism. It is an argument that needs to be carefully examined. Nyerere
has never seen himself as a cypher, whose role is simply to transpose the
wishes of the people into laws and government actions. His populism has
not been a simple judgment that the people are always right. Neither has
Nyerere seen his primary function as that of finding effective and lasting
compromises between the main interest groups in Tanzania. Such a
conception of democratic leadership is a product of economically developed plural societies. It is inappropriate in countries such as Tanzania

which still lack the institutions and the skills that would make it possible for their peoples to lift themselves from their present extremely low living standards. These societies need more than the provision of services, the maintenance of law and order, and the negotiation of working compromises. They need new enthusiasms, new capacities for collective action, a new receptivity to innovation and a new attitude towards work. They need new political institutions and wider loyalties, and a more acute awareness of the international dimensions to the continuance of their poverty. They are, to put it briefly, societies that need to be transformed. They are societies which need leaders who are men of vision who can see a way forward for their people, can define that path in terms that will win the understanding and support of ordinary men and women and can lead them towards it.

Nyerere is one such leader. He sees himself as the leader of a people who are groping their way forward towards a better future. He is not just the servant of his people. He has always been a leader with strong convictions about his people's needs. Nyerere has been, above all, a teacher, a *mwalimu*. He is a teacher of a special sort. He is a teacher of morality. However, Nyerere is not just a *mwalimu*. He is a *mwalimu*-in-power – a moral teacher who is also a political leader with a great deal of authority and power. He has not needed to confine himself to teaching by example and by precept. He has been able to manipulate the circumstances of politics, in order to lead his people to moral perceptions which as yet they only imperfectly comprehend. His purpose has not been to deceive either Tanzanians or outsiders. His purpose has been to bring Tanzanians to an increasingly profound commitment to pursue a democratic and socialist society.

In doing this Nyerere has been willing to use the opportunities which are his as President to set the stage for decision-making, to influence its timing and to define the issues in ways that will increase the likelihood that the people will decide along the lines he feels are necessary. He did this, for example, to win TANU support for a form of one-party state which was acceptable to him and he did it again to assure formal TANU support for the *ujamaa* villages. These two major decisions and many minor ones illustrate that Nyerere has used great political skill to win TANU support for decisions which he has felt were needed.

He has guided and he has manipulated, in addition to merely teaching and advocating. For some, perhaps, this will mean that he is not a democrat. But in a society that needs transformation someone must strive to define the society's needs for it. In a society in which national political institutions are still imperfectly structured and inadequately rooted in the life of the society, strong leadership may be the only way in which a national consensus can be obtained on essential issues. To be a political leader in such a society is inevitably to be open to the charge of elitism.

More important therefore than any discussion of whether Nyerere exhibits such paternalism towards his people (which he surely does) is a consideration of the techniques which he is willing to use, as well as those which he will not use, to win people to his perception of their needs. It is not what distinguishes Nyerere from the pure populist or from the liberal democrat that is important so much as what distinguishes him from the ideological authoritarian. This, the more important distinction, rests upon his continued insistence that democratic participation, including popular electoral participation, is an essential feature of the transition to socialism. The authoritarian socialist takes an instrumental view of participation, valuing it to the extent that it will contribute to the achievement of socialist objectives as these are identified by a committed and ideologically sound elite, the benevolent leadership, to use John Saul's flattering phrase. In contrast to that position, Nyerere regards democratic participation as intrinsically valuable and strategically essential.

Democracy, however, has not been easily achieved in Tanzania. There has been a persistent tendency towards oligarchy and authoritarian rule. There have been cultural barriers to overcome before the people are likely to assert their rights against the leadership. The institutions of constitutional democracy with which Tanzania began its independence were inappropriate to a society whose national integration was not yet firm. They were also unsuited to the closely integrated socialist society which TANU hoped to develop in Tanzania. As a result, Nyerere has long searched for institutional forms of democracy which would be appropriate to its needs and consonant with its values. The democratic one-party state was but the most important of the initiatives in the period covered by this study which issued from that concern.

Nyerere has continued to seek ways to make democratic participation and control effective in Tanzania. He has seen Parliament, even after the 1965 constitutional changes, fail to become a significant instrument of policy-making, policy-review or public accountability. He has seen local representative councils flounder ineffectively in the area of local government. He has seen electoral processes in both the party and in Parliament produce representatives who quickly pursue interests that are separate and different from those of the people. Under these pressures, his ideas on democratic participation have grown complex and more sophisticated. In particular, three ideas have acquired more prominence in his writings in recent years and have had a significant influence upon policy.

First, Nyerere, like so many thinkers whose concern with participation is genuine, has returned to the importance of government at the local level. At one point, for example, he spoke of his longer-term vision of Tanzanian life in terms of 'rural economic and social communities where people live together and work together for the good of all and which are inter-locked so that all the different communities also work together in cooperation for the common good of the nation as a whole'.[84] This was not a casual fantasy. Two of Nyerere's most important Presidential initiatives since 1967, the *ujamaa* villages and decentralization, are in part an expression of this interest.

Second, Nyerere has come in recent years to see wide income differentials as an important obstacle to the effective operation of democratic institutions. The point involved has not only been that those with much more economic power are likely to dominate the political process. It is also and perhaps more important, that if those with political and government power have significantly higher incomes than ordinary citizens, they are likely to constitute a 'new class'. Greater equality as between ruler and ruled is an important restraint upon such a development. If ruler and ruled are of the same class, if the leaders are truly of and with the people in their daily living, then government is more likely to be responsive to popular needs.

Greater equality is thus not only a desirable social objective, it is also an important aid to effective democratic government. The Arusha Declaration rules, to give a specific policy application, even though they exclude from political and public office any who offend them, are nevertheless an expression of a commitment to democracy. These rules are the expression of a widely shared ethic. To the extent that they are enforced they lessen the risk that leaders will develop interests which will conflict with those of the ordinary voter. They can therefore legitimately be seen as an aid to democracy rather than a limitation upon it.

Finally, Nyerere has increasingly stressed the importance of the party as the structure that is closest to the people and most representative of the people. In contrast to TANU, Parliament is an aloof and distant institution while the government, however led, is always to some extent a power that is outside of and over the people. TANU leaders during the struggle for independence were in close harmony with the ordinary citizens. That closeness can be recreated. The party must strive to be the organized voice of the people. 'When we argue for the sovereignty of the party I want us to mean by this the sovereignty of the people.'[85]

It was suggested earlier that Parliament had not become an adequate instrument for the democratic control of government policies and the political leadership.[86] The argument was offered that if the democratic purposes of the 1965 Constitution were to be realized, TANU must itself become more democratic. This has, in fact, been one of the most important of the issues to which Nyerere has devoted his time, particularly in the years between 1965 to 1969. Quietly but effectively the party's competence as an organization was greatly strengthened. Then, in 1968 and 1969, Nyerere, as President of TANU, effected a democratic revolution within TANU. The main components of the parliamentary electoral system were transplanted into the party. A wide range of posts, including much of the membership of the Party Conference, the National Executive Committee, the Central Committee and the Regional party conferences and the District and Regional Chairmen are now filled through an election process which includes the same four stages as the national elections. There are now nominations, a preliminary ranking of candidates by a local party gathering, the scrutiny of the list of candidates and the selection by a superior party organ of two candidates for the final election, and, finally, voting on these two candidates by a more representative electorate. These reforms have significantly increased internal democracy within the party and are an integral part of the strategy developed by Nyerere for the transition to socialism.

One development might seem to contradict this view that Nyerere's socialist strategy has involved a move towards increased democratic participation within the party. This is the power which the National Executive Committee or the Central Committee have to veto candidates for election to the National Assembly and to any of the important elected positions within TANU. Certainly if this power were used to secure a close conformity to a detailed ideology it would quickly transform TANU into something close to a vanguard party. One can only say that this does not appear to have happened yet, despite the support for such a development from Marxists and from authoritarians in the party who have long supported developments that would confirm and consolidate their hold on power. The democratic traditions within the party, the mass support for meaningful elections and Nyerere's continuous championing of democratic controls have held in check this particular authoritarian development.[87]

There are few elements in Nyerere's political thought which are repeated more insistently and more forcefully than the conviction that there can be neither socialism nor the beginnings of a transition to socialism without democracy. These brief quotations illustrate this:

The people must make the decisions about their own future through democratic procedures. Leadership cannot replace democracy, it must be part of democracy.

Socialism is not an alternative to political democracy; it is an extension of it. . .Socialism means the extension of political democracy to include economic democracy.

The people's freedom to determine their own priorities, to organize themselves and their own advance in welfare, is an important part of our objective. It cannot be postponed to some future time. The people's active and continued voluntary participation in the struggle is an important part of our objective because only through this participation will the people develop.[88]

These quotations are each from a different major Presidential statement made between 1968 and 1971. They could be matched by others equally unequivocal. Their meaning is clear. Democracy is an essential feature of the transition to socialism.

But what if the practice of democracy threatens an important socialist measure or is but an occasion for the voicing of inconsequential or even divisive interests? In 1965 Nyerere had given this reply: 'If the people did make a mistake, it is their right to do so...It is arrogance for anyone to think that they can choose on behalf of the people better than the people can choose for themselves.'[89] Five years later his position had not really altered:

> I know that there are, even in Tanzania, some beliefs that periodic
> elections are dangerous. It is said that they give to the enemies of our
> people and of our political system an opportunity to sow confusion: it is
> said that they could be used to destroy our unity; that they could be
> used to get rid of good leaders and replace them with bad leaders...I
> myself am aware that periodic elections do bring these dangers. Yet I
> am quite unable to see what we can put in their place.[90]

Nyerere could see nothing to put in the place of democracy because, as he went on to explain, 'only while there is this kind of recurring opportunity for choice...are we, their [the people's] representatives, forced to overcome our indolence or our selfishness and serve them [the people] to the best of our ability'.[91]

There is on this issue a key divide which separates the socialist whose primary commitment is to a doctrine (however much he feels that this doctrine reflects the true interests of the people) and the socialist whose primary commitment is to the people themselves as they now are, warts and all. No state can achieve its communal objectives without relying upon political, administrative and technological 'experts'. Yet to rely upon 'experts' is to risk oppression by these 'experts'. Some socialists would seek to minimize this risk primarily by an emphasis on ideology, arguing that if the 'experts' are ideologically well trained and the leaders are a committed socialist vanguard the risks will be minimal.

At this divide in socialist thought, Nyerere takes, instead, the democratic path. He would prefer to run the risk of the people misusing their power than the risk of a 'benevolent leadership' abusing its power. He would minimize the risk of oppression by 'experts' by assuring as best he can that they are not so well rewarded as to constitute a separate class and that they are electorally answerable to the people. 'All of us', he has said, 'everywhere, have to wage a constant struggle to support the supremacy of the people. We have to be constantly vigilant to ensure that the people are not used by the individuals to whom they have entrusted power.'[92]

This constant vigilance is to be directed at least as much towards the potential political 'new class' as towards the bureaucratic bourgeoisie. Nyerere has never supported the argument that TANU should become a vanguard party, a party that is which would be a closed party of committed socialists, admitting to its elite membership only those who it feels are committed to its doctrines. This has never been Nyerere's position. His reason is simple. A vanguard party would need to be a party of angels and 'We are not angels.'[93]

The fact that Nyerere hopes for an increasing number of committed socialists within the leadership of TANU in no way means that he is in effect advocating a vanguard within a mass party that would be little different from a vanguard party within a mass society. The difference is in fact crucial. In the former case the leadership would not be a closed elite but would be open to anyone in the party who could win the confidence of his fellow party members while the people themselves would have a structure, the party, and a process, the elections, through which to assert their rights and to exercise a final control upon the leadership. For Nyerere, all of this is particularly relevant to the transition to socialism for in that transition the power of the state is likely to increase and the risk of oppression, or at least the potential for it, will therefore be greater. 'State ownership and control of the key points of the economy can, in fact, lead to a greater tyranny if the state is not itself controlled by the people who exercise this control for their own benefit and on their own behalf.'[94] Democracy, in consequence, including the recurrent election of leaders in free elections, is thus an important component of his political strategy for the transition to socialism.

Political ideologists and theorists of widely differing persuasions tend to have in common one basic characteristic when they consider the politics of economically poor societies. All are convinced that the policies they are promoting are in the best interests of the great mass of the people. All are anxious to provide for the active participation of ordinary citizens to the extent, but only to the extent, that this participation will further the implementation of these policies. All are confident that in the long run the wisdom of these policies will be recognized by the mass of the people and that their continued implementation can then be entrusted to a fully democratic system. However in the interim, the 'critical phase', they are ready to override popular opinion in order to assure the continued promotion of the policies which they identify as being in the general interest.

This underlying similarity, this active, operational elitism is a feature of writers, political leaders and administrators whose views otherwise differ widely one from the other. This similarity has been observed before by other observers of the African scene. Coleman and Rosberg for example have noted the parallels between colonial rule and the style and structure of government in many independent African states.[95] Jonathan Barker has drawn out the parallels between Lenin's view of the need for an autonomous political force in revolutionary social situations and the role of rural *animateurs* in the rural development program in Senegal.[96] In the particular case of Tanzania, James Finucane has compared the attitude towards mass participation held by the Tanzanian bureaucracy and by many Tanzanian political leaders with that of the theorists of the 'human relations' school of management such as Martin Oppenheimer and Douglas MacGregor.[97]

Similarities and parallels of this sort are worth noting in the specific context of Tanzania. The British colonial rulers sought to provide a degree of popular participation after 1945 only to the extent that it did not conflict with the promotion of policies which they judged to be important. Soon after 1961, many nationalists took essentially the same position. They tended to feel that they did not need to be answerable to the people through competitive and democratic elections, though electoral arrangements which might help to legitimize their rule were desirable. A group of liberal American social scientists took a position close to the classic defence of controlled participation under the direction of an administrative state when they declared, 'The problem remains one of increasing the feeling of participation without necessarily increasing the local input into decision making.'[98] This view in turn could easily be a paraphrase of the position taken by John Saul who has argued that the pursuit of socialism in Tanzania is likely to require that a socialist leadership be ready to act without popular support in order to promote social change which will, he hopes, then lead to a situation of 'congruent socialism', a happy situation in which the socialist leadership and the mass of the people are in agreement on the objectives of social and economic policies.[99]

All these positions, the colonial, the nationalist, the administrative, and the Marxist, though differing in many fundamental ways, are in agreement that for an indeterminate period, hopefully finite but of significant length, a group in power which knows best must be ready to override the wishes and sentiments of the people. Popular recognition of the wisdom and historical necessity of this elite's role will come later. For the moment however that elite must rule according to its own prescriptions and pursue its own vision of the future.

In taking such a position each of these schools stands in sharp contrast to the position taken by Julius Nyerere. He has always seen the transition to a socialist society in terms of a gradual actualization in contemporary Tanzania of the values that will finally predominate in a socialist Tanzania. To advance towards socialism is to begin to act as socialists. One essential feature of such a transition to socialism is the participation of ordinary citizens in the nation's political processes. Nyerere has never meant by this merely participation to the extent that it supports his rule. Nyerere is often a vigorous leader, moving far ahead of the sentiments and perceived needs of his people. However, he has never seen participation merely as a mobilized ratification of whatever the leadership proposes. He has at times come close to that position, particularly in recent years when his socialist convictions have become firmer and more clearly defined. He has always returned to the view that participation must mean active and direct popular involvement in politics, including the regular, recurrent choice of political leaders through democratic elections.

This continuing democratic component in his political ideas is not the result of a simplistic populism. Nyerere has recognized that the unity of Tanzania is still fragile and that a demagogue could destroy much that has been laboriously constructed. He has had to maintain the loyalty of many colleagues who have been sceptical of democratic participation at this stage. Although profoundly committed to an egalitarian society, he has witnessed developments that would seem to lessen the likelihood of Tanzania's achieving such an objective. Nevertheless he has remained committed to democratic participation as an essential feature of Tanzania's lengthy transition to socialism. His belief in democracy has persisted. He has recurringly refused to allow himself or his government to become so certain of their own integrity, of the validity of their vision and the adequacy of their means as to feel that extensive coercion is justified. This is, perhaps, the characteristic of Tanzanian socialism which explains more than any other the international interest which it has attracted.

Marxist commentators tend to identify the bureaucracy as the source of the major threat to the achievement of socialism in Tanzania. They fear that senior officials in the public service are increasingly hostile to socialism and are determined to bend the policies of government to suit their interests as an emerging dominant class. This certainly is one of the risks that must concern the political leadership in Tanzania. It is an almost unavoidable risk in any third-world country that seeks a peaceful transition to socialism. However, this study would seem to suggest that there are two continuing threats to a successful transition to socialism in Tanzania which, though more traditional-sounding and less sophisticated in conception, are nevertheless at least as serious as any that may emerge from the bureaucracy.

The first of these is the tendency to authoritarian rule which still persists within the middle and senior ranks of TANU and which the politicization of the army and the greater emphasis on social discipline may be intensifying. The second is the threat of economic and administrative failures of such an extent as finally to alienate mass support and leave the leadership prone either to self-transformation into an authoritarian oligarchy, or to replacement by a new set of men who would constitute such an oligarchy.

These variations in the judgment of commentators about the main threats to Tanzanian socialism are, unfortunately, not merely of academic consequence. They lead to different and in part contradictory policy recommendations. Marxists emphasize the need for a vanguard party and the deliberate intensification of mass antagonisms towards the bureaucracy and the successful peasant farmer. These two recommendations, if pursued, might well help to check the emergence of a bureaucratic bourgeoisie but they would also be likely to increase the risk of authoritarian rule and of serious economic and governmental failures. A parallel point is equally valid. The policy recommendations which are implicit in the identification of authoritarian rule and governmental and economic failure as the immediate major threats are, if implemented, likely to increase the risk of an entrenchment of the bureaucracy as a ruling class. If all three of these risks are in fact real and threatening, then any exclusive preoccupation by the government with only one or two of them would increase the likelihood that the unnoticed third threat would in fact become the most important.

This leads to a final observation and conclusion. The strategy for the transition to socialism which emerged after 1967 cannot be dismissed as an intriguing mutation, an odd and unique consequence of the particular set of intellectual and ethical influences which shaped Nyerere's political values. The emphasis in that strategy on equality, on self-reliance, on democracy and on a unity which includes the bureaucrat and the cash-crop farmer rather than on a unity which is sought in opposition to them, entails an effort to hold in check all three of the central threats to the success of Tanzania's transition to socialism which have just been identified. It is thus fair to suggest as the final conclusion to this volume, that however difficult and precarious its pursuit, the strategy for the transition to socialism which was initially largely shaped by Nyerere, was a subtle and realistic response to the complex set of challenges which face Tanzanian society.

NOTES

Chapter 1. Themes and perspectives

1 Amir H. Jamal, *The Critical Phase of Emergent African States* (Nairobi, 1965).
2 *Ibid.* pp. 10–11.
3 This is the title of an address given by Nyerere in July 1961. It is reprinted in Nyerere, *Freedom and Unity: Uhuru na Umoja* (London, 1966), pp. 119–23.
4 This plasticity has been commented upon also by Roger Murray in his 'Second Thoughts on Ghana', *New Left Review*, 42 (March–April 1967), 25–39.
5 Karl Marx, 'Economic and Philosophical Manuscript', as quoted in Erich Fromm, *Beyond the Chains of Illusion* (New York, 1962), p. 67.
6 *Freedom and Socialism: Uhuru na Ujamaa* (Dar-es-Salaam, 1968), Introduction.

Chapter 2. British strategies and African nationalism in Tanganyika 1945–58

1 '...there is perhaps less divergence between government policy and nationalist policy than one might imagine. The announced goal of both is self-government, and although there are differences relating to timing of "when they are ready for it" and a question also of who will take over the reins of government, the ends are similar.' Roland Young and Henry A. Fosbrooke, *Smoke in the Hills* (Evanston, Ill., 1960), p. 177.
2 Margery Perham, *The Colonial Reckoning* (London, 1962), p. 70; emphasis added.
3 *Ibid.* p. 73.
4 *Ibid.* pp. 73–4 Lady Listowel in *The Making of Tanganyika* (London, 1965) provides at some length a similar interpretation of this period. I believe she has romanticized the relationship between these two men and has attached too much importance to the fact that each is an urbane and civilized individual.
5 This was the pattern referred to in the Rhodesias and Nyasaland as 'racial partnership' and in East Africa as 'multiracialism'. These terms are, of course, the identifications given to the policies by the British.
6 Lord Hailey, *Native Administration and Political Development in British Tropical Africa* (London, 1940–2).
7 Andrew Cohen (later Sir Andrew) was to become Governor of Uganda from 1952 to 1957.
8 This campaign included the famous dispatch of the Secretary of State of 25 Feb. 1947, the launching of annual conferences at Cambridge for senior

members of the administration in British African territories, a conference of Governors in 1947 and of colonial legislators in 1948, and the publication of a new quarterly journal, *The Journal of African Administration*, in 1949.

9 Hailey, *Native Administration and Political Development*, p. 50.

10 Secretary of State for the Colonies Despatch of 25 February 1947, para. 4.

11 Hailey, *Native Administration and Political Development*, p. 52.

12 United Kingdom Goverment, 'Papers Presented to the Africa Conference', A.C. 4811, p. 22.

13 Mrs Ursula Hicks, on very little evidence, suggests that this last concern was the main explanation for the interest of the Secretary of State and the Colonial Office in the development of local government in Africa. *Development from Below* (London, 1961), esp. ch. 1.

14 Kenya, *From the Governor of Kenya to the Secretary of State for the Colonies*, 30 May 1947, Despatch No. 16, 1947.

15 *Ibid.*

16 *Ibid.*

17 *Ibid.* Appendix 2.

18 'The Acting Governor of Tanganyika to the Secretary of State for the Colonies', Confidential No. 144, 8 November 1947.

19 In 1954, for example, the Commission on the East African Civil Services pointed out how very few Africans were qualified for admission to the administrative service but concluded from this fact, not that alternative arrangements were required to secure African candidates but rather that overseas recruitment would therefore be necessary for a long time. See United Kingdom Government, *Report of the Commission on the Civil Services of the East African Territories and the East African High Commission 1953–54* (London, 1954), particularly vol. 1, ch. 3.

20 The first Makerere graduate to be appointed to the administrative service in Tanganyika was not appointed until April 1959 and even then the appointment was only to a training grade. In May 1959, B. Lukindo and B. Mulokozi were each appointed as district officers (training grade). Two months later C. Y. Mgonja was also appointed. These were the first Makerere graduates to join the administrative service. Tanganyika, *Staff List 1959* (Dar-es-Salaam, 1959), p. 21.

21 Hailey, *Native Administration and Political Development*, p. 47.

22 United Kingdom Government, 'Despatch from the Governor of Tanganyika to the Secretary of State for the Colonies, No. 88, 20 Sept. 1950', in *Development of African Local Government in Tanganyika*, Colonial No. 277 (London, 1951), p. 10.

23 Even a commentator as sympathetic to the colonial administration in Tanganyika as Robert Heussler commented that 'People spoke about African self-rule, but somewhat as clergymen talk of an after life: euphorically and not as a discrete end toward which one marched by definite stages'. Robert Heussler, *British Tanganyika: An Essay and Documents on District Administration* (Durham, N.C., 1971), p. 66.

24 Cyril Ehrlich and John Iliffe have each written with much insight on the economic policies of the government of Tanganyika between the years 1945 and 1960. See Cyril Ehrlich, 'Some Aspects of Economic Policy in Tanganyika, 1945–60', *Journal of Modern African Studies*, 11 (July 1964), 265–78, and John Iliffe, *Agricultural Change in Modern Tanganyika: An Outline History*, Historical Association of Tanzania Paper No. 10 (Dar-es-Salaam, 1971). A major study of the economic aspects of colonial rule in East Africa is badly needed to correct the preoccupation with its political aspects which

has dominated scholarly writings on the colonial period in Tanganyika, a preoccupation which this book reflects and perpetuates. As the writing of this volume was completed, Anthony Brett's *Colonialism and Underdevelopment in East Africa* (London, 1973) appeared. It goes a long way to meet this need although it occasionally misses some of the nuances of earlier policy debates and decisions because of Brett's tendency to test earlier policies against contemporary preconceptions.

25 This quotation is from Dr Ehrlich's 'The Tanganyikan Economy 1945 to 1960' which is to appear in the third volume of the *History of East Africa* which is being published by Clarendon Press, Oxford.

26 International Bank for Reconstruction and Development, *The Economic Development of Tanganyika: A Report of a Mission Organized by the International Bank for Reconstruction and Development* (Baltimore, 1961), pp. 230, 476–7.

27 Tanganyika, *Annual Report of the Department of Education, 1956* (Dar-es-Salaam, 1957), p. 3.

28 Tanganyika, *African Census Report 1957* (Dar-es-Salaam, 1963), p. 67.

29 Bruce M. Russett *et al.*, *World Handbook of Political and Social Indicators* (New Haven, Conn., 1964), part A, section III, tables 37 and 38.

30 United Nations, *World Communications* (Paris, 1956), p. 57. This publication put Uganda's literacy at between 25% and 30% and the Gold Coast's at between 20% and 25%. Stephens estimates adult literacy in Tanganyika in 1960 to have been 16%. Hugh Stephens, *The Political Transformation of Tanganyika, 1920–67* (New York, 1968), p. 115. This book contains a comprehensive compilation of a variety of indices of social mobilization in Tanganyika.

31 International Bank for Reconstruction and Development, *Economic Development of Tanganyika*, p. 462.

32 Stephens, *Political Transformation of Tanganyika*, p. 38.

33 Tanganyika, *Statistical Abstract 1958* (Dar-es-Salaam, 1958), p. 66.

34 Tanganyika, *High-Level Manpower Requirements and Resources in Tanganyika, 1962–67*, by George Tobias, Government Paper No. 2 of 1963 (Dar-es-Salaam, 1963).

35 See, for example, International Bank for Reconstruction and Development, *Economic Development of Tanganyika*, p. 231.

36 *Ibid.* p. 27.

37 Iliffe, *Agricultural Change*, pp. 29–31.

38 There is need for a detailed history of African nationalism in Tanganyika such as G. Andrew Maguire has so ably written of the rise of nationalism within Sukumaland in his *Towards 'Uhuru' in Tanzania: The Politics of Participation* (Cambridge, 1969). There are interesting, relevant essays by Terence Ranger, John Iliffe and A. J. Temu in I. N. Kimambo and Temu (eds.), *A History of Tanzania* (Nairobi, 1969). As well, there are two important articles, Lionel Cliffe's 'Nationalism and the Reaction to Enforced Agricultural Change in Tanganyika during the Colonial Period', paper presented to the East African Institute of Social Research Conference, 1964, and John Iliffe's 'The role of the African Association in the Formation and Realization of Territorial Consciousness in Tanzania' (University of East Africa Social Science Conference, 1968). Much that had been written about the early years of TANU before these publications has now been superseded by their more detailed scholarship. One earlier work however is still of value because of the detail it includes of the original research done by its author in 1957. This is Martin Lowenkopf's 'Political Parties in Uganda and

Tanganyika', unpublished M.A. thesis, University of London, 1961.

39 In his chapter in Kimambo and Temu (eds.), *History of Tanzania*.

40 John Iliffe argues convincingly that a major reason why a single nationalist movement, TANU, rather than a number of rival ethnic-based parties, dominated the political scene in the 1950s was because TANU was the heir to the TAA which had already established itself as the 'Association of the Africans'. See his 'Role of the African Association'.

41 Tanganyika, *Provincial Commissioners Annual Reports 1946* (Dar-es-Salaam, 1947), p. 84.

42 Quoted in Maguire, *Towards 'Uhuru'*, p. 28.

43 'The Acting Governor of Tanganyika to the Secretary of State for the Colonies', Confidential No. 144, 8 November 1947.

44 This development scheme is discussed by Peter McLoughlin in his 'Tanzania: Agricultural Development in Sukumaland' in John C. de Wilde *et al.*, *Experiences with Agricultural Development in Tropical Africa*, vol. 2 (Baltimore, 1967), and Maguire, *Towards 'Uhuru'*.

45 The full text of all the rules being applied in Sukumaland in 1955 had been mimeographed and circulated within Sukumaland in that year. The above summary of these rules is based upon that mimeographed text.

46 This scheme is discussed in Young and Fosbrooke, *Smoke in the Hills*, ch. 7.

47 Young and Fosbrooke, *Smoke in the Hills*, p. 149.

48 In interviews with the author, May 1959.

49 This statement was quoted by the Governor in the Legislative Council in September 1955. *Tanganyika Standard*, 11 Sept. 1955. The Governor added, 'Although I do not consider this [i.e., parity] by any means perfect, I do think that it suits the conditions of Tanganyika at this stage of its progress and is likely to continue to be the best arrangement for a long time to come.'

50 Under the 1948 constitution, there were fourteen unofficial members of the Northern Rhodesia Legislative Council. Ten of these were elected Europeans, two were Europeans nominated by the Governor to represent African interests and two were Africans appointed by the Governor on the recommendation of the African Representative Council, a council whose membership was made up of Native Authorities. See David C. Mulford, *Zambia: The Politics of Independence 1957–64* (London, 1967), p. 12.

51 Twining's dispatch to Cohen and Cohen's reply are dated 11 October 1949 and 1 November 1949. *Committee on Constitutional Development: Report and Despatches to the Secretary of State*, file no. 1146–6. Dar-es-Salaam Secretariat Library (consulted in 1959).

52 In 1951 Twining acquiesced to European pressure and accepted a ratio of African to European to Asian members of 1 : 1 : 1 rather than the 2 : 1 : 1 which he had originally proposed.

53 Six of these submissions came from branches of the TAA, nine from welfare societies, fifteen from Native Authorities and twenty-two from prominent individuals. *Committee on Constitutional Development: Report and Despatches to the Secretary of State*, file no. 1146–6.

54 *Ibid.* part 3, fo. 76. This submission was signed by V. Kyaruzi, H. K. Mwapachu, John Rupia, S. Mhando, A. W. Sykes, S. Chaurambo and Sheikh Hassa Ameri.

55 Tanganyika, *Report of the Committee on Constitutional Development* (Dar-es-Salaam, [1951]). The Committee's chairman, Sir Charles Mathew, mentioned the African submissions to the Committee only in his preface to the report. In two sentences he succeeded in being both misleading and inaccurate, providing another example of the disdain shown by senior administrators

towards independent African opinion. He wrote, '...generally speaking, informed opinion of all races is that the economic and political development of
the Territory must depend on a working partnership between the three main
races based on mutual confidence and trust. The few who expressed a contrary
view were groups of Africans from Bukoba and Moshi who stated that all
other races should eventually lose all political rights.'

56 It had, however, been recommended to the government of Nyasaland by a
senior Colonial Office official, R. G. Hudson, in 1951. United Kingdom Government, 'Report on the Development of Local Government in Nyasaland'
(London, 1951). Hudson came to Tanganyika in 1952 to assist W. J. M.
Mackenzie, who was appointed a Special Commissoner on constitutional
matters. His report in 1953 offered detailed recommendations relating to the
introduction of multiracial county councils.

57 This quotation is from the memorandum 'Future Constitutional Development
in Tanganyika', dated 18 November 1949, which was prepared for the Constitutional Development Committee as a statement of the views of the
government. *Committee on Constitutional Development: Report and Despatches to the Secretary of State*, file no. 1146–6. Dar-es-Salaam Secretariat
Library (consulted in 1959).

58 *Committee on Constitutional Development: Proceedings of the Committee*,
file no. 1146–4, vol. 1, fo. 86. Secretariat Library, Dar-es-Salaam (consulted in
1959).

59 The quotations in this paragraph are from the United Kingdom Government,
'Despatch from the Governor of Tanganyika', No. 88, 1950, in *Development
of African Local Government in Tanganyika*, p. 5.

60 Tanganyika, *Legislative Council Official Report*, 27th Session, col. 246,
9 July 1953.

61 Minister of Local Government and Administration, in Tanganyika, *Legislative
Council Official Report*, 30th Session, vol. 1, col. 330, 14 Dec. 1955.

62 Tanganyika, 'Interim Report on the County Council in Tanganyika, 1951–56',
by S. H. Page-Jones, Member for Local Government (Dar-es-Salaam, 1956),
p. 12.

63 The South-East Lake County Council had a standing executive committee
which consisted of four officials and six unofficials, two of these being drawn
from each of the racial communities. This committee met ten times in 1958.
At seven of these meetings neither African member was present and at no
meeting were they both present. Tanganyika, 'South-East Lake County
Council, Report of the Clerk of the Council' (Mwanza, 1958).

64 The County Council experiment, and the effort to introduce multiracialism at
the District level after that experiment had collapsed, are analyzed in some
detail in my '"Multiracialism" and Local Government in Tanganyika',
Race, II (Nov. 1960), 33–49.

65 This was the phrase used by the Provincial Commissioner, Western Province,
in January 1957 when recommending the policy to the attention of the
District Commissioner, Tabora. Tabora Provincial Commissioner's Office file
CL5/1 *Local Government*, vol. IV (consulted in 1959).

66 Tanganyika, 'Interim Report on the County Council 1956–57', by S. H.
Page-Jones (Dar-es-Salaam, 1957), p. 9.

67 'It need mean no more than one white face and one brown face', the District
Commissioner, Tabora, was told by his Provincial Commissioner in January
1957. See Tabora Provincial Commissioner's Office file CL5/1 *Local
Government*, vol. IV (consulted in 1959).

68 This was Nyerere's judgment in an interview in May 1959. Its validity is

borne out by the fact that when the threat of a British imposed 'multiracialism' was lifted in October 1958, relations between TANU and the colonial government were immediately remarkably improved. This is discussed in chapter 3 below.

69 Martin Lowenkopf, 'Political Parties', pp. 160–2.

70 Joan Wicken, 'Report from Tanganyika' (London, 1957).

71 From a speech to the Legislative Council quoted in Maguire, *Towards 'Uhuru'*, p. 172.

72 Iringa District Office, file C-A-2: *African Administration and Affairs*, fo. dated 15 June 1958 (consulted in 1959).

73 This paragraph summarizes the main points in a memorandum dated April 1956 from the Ministry of Local Government and Administration which was in Kondoa District Offices, file C-L-5 (consulted in 1959).

74 Tanganyika, *Membership of Political Associations*, Tanganyika Government Circular No. 5 (1 August 1953) (Dar-es-Salaam, 1953).

75 Ordinance No. 13 of 1954.

76 From the *Report of the Registrar General 1955* referred to by Margaret Bates in her 'Tanganyika' in Gwendolen Carter (ed.), *African One-Party States* (Ithaca, N.Y., 1962), p. 423.

77 George Bennett, *An Outline History of TANU*, Oxford University Institute of Commonwealth Studies Series, no. 31 (1965), p. 7. This article was first printed in *Makerere Journal*, no. 7 (1963).

78 Section 63(b) of the Penal Code, as amended by the Penal Code (Amendment) Ordinance 1955.

79 The Attorney-General, as quoted in *Tanganyika Standard*, 3 Nov. 1955.

80 Quoted in Maguire, *Towards 'Uhuru'*, p. 172.

81 In May of that year, *The Times* of London commented on the appearance of political repression in Tanganyika (24 May 1957, p. 4).

82 Section 3(1)(C)(I) of the African Chiefs (Special Powers) Ordinance No. 42 of 1957.

83 Kondoa District Office, file C-A-2 *African Affairs and Administration*, Memorandum from the Minister of Local Government and Administration to District Commissioners (consulted in 1959).

84 Dar-es-Salaam Secretariat Library, file C-C-5/1, confidential Minute on the first meeting of the Chiefs' Convention by C. M. Meek, then Acting Principal Assistant Secretary, Ministry of Local Government and Administration (consulted in 1959).

85 Tanganyika, *Report of the Special Commissioner Appointed to Examine Matters Arising out of the Report of the Committee on Constitutional Development* (Dar-es-Salaam, 1953), ch. 20.

86 *Report of the Committee on Voters' Qualifications*, Government Paper No. 1 of 1957 (Dar-es-Salaam, 1957).

87 Quoted by Young and Fosbrooke, *Smoke in the Hills*, p. 180.

88 Dar-es-Salaam Secretariat file C-C-5/1, C. M. Meek, *Confidential Memorandum to the Third Chiefs' Convention* (consulted in 1959).

89 Tanganyika, *Legislative Council Official Report*, 34th Session (1st Meeting), vol. 1, col. 5, 14 Oct. 1958.

90 *Ibid.* col. 3.

Chapter 3. Shifting strategies 1958–61

1 Tanganyika, *Legislative Council Official Report*, 34th Session, vol. i, cols. 7–8, 15 Oct. 1958.
2 See, for example, Nyerere's statement to the Trusteeship Council, 18 June 1957, quoted in Nyerere, *Freedom and Unity*, p. 47.
3 *Ibid.* p. 78.
4 See below, pp. 53–5.
5 This is reported in John Stonehouse, *Prohibited Immigrant* (London, 1960), p. 137.
6 Tanganyika, *Legislative Council Official Report*, 34th Session, vol. ii, Question No. 42, 9 Dec. 1958.
7 *Ibid.*
8 Tanganyika, *Legislative Council Official Report*, 34th Session, vol. iii, Question No. 64.
9 This was reported to me by R. de Z. Hall, Provincial Commissioner of the Lake Province, at an interview in May 1959. Nyerere was reported as having spoken at length on the need for law and order in a major speech in Mwanza in November 1958. *Tanganyika Standard*, 25 Nov. 1958.
10 This impression was unmistakably gained in an interview with Mahada in May 1959.
11 Political history of these years in Geita District and elsewhere in Sukumaland is well described in Maguire's *Towards 'Uhuru'*.
12 In an interview with the author, June 1959.
13 This paragraph and the preceding one summarize the author's impression of the values and viewpoints of government officers as these were observed in 1959 and confirmed in 1961–5 in extended conversations about the colonial period with officers who were still in Tanzania.
14 This paragraph summarizes chapter 15 of E. G. Rowe, 'Decentralization to Provinces in Tanganyika' (Dar-es-Salaam, undated but *circa* 1958).
15 The confidential report on the fourth convention of chiefs which was held in December 1958 reported to its restricted audience that the Governor had expressed to the chiefs the supposition that some of them would live to see an independent Tanganyika and that in any case their children would. *Chiefs' Convention, Fourth Meeting*, 17–20 Dec. 1958, Confidential Report. Ministry of Local Government and Administration, file C-C-5/1, Dar-es-Salaam, Secretariat Library (consulted in 1959).
16 Tanganyika, *Report of the Post-Elections Committee* (Dar-es-Salaam, 1959), p. 3.
17 For a brief period there were both an Executive Council and a Council of Ministers in Tanganyika. The Executive Council consisted of all the official Ministers. The Council of Ministers consisted of these official Ministers along with the elected Ministers. In that way the Governor was able to consult his British colleagues and come to a common view with them before taking the issues concerned to the Council of Ministers.
18 Immediately after the October election, the Tanganyikan-Elected Members Organization (TEMO) was formed. The Asian and European members all joined this organization and unanimously supported Nyerere as its President. The African members in turn supported Derek Bryceson as the Vice-President and Al Noor Kassum as one of its parliamentary whips. TEMO, rather than TANU, decided upon the tactics which the elected members would follow in the legislature

19 Turnbull's previous offer had been four elected members in a nine-man Council of Ministers. By increasing the size of the Council to twelve at the same time as he conceded an extra elected Minister, he assured that elected Ministers would not thereby gain extra power within the Council. That Nyerere did not object to this manoeuvre shows that his concern was not with the balance of numbers between elected and official Ministers but with the principle of a clear African majority amongst the elected Ministers.

20 'We had to prove that we were good boys' is how Nyerere explained his first appointments. Interview with the author, June 1966.

21 In an interview with the author, June 1959.

22 The arguments of this and the next paragraph were made to the author by Nyerere in June 1959.

23 Tanganyika, *Legislative Council Official Report*, 35th Session, vol. I, col. 75, 14 Oct. 1959.

24 Tanganyika, *Legislative Council Official Report*, 34th Session, vol. III, col. 6, 17 Mar. 1959.

25 Lady Listowel reports that it was the intention of the British government at that date to concede responsible government by 1963–4 and to grant independence in 1970. Listowel, *The Making of Tanganyika*, p. 351.

26 Tanganyika, *Report of the Post-Elections Committee*, p. 14.

27 Tanganyika, *Legislative Council Official Report*, 35th Session, vol. II, col. 3, 15 Dec. 1959. It is worth noting that Turnbull chose to use the term 'people' rather than 'peoples', thus subtly indicating that the British government had finally abandoned any effort to treat Tanganyika as a land of several different peoples each with rights as a separate community.

28 The local TANU constituency organization had nominated a popular local figure, H. E. Sarwatt. The National Executive Committee of TANU, which reviewed all local TANU nominations, rejected this nomination alleging that tribalism had influenced the selection. Sarwatt then stood as an independent and defeated the official TANU candidate by a vote of 7,860 to 6,520.

29 After this date the Governor no longer presided over the Council of Ministers and was in effect the titular Head of State on all matters internal to the country. Nyerere became Prime Minister and the Council of Ministers was composed entirely of unofficial members of the Legislative Council selected by him. The Governor retained control over the armed forces and External Affairs until the granting of full independence in December 1961.

30 The Secretary of State is quoted to this effect by Sir Andrew Cohen in a speech to the Twenty-sixth Session of the Trusteeship Council. 'United Nations Visiting Mission to Trust Territories in East Africa, 1960, Report on Tanganyika', in *Trusteeship Council, Official Records: Twenty-sixth Session* (14 April–30 June 1960), Supplement No. 2 (New York, 1960), pp. 42–54. Lord Perth, when Minister of State for Colonial Affairs, is similarly quoted in Claggart Taylor, *The Political Development of Tanganyika* (Stanford, Calif., 1963), p. 188.

31 In his statement to the United Nations Trusteeship Council, June 1960. 'United Nations Visiting Mission', p. 50.

32 *Ibid.* pp. 50–1.

33 *Ibid.* p. 50.

34 This famous equation was presented to the *Force Publique* by its Belgian commanding officer several days after independence and just before the Force rioted. Crawford Young, *Politics in the Congo* (Princeton, 1964), p. 316.

Chapter 4. Nyerere's political thought 1954–62

1 From Nyerere's address in the Legislative Council on 16 December 1959. The text of this address is in Nyerere, *Freedom and Unity*, pp. 75–80.

2 *Ibid.* p. 70.

3 This issue is discussed in greater detail in chapter 5 below, pp. 112–13.

4 Tanganyika, *National Assembly Official Report*, 36th Session, vol. 1, cols. 334–5, 18 Oct. 1960.

5 Nyerere, 'The Entrenchment of Privilege', *Africa South*, II, 2 (January–March 1958), 47.

6 From Nyerere's speech in response to the government's proposals for the introduction of responsible government in December 1959. The speech is reproduced in Nyerere, *Freedom and Unity*, pp. 75–80.

7 Nyerere, *Democracy and the Party System* (Dar-es-Salaam, January 1963), p. 16.

8 See for example 'One-Party Government', *Spearhead*, I, 1 (November 1961), 7–10; 'Africa's Bid for Democracy', *African and Colonial World*, VIII, 3 (July 1960), 70–4; 'Africa's Place in the World', in *Symposium on Africa* (Wellesley, Mass., 1960), pp. 153–64; 'Will Democracy Work in Africa?', *Africa Report*, v, 2 (February 1960), 4–5; 'Democracy in Africa', *Tribune* (London), June 1960; and *Democracy and the Party System*.

9 Nyerere, *Democracy and the Party System*, p. 27.

10 Nyerere, 'One-Party Government', p. 8.

11 Portions of this article were reprinted in *East Africa and Rhodesia*, 36 (9 June 1960), 968.

12 Nyerere, 'One-Party Government', p. 9.

13 Nyerere, *Democracy and the Party System*, p. 22.

14 In *Democracy and the Party System* (p. 25) Nyerere even recommended that the people as a whole should be permitted to remove their leaders at any time that they lose confidence in them.

15 Nyerere, *Ujamaa, The Basis of African Socialism* (Dar-es-Salaam, 1962), pp. 7, 11.

16 *Ibid.* p. 1.

17 Harvey Glickman's paraphrase of President Nyerere's observation to him in an interview. See Glickman, 'Dilemmas of Political Theory in an African Context: The Ideology of Julius Nyerere', in Jeffrey Butler and A. A. Castagno, *Boston University Papers on Africa: Transition in African Politics* (New York, 1967), p. 203.

18 Nyerere, *Democracy and the Party System*, pp. 22–3.

19 Tanganyika, *National Assembly Official Report, 1st Session*, vol. II, col. 1105, 28 June 1962.

20 See for example Thomas Hodgkin, 'A Note on the Language of African Nationalism', in K. Kirkwood (ed.), *African Affairs No. 1*, St Antony Papers No. 10 (London, 1961); and Glickman, 'Dilemmas of Political Theory'.

21 Nyerere, 'Africa's Place in the World', p. 155.

22 Nyerere, 'The African and Democracy', in James Duffy and Robert Manners (eds.), *Africa Speaks* (New York, 1961), pp. 30–2.

23 Nyerere, 'Africa's Place in the World', p. 157.

24 *Political Order in Changing Societies* (New Haven, Conn., 1968), pp. 10–11.

25 Nyerere, 'Will Democracy Work in Africa?', p. 5, and quoted again in *Africa Report*, VI, 11 (December 1961), 6.

26 Glickman, 'Dilemmas of Political Theory', pp. 216–17.

27 Nyerere, *Democracy and the Party System*, p. 22.
28 Glickman, 'Dilemmas of Political Theory', p. 200. Although I am critical of several aspects of Glickman's analysis of Nyerere's political theory, it is an outstanding article.
29 *Ibid*. p. 200.
30 See Henry Bienen, *Tanzania: Party Transformation and Economic Development*, 2nd ed. (Princeton, N.J., 1970), p. 69.
31 This episode is discussed in William H. Friedland, 'Co-operation, Conflict, and Conscription: TANU–TFL Relations 1955–1964', in Butler and Castagno, *Boston University Papers on Africa*, p. 71.
32 Glickman, 'Dilemmas of Political Theory', p. 217.
33 The concluding section of the final chapter of this book considers whether Nyerere became more prone to authoritarian attitudes over the years 1962–7.
34 Nyerere, *Democracy and the Party System*, p. 24.
35 Nyerere, *Freedom and Unity*, p. 121.
36 'We Cannot Afford to Fail', *Africa Special Report*, iv, 12 (December 1959), 10.
37 These questions are examined in greater detail in chapter 5 below.
38 Quoted in *East Africa and Rhodesia*, 13 August 1959, p. 1404.
39 Quoted in Nyerere, *Freedom and Unity*, p. 76.
40 Quoted in *East Africa and Rhodesia*, 24 December 1959, p. 412.
41 Tanganyika, *Legislative Council Official Report*, 36th Session, vol. i, cols. 390–1, 20 Oct. 1960.
42 The suggestion here that Nyerere had briefly contemplated a longer period of responsible government under a final British authority is borne out by the observation of the Visiting Mission that both TANU and Nyerere had come to view early independence as a much more urgent matter than Nyerere had earlier suggested. See 'United Nations Visiting Mission', p. 5.
43 From a pamphlet of Nyerere's entitled 'Barriers to Democracy'. This passage is quoted by Martin Lowenkopf in his 'Political Parties in Uganda and Tanganyika', p. 187.
44 In a speech to the Legislative Council, 16 December 1959, quoted in Nyerere, *Freedom and Unity*, p. 79.
45 Nyerere, 'We Cannot Afford to Fail', p. 9.
46 Quoted in Sophia Mustafa, *The Tanganyika Way* (Dar-es-Salaam, 1961), p. 128.
47 Quoted by Mrs Mustafa from a Tanganyika government press release of 5 September 1960, *ibid*. p. 30.
48 Nyerere, 'We Cannot Afford to Fail', pp. 9–10.
49 This was relvealed in a number of ways. He corresponded closely with friends in the Labour Party, the Fabian Colonial Bureau and the Africa Bureau during the period in which he was struggling against Twining. (Maguire has had access to some of this correspondence and used it effectively in *Towards 'Uhuru'*.) British critics of colonial rule were heavily represented as honoured guests at the Independence celebrations on 9 December 1961. In the first year of responsible government he was able to find time for extended conversations with such British critics of colonial rule as Margery Perham, Thomas Hodgkin, Michael Scott, Basil Davidson and Colin Legum. It was at this time and from this group of intellectuals that he recruited Joan Wicken who was to be his Personal Assistant and Roland Brown, his Attorney-General, two of the ablest, most sensitive and most self-effacing of the many expatriates who have served in his government.
50 Tanganyika, *Legislative Council Official Record*, 35th Session, vol. i, col. 11, 23 Oct. 1959.

Chapter 5. The operation and abandonment of a dependent relationship 1959–62

1 Quoted in *East Africa and Rhodesia*, 36, 1826 (19 November 1959).
2 The details in this paragraph have been compiled from Tanganyika, *Staff List 1959*.
3 Compiled from Tanganyika, *Staff List 1961* (Dar-es-Salaam, 1961).
4 *Ibid.*
5 *Ibid.*
6 Tanganyika, 'Draft Five-Year Africanization Programme for the Civil Service' (Dar-es-Salaam, 1962), p. 89.
7 Tanganyika, *Report of the Tanganyika Salaries Commission, 1961* (The Adu Report) (Dar-es-Salaam, 1961), p. 11.
8 The information on enrollments and graduations for the years 1958 and 1959 is from Tanganyika, *Ministry of Education Triennial Survey of Education in the Years 1958–60* (Dar es-Salaam, 1960), p. 10. The figures for 1962 are from George Skorov, *Integration of Educational and Economic Planning in Tanzania* (Paris, 1966), p. 39.
9 Tanganyika, *High-Level Manpower Requirements*, p. 40.
10 United Nations, 'Report of the UNESCO Educational Planning Mission for Tanganyika, June–October 1962' (Paris, 1963), p. 51.
11 These four Ministers were George Kahama, Chief Fundikira, Derek Bryceson and Amir Jamal. The fifth elected Minister from the previous Executive Council, Eliufoo, had been elected head of the Chagga tribe.
12 Tanganyika, *Development Plan for Tanganyika 1961–62 to 1963–64* (Dar-es-Salaam, 1961).
13 *Ibid.* p. 74.
14 Nyerere, *Freedom and Unity*, p. 105.
15 Although the Cabinet system was a British legacy, it met several immediate and obvious political requirements in Tanganyika. These are discussed in my article 'The Cabinet and Presidential Leadership in Tanzania: 1960–1966', in Lofchie (ed.), *The State of the Nations*, esp. pp. 93–6.
16 Nyerere, 'Chief Minister's Circular No. 1' (1960), reprinted in *Journal of African Administration*, XIII, 2 (April 1961), 108–11.
17 *Ibid.* p. 111.
18 From his Independence Day Message to TANU, December 1961, quoted in Nyerere, *Freedom and Unity*, p. 140.
19 Nyerere, 'Chief Minister's Circular No. 1', p. 108.
20 Quoted in *East Africa and Rhodesia*, 36, 1808 (13 August 1969), 1404.
21 This was done by permitting the Governor to retain responsibility for the appointment, promotion and dismissal of public officers until May 1961 and then creating a Public Service Commission with wide executive responsibilities. For the arrangements prior to May 1961, see Tanganyika (Public Service Commission) Order-in-Council 1960, Government Notice No. 310, 1960. Published in Tanganyika, *Constitutional Documents 1960* (Dar-es-Salaam, 1960), pp. 51–7. The arrangements thereafter were entrenched within the Independence Constitution, sections 74 and 75.
22 Nyerere, 'Chief Minister's Circular No. 1', p. 108.
23 These arrangements applied to all the African territories and to most other colonial and previously colonial territories. The details are presented in United Kingdom Government, *Colonial Office: Service with Overseas Governments*, Cmnd. 1193 (London, 1960).

24 Tanganyika, *Legislative Council Official Report*, 36th Session, vol. II, col. 127, 8 Dec. 1960.

25 Turnbull's first presentation of the British position called for compensation for officers prematurely retired but made no mention of compensation for loss of career for officers who chose to quit. *East Africa and Rhodesia*, 36, 1836 (17 December 1969), 396.

26 This is not an insubstantial point. Nine million pounds of the £19.85m of that settlement were grants or loans related to the retirement benefits and the pension commutation.

27 Tanganyika, *National Assembly Official Report*, 36th Session, vol. IV, col. 54, 16 May 1961.

28 Quoted in Listowel, *The Making of Tanganyika*, p. 395.

29 In March 1959 there were 203 Africans in the middle and senior positions in the civil service. They therefore occupied about 5% of the total of these positions in the service. See the information given by the Minister without Portfolio to the National Assembly. Tanganyika, *National Assembly Official Report*, 36th Session, vol. IV, col. 86, 17 May 1961.

30 Tanganyika, *Legislative Council Official Report*, 36th Session, vol. II, col 131, 19 Oct. 1960.

31 *Ibid.*, col. 375, 19 Oct. 1960.

32 Tanganyika, *Legislative Council Official Report*, 36th Session, vol. II, col. 131, 8 Dec. 1960.

33 Tanganyika, 'Human Resources and Manpower Planning in Tanganyika', by J. L. Thurston (Dar-es-Salaam, 1960), and Tanganyika, 'Some Problems Associated with Localisation of the Tanganyika Civil Service', by J. Donald Kingsley and J. L. Thurston (Dar-es-Salaam, May 1961).

34 Tanganyika, 'Some Problems Associated with Localisation', by Kingsley and Thurston, pp. 5–6. They recommended a variety of emergency measures including a relaxation of entry requirements, special and highly specific training programs, and the identification of those positions that must be given highest priority in the allocation of scarce African senior staff.

35 Indeed, he had secured the service of David Anderson, a senior expatriate officer provided by the Ford Foundation as a special adviser on staff development. Anderson had previously been intimately involved in the successful administration of the Africanization program in Ghana.

36 *Tanganyika Standard, 21 November* 1960, p. 1.

37 This is a paraphrase taken from notes of a conversation with Nyerere in October 1961.

38 Tanganyika, *Legislative Council Official Report*, 36th Session, vol. I, col. 385, 19 Oct. 1960.

39 Tanganyika, *National Assembly Official Report*, 36th Session, vol. V, col. 101, 11 Oct. 1961.

40 Nyerere as quoted in *East Africa and Rhodesia* (18 February 1960), p. 592.

41 The most detailed study of the trade union activities in this period is in William Friedland, 'Cooperation, Conflict, and Conscription'.

42 Tanganyika, *Report of the Committee on the Integration of Education, 1959* (Dar-es-Salaam, 1960). This Committee would have given priority still in primary school admissions to the children 'of the community for whom the school was established' (p. 10).

43 Tanganyika, *Legislative Council Official Report*, 36th Session, vol. II, col. 115, 7 Dec. 1960.

44 Tanganyika, *Legislative Council Official Report*, 36th Session, vol. I, cols. 374–392, 19 Oct. 1960.

45 Tanganyika, *National Assembly Official Report*, 36th Session, vol. v, col. 333, 18 Oct. 1961.
46 See above, ch. 4, pp. 64–5, for Nyerere's response in the House.
47 Tanganyika, *National Assembly Official Report*, 36th Session, vol. v, col. 335, 18 Oct. 1961.
48 These quotations from *Uhuru* are from translations which appeared in the *Tanganyika Standard*, 25 January 1962.
49 *Tanganyika Standard*, 17 January 1962.
50 *Tanganyika Standard* 23 January 1962.
51 *Tanganyika Standard*, 23 January 1962.
52 From a transcript of interviews with President Nyerere on 8 and 9 September 1966.
53 These were the English-language pamphlet *Ujamaa, The Basis of African Socialism*, which has already been discussed above (pp. 70–1), and two Swahili pamphlets, *TANU na Raia* [TANU and the People] (Dar-es-Salaam, [1962]) and *Tujisahihishe* [Self-Criticism] (Dar-es-Salaam [1962]).
54 *Ujamaa, The Basis of African Socialism*, pp. 5–6.
55 *TANU na Raia*, p. 6.
56 *Ibid.* p. 4.
57 From a record of an interview with the President on 8 and 9 September 1966.
58 The third new Minister was Solomon Eliufoo, who was appointed Minister of Education. Eliufoo was the recently elected head of the Chagga tribe and an experienced secondary school teacher.
59 In particular, in March 1962 the Development Committee of the Cabinet which Vasey had chaired was replaced by an Economic Commission of the Cabinet which Kawawa chaired.
60 These men were Rowland Mwanjisi, P. C. Walwa, and E. Kisenge.
61 This combination of a wide ideological latitude within the ruling group with strong opposition to any who challenge the legitimacy of their right to rule was an early feature of TANU. It is discussed above (pp. 79–80) where it is seen to be compatible with a strand within Nyerere's political ideology.
62 These opponents included Christopher Tumbo, General Secretary of the Tanganyikan African Railways Union until February 1962, Katungutu, Tumbo's successor after that date, Hassan Khupe, President of the Mine Workers Union, Victor Mkello, head of the Plantation Workers Union, and President of the Tanganyika Federation of Labour (T.F.L.) and John Magongo, General Secretary of the T.F.L. and of the Tanganyika Union of Public Employees.
63 The details of this period are summarized in Friedland, 'Cooperation, Conflict, and Conscription'.
64 The Severance Allowance Act of 1962 and the Employment Ordinance (Amendment) Act of 1962.
65 The officer was David Anderson. See fn. 35, p. 276.
66 From the terms of reference of the Commission quoted in Tanganyika, *Report of the Africanisation Commission, 1962* (Dar-es-Salaam, 1963), p. 1.
67 By the end of 1964 only one Principal Secretary was an expatriate. Tanzania, 'Establishment Circular Letter No. 21 of 1965' (Dar-es-Salaam, 15 November 1965).
68 These figures are calculated from Tanganyika, *Staff List 1961,…1962,…1963.*
69 His opponent was Z. Mtemvu of the African National Congress. The vote was Nyerere, 1,127,978; Mtemvu, 21,276. Bienen points out that as only 25% of the potential voters actually voted, this result suggests that TANU had not been very effective at mobilizing rural support. Bienen, *Tanzania*, p. 56.

Chapter 6. A loss of innocence 1963–8

1 Nyrere, *Freedom and Unity*, pp. 314–15.
2 Tanganyika, *Tanganyika Five Year Plan for Economic and Social Development 1st July, 1964–30th June, 1969*, vol. 1, Analysis (Dar-es-Salaam, 1964), p. 86.
3 This is discussed in ch. 5, p. 124.
4 Tanzania, 'Annual Manpower Report to the President 1965' (Dar-es-Salaam, 1965), p. 20.
5 The figures in this paragraph have been calculated from Tanzania, *Staff List as at September 1965* (Dar-es-Salaam, 1965).
6 See, for example, the opinion expressed in the 'Report of the British Economic Mission on the Tanzanian Five Year Development Plan' (London, 1965), ch. 8. The Ministry of Economic Affairs and Development Planning reported in April 1967 that the investment performance of the government in the first half of the period of the Five Year Plan had been only fifty to fifty-five per cent of the Plan's expectations. It attributed this serious failure not to any shortage of external capital assistance but rather to two basic bottlenecks. The first of these was 'a shortage of skilled and technical manpower which has not permitted advance project preparation and affected seriously the rate of physical implementation'. The second bottleneck was a severe failing in capital budgeting which resulted in substantial sums being tied up for long periods in slow-moving projects while other projects had to be delayed for want of capital funds. This failure was itself partly a result of the severe under-staffing in the Ministry of Economic Affairs and Development Planning after the publication of the Five Year Plan. Tanzania, *A Mid-term Appraisal of the Achievements under the Five Year Plan, July 1964 to June 1969* (Dar-es-Salaam, 1967), p. 13.
7 The 1966 figure was obtained by interview with Mr Walter Grieves, who was the official in the Office of the British High Commissioner in Dar-es-Salaam primarily responsible for British technical assistance. The 1968 figure was obtained by interview from Mr Frank Glynn, who was the staff development officer in the Central Establishment's Division of the Office of the President in Dar-es-Salaam.
8 Interview with Mr Frank Glynn.
9 Tanzania, 'Annual Manpower Report to the President 1966' (Dar-es-Salaam, 1967), p. 20. Of the balance of the expatriates, Denmark provided 12, U.N. agencies 12, the U.S.A. 9, Poland 4, Yugoslavia 2, Czechoslovakia 1, Germany 1 and Italy 1. The report leaves five expatriates unidentified by nationality.
10 Under the main British scheme, the Overseas Service Assistance Scheme, the British government paid an inducement allowance, half the travel costs of the appointee and his family and an educational allowance for any of his children being educated in Britain for every British national recruited for service in countries such as Tanzania.
11 There were 207 American teachers in Tanzanian secondary schools on two-year renewable contracts between 1961 and 1964. In 1965 the Peace Corps took over this responsibility and in that year there were 338 Peace Corps volunteers in Tanzania, a high majority of them as teachers. International Bank for Reconstruction and Development, 'Consultative Group for East Africa: Information on Financial and Technical Assistance' (Washington, D.C., 1968), part 1, sect. 4.
12 Requests for technical assistance personnel were normally sent to a number of

different countries in regard to each of the job categories in which expatriate staff were being recruited. A review of the report on overseas recruitment for August 1968 shows that Tanzania was seeking candidates for 295 posts in 75 job categories. Sweden had been asked to help in the case of 43 job categories, Denmark, 18, Czechoslovakia, 16, Yugoslavia, 15, the United States of America, 2 and West Germany, 2. In contrast Britain, with whom relations were otherwise badly strained, had been asked for assistance in 64 of these 75 categories.

13 The treatment here of these issues is in each case related to their impact upon Tanzania's perception of contemporary international politics. The fullest treatment of Tanzanian foreign policy is provided by T. C. Niblock's able 'Aid and Foreign Policy in Tanzania, 1961–68', unpublished Ph.D. thesis, University of Sussex, 1972. See also Catherine Hoskyns' perceptive article 'Africa's Foreign Policy: The Case of Tanzania', *International Affairs*, 44 (July 1968) and Timothy Shaw, 'The Foreign Policy of Tanzania', unpublished Ph.D. thesis, Makerere University, 1972. George T. Yu's *China and Tanzania: A Study in Comparative Interaction* (Berkeley, Calif., 1970) provides a thorough study of one important aspect of Tanzanian foreign policy.

14 From Nyerere's address to the United Nations General Assembly on 14 December 1961, quoted in Nyerere, *Freedom and Unity*, p. 152.

15 *Tanganyika Standard*, 25 July 1963, p. 1.

16 *An Address to the Norwegian Students' Association in Oslo* (Dar-es-Salaam, 1963).

17 The classic statement of this continuing willingness to negotiate a peaceful transition to majority rule in southern Africa is the Lusaka Manifesto, drafted by Nyerere and accepted by the heads of government of fourteen East and Central African states. The Manifesto has been frequently reprinted. See, for example, Colin Legum and John Drysdale (eds.), *Africa Contemporary Records: Annual Survey and Documents 1968–69* (London, 1969).

18 From an interview with Colin Legum, *Observer*, 20 April 1965.

19 *Stability and Change in Africa* (Dar-es-Salaam, 1969), p. 12. Nyerere went on to comment that the final irony in that sad eventuality would be that liberal Western humanitarians would find themselves grateful to the Russian and East European Communists as it would be their support for the liberation movements which alone would break this colour pattern.

20 *Ibid.* p. 13.

21 *The New York Times* estimated the numbers killed at over 10,000 (8 April 1964). John Okello, in his curious autobiography, makes the oddly precise comment that 'the total reported killed then was 13,635'. *Revolution in Zanzibar* (Nairobi, 1967), p. 160.

22 'It seemed that the brightest spark in Africa had been snuffed when the news came through of the Tanganyika–Zanzibar anschluss.' Lucien Rey, 'The Revolution in Zanzibar', *New Left Review*, 25 (May–June 1964), 29.

23 Colin Legum, 'How Nyerere Out-manoeuvred Babu of Zanzibar', *Observer*, 26 April 1964.

24 Russia, China and the German Democratic Republic had recognized the new government immediately and had given it assistance at a time when this was most needed. Tanganyika urged the Western powers to do the same so as to prevent any possibility of this nationalist revolution even appearing to be taken over by one bloc in the cold war.

25 Quoted by S. G. Ayany, *A History of Zanzibar* (Nairobi, 1970), p. 1421.

26 *The Nationalist* (Dar-es-Salaam), 6 May 1964.

27 Quoted by Niblock, in his 'Aid and Foreign Policy in Tanzania, 1961–68',

p. 232. This excellent study includes an extensive section (pp. 215–63) on the crises with West Germany over the status of the East German representation.

28 The author was in Dar-es-Salaam at the time and remembers well frequent conversations about disagreements within the Cabinet on this issue.

29 This also the author recalls from conversations at the time in Dar-es-Salaam.

30 The need for this was explained to the author in a personal memorandum from the Ambassador of the Federal Republic of Germany to Dar-es-Salaam in these terms: 'Under the circumstances, the federal government is unfortunately prevented from making new commitments to Tanzania, since this would not be understood by the friendly African states which have not entered into any relations with the Ulbricht regime.'

31 'Background Paper on the East/West German Problem in Tanzania' (Dar-es-Salaam, 17 Mar. 1965), p. 3.

32 President Nyerere once called Dar-es-Salaam 'Rumourville'. This particular crisis in Tanzanian–American relations is a good example of an important incident about which there were and are very few hard facts. The account which is given here is based upon hearsay, tested where feasible by interview. It is consistent with the known facts and with the wording of Nyerere's final decision relating to it.

33 First Secretary McNamara of the U.S. Embassy confirmed to the author in an interview in May 1966 that Nyerere never intimated to the American Ambassador that he did not personally believe the accusations.

34 A good impression of the intensity of African reactions even at high official level can be gained from the excerpts from the United Nations Security Council debate on the Congo in December 1964 which are given in Catherine Hoskyns' excellent case study, *The Organization of African Unity and the Congo Crisis, 1964–65*, Case Studies in African Diplomacy No. 1 (Dar-es-Salaam, 1969), pp. 50–62.

35 *East African Standard*, 27 November 1964, p. 5.

36 The account which follows is based upon press reports at the time supplemented by interviews in 1966 and again in 1968. The various accounts were essentially very similar.

37 Kambona recounted this episode to the author in an interview in London in June 1968.

38 This quotation is from an English translation in the author's possession of a tape of the President's speech at Jangwani Playing Fields in Dar-es-Salaam on 15 November 1964.

39 *Ibid.*

40 *East African Standard*, 10 December 1964, p. 1.

41 From an interview with First Secretary McNamara of the U.S. Embassy, May 1966. A similar story was told to me by Kambona in London in 1968 when he expressed deep disappointment at not being supported by Nyerere over the plot.

42 Kambona, for example, in a speech in August 1965 said, 'Independent African states. . .must work ceaselessly for the preservation of their independence from their erstwhile masters. . .They have to extricate themselves from the ties which might cripple their determination to make their own decisions. Independent African states make it a point to sunder such stifling ties as existed prior to independence with their metropolitan countries.' Quoted in *External Affairs Bulletin*, Tanzania, 1, 3 (October 1965), 17.

43 From the speech of 15 November 1964 (see note 38 above).

44 Duncan Sandys wrote to Ian Smith in December of 1963 that 'the present difficulty arises from your desire to secure independence on the basis of a

franchise which is incomparably more restrictive than that of any other British territory to which independence had hitherto been granted'. United Kingdom Government, *Southern Rhodesia – Documents Relating to the Negotiations between the United Kingdom and Southern Rhodesian Government*, Cmnd. 2807 (London, 1965), p. 16.

45 From a paper, 'Rhodesia', submitted by Nyerere to a meeting of heads of government of East and Central Africa in March 1966.

46 This became public knowledge late in 1965 with the publication of the United Kingdom Government's *Southern Rhodesia*, Cmnd. 2807.

47 This decision and related matters are discussed in R. C. Pratt, 'African Reactions to the Rhodesian Crisis', *International Journal*, XXI, 2 (Spring 1966), 186–98.

48 From the text of the final communiqué of the Commonwealth Conference held in London. *Times*, 15 September 1966, p. 9.

49 From the text of the final communiqué of the Commonwealth Conference held in Lagos. *Times*, 13 January 1966, p. 7.

50 See the text of his address to a mass rally in Dar-es-Salaam, in Yu, *China and Tanzania*, appendix 3, pp. 86–90.

51 Henry Bienen discusses the Marxian influence on *The Nationalist* in his *Tanzania*, pp. 207, 209–10.

52 The most prolific and consistently insightful of these Marxist commentators has been John Saul, whose articles on Tanzania constitute a sophisticated and well-integrated view of the determinants and dynamics of Tanzanian politics.

53 Giovanni Arrighi and John Saul, 'Nationalism and Revolution in Sub-Saharan Africa' in Ralph Miliband and John Saville (eds.), *The Socialist Register 1969*, (London, 1969).

54 *Tanzania Policy on Foreign Affairs*. Address by the President Mwalimu Julius K. Nyerere at the Tanganyika African National Union National Conference, 16 Oct. 1967 (Dar-es-Salaam, October 1967), reprinted in Nyerere, *Freedom and Socialism*, p. 374.

55 Nyerere, *Stability and Change*, pp. 6–7.

56 Ghana, *Nkrumah's Subversion in Africa* (Accra, 1966).

57 'Tanzania Policy on Foreign Affairs' in *Freedom and Socialism*, p. 379.

58 *Ibid.* p. 380.

59 *Stability and Change in Africa*, p. 6.

60 'Tanzania Policy on Foreign Affairs' in *Freedom and Socialism*, pp. 368–9.

61 'Principles and Development' (1966) in Nyerere, *Freedom and Socialism*, p. 192.

62 *Ibid.* p. 192.

63 From the translation of the recorded text of Nyerere's speech on 15 November 1964 at the Jangwani Playing Fields, Dar-es-Salaam.

64 Teachers formed a substantial majority of the civilian personnel provided to Tanzania by the Canadian aid program. In 1967–8 for example there were 33 secondary school teachers, 11 teacher trainers and 5 professors who were provided by Canada in contrast to a total of 16 Canadian advisers outside the field of education. Five of these 16 were in agriculture, 3 in wildlife and conservation, 2 in forestry, 3 in social services, 2 in development planning and 1 in cooperatives. International Bank for Reconstruction and Development, 'Consultative Group for East Africa', part 1, section 10. In addition to these experts, who were fully paid by the Canadian government, there were between 30 and 40 young Canadians employed at local salaries by the Tanzanian government and recruited for service overseas by the Canadian University Service Overseas.

65 From information provided by Mr Allan McGill, Canadian High Commissioner to Tanzania at the time, and political scientist Linda Freeman.
66 This information on Swedish technical assistance has been drawn from a memorandum to the author from the Royal Swedish Embassy in Dar-es-Salaam dated November 1966 and supplemented by information from the International Bank for Reconstruction and Development, 'Consultative Group for East Africa', part 1, sect. 3.
67 From information supplied to the author by Mr David Thorup, the Assistant Resident Representative of the United Nations Development Program in a letter of 25 August 1966. The three agencies were the Food and Agriculture Organization, the U.N. Technical Assistance Agency and UNESCO, which in part operated as a recruiting agency for the U.N. Special Fund.
68 From a typescript summary of Vice-President Kawawa's remarks.
69 *Ibid.*
70 Tanzania, *The Appropriation Accounts of Tanzania for the Year 1968–69* (Dar-es-Salaam, 1970), pp. 14, 17.
71 From information obtained from interviews within the Ministry of Economic Affairs and Development Planning, May 1966 and September 1968.
72 Yu, *China and Tanzania*, p. 41.
73 From Nyerere's speech at the banquet upon the conclusion of his visit to China in 1968. Quoted in Yu, *China and Tanzania*, p. 99.
74 This report, which was prepared by Robert Sadove, has never been made public. It is discussed in Richard Hall's *The High Price of Principles: Kaunda and the White South* (London, 1969), ch. 15.
75 United Nations, *Report of the U.N./ECA/FAO Economic Survey Mission on the Economic Development of Zambia* (Ndola, 1964).
76 *A British–Canadian Report on an Engineering and Economic Feasibility Study for a Proposed Zambia and East Africa Rail Link Prepared by Canadian Area Services, Ltd., Livesey and Henderson, Maxwell Stamp Associates Ltd., and Sumption, Berkeley and Co. Ltd.* (London, 1966).
77 Michael J. Weil, 'The Tan-Zam Railroad: A Case Study in Project Evaluation and Development', unpublished M.A. thesis, University of Sussex, August 1972.
78 This paragraph summarizes Nyerere's remarks in an interview with the author, June 1968.
79 These figures are taken from Tanzania, *Budget Survey 1965–66* and *Background to the Budget 1967–68* and from Tanzania, *The Economic Survey and Second Annual Plan 1970–71* (Dar-es-Salaam, 1970), table 68.
80 Gerald Helleiner, in his important contribution to the discussion in Tanzania of the significance of foreign assistance, estimated that such tying arrangements typically cut the value to Tanzania of a foreign loan by twenty per cent. His paper, which was originally delivered as a public lecture in Dar-es-Salaam and was then widely circulated within the Tanzanian government, is published as 'Trade, Aid and Nation-Building in Tanzania', in Anthony Rweyemamu (ed.), *Nation-Building in Tanzania* (Nairobi, 1970).
81 Hoskyns, 'Africa's Foreign Policy', p. 103.

Chapter 7. The prelude to a socialist strategy 1963–7

1 From the 1954 TANU Constitution, which is quoted at length in Lowenkopf, 'Political Parties', pp. 132–4.
2 TANU Constitution (Dar-es-Salaam, 1962), pp. 1–2.

3 It is reprinted in William Tordoff, *Government and Politics in Tanzania* (Nairobi, 1967), pp. 236–57.

4 This point is given prominence in several sections of the first five year plan, 1964–9. See for example Tanganyika, *Tanganyika Five Year Plan*, pp. 3, 12, 42.

5 *Ibid*. p. 38.

6 These various estimates appear in Tanzania, *Report to the Government of the United Republic of Tanzania on Wages, Incomes and Prices Policy*, by the International Labour Office, Government Paper No. 3 of 1967 (Dar-es-Salaam, 1967), p. 31. The report goes on to contrast this estimate of retained profits with the figure of Shs.1,400m which was the total value of wages and salaries paid in the same year.

7 Tanzania, *Annual Economic Survey 1968*, tables 2 and 3, pp. 5 and 6.

8 Tanzania, *Background to the Budget, An Economic Survey 1968–69* (Dar-es-Salaam, 1968), table 10, p. 18.

9 *Ibid*. table 8, p. 18. Between 1963 and 1967, Tanzania lost an estimated Shs.450m from these adverse shifts in the terms of trade. This amount was significantly more than twice the foreign assistance Tanzania had received over the same period. *Ibid*. p. 20.

10 *Ibid*. table 3, p. 10.

11 Tanzania, *Tanzania Second Five Year Plan*, vol. I, p. xiii.

12 There are a great many able studies on various aspects of East African cooperation in these years. Perhaps the most helpful for the purposes of this book are Colin Leys' 'Recent Relations between the States of East Africa', *International Journal*, xx, 4 (Winter 1965), 510–23, and Arthur Hazelwood's chapter on East Africa in Hazelwood (ed.), *African Integration and Disintegration* (London, 1968). Donald Rothchild has edited a fine collection of essential primary material and of extracts from relevant academic articles in his *Politics of Integration* (Nairobi, 1969).

13 The text of this address is in *Freedom and Unity*, pp. 176–87.

14 Tanzania, *Statistical Abstract, 1964* (Dar-es-Salaam, 1965), p. 96.

15 The army mutiny in Tanzania is discussed most fully in Henry Bienen, 'Public Order and the Military in Africa' in the volume which he edited, *The Military Intervenes: Case Studies in Political Development* (New York, 1968), and in Harvey Glickman, *Some Observations on the Army and Political Unrest in Tanganyika* (Pittsburgh, 1964).

16 The background to this union is discussed in ch. 6 above, pp. 137–9.

17 Presidential Decree No. 8 of 1964, Legal Supplement (Part 1) to the *Zanzibar Gazette*, LXXIII, 4347 (21 March 1964).

18 In 1964 there were 49 confiscation notices published in the *Zanzibar Gazette* and 51 additional notices in 1965. Most of these notices included long lists of individual properties. Confiscation Order No. 62 of 1965, for example, identified 236 different properties which were to be confiscated by that one Order.

19 From the address by the President to Parliament, 12 May 1964, which is printed as a preface to Tanzania, *Tanzania Second Five Year Plan*, p. vii.

20 These several paragraphs summarize the analysis of development planning in Tanzania which is developed in my article 'The Administration of Economic Planning in a Newly Independent State: The Tanzanian Experience, 1963–66', *Journal of Commonwealth Political Studies*, v, 1 (March 1967), 38–59.

21 Their report, the 'Report of the British Economic Mission on the Tanzanian Five Year Development Plan', was presented in December 1965 just at the

time when Tanzania broke diplomatic relations with Britain. It is an interesting indication of the ability of the Tanzanians to distinguish between governments and their citizens that the Tanzanians were willing, despite the break in diplomatic relations, to treat this report as seriously as they did.

22 See Tanzania, *Report of the Presidential Special Committee of Inquiry into Co-operative Movement and Marketing Boards* (Dar-es-Salaam, 1966) and *Report of the Presidential Commission on the National Union of Tanganyika Workers* (Dar-es-Salaam, 1967).

23 *President Nyerere Opens Dar-es-Salaam University College Campus* (Dar-es-Salaam, 1964), pp. 16–17. This address is reprinted in Nyerere, *Freedom and Unity*, pp. 305–15; the quotation appears on p. 312.

24 The Preventive Detention Act, No. 60 of 1962.

25 *Ibid.* sect. 2(1)(a) and (b).

26 The Preventive Detention (Communication with Detainees) Regulations, 1963, Government Notice No. 203, *Tanganyika Gazette*, XLIV, 27 (Dar-es-Salaam, 17 May 1963).

27 The restriction of Chief Makwaia is discussed in some detail in Maguire's *Towards 'Uhuru'*, pp. 354–6.

28 Nyerere wrote in 1967, 'The danger that self-seeking men will mislead the people can finally only be avoided when a people are ready to assert their control over their leaders.' *Freedom and Socialism*, p. 26.

29 This speech was recorded at the time and could therefore be transcribed and translated into English. Nyerere himself comments that it is typical of his political speeches outside of Dar-es-Salaam and of the kind of teaching which he always undertakes. *Freedom and Socialism*, pp. 136–42.

30 *Ibid.* pp. 139–41. A further and important indication that Nyerere was concerned to encourage citizens to stand up for their rights was his support for the establishment of a Tanzanian 'ombudsman'. From its creation in 1966, Nyerere has taken a close interest in the work of the Permanent Commission of Enquiry and has been its patron. The Commission is discussed in several able articles. See in particular Helge Kjekshus, 'The Ombudsman in the Tanzanian One-Party System', *African Review*, I, 2 (September 1971) and J. P. W. B. McAuslan and Yash Ghai, 'Constitutional Innovation and Political Stability in Tanzania: A Preliminary Assessment', *Journal of Modern African Studies*, IV, 4 (December 1966), 479–515.

31 National Union of Tanganyika Workers (Establishment) Act, No. 18 of 1964. First Schedule, sect. 3.

32 Friedland, 'Cooperation, Conflict, and Conscription', p. 94. These events are effectively discussed in William Tordoff, *Government and Politics in Tanzania*, ch. 4.

33 The National Union of Tanganyika Workers Act, First Schedule, sect. 3(3)(a).

34 *Ibid.* First Schedule, Rule 36(2).

35 Tanzania, *Report of the Presidential Commission on the National Union of Tanganyika Workers*.

36 Nyerere initiated a fresh effort to create workers' committees in 1970 by his Presidential Circular No. 1 of 1970. These more recent developments are ably discussed in Henry Mapolu, 'The Organization and Participation of Workers in Tanzania', *African Review*, II, 3 (1972), 381–416.

37 Tanzania, *Report of the Presidential Special Committee of Inquiry into Cooperative Movement and Marketing Boards*, p. 5.

38 Tanzania, 'Proposals for Reorganization of the Cooperative Movement in Tanzania', by A. M. Babu (Dar-es-Salaam, 1965).

39 These and other aspects of the cooperative movement in Tanzania are

discussed in a particularly insightful fashion in John Saul's 'Marketing Cooperatives in a Developing Country: The Tanzanian Case', in P. M. Worsley (ed.), *Two Blades of Grass* (Manchester, 1970), pp. 347–70.

40 Tanzania, 'Interim Report No. 2 of the Presidential Commission of Enquiry into the Cooperative Movement and the Marketing Boards' (Dar-es-Salaam, 1966).

41 Tanzania, *Report of the Presidential Special Committee of Inquiry into Cooperative Movement and Marketing Boards.*

42 African Chiefs Ordinance (Repeal) Act, 1963. The political and administrative consequences of this Act were noted by the government's simultaneous decision to use many chiefs as individuals in a variety of important ways. Many were appointed as Divisional Executive Officers which was the new administration position replacing the Native Authorities. A number of senior chiefs were appointed to prominent public offices of a non-political kind – the Speaker of the National Assembly, the Chairman of the Local Government Services Commission, the Chairman of the Tourist Board and, at one point, the Ambassador to the United Nations were all prominent chiefs.

43 There are good general discussions of local government in Tanzania in Lionel Cliffe and John Saul, 'The District Development Front in Tanzania', *African Review*, II, 1 (June 1972), 65–104, and in Tordoff, *Government and Politics in Tanzania*. See also Stanley Dryden's *Local Administration in Tanzania* (Nairobi, 1968). More specialized analyses are given by Eugene Lee, *Local Taxation in Tanzania* (Nairobi, 1965) and R. G. Penner, *Financing Local Government in Tanzania* (Nairobi, 1970).

44 These figures were provided to the author in June 1969 by the Ministry of Regional Administration and Rural Development.

45 Interview with A. G. Kalleghe, then Principal Secretary, Ministry of Regional Administration and Local Government, June 1966.

46 There is much valuable information and analysis relating to politics and development in rural Tanzania in a number of studies that have concentrated upon a particular District or area within Tanzania. Their narrower focus is often their great strength for their authors are able to grasp the dynamics of Tanzanian rural politics with a confidence that only comes from intensive study. These include Jean Fox O'Barr, 'Ten House Party Cells and Their Leaders: Micro-Politics in Pare District, Tanzania', unpublished Ph.D. thesis, Northwestern University, 1970; Joel Samoff, 'Politics, Politicians, and Party: Moshi, Tanzania 1968–69', unpublished Ph.D. thesis, University of Wisconsin, 1972; James Finucane, 'Bureaucracy and Development in Rural Tanzania: The Case of Mwanza Region', unpublished Ph.D. thesis, University of London, 1972; Goran Hyden, *TANU Yajenga Nchi: Political Development in Rural Tanganyika* (Lund, 1968); Dean McHenry, 'Tanzania, the Struggle for Development: A Study of Attempts to Establish a Fishermen's Cooperative and to Introduce Cotton Growing in Kigoma Region of Western Tanzania', unpublished Ph.D. thesis, Indiana University, 1971; and Maguire, *Towards 'Uhuru'.*

47 Ministry of Local Government, file LGC12/127/08, 1963. The further information on these tensions which follows is also drawn from the Ministry files.

48 Ministry of Local Government, file LGC51/01, Secretary to the Cabinet to Principal Secretary, Ministry of Local Government, 8 Sept. 1963.

49 Ministry of Local Government, file LGC51/01, Principal Secretary, Ministry of Local Government to Secretary to the Cabinet, 18 Sept. 1963.

50 Tanzania, *Report of the Presidential Commission on the Establishment of a Democratic One Party State* (Dar-es-Salaam, 1965), p. 25.

51 Tanzania, *Proposals of the Tanzanian Government on Local Government Councils*, Government Paper No. 1 of 1966 (Dar-es-Salaam). The final recommendation mentioned above is particularly interesting as it resulted in a significant increase in the popular component of that party structure which not only selects the District Chairman of the party but which also votes its preferences for the candidates for the National Assembly.

52 The previous several paragraphs summarize the state of local government as it was observed by the author in May and June 1969, while a member of the Presidential team reporting on the possible decentralization of the government of Tanzania.

53 *Socialism and Rural Development* (Dar-es-Salaam, 1967), p. 11; reprinted in *Freedom and Socialism*, pp. 337–84.

54 Nyerere, *Decentralization* (Dar-es-Salaam, 1972).

55 These ideas were developed by Nyerere in *Democracy and the Party System*. Nyerere's views on democracy are analyzed in ch. 4 above, pp. 67–70.

56 The argument of this last paragraph is a paraphrase of Nyerere's exposition of his views on democracy in an interview with the author in May 1968.

57 This delay was due to Nyerere's recognition that the introduction of a single-party system in Tanzania in 1963 would have been a further and important obstacle to the creation of an East African Federation. By the end of 1963 it was clear that neither Kenya nor Uganda was seriously interested in the establishment of such a federation. Nyerere therefore felt able to go ahead with the creation of the Commission on the Democratic One Party State.

58 Tanzania, *Report of the Presidential Commission on the Establishment of a Democratic One Party State*, p. 3.

59 *Ibid.* p. 5.

60 *Ibid.* pp. 4–5.

61 *Ibid.* p. 5.

62 This is in fact the case even though his name was included as a signatory in the published report. He also did not accompany the Commission when its members presented the report to President Nyerere.

63 The summary of this evidence which follows is based upon interviews with several of the Committee members and a reading of a detailed summary of the evidence which the Commission received. That summary appears in a condensed form in Tanzania, *Report of the Presidential Commission on the Establishment of a Democratic One Party State*, pp. 7–13.

64 *Ibid.* p. 16.

65 The fullest and best exposition of the democratic one-party state in Tanzania is still Lionel Cliffe (ed.), *One Party Democracy* (Nairobi, 1967). There have been many interesting analyses and commentaries on the Constitution and the election held under it. See for example, Colin Leys and Goran Hyden, 'Elections and Politics in Single-Party Systems: The Case of Kenya and Tanzania', *British Journal of Political Science*, 1, 2 (1972), 389–420. William Tordoff and Henry Bienen have each considered the elections in their respective books on Tanzanian politics to which references have already been made. For an exposition of the democratic one-party state which is somewhat abstracted from the details and cast in ideological terms see John Saul, 'The Nature of Tanzania's Political System, Issues Raised by the 1965 and 1970 Elections', Parts 1 and 11, *Journal of Commonwealth Political Studies*, v, 2, 3 (July, November 1972), 113–29, 198–221.

66 The 1965 Constitution provided for the appointment by the President of up to 35 nominated members of the Assembly, including up to 20 Zanzibaris. It also provided that up to 32 members of the Revolutionary Council could be

appointed to the Assembly and that there could be a maximum of 15 national members elected indirectly by the Assembly. The actual numbers given above are from Tanzania, *Majadiliano ya Bunge* (Hansard), 10–30 June 1966 (Dar-es-Salaam, 1966).

67 Tanzania, *Report of the Presidential Commission on the Establishment of a Democratic One Party State*, p. 18.

68 This is a conclusion common to the major studies which have been made of the National Assembly. See for example 'Parliament and Party, October 1960 to July 1965' in Tordoff, *Government and Politics in Tanzania*, McAuslan and Ghai, 'Constitutional Innovation and Political Stability in Tanzania', Raymond Hopkins, *Political Roles in a New State: Tanzania's First Decade* (New Haven, Conn., 1971), and Helge Kjekshus, 'The Question Hour in Tanzania's Bunge', *African Review*, II, 3 (1972), 351–80.

69 Hopkins, *Political Roles*, p. 153. McAuslan and Ghai come to a similar conclusion in their article 'Constitutional Innovation and Political Stability in Tanzania', p. 496.

70 These events and their background are effectively discussed by H. U. E. Thoden van Velzen and J. J. Sterkenburg in two articles, 'Stirrings in the Tanzanian National Assembly' and 'The Party Supreme', in Lionel Cliffe and John Saul (eds.), *Socialism in Tanzania*, vol. I (Dar-es-Salaam, 1972), pp. 248–53, 257–64.

71 See above, ch. 5, pp. 95–8.

72 See for example Tanganyika, *Proposals of the Tanganyika Government for a Republic*, Government Paper No. 1 of 1962 (Dar-es-Salaam, 1962), p. 3, and speech by Kawawa as Prime Minister introducing these proposals to the Assembly. Tanganyika, *National Assembly Official Report*, 1st Session, vol. I, col. 1085, 28 June 1962.

73 The best detailed study of the institutions of TANU continues to be Henry Bienen's *Tanzania*. The composition of the National Conference (called the Annual Conference until 1965) and of the NEC are set out in Article IV, Section E, of the TANU Constitution. The 1965 version of that Constitution is reprinted as an appendix in Tordoff's *Government and Politics in Tanzania*, pp. 236–51.

74 Cliffe reports that of the 101 members elected in the seats which were contested in 1965, 16 had university or other post-secondary education, 56 had had secondary school education, 19 upper primary education, 3 had had 4 or less years of formal schooling and 7 had not attended any school. Cliffe, *One Party Democracy*, p. 263.

75 *Ibid.* p. 267.

76 This information on the members of the National Executive Committee was made available to me at TANU headquarters in May 1968.

77 This shift is discussed in my 'The Cabinet and Presidential Leadership in Tanzania: 1960–66'. Recent and fuller treatment of it is given in Pius Msekwa's excellent 'Towards Party Supremacy: The Changing Pattern of Relationships between the National Assembly and the National Executive Committee of TANU before and after 1965', unpublished M.A. thesis, University of Dar-es-Salaam, 1974.

78 Act No. 49 of 1965.

79 Tanzania, *Report of the Presidential Commission on the Establishment of a Democratic One Party State*, p. 16.

80 Quoted in Hopkins, *Political Roles*, p. 192.

81 Quoted by Msekwa, 'Towards Party Supremacy', p. 33.

82 Tanzania, *Background to the Budget 1967–68*, p. 85.

83 Tanganyika, *Report of the Territorial Minimum Wage Board* (Dar-es-Salaam, 1962).
84 Colin Leys, 'The Analysis of Planning', in Leys (ed.), *Politics and Change in Developing Countries* (Cambridge, 1969), p. 269.
85 The literature on class stratification in rural Africa is still not as extensive as it might be. This literature is ably discussed with particular reference to Tanzania in Gavin N. Kitching, 'The Concept of Class and the Study of Africa', *African Review*, II, 3 (1972), 327–50. Lionel Cliffe has summarized the scattered evidence on the emergence of more severe class differentiation in rural Tanzania in his 'The Policy of Ujamaa Vijijini and the Class Struggle in Tanzania', in Cliffe and Saul (eds.), *Socialism in Tanzania*, vol. II, pp. 195–214. Manuel Gottlieb has brilliantly analyzed the results of the 1967 census which covered a wide variety of economic data to produce a statistically based assessment of the extent and character of the reorientation that has occurred. See his 'The Extent and Character of Differentiation in Tanzanian Agricul-tural and Rural Society 1967–69' in *African Review*, III, 2 (June 1973), 241–62.
86 These developments are discussed by H. U. E. Thoden van Velzen in his brilliant 'Staff, Kulaks and Peasants', in Cliffe and Saul (eds.), *Socialism in Tanzania*, vol. II, pp. 153–79.
87 Hans Ruthenburg, 'Coffee and Banana Farms at Mount Kilimanjaro' in Ruthenburg (ed.), *Smallholder Farming and Smallholder Development in Tanzania* (Munich, 1968), pp. 213–18.
88 Cliffe calls these areas 'frontier areas' and discusses them in his article 'The Policy of Ujamaa Vijijini'.
89 Gottlieb, 'Extent and Character of Differentiation in Tanzanian Agricultural and Rural Society', p. 254.
90 *Ibid.* pp. 246–7.
91 John Saul, in a 1966 paper, was one of the first commentators to identify this trend in rural leadership in Tanzania and to note its significance. See his 'Marketing Cooperatives in Tanzania: A Case Study in Resource Allocation and Inequality', East African Institute of Social Research Conference paper, 1966.
92 From Nyerere's speech during the budget debate in June 1959. Quoted in *East Africa and Rhodesia*, 25 June 1959.
93 Tanganyika, *Report of the Tanganyika Salaries Commission, 1961*, p. 1. The terms of reference of the Commission were determined in January 1961 and its members were appointed in March of that year. The other members of the Commission were Rawle Fairley, a West Indian economist, Jacob Namfua, then a young Tanzanian trade union leader, and M. N. Devani, a Tanganyikan Asian. Mwai Kibaki, who was at that time Executive Officer of the Kenya African National Union, was also to have been a member of the Commission. However he resigned from it before it began its work.
94 *Ibid.* p. 24.
95 This was the estimate given by a Minister without Portfolio to the National Assembly in October 1961. This estimate assumes that the new salary scales would be extended to teachers employed by the voluntary agencies though paid by the Ministry of Education. Tanganyika, *National Assembly Official Report*, 36th Session, vol. V, cols. 41–2, 10 Oct. 1961.
96 *Ibid.* col. 101.
97 Tanganyika, *High Level Manpower Requirements*, p. 38.
98 Tanzania, *Background to the Budget 1967–68*, p. 82.
99 Tanganyika, *Legislative Council Official Report*, 36th Session, vol. III, cols. 56, 59, 14 Feb. 1961.

100 See for example Issa Shivji *et al.*, *The Silent Class Struggle* (Dar-es-Salaam, 1973) and John Saul, 'African Socialism in One Country: Tanzania', in Giovanni Arrighi and John Saul (eds.), *Essays on the Political Economy of Africa* (New York, 1973), pp. 237–335.

101 'An Index of the Cost of Goods and Services Consumed by Middle Grade Civil Servants' shows a 30% increase in their cost of living between September 1963 and September 1968. Tanzania, *Annual Economic Survey 1968*, p. 36.

102 K. Ngobale-Mwiru, 'The Arusha Declaration on Ujamaa na Kujitegemea and the Perspectives for Building Socialism in Tanzania', in Cliffe and Saul (eds.), *Socialism in Tanzania*, vol. II, p. 57.

103 Tanzania, *Background to the Budget 1968–69*, table 28, p. 36.

104 A. P. van der Laar, 'Arusha: Before and After', *East African Journal*, V, 11 (November 1968), 18. Van der Laar, however, does not provide any of this evidence in this article.

105 The author did this while in Tanzania in that year as a member of a Presidential team considering the possible decentralization of the government.

106 In 1964, all fees were abolished for the regular secondary schools. However, fees at Ilyunga remained at Shs.480 per annum for tuition plus Shs.1,400 for board and lodging. (Government Notice No. 679 of 1964.) This school, however, has since been closed.

107 From a speech by Nyerere in February 1963 which was reprinted in full in *Vigilance Africa*, I, 3 (4 Nov. 1964), 10–11. This speech appears in an abbreviated form which excludes the passages quoted, in Nyerere, *Freedom and Unity*, pp. 208–11.

Chapter 8. The commitment to socialism 1967–8

1 Tanzania, *Report to the Government of the United Republic of Tanzania on Wages, Incomes and Prices Policy.*

2 This is also the judgment of Justinian Rweyemamu in his *Underdevelopment and Industrialization in Tanzania* (Nairobi, 1973). In Part One of this book, Rweyemamu ably surveys a number of the same issues which are being raised here.

3 They are briefly mentioned above in chapter 6, p. 153. The few scholars from socialist countries tended to be much more hesitant to involve themselves in contemporary Tanzanian political affairs than Western Marxists (or for that matter than some Western democratic socialists and liberals as well).

4 *Tanganyika Standard*, 25 June 1966, p. 3.

5 See for example his introduction to *Freedom and Socialism*, pp. 26–7 and his opening speech to the special TANU Conference in March 1967, in Tanzania, *Majadiliano ya Mkutano Mkuu wa TANU*, 27 Feb. to 3 Mar. 1967 (Dar-es-Salaam, 1967).

6 See for example 'After the Arusha Declaration', reprinted in *Freedom and Socialism*, p. 405.

7 In the introduction to *Freedom and Unity*, pp. 17, 6–7.

8 *Tanzania Ten Years after Independence* (Dar-es-Salaam, 1971), p. 14.

9 *Socialism and Rural Development*, p. 8; reprinted in *Freedom and Socialism*.

10 From several interviews with James Skinner, then Acting Managing Director of the National Development Corporation, June and July 1966.

11 There is much contemporary evidence confirming that Nyerere regarded these two sections as being the most important parts of the Declaration. See for example Nyerere's speech opening the special TANU Conference to consider the Arusha Declaration in Tanzania, *Majadiliano ya Mkutano Mkuu wa*

> *TANU*, cols. 1–21; his speech at the university on 5 August 1967, 'The Purpose Is Man', reprinted in *Freedom and Socialism*, pp. 315–26, and his speech 'After the Arusha Declaration', to the TANU National Conference in October 1967, also reprinted in *Freedom and Socialism*, pp. 385–409. The same emphasis was given by the President in a major press conference on 4 March 1967, a tape of which is in the author's possession. In two widely separated interviews, one in June 1968 and one in June 1974, Nyerere also reiterated that these two sections were the most important in the Declaration.

12 The Arusha Declaration, Part IV. The Declaration appears in Nyerere's *Freedom and Socialism*, pp. 230–50.

13 See in particular Henry Bienen, *Tanzania*, ch. 13; John Saul, 'African Socialism in One Country'; Reginald Green, 'Political Independence and the National Economy: An Essay on the Political Economy of Decolonization', in Christopher Allen and R. W. Johnson (eds.), *African Perspectives* (Cambridge, 1970); Justinian Rweyemamu, *Underdevelopment and Industrialization in Tanzania*, ch. 2.

14 From the Arusha Declaration, reprinted in Nyerere's *Freedom and Socialism*, p. 238.

15 Tanzania, *Majadiliano ya Mkutano Mkuu wa TANU*, col. 12.

16 From an interview with Nyerere, June 1968.

17 This is mentioned above, pp. 109–10.

18 Interview with Joseph Namata, Principal Secretary to the President, June 1965. Some of these incidents are discussed briefly in my 'The Cabinet and Presidential Leadership'.

19 National Service (Amendment) Act, 1966 (No. 64 of 1966).

20 The details are set out in Tanzania, *National Service*, Staff Circular No. 5 of 1967 (Dar-es-Salaam, 17 July 1967).

21 From a transcript of a tape of the confrontation between the students and the President, 22 October 1966. A copy of this tape is in the author's possession.

22 *Ibid.*

23 *Ibid.*

24 These items are a summary of the list which appears in Part V of the Arusha Declaration. They were to apply to 'Members of the National Executive Committee of TANU, Ministers, Members of Parliament, senior officials of organizations affiliated with TANU, senior officials of parastatal bodies; all those appointed or elected under any clause of the TANU constitution; councillors; and civil servants in the high and middle cadres'. Nyerere, *Freedom and Socialism*, p. 249.

25 From the transcript of a press conference on 4 March 1967.

26 See ch. 5 above, pp. 119–21 where the content of these pamphlets is summarized.

27 From the transcript of the press conference given by Nyerere on 4 March 1967 in Dar-es-Salaam.

28 From an interview with Nyerere, June 1974.

29 That leaders and government officials can come to socialist positions without prior indoctrination has been shrewdly commented on by Tamas Szentes in his '"Status Quo" and Socialism' in Shivji *et al.*, *The Silent Class Struggle*, pp. 97–8.

30 He talked of this aspect of the Arusha Declaration in an interview in June 1974.

31 This fact is referred to by Nyerere in his opening speech to the special March Conference of TANU. Tanzania, *Majadiliano ya Mkutano Mkuu wa TANU*,

cols. 1–21. Some flavour of the individual concerns of members can be gathered from an extraordinary pamphlet which provides the questions which MPs submitted to Nyerere concerning the Declaration and his replies to these questions. *Arusha Declaration: Answers to Questions* (Dar-es-Salaam, 1967).

32 Nyerere agreed that this was a valid point, though he said that the nationalizations had not been deliberately introduced for that tactical purpose. They were, however, an integrated package and without the more popular components the less popular ones would have been more difficult to implement. Interview with Nyerere, June 1974.

33 'Political Independence and the National Economy', p. 318.

34 In an interview with the author, June 1974.

35 In a speech on 28 February 1967, quoted in *Freedom and Socialism*, pp. 262, 264.

36 The preceding several pages summarize my sense of the mood of Tanzanian political leaders and civil servants as I observed it in the years 1965 to 1968 and as politicians and civil servants later recalled it in interviews. They are inevitably impressionistic. However, the phenomenon they seek to account for, the positive response of TANU and government leaders to the Arusha Declaration, is of real importance.

37 From the transcript of the press conference on 4 March 1967.

38 *Ujamaa, The Basis of African Socialism*, p. 1.

39 See for example his address in April 1967 at the University of Cairo which is reprinted in *Freedom and Socialism*, pp. 300–10.

40 In an address at the University of Dar-es-Salaam, August 1967, *ibid.* p. 324.

41 August 1968. Introduction to *Freedom and Socialism*, p. 4.

42 This argument was developed fully by Nyerere in his speech to the special TANU Conference in March 1967 when he introduced the Arusha Declaration. Tanzania, *Majadiliano ya Mkutano Mkuu wa TANU*, cols. 1–20.

43 Nyerere, *Freedom and Socialism*, pp. 340, 344.

44 Introduction to *Freedom and Unity*, p. 13.

45 Nyerere, in his address to Parliament on 6 July 1970. Reprinted in *Freedom and Development: Uhuru na Maendeleo* (Dar-es-Salaam, 1973), p. 197.

46 See for example *Freedom and Socialism*, pp. 13–14.

47 *Ibid.* p. 23.

48 *Ibid.* p. 25.

49 Tanzania, *Majadiliano ya Mkutano Mkuu wa TANU*, col. 99.

50 Nyerere, *Freedom and Socialism*, p. 341.

51 *Tanzania Standard*, 11 February 1967, p. 1.

52 The latter position is taken by Shivji in Shivji *et al., The Silent Class Struggle*, p. 39.

53 Tanzania, *Majadiliano ya Mkutano Mkuu wa TANU*, cols. 90–5.

54 *Ibid.* col. 102.

55 *Ibid.* col. 106.

56 Nyerere in his speech to the October 1967 TANU Conference, *Freedom and Socialism*, p. 395.

57 *Freedom and Socialism*, p. 325.

58 In his speech 'After the Arusha Declaration' to the TANU National Conference, October 1967, *ibid.* p. 403.

59 Knud Erik Svendsen, 'Socialism in a Poor Peasant Economy', in Idrian Resnick (ed.), *Tanzania: Revolution by Education* (Arusha, 1968), p. 86.

60 These estimates were prepared by Reginald Green, Economic Adviser to the Treasury, June 1974. They include fringe benefits.

61 This fall in real income has been due to cost-of-living increases, particularly

since 1971, to the salary cuts, ranging from 3% to 20%, introduced in 1966, and to tax increases. These were at first largely offset by promotions. However, in recent years many senior officials have had to adjust to a falling standard of living. Green estimates that a person in the same senior post from 1967 to 1973 would have experienced a 25% fall in his living standards. Salaries in the Kenyan civil service were on the average 25% higher than in Tanzania (United Nations, *Wages and Salary Policies of the East African Community* (Geneva, 1974)). As the Tanzanian minimum wage exceeded the Kenyan, the differentials in the higher brackets must be very significantly higher than 25%.

62 From a speech on 28 February 1967, reprinted in *Freedom and Socialism*, p. 264.

63 *Freedom and Development* (Dar-es-Salaam, 1968), p. 6.

64 'Socialism in a Poor Peasant Economy', p. 87.

65 Interview, *The Daily Nation* (Nairobi), 7 August 1968.

66 This is I believe the interpretation which a number of Marxist commentators have read into the concept of 'self-reliance'. In some cases they have wished merely to argue that it should have this meaning. Others however seem to be suggesting that this was in fact part of the original meaning of self-reliance. This latter position is untenable. For the varying shades of Marxian emphasis on this important question see, for example, Giovanni Arrighi and John Saul, 'Socialism and Economic Development in Tropical Africa' and Saul, 'African Socialism in One Country: Tanzania', in Arrighi and Saul (eds.), *Essays on the Political Economy of Africa*; Issa Shivji *et al.*, *The Silent Class Struggle*; Justinian Rweyemamu, *Underdevelopment and Industrialization in Tanzania*; and S. M. Mbilinyi, R. Mabele and M. L. Kyomo, 'Economic Struggle of TANU Government', in Gabriel Ruhumbika (ed.), *Towards Ujamaa: Twenty Years of TANU Leadership* (Nairobi, 1974).

67 *Freedom and Socialism*, p. 321.

68 Nyerere, *Non-Alignment in the Seventies* (Dar-es-Salaam, 1970), pp. 6–7.

69 Nyerere, *Tanzania Policy on Foreign Affairs*.

70 Nyerere, *Non-Alignment in the Seventies*.

71 See the text of this address in Yu, *China and Tanzania*, appendix 8.

72 No effort can be made here to assess the initial consequences of these initiatives. What is important for the argument here is that they were very much Presidential initiatives in the first instance and that they constituted an integral part of a coherent social strategy. This judgment is confirmed by one of the ablest scholars presently writing on Tanzanian affairs, Helge Kjekshus, in 'Perspectives on the Second Parliament, 1965–1970', in the excellent volume by the Election Studies Committee, *Socialism and Participation: Tanzania's 1970 National Elections* (Dar-es-Salaam, 1974), pp. 60–95.

73 See pp. 77–82.

74 Nyerere argued both these points in his opening speech to the special TANU Conference, March 1967. Tanzania, *Majadiliano ya Mkutano Mkuu wa TANU*.

75 See for example his rejection of this line of argument in *Freedom and Socialism*, pp. 14–17.

76 *Freedom and Socialism*, p. 367.

77 *Freedom and Development* (1973), p. 186.

78 This quotation is from one of Nyerere's most thoughtful policy papers, *Freedom and Development* (Dar-es-Salaam, 1968), reprinted in *Freedom and Development* (1973), pp. 58–71. The quotation appears on p. 3 of the original pamphlet (1968) and on p. 60 of the later (1973) volume.

79 These quotations are from Nyerere's important policy paper *Socialism and Rural Development*, which is reprinted in *Freedom and Socialism*.
80 'Socialism and Rural Development', in *Freedom and Socialism*, p. 346.
81 *Ibid.* p. 356.
82 Indeed he announced in November 1973 that TANU had decided that all peasants must live in villages by 1976! *Daily News* (Dar-es-Salaam, 7 November 1973, p. 1.
83 The argument of this paragraph summarizes the point of view expressed by Nyerere in an interview with the author in June 1974.
84 From 'Socialism and Rural Development', in Nyerere, *Freedom and Socialism*, p. 348.
85 In an interview, June 1974. This paragraph relies in part upon Nyerere's explanation of his views in that interview. He also discusses the role of the party in his introduction to *Freedom and Socialism*, in particular on pp. 30–2.
86 See ch. 7, above, especially pp. 208–10.
87 Marxian analysis is, of course, not intended to reinforce oligarchic tendencies within the party. We are however talking of an area of political practice where the slippage between intention and reality can be very great. If the effort were in fact made to convert TANU into a vanguard party the result might very well be the full entrenchment of a political oligarchy free of the encumbrance of the existing democratic constraints, an oligarchy which utilizes a socialist rhetoric without real commitment to it.
88 Nyerere, *Freedom and Development* (1973), pp. 66, 179, 333.
89 *Freedom and Socialism*, p. 91.
90 *Freedom and Development* (1973), pp. 184–5.
91 *Freedom and Development* (1973), p. 186.
92 *Ibid.* p. 37.
93 In an interview, June 1974.
94 *Freedom and Development* (1973), p. 179.
95 James S. Coleman and Carl G. Rosberg (eds.), *Political Parties and National Integration in Tropical Africa* (Berkeley, Calif., 1964), pp. 659ff.
96 Jonathan Barker, 'Local–Central Relations in Senegal', in Lofchie (ed.), *The State of the Nations*, p. 56.
97 See Finucane, 'Bureaucracy and Development in Rural Tanzania', ch. 1.
98 This view is attributed to a group of 17 social scientists which included Douglas Ashford, Henry Bienen, Martin Kilson, Arthur Lewis and Aristide Zolberg, in a summary of a conference held in 1967. It is quoted by Finucane, *ibid.* pp. 19–20.
99 Saul, 'The Nature of Tanzania's Political System', part 1, pp. 113–29.

BIBLIOGRAPHY OF WORKS CITED

The works cited here include all items cited in the notes except the government files consulted by the author in 1959, government Acts and Ordinances, official Gazettes, contemporary newspaper accounts and, of course, personal communications to the author.

Arrighi, Giovanni and Saul, John. 'Nationalism and Revolution in Sub-Saharan Africa', in Ralph Miliband and John Saville (eds.), *The Socialist Register 1969*. London: Merlin Press, 1969, pp. 137–88.
  'Socialism and Economic Development in Tropical Africa', in Arrighi and Saul (eds.), *Essays on the Political Economy of Africa*.
Arrighi, Giovanni and Saul, John (eds.). *Essays on the Political Economy of Africa*. New York: Monthly Review Press, 1973.
Ayany, S. G. *A History of Zanzibar*. Nairobi: East African Literature Bureau, 1970.
Barker, Jonathan. 'Local–Central Relations in Senegal', in Lofchie (ed.), *The State of the Nations*, pp. 47–63.
Bates, Margaret. 'Tanganyika', in Gwendolyn Carter (ed.), *African One-Party States*. Ithaca, N.Y.: Cornell University Press, 1962, pp. 395–483.
Bennett, George. 'An Outline History of TANU'. *Makerere Journal*, no. 7 (1963), 1–18; reprinted in Oxford University Institute of Commonwealth Studies Reprint Series, no. 31, 1965.
Bienen, Henry. 'Public Order and the Military in Africa', in Bienen (ed.), *The Military Intervenes: Case Studies in Political Development*. New York: Russell Sage Foundation, 1968, pp. 35–69.
  Tanzania: Party Transformation and Economic Development, 2nd ed. Princeton, N.J.: University Press, 1970.
Brett, Anthony. *Colonialism and Underdevelopment in East Africa*. London: Heinemann, 1973.
A British–Canadian Report on an Engineering and Economic Feasibility Study for a Proposed Zambia and East Africa Rail Link Prepared by Canadian Area Services Ltd., Livesay and Henderson, Maxwell Stamp Associates Ltd., and Sumption, Berkeley and Co. Ltd. London, 1966.
'The Capital Development Programme of the University College, 1964–1967'. Dar-es-Salaam: University of Dar-es-Salaam, 1963. Mimeographed.
Cliffe, Lionel. 'Nationalism and the Reaction to Enforced Agricultural Change in Tanganyika during the Colonial Period'. Paper presented to the East African Institute of Social Research Conference, 1964. Mimeographed.
  'The Policy of Ujamaa Vijijini and the Class Struggle in Tanzania', in Cliffe and Saul (eds.), *Socialism in Tanzania*, vol. II, pp. 195–214.
Cliffe, Lionel (ed.). *One Party Democracy*. Nairobi: East African Publishing House, 1967.

Cliffe, Lionel and Saul, John. 'The District Development Front in Tanzania'. *African Review*, II, 1 (June 1972), 65–104.
Cliffe, Lionel and Saul, John (eds.). *Socialism in Tanzania*, 2 vols. Dar-es-Salaam: East African Publishing House, 1972–3.
Coleman, James S. and Rosberg, Carl G. (eds.). *Political Parties and National Integration in Tropical Africa*. Berkeley: University of California Press, 1964.
Dryden, Stanley. *Local Administration in Tanzania*. Nairobi: East African Publishing House, 1968.
Ehrlich, Cyril. 'Some Aspects of Economic Policy in Tanganyika 1945–60'. *Journal of Modern African Studies*, II (July 1964), 265–78.
'The Tanganyikan Economy 1945 to 1960'. Typescript undated but *circa* 1965.
Election Studies Committee, University of Dar-es-Salaam. *Socialism and Participation: Tanzania's 1970 National Elections*. Dar-es-Salaam: Tanzania Publishing House, 1974.
Finucane, James. 'Bureaucracy and Development in Rural Tanzania: The Case of Mwanza Region'. Unpublished Ph.D. thesis, University of London, 1972.
Friedland, William H. 'Co-operation, Conflict, and Conscription: TANU–TFL Relations 1955–1964', in Jeffrey Butler and A. S. Castagno (eds.), *Boston University Papers on Africa: Transition in African Politics*. New York: Praeger, 1967, pp. 67–103.
Ghana. *Nkrumah's Subversion in Africa*. Accra: Ghana Ministry of Information, 1966.
Glickman, Harvey. 'Dilemmas of Political Theory in an African Context: The Ideology of Julius Nyerere', in Jeffrey Butler and A. S. Castagno (eds.), *Boston University Papers on Africa: Transition in African Politics*. New York: Praeger, 1967, pp. 195–223.
Some Observations on the Army and Political Unrest in Tanganyika. Pittsburgh: Duquesne University Press, 1964.
Gottlieb, Manuel. 'The Extent and Character of Differentiation in Tanzanian Agricultural and Rural Society 1967–69'. *African Review*, III, 2 (June 1973), 241–62.
Green, Reginald. 'Political Independence and the National Economy: An Essay on the Political Economy of Decolonization', in Christopher Allen and R. W. Johnson (eds.), *African Perspectives*. Cambridge: University Press, 1970.
Hailey, Lord. *Native Administration and Political Development in British Tropical Africa*. London: HMSO, 1940–2.
Hall, Richard. *The High Price of Principles: Kaunda and the White South*. London: Hodder and Stoughton, 1969.
Hazelwood, Arthur (ed.). *African Integration and Disintegration*. London: Oxford University Press, 1968.
Helleiner, Gerald. 'Trade, Aid and Nation-Building in Tanzania', in Anthony Rweyemamu (ed.), *Nation-Building in Tanzania*. Nairobi: East African Publishing House, 1970, pp. 61–78.
Heussler, Robert. *British Tanganyika: An Essay and Documents on District Administration*. Durham, N.C.: Duke University Press, 1971.
Hicks, Ursula. *Development from Below*. London: Oxford University Press, 1961.
Hodgkin, Thomas. 'A Note on the Language of African Nationalism', in Kenneth Kirkwood (ed.), *African Affairs No. 1*. St Antony Papers No. 10. London: Chatto and Windus, 1961, pp. 22–40.
Hopkins, Raymond. *Political Roles in a New State: Tanzania's First Decade*. New Haven, Conn.: Yale University Press, 1971.
Hoskyns, Catherine. 'Africa's Foreign Policy: The Case of Tanzania'. *International Affairs*, 44, 3 (July 1968), 446–62.

The Organization of African Unity and the Congo Crisis, 1964–65. Case Studies
  in African Diplomacy No. 1. Dar-es-Salaam: Oxford University Press, 1969.
Hudson, R. G., *see* United Kingdom Government, 'Report on the Development...'
Huntington, Samuel. *Political Order in Changing Societies.* New Haven, Conn.:
  Yale University Press, 1968.
Hyden, Goran. *TANU Yajenga Nchi: Political Development in Rural Tanganyika.*
  Lund: Scandinavian University Books, 1968.
Iliffe, John. *Agricultural Change in Modern Tanganyika: An Outline History.*
  Historical Association of Tanzania, Paper No. 10. Dar-es-Salaam: East African
  Publishing House, 1971.
  'The Role of the African Association in the Formation and Realization of
  Territorial Consciousness in Tanzania'. University of East Africa Social Sciences
  Conference, 1968. Mimeographed.
International Bank for Reconstruction and Development. 'Consultative Group for
  East Africa: Information on Financial and Technical Assistance'. Washington,
  D.C., 1968. Mimeographed.
  *The Economic Development of Tanganyika: A Report of a Mission Organized
  by the International Bank for Reconstruction and Development.* Baltimore:
  Johns Hopkins University Press, 1961.
International Labour Office, *see* Tanzania, *Report to the Government...*
Jamal, Amir H. *The Critical Phase of Emergent African States.* Nairobi: East
  African Institute Press, 1965.
Kimambo, N. N. and Temu, A. J. (eds.). *A History of Tanzania.* Nairobi: East
  African Publishing House, 1969.
Kingsley, J. Donald and Thurston, J. L., *see* Tanzania, 'Some Problems...'
Kitching, Gavin N. 'The Concept of Class and the Study of Africa'. *African
  Review*, II, 3 (1972), 327–50.
Kjekshus, Helge. 'The Ombudsman in the Tanzanian One-Party System'. *African
  Review*, I, 2 (Sept. 1971), 13–29.
  'Perspectives on the Second Parliament, 1965–1970', in Election Studies Committee,
  Socialism and Participation: Tanzania's 1970 National Elections, pp. 60–95.
  'The Question Hour in Tanzania's Bunge'. *African Review*, II, 3 (1972), 351–80.
Lee, Eugene. *Local Taxation in Tanzania.* Nairobi: Oxford University Press, 1965.
Legum, Colin. 'How Nyerere Out-manoeuvred Babu of Zanzibar', *Observer*,
  26 April 1964.
Legum, Colin and Drysdale, John (eds.). *Africa Contemporary Records: Annual
  Survey and Documents 1968–69.* London: Rex Collings, 1969.
Leys, Colin. 'Recent Relations between the States of East Africa'. *International
  Journal*, xx, 4 (Winter 1965), 510–23.
Leys, Colin (ed.). *Politics and Change in Developing Countries.* Cambridge:
  University Press, 1969.
Leys, Colin and Hyden, Goran. 'Elections and Politics in Single-Party Systems: The
  Case of Kenya and Tanzania'. *British Journal of Political Science*, I, 2 (1972),
  389–420.
Listowel, Lady, *The Making of Tanganyika*, London: Chatto and Windus, 1965.
Lofchie, Michael (ed.). *The State of the Nations: Constraints on Development in
  Independent Africa.* Los Angeles: University of California Press, 1971.
Lowenkopf, Martin. 'Political Parties in Uganda and Tanganyika'. Unpublished
  M.A. thesis, University of London, 1961.
'Lusaka Manifesto', reprinted in Legum and Drysdale (eds.), *Africa Contemporary
  Records...1969–70.* London: Rex Collings, 1970.
Maguire, G. Andrew. *Towards 'Uhuru' in Tanzania: The Politics of Participation.*
  Cambridge: University Press, 1969.

Mapolu, Henry. 'The Organization and Participation of Workers in Tanzania'. *African Review*, II, 3 (1972), 381–416.

Mazrui, Ali. 'Tanzania verus East Africa'. *Journal of Commonwealth Political Studies*, III, 3 (Nov. 1965), 209–25.

Mbilinyi, S. M., Mabele, R. and Kyomo, M. L. 'Economic Struggle of TANU Government', in Gabriel Ruhumbika (ed.), *Towards Ujamaa: Twenty Years of TANU Leadership*. Nairobi: East African Literature Bureau, 1974.

McAuslan, J. P. W. B. and Ghai, Yash. 'Constitutional Innovation and Political Stability in Tanzania: A Preliminary Assessment'. *Journal of Modern African Studies*, IV, 4 (Dec. 1966), 479–515.

McHenry, Dean. 'Tanzania, The Struggle for Development. A Study of Attempts to Establish a Fishermen's Cooperative and to Introduce Cotton Growing in Kigoma Region of Western Tanzania'. Unpublished Ph.D. thesis, Indiana University, 1971.

McLoughlin, Peter. 'Tanzania: Agricultural Development in Sukumaland', in John C. de Wilde *et al.*, *Experiences with Agricultural Development in Tropical Africa*, vol. 2. Baltimore: Johns Hopkins University Press, 1967, pp. 415–50.

Mitchell, Sir Philip. *Native Administration*. Entebbe: Government Printer, 1939.

Msekwa, Pius. 'Towards Party Supremacy: The Changing Pattern of Relationships between the National Assembly and the National Executive Committee of TANU before and after 1965'. Unpublished M.A. thesis, University of Dar-es-Salaam, 1974.

Mulford, David C. *Zambia: The Politics of Independence 1957–64*. London: Oxford University Press, 1967.

Murray, Roger. 'Second Thoughts on Ghana'. *New Left Review*, 42 (March–April 1967), 25–39.

Mustafa, Sophia. *The Tanganyika Way*. Dar-es-Salaam: East African Literature Bureau, 1961.

Ngobale-Mwiru, K. 'The Arusha Declaration on Ujamaa na Kujitegemea and the Perspectives for Building Socialism in Tanzania', in Cliffe and Saul (eds.), *Socialism in Tanzania*, vol. II, pp. 52–60.

Niblock, T. C. 'Aid and Foreign Policy in Tanzania, 1961–68', Unpublished Ph.D. thesis, University of Sussex, 1972.

Nyerere, Julius K. *An Address to the Norwegian Students' Association in Oslo*. Dar-es-Salaam: Tanganyika Information Services, 1963.

  'The African and Democracy', in James Duffy and Robert Manners (eds.), *Africa Speaks*. New York: Van Nostrand, 1961, pp. 28–34.

  'Africa's Bid for Democracy', *Africa and the Colonial World*, VIII, 3 (July 1960).

  'Africa's Place in the World', in *Symposium on Africa*. Wellesley, Mass.: Wellesley College, 1960, pp. 147–62.

  Arusha Declaration: Answers to Questions. Dar-es-Salaam: Government Printer, 1967.

  'Chief Minister's Circular No. 1' (1960). *Journal of African Administration*, XIII, 2 (April 1961), 108–11.

  Decentralization. Dar-es-Salaam: Government Printer, 1972.

  Democracy and the Party System. Dar-es-Salaam: *Tanganyika Standard* (January 1963).

  'Democracy in Africa'. *Tribune* (London), June 1960.

  'The Entrenchment of Privilege'. *Africa South*, II, 2 (January–March 1958), 85–92.

  Freedom and Development. Dar-es-Salaam: Government Printer, 1968; reprinted in Nyerere, *Freedom and Development: Uhuru na Maendeleo*, pp. 58–71.

  Freedom and Development: Uhuru na Maendeleo. Dar-es-Salaam: Oxford University Press, 1973.

Freedom and Socialism: Uhuru na Ujamaa. Dar-es-Salaam: Oxford University Press, 1968.
Freedom and Unity: Uhuru na Umoja. London: Oxford University Press, 1966.
'Groping Forward', in Nyerere, *Freedom and Unity*, pp. 119–23.
Non-Alignment in the Seventies. Dar-es-Salaam: Government Printer, 1970.
'One-Party Government'. *Spearhead*, 1, 1 (November 1961), 7–10.
President Nyerere Opens Dar-es-Salaam University College Campus. Dar-es-Salaam: Ministry of Information and Tourism, 1964; reprinted in Nyerere, *Freedom and Unity*, pp. 305–15.
Socialism and Rural Development. Dar-es-Salaam: Government Printer, 1967; reprinted in Nyerere, *Freedom and Socialism*, pp. 337–84.
'The Socialist Way'. *Vigilance Africa*, 1, 3 (November 1964), 10–11.
Stability and Change in Africa. Dar-es-Salaam: Government Printer, 1969.
TANU na Raia [TANU and the People]. Dar-es-Salaam: Tanganyika African National Union Press [1962].
Tanzania Policy on Foreign Affairs. Address by the President Mwalimu Julius K. Nyerere at the Tanganyika African National Union National Conference, 16 October 1967. Dar-es-Salaam: Ministry of Information and Tourism, 1967; reprinted in Nyerere, *Freedom and Socialism*, pp. 367–84.
Tanzania Ten Years after Independence. Dar-es-Salaam: Government Printer, 1971.
Tujisahihishe [Self-Criticism]. Dar-es-Salaam: Tanganyika African National Union Press [1962].
Ujamaa, The Basis of African Socialism. Dar-es-Salaam: *Tanganyika Standard*, 1962.
'We Cannot Afford to Fail'. *Africa Special Report*, IV, 12 (December 1959), 8–10.
'Will Democracy Work in Africa?' *Africa Report*, V, 2 (February 1960), 4–5.
O'Barr, Jean Fox. 'Ten House Party Cells and Their Leaders: Micro-Politics in Pare District, Tanzania'. Unpublished Ph.D. thesis, Northwestern University, 1970.
Okello, John. *Revolution in Zanzibar*. Nairobi: East African Publishing House, 1967.
Page-Jones, S. H., *see* Tanganyika, 'Interim Report on the County Council...'
Penner, R. G. *Financing Local Government in Tanzania*. Nairobi: East African Publishing House, 1970.
Perham, Margery. *The Colonial Reckoning*. London: Collins, 1962.
Pratt, R. C. 'The Administration of Economic Planning in a Newly Independent State: The Tanzanian Experience, 1963–66'. *Journal of Commonwealth Political Studies*, V, 1 (March 1967), 38–59.
'African Reactions to the Rhodesian Crisis', *International Journal*, XXI, 2 (Spring 1966), 186–98.
'The Cabinet and Presidential Leadership in Tanzania: 1960–1966', in Lofchie (ed.), *The State of the Nations*, pp. 93–118.
' "Multi-Racialism" and Local Government in Tanganyika'. *Race* (London), II (Nov. 1960), 33–49.
'Report of the British Economic Mission on the Tanzanian Five Year Development Plan'. London, 1965. Mimeographed.
Rey, Lucien. 'The Revolution in Zanzibar'. *New Left Review*, no. 25 (May–June 1964), 29–32.
Rothchild, Donald. *Politics of Integration*. Nairobi: East African Publishing House, 1969.
Rowe, E. G., *see* Tanganyika, 'Decentralization to Provinces...'
Russett, Bruce M. *et al*. *World Handbook of Political and Social Indicators*. New Haven, Conn.: Yale University Press, 1964.

Ruthenburg, Hans. 'Coffee and Banana Farms at Mount Kilimanjaro', in
   Ruthenburg (ed.), *Smallholder Farming and Smallholder Development in
   Tanzania*. Munich: Weltforum Verlag, 1965.
Rweyemamu, Justinian. *Underdevelopment and Industrialization in Tanzania*.
   Nairobi: Oxford University Press, 1973.
Samoff, Joel. 'Politics, Politicians, and Party: Moshi, Tanzania 1968–69', Unpub-
   lished Ph.D. thesis, University of Wisconsin, 1972.
Saul, John. 'African Socialism in One Country: Tanzania', in Arrighi and Saul
   (eds.), *Essays on the Political Economy of Africa*, pp. 237–335.
   'Marketing Cooperatives in a Developing Country: The Tanzanian Case', in
   P. M. Worsley (ed.), *Two Blades of Grass*. Manchester: University Press, 1970,
   pp. 347–70.
   'Marketing Cooperatives in Tanzania: A Case Study in Resource Allocation and
   Inequality'. East African Institute of Social Research Conference paper, 1966.
   Mimeographed.
   'The Nature of Tanzania's Political System: Issues Raised by the 1965 and 1970
   Elections', Parts I, II. *Journal of Commonwealth Political Studies*, v, 2 and 3
   (July, November 1972), 113–29, 198–221.
Shaw, Timothy. 'The Foreign Policy of Tanzania'. Unpublished Ph.D. thesis,
   Makerere University, 1967.
Shivji, Issa. 'The Class Struggle Continues'. Dar-es-Salaam: Department of Develop-
   ment Studies, University of Dar-es-Salaam, 1973. Mimeographed.
Shivji, Issa *et al. The Silent Class Struggle*. Dar-es-Salaam: Tanzania Publishing
   House, 1973.
Skorov, George. *Integration of Educational and Economic Planning in Tanzania*.
   Paris: UNESCO International Institute for Educational Planning, 1966.
Skottan, S. B. 'Report on Local Government Taxation in Tanzania'. Washington,
   D.C.: International Monetary Fund, 1969. Mimeographed.
Stephens, Hugh W. *The Political Transformation of Tanganyika, 1920–67*. New
   York: Praeger, 1968.
Stonehouse, John. *Prohibited Immigrant*. London: Bodley Head, 1960.
Svendsen, Knud Erik. 'Socialism in a Poor Peasant Economy', in Idrian Resnick
   (ed.), *Tanzania: Revolution by Education*. Arusha: Longman, 1968, pp. 85–93.
Szentes, Tamas. '"Status Quo" and Socialism', in Shivji *et al., The Silent Class
   Struggle*, pp. 78–117.
Tanganyika. *African Census Report 1957*. Dar-es-Salaam: Government Printer, 1963.
   Africanisation of the Civil Service, Annual Report 1963. Dar-es-Salaam: Govern-
   ment Printer, 1963.
   Annual Report of the Department of Education, 1956. Dar-es-Salaam: Government
   Printer, 1957.
   Budget Survey, 1962–63...1964–65. Dar-es-Salaam: Government Printer, 1962,
   1964.
   Constitutional Documents 1960. Dar-es-Salaam: Attorney-General's Chambers,
   1960. Mimeographed.
   'Decentralization to Provinces in Tanganyika', by E. G. Rowe. Dar-es-Salaam:
   Government Printer, undated but *circa* 1958. Mimeographed.
   Development Plan for Tanganyika, 1961–62 to 1963–64. Dar-es-Salaam: Govern-
   ment Printer, 1961.
   'Draft Five-Year Africanisation Programme for the Civil Service'. Dar-es-Salaam:
   Establishment Division, Prime Minister's Office, 1961. Mimeographed.
   High-Level Manpower Requirements and Resources in Tanganyika, 1962–67, by
   George Tobias. Government Paper No. 2 of 1963. Dar-es-Salaam: Government
   Printer, 1963.

'Human Resources and Manpower Planning in Tanganyika', by J. L. Thurston. Dar-es-Salaam: Ministry of Finance, 1960. Mimeographed.

'Interim Report on the County Council in Tanganyika, 1951–56', by S. H. Page-Jones. Dar-es-Salaam: Department of Local Government, 1956. Mimeographed.

'Interim Report on the County Council in Tanganyika, 1956–57', by S. H. Page-Jones. Dar-es-Salaam: Department of Local Government, 1957. Mimeographed.

Legislative Council Official Report, 27th Session (1952–3); 30th Session (1955–6); 34th Session (1958–9), vol. i (1st Meeting, 14–18 Oct. 1958), vol. ii (2nd Meeting, 9–12 Dec. 1958), vol. iii (3rd Meeting, 17–20 Mar. 1959); 35th Session (1959–60), vol. i (1st Meeting, 20–5 Oct. 1959), vol. ii (2nd Meeting, 16–18 Dec. 1959); 36th Session (1960–1), vol. i (1st Meeting, 11–20 Oct. 1960), vol. ii (2nd Meeting, 6–9 Dec. 1960), vol. iii (3rd Meeting, 14–16 Feb. 1961). Dar-es-Salaam: Government Printer, 1953–61.

Membership of Political Associations. Tanganyika Government Circular No. 5 of 1953. Dar-es-Salaam: Government Printer, 1 August 1953.

Ministry of Education Triennial Survey of Education in the Years 1958–60. Dar-es-Salaam: Government Printer, 1960.

National Assembly Official Report, 36th Session (1960–1), vol. iv (4th Meeting, 16 May–6 June 1961), vol. v (5th Meeting, 10–20 Oct. 1961); 1st Session (1961–2), vol. ii (2nd Meeting, 5 June–3 July 1962). Dar-es-Salaam: Government Printer, 1961–2.

Proposals of the Tanganyika Government for a Republic. Government Paper No. 1 of 1962. Dar-es-Salaam: Government Printer, 1962.

Provincial Commissioners Annual Reports 1946. Dar-es-Salaam: Government Printer, 1947.

Report of the Africanisation Commission, 1962. Dar-es-Salaam: Government Printer, 1963.

Report of the Committee on Constitutional Development. Dar-es-Salaam: Government Printer [1951].

Report of the Committee on the Integration of Education, 1959. Dar-es-Salaam: Government Printer, 1960.

Report of the Committee on Voters' Qualifications. Government Paper No. 1 of 1957. Dar-es-Salaam: Government Printer, 1957.

Report of the Post-Elections Committee. Dar-es-Salaam: Government Printer, 1959.

Report of the Special Commissioner Appointed to Examine Matters Arising out of the Report of the Committee on Constitutional Development. Dar-es-Salaam: Government Printer, 1953.

Report of the Tanganyika Salaries Commission, 1961 (The Adu Report), vol. i. Dar-es-Salaam: Government of Tanganyika, 1961. Mimeographed.

Report of the Territorial Minimum Wage Board. Dar-es-Salaam: Government Printer, 1962.

'Scheme of Retirement Benefits for Members of H.M.O.C.S. and Officers Designated under the Overseas Service Aid Scheme'. Staff Circular No. 4 of 1961. Dar-es-Salaam: Establishment Division, Office of the Chief Minister, 1961.

'Some Problems Associated with Localisation of the Tanganyikan Civil Service', by J. Donald Kingsley and J. L. Thurston. Dar-es-Salaam: Ministry of Finance, 28 April 1961. Mimeographed.

'South-East Lake County Council, Report of the Clerk of the Council'. Mwanza, 1958. Mimeographed.

Staff List 1959...1961...1962...1963. Dar-es-Salaam: Government Printer, 1959–63.

Statistical Abstract 1958...1962. Dar-es-Salaam: Government Printer, 1958, 1962.
*Tanganyika Five Year Plan for Economic and Social Development 1st July, 1964–
30th June, 1969,* vol. 1, Analysis. Dar-es-Salaam: Government Printer, 1964.
Tanganyika African National Union. 'TANU Constitution'. Dar-es-Salaam, 1962.
Mimeographed.
Tanzania. *The Annual Economic Survey 1968 (A Background to the 1969–70
Budget).* Dar-es-Salaam: Government Printer, 1969.
  'Annual Manpower Report to the President 1965'. Dar-es-Salaam: Directorate of
  Economic Affairs and Development Planning, 1965...1966...1969. Dar-es-
  Salaam: Ministry of Economic Affairs and Development Planning, 1967, 1969.
  Mimeographed.
  *The Appropriation Accounts of Tanzania for the Year 1965–66...1966–67...
  1967–68...1968 69.* Dar-es-Salaam: Government Printer, 1967–70.
  'Background Paper on the East/West German Problem in Tanzania'. Dar-es-
  Salaam: Office of the President, 17 March 1965. Mimeographed.
  Background to the Budget, An Economic Survey 1966–67...1967–68...1968–69.
  Dar-es-Salaam: Government Printer, 1966–8.
  Budget Survey, 1964–65...1965–66. Dar-es-Salaam: Government Printer, 1964,
  1965.
  The Economic Survey and Second Annual Plan 1970–71. Dar-es-Salaam:
  Government Printer, 1970.
  'Establishment Circular Letter No. 21 of 1965'. Dar-es-Salaam: Chief Establishment
  Division, President's Office, 15 Nov. 1965.
  'Interim Report No. 2 of the Presidential Commission of Enquiry into the
  Cooperative Movement and the Marketing Boards'. Dar-es-Salaam: Ministry of
  Agriculture, 1966. Mimeographed.
  Majadiliano ya Bunge (Hansard), 10–30 June 1966. Dar-es-Salaam: Government
  Printer, 1966.
  Majadiliano ya Mkutano Mkuu wa TANU, 27 February–3 March 1967. Dar-es-
  Salaam: Government Printer, 1967.
  *A Mid-Term Appraisal of the Achievements under the Five Year Plan, July 1964
  to June 1969.* Dar-es-Salaam: Ministry of Economic Affairs and Development
  Planning, 1967.
  National Service. Staff Circular No. 5 of 1967. Dar-es-Salaam: Central Establish-
  ment Division, 17 July 1967.
  Proposals of the Tanzania Government on Local Government Councils. Govern-
  ment Paper No. 1 of 1966. Dar es-Salaam: Government Printer, 1966.
  'Proposals for Reorganization of the Cooperative Movement in Tanzania', by
  A. M. Babu. Dar-es-Salaam: Ministry of Commerce and Cooperatives, 1965.
  Mimeographed.
  *Report of the Presidential Commission on the Establishment of a Democratic
  One Party State.* Dar-es-Salaam: Government Printer, 1965.
  *Report of the Presidential Commission on the National Union of Tanganyika
  Workers.* Dar-es-Salaam: Government Printer, 1967.
  *Report of the Presidential Special Committee of Inquiry into Cooperative Move-
  ment and Marketing Boards.* Dar-es-Salaam: Government Printer, 1966.
  *Report to the Government of the United Republic of Tanzania on Wages, Incomes
  and Prices Policy,* by the International Labour Office. Government Paper No.
  3 of 1967. Dar-es-Salaam: Government Printer, 1967.
  *Speech by the Honourable the Minister for Finance Introducing the Estimates of
  Revenue and Expenditure, 1967/68 to the National Assembly, on 14th June,
  1967...1968–69...on 18th June, 1968.* Dar-es-Salaam: Government Printer,
  1967, 1968.

Staff List as at September 1965. Dar-es-Salaam: Government Printer, 1965.
Statistical Abstract, 1964. Dar-es-Salaam: Government Printer, 1965.
Survey of Employment and Earnings, Tanzania, 1970. Dar-es-Salaam: Bureau of
   Statistics, Ministry of Economic Affairs and Development Planning, 1972.
*Tanzania Second Five Year Plan for Economic and Social Development, July 1,
   1969–June 30, 1974*, vol. I, General Analysis. Dar-es-Salaam: Government
   Printer, 1969.
Taylor, Claggart. *The Political Development of Tanganyika*. Stanford, Calif.:
   University Press, 1963.
Thurston, J. L., *see* Tanganyika, 'Human Resources and Manpower Planning...'
Tobias, George, *see* Tanganyika, *High-Level Manpower Requirements*...
Tordoff, William. *Government and Politics in Tanzania*. Nairobi: East African
   Publishing House, 1967.
United Kingdom Government. *Colonial Office: Service with Overseas Governments*.
   Cmnd. 1193. London: HMSO, 1960.
'Despatch from the Governor of Tanganyika to the Secretary of State for the
   Colonies, No. 88, 20 Sept. 1950', in *Development of African Local Government
   in Tanganyika*, Colonial No. 277. London: HMSO, 1951, pp. 3–12.
'Papers Presented to the Africa Conference'. A.C. 4811. London: African Studies
   Branch, Colonial Office, 1947. Mimeographed.
*Report of the Commission on the Civil Services of the East African Territories
   and the East African High Commission 1953–54*, 2 vols. London: HMSO,
   1954.
'Report on the Development of Local Government in Nyasaland', by R. G.
   Hudson. London: Colonial Office, 1951. Mimeographed.
'Secretary of State for the Colonies Despatch of 25 February 1947', confidential
   publication of the Colonial Office, London, 1947.
*Southern Rhodesia – Documents Relating to the Negotiations between the
   United Kingdom and the Southern Rhodesian Government*. Cmnd, 2807.
   London: HMSO, 1965.
United Nations. *Report of the U.N./ECA/FAO Economic Survey Mission on the
   Economic Development of Zambia*. Ndola: Falcon Press, 1964.
'Report of the UNESCO Educational Planning Mission for Tanganyika, June–
   October 1962'. Paris: UNESCO, 1963. Mimeographed.
'United Nations Visiting Mission to Trust Territories in East Africa, 1960, Report
   on Tanganyika', in *Trusteeship Council, Official Records: Twenty-Sixth
   Session* (14 April–30 June 1960), Supplement No. 2. New York: United Nations
   Organization, 1960.
Wages and Salary Policies of the East African Community. Geneva: United
   Nations Development Program, 1974.
World Communications. Paris: UNESCO, 1956.
Van de Laar, A. P. 'Arusha: Before and After'. *East African Journal*, v, 11
   (November 1968), 15–25.
van Velzen, H. U. E. Thoden. 'Staff, Kulaks and Peasants', in Cliffe and Saul (eds.),
   Socialism in Tanzania, vol. 11, pp. 153–79.
van Velzen, H. U. E. Thoden and Sterkenburg, J. J. 'The Party Supreme', in
   Cliffe and Saul (eds.), *Socialism in Tanzania*, vol. 1, pp. 257–64.
'Stirrings in the Tanzanian National Assembly', in Cliffe and Saul (eds.),
   Socialism in Tanzania, vol. 1, pp. 248–53.
Weil, Michael J. 'The Tan-Zam Railroad: A Case Study in Project Evaluation and
   Development'. Unpublished M.A. thesis, University of Sussex, August
   1972.
Wicken, Joan. 'Report from Tanganyika'. London, 1957. Mimeographed.

Young, Crawford. *Politics in the Congo*. Princeton, N.J.: University Press, 1964.

Young, Roland and Fosbrooke, Henry A. *Smoke in the Hills*. Evanston, Ill.; Northwestern University Press, 1960.

Yu, George T. *China and Tanzania: A Study in Comparative Interaction*. Berkeley: University of California Press, 1970.

INDEX

African Chiefs (Special Powers) Act (1957), 38

Africanization, British attitude towards, 17–18, 105–6; Ford Foundation advisers on, 107–8; and non-African citizens, 106–7; progress of, (1959–61) 91–4, (1962) 124–6, (1963–9) 128–33, 218–21; TANU policy towards, 105–7, 110, 124–6

Anderson, David, 107n, 124n

Arusha Declaration, 227–43 *passim*; background to, 227–8, 232–5; implementation of (1967), 238–41; Nyerere and, 228–31; objectives of, (equality) 232–6, 238–9, (self-reliance) 231–2, (socialism) 237; reception of, 237–8, 239–43; timing of, 242–3

Babu, A. M., 137, 162, 181, 192

Barker, Jonathan, 261

Bennett, George, 37

Bomani, Paul, 95, 121, 140, 183, 191

Brett, Anthony, 20n

British administration in Tanganyika, African nationalism, policy towards, 18, 35–6, 48–9; Africanization, policy towards, 16–18, 98–9, 105–6; economic policies of, 19–20; multiracialism promoted by, (Legislative Council) 28–31, 38–9, 41–2, (District Councils) 31–4, 39–41; TANU, policies to counter, (decentralization) 48, (chiefs) 37–8, 40, (repression) 37, (United Tanganyika Party) 38–9; transition to independence, policies regarding, 17–19, 49–59, (British officers) 99–102, (financial settlement) 102–3

British Economic Mission, 183

British government, African nationalism, policy towards, 11–13; East Africa, policy regarding (1945–50), 13–19; and the Rhodesian crisis, 147–50; Tanzania, relations with, 87–8, 127, 147–52 *passim*, 178–9

Brown, Roland, 88n, 138, 203

Bryceson, Derek, 51, 121, 191

Burengelo, Frederick, 197–8

Cabinet, civil service, relations with, 182; establishment of, 95; Kawawa, leadership in (1962), 121–3; TANU, relations with, 212–13

Canada, military aid program, 157–8; technical assistance, 157

capital assistance, (1961–5) 133–4, (1965–9) 166–70; British, 102–3, 133–4, 149; Chinese, 161–6; I.D.A., 158; Scandinavian, 158; Soviet and East European, 158–61; terms of, 166–70

Chiefs, in Convention, 1958–60, 38, 40–1; removal from local government, 108, 194; TANU's use of, 194n

China, People's Republic of, capital projects in Tanzania, 163–4; grants and loans, 162–3, 165–6; military assistance, 148, 165; and railway to Zambia, 164–6; and Tanzanian non-alignment, 166, 250

Chiume, Kenayama, 44–5

citizenship debate (1961), 112–13

civil service and the Arusha Declaration, 235–6, 241–3; Asians, policy towards, 106; expatriates' role within, 91–3, 98–101, 129–33; independence, problems at the time of, 91–4; as an oligarchy, 221–6, 232–3, 235–7, 263; salaries of,

Uhuru (Swahili party paper), 113, 122
ujamaa vijijini (socialist villages), 253–5
Uluguru Land Usage Scheme, 26–7
United States of America, aid, 132–3,
157, 168; Congo, role in, 142–4; crisis
with Tanzania, 141–2; 'plot' against
Nyerere, 144–7
United Tanganyika Party, 38–9, 41
University College, Dar-es-Salaam, 178,
184–5; student crisis (1966), 233–5

Vasey, Sir Ernest, 95–6, 102–3, 122
village resettlement, 178, 183

Wambura, Joseph, 112

Wicken, Joan, 35, 88n
Workers' Development Corporation, 190
World Bank assistance (I.D.A.), 158, 168

Zambia, rail link with Dar-es-Salaam,
164–5; crisis over Rhodesian independence, 148; *see also* Tanzara Railway
Zanzibar, 137–42 *passim*; colonial
politics in, 137–9; Communist role in,
139–40; dispute over East German
embassy in, 139–41; revolution in,
138; Revolutionary Council of, 180,
206, 214; union with Tanganyika,
138–9, 179–81